R0061517157

01/2012

D0932622

THE *elephant,* THE *tiger,*
AND THE *cell phone*

PALM BEACH COUNTY
LIBRARY SYSTEM
3650 Summit Boulevard
West Palm Beach, FL 33406-4198

Also by Shashi Tharoor
(published by Arcade)

Bookless in Baghdad
The Five-Dollar Smile
The Great Indian Novel
India
Nehru
Riot
Show Business

THE *elephant*, THE *tiger*, AND THE *cell phone*

Reflections on INDIA

THE EMERGING 21ST-CENTURY POWER

Shashi Tharoor

ARCADE PUBLISHING • NEW YORK

Copyright © 2007, 2011 by Shashi Tharoor

All Rights Reserved. No part of this book may be reproduced in any manner without the express written consent of the publisher, except in the case of brief excerpts in critical reviews or articles. All inquiries should be addressed to Arcade Publishing, 307 West 36th Street, 11th Floor, New York, NY 10018.

Arcade Publishing books may be purchased in bulk at special discounts for sales promotion, corporate gifts, fund-raising, or educational purposes. Special editions can also be created to specifications. For details, contact the Special Sales Department, Arcade Publishing, 307 West 36th Street, 11th Floor, New York, NY 10018 or info@skyhorsepublishing.com.

Arcade Publishing® is a registered trademark of Skyhorse Publishing, Inc.®, a Delaware corporation.

Earlier versions of essays in this book have appeared, in somewhat different form, in the author's columns in the *Hindu*, the *Indian Express*, the *Times of India*, and in the following publications: *The New York Times*, the *Washington Post*, the *Los Angeles Times*, the *International Herald Tribune*, *India Today Plus*, *Time*, and *Global Asia*. Permission to reproduce previously published material is gratefully acknowledged.

Visit our website at www.arcadepub.com.

10 9 8 7 6 5 4 3 2 1

Library of Congress Cataloging-in-Publication Data is available on file.

ISBN: 978-1-61145-291-4

Printed in the United States of America

To my wife, Christa,
in the hope of introducing her to my India

Contents

Part Three   Indians Who Made My India

Part Four   Experiences of India

Part Five   The Transformation of India

Part Six   An *A* to *Z* of Being Indian

Preface

Why India Matters

On August 15, 2007, independent India turned sixty years old. What does the twenty-first century hold for India? And why should the answer to this question matter?

India is, in the words of the British historian E. P. Thompson, "the most important country for the future of the world." I would not presume to make such a judgment myself, but in my book *India: From Midnight to the Millennium and Beyond*, I saw Indians standing at the intersection of four of the most important debates facing the world at the end of the twentieth century:

- The bread vs. freedom debate: Can democracy "deliver the goods" to alleviate desperate poverty, or does its inbuilt inefficiencies only impede rapid growth? Is the instability of political contention (and of makeshift coalitions) a luxury a developing country cannot afford? As today's young concentrate on making their bread, should they consider political freedom a dispensable distraction?
- The centralization vs. federalism debate: Does tomorrow's India need to be run by a strong central government able to transcend the fissiparous tendencies of language, caste, and region, or is a government best that centralizes least? Does

every decision affecting Dharwar or Daman have to be taken in Delhi?

• The pluralism vs. fundamentalism debate: Is the secularism established in India's constitution, and now increasingly attacked as a westernized affectation, essential in a pluralist society, or should India, like many other third world countries, and almost all its neighbors, find refuge in the assertion of its own religious identity?

• The "coca-colonization" debate, or globalization vs. self-reliance: Should India, where economic self-sufficiency has been a mantra for more than four decades, open itself further to the world economy, or does the entry of Western consumer goods bring in alien influences that threaten to disrupt Indian society in ways too vital to be allowed? Should we raise the barriers to shield our youth from the pernicious seductions of MTV?

There is also a fifth debate that I did not discuss in my book, out of deference to the restraint expected by my then-employer, the United Nations: what one might call the "guns vs. butter" debate, the case for expenditure on defense against spending on development. With the twenty-first century having begun amid new threats of terrorism and renewed talk of nuclear confrontation, there is an ideological battle looming between advocates of military security (freedom from attack and conquest) and those of human security (freedom from hunger and hopelessness). It is difficult to deny that without adequate defense, a country cannot develop freely, according to its own rights; it is equally impossible to deny that without development, there will not be a country worth defending.

These are not merely academic debates: they are now being enacted on the national and world stage, and the choices we make will determine the kind of India our children will inherit in the twenty-first century. And since the century began with Indians accounting for one-sixth of the world's population, their choices will resonate throughout the globe.

In the present volume, I have tried to bring together material I have published in the last half-dozen years on subjects related to contemporary India, with these debates always (but not always explicitly) in mind. This book is not a survey of modern Indian history or politics; to become familiar with many of the principal events of the last six decades, the reader is advised to pick up *India: From Midnight to the Millennium and Beyond.* It is not "reportage," though I do draw anecdotally upon my own travels and conversations in India and my exchanges with ordinary Indians who have communicated with me over the past few years. It is, I hope, both informed and impassioned, organized thematically but covering a broad range of subjects — from the very notion of "Indianness" in a pluralist society, to the lives of the men and women who helped shape my India, to whimsical and often tongue-in-cheek pieces on cricket or the national penchant for holidays. Almost all of these espouse a point of view: they reflect my taste for advocacy. Do not look here for dispassionate and neutral analysis. But each chapter, whether long or short, may be read in isolation.

India in the first decade of the twenty-first century is a young country, an optimistic country, a country marching confidently toward the future. This book reflects something of the assumptions and the worldview of the English-speaking, educated, professional, and entrepreneurial classes who are driving change and prosperity in India. But it is still a land of contrasts, where millions live wretched lives amid poverty and neglect even as India boasts the largest number of billionaires of any country in Asia, higher than either Japan or China. As one who loves and believes in my country, I have not allowed myself to forget those who have not been able to benefit from the dramatic changes taking place there. The book concludes on a sobering note that is not meant to undermine the message of the earlier chapters. Rather, it points to the necessity of entering the sunlit uplands with eyes wide open to the dangers lurking in the shadows.

This is a book oriented toward the future, but one in which issues of history and identity make more than an occasional appearance. Whether through elections or quotas, political mobilization in contemporary India has asserted the power of old identities, habits, faiths, and prejudices. Transcending them will be the major challenge for the Indian polity in the twenty-first century. India must rise above the past if we are to conquer the future.

Shashi Tharoor
New York, 2007

Introduction

The Elephant Who Became a Tiger

ONCE UPON A TIME, in a hot and humid jungle (though one with stretches known better for heat and dust), there lived an old elephant. She was a big, slow, lumbering elephant, with a long but not always happy history, and it was widely accepted that she had known better days. She was prone, the other animals knew, to lie back and scratch herself and talk nostalgically about the glorious past, her great accomplishments in times long gone by, but when the other animals listened they did not forget that that was really a long time ago. After all, for some time, the elephant's own stretch of the jungle had come under the sway of a fierce lion from far away. Despite her size and strength, the elephant had proved no match for the lion and had been cowed into submission, until the day when the lion, tired of subduing distant lands, had finally slunk away.

Despite this experience, the elephant tended to lecture the other animals, secure in the conviction that she had all the answers. She would raise her trunk and trumpet her views about the right way to do things, the correct manner of living, the ideal principles according to which to organize the jungle, and the other animals would nod politely, trying not to point out that the elephant herself hadn't done all that well, and that she was visibly becoming a bit

1

mangy and flea-infested. She certainly was not the strongest animal in the jungle, for her way of doing things meant that she did not grow as big and strong as she might have. (The other animals, not entirely kindly, spoke somewhat patronizingly of "the elephant's rate of growth.") She was large, of course, and that meant she could never be entirely ignored; as she came steadily, unblinkingly (and unthinkingly) on, the smaller animals at least had to get out of the way. But the number of animals who did as she did, and lived as she told them to, dwindled with each passing season.

In another part of the jungle, to the southeast, another group of animals was faring much better than our elephant. They were a sleek band of tigers, their stripes glistening in the sun that seemed inevitably to shine on their patch of forest. The tigers were lithe and well muscled; they ate well, they bounded about, and they grew strong and contented. Though tourists still came occasionally to photograph the elephant, the tigers attracted swarms of visitors, who took pictures and films that framed the tigers' fearful symmetry. The visitors also gushed about the greenness of the grass the tigers grazed on, brought them ever more food and water, and stroked their backs till their coats glittered. If the elephant noticed what was going on, she pretended not to; far from wondering what shoulder and what art might have twisted the sinews of the tigers' heart, she acted as if the good fortune of such small, little creatures was of no consequence for an animal as large and important as an elephant.

But then, one day, she fell ill. She lay down and bellowed, until the veterinarians from the big animal hospital came running to see what the matter was. And when they had examined her, they told her the sad truth: either she would have to change the way she was living, allow others into her patch of jungle, and pay attention to the needs of the other animals (needs she could help them fulfill), or she would soon have to sell her tusks to be made into ivory trophies for the mantels of distant humans. "My tusks?!" she exclaimed in consternation (and horror). "I'll never sell my tusks!"

"Why, then," the vets said, "you must change. You must become more like the tigers."

The elephant blanched (which looked particularly awful under the gray pallor of her mottled skin), but said nothing. She lumbered heavily to her feet and plodded uncertainly toward her new destiny. Slowly, very slowly, but with the deliberateness for which she was known, she began to change.

As the seasons passed, the other animals began to notice that there was something different about the old elephant. She brushed off the fleas that had begun feasting on her. A certain sprightliness entered her step. She still moved with that familiar elephantine gait, but there was a pronounced sway from side to side now, as though she were prepared to entertain all possibilities. The old fat began to give way to muscle. Her ears flapped in a way that suggested she was — surprise! — actually listening, instead of merely lecturing others. She dipped her trunk into clean water and sprayed it liberally on herself, washing away decades of dirt and mud (though some clumps still stubbornly clung to her). She began to grow — how she began to grow! Soon the visitors started crossing over from the tigers' sanctuary to take a look. And they started chattering to one another in excitement, since they could not believe what they were seeing. For, appearing on the elephant's back, at first faint but soon clearly visible, was the unmistakable sign of stripes. Large black stripes swirled confidently around her torso. And then, even as the visitors gawked with disbelief, the elephant's dirty gray skin began to acquire a distinctly golden hue.

There was no doubt about it. The elephant was becoming a tiger.

Miracle of miracles! All the animals came to look, and admire. Some were afraid: imagine the strength of a tiger within the size of an elephant! What would happen to the rest of the jungle? Others said there was no reason to worry: whatever stripes she grew, the elephant would always be an elephant at heart. And still others said, it can't last; the stripes will fade away soon enough, and we will again see the comforting sight of our old plodding, stumbling friend.

Which of the animals would be right? Who knows? Tune in a few years from now, when we will recount the next episode of our favorite animal fable.

1

Ideas of Indianness

1

The Invention of India

I N A PASSAGE OF HIS MUCH-MISUNDERSTOOD NOVEL *The Satanic Verses*, Salman Rushdie writes of "the eclectic, hybridized nature of the Indian artistic tradition." Under the Mughals, he says, artists of different faiths and traditions were brought from many parts of India to work on a painting. One hand would paint the mosaic floors, another the human figures, a third the cloudy skies: "Individual identity was submerged to create a many-headed, many-brushed Overartist who, literally, *was* Indian painting."

This evocative image could as well be applied to the very idea of India, itself the product of the same hybrid culture. How, after all, can one approach this land of snow peaks and tropical jungles, with twenty-three major languages and 22,000 distinct dialects (including some spoken by more people than Danish or Norwegian), inhabited in the first years of the twenty-first century by a billion individuals of every ethnic extraction known to humanity? How does one come to terms with a country whose population is 40 percent illiterate but which has educated the world's second-largest pool of trained scientists and engineers, whose teeming cities overflow while two out of three Indians still scratch a living from the soil? What is the clue to understanding a country rife with despair and disrepair, which nonetheless moved a Mughal emperor to declaim, "If on earth there be paradise of bliss, it is this, it is this, it is this"? How does one gauge a culture that elevated nonviolence to an effective moral principle, but whose freedom was born in blood and whose independence still soaks in it? How does one explain a land where peasant organizations and suspicious officials attempt to close down Kentucky Fried Chicken™ as a threat to the nation, where a former prime minister bitterly criticizes the sale of Pepsi-Cola™ "in a country where villagers don't have clean drinking water," and yet invents more sophisticated software for U.S. computer manufacturers than any other country in the world? How can one portray an ageless civilization that was the birthplace of four major religions, a dozen different traditions of classical dance, eighty-five political parties, and three hundred ways of cooking the potato?

The short answer is that it can't be done — at least not to everyone's satisfaction. Any truism about India can be immediately contradicted by another truism about India. The country's national motto, emblazoned on its governmental crest, is "*Satyameva Jayaté*" — Truth alone triumphs. The question remains, however, whose truth? It is a question to which there are at least a billion answers — if the last census hasn't undercounted us again.

For the singular thing about India, as I have written elsewhere, is that you can only speak of it in the plural. There are, in the hackneyed phrase, many Indias. If India were to adopt the well-known U.S. motto, it would have read "*E Pluribis Pluribum.*" Everything exists in countless variants. There is no single standard, no fixed stereotype, no "one way." This pluralism is acknowledged in the way India arranges its own affairs: all groups, faiths, tastes, and ideologies survive and contend for their place in the sun. The idea of India is that of a land emerging from an ancient civilization, united by a shared history, sustained by pluralist democracy, but containing a world of differences. It is not surprising, then, that the political life of modern India has been rather like traditional Indian music: the broad basic rules are firmly set, but within them one is free to improvise, unshackled by a written score.

When India celebrated the forty-ninth anniversary of its independence from British rule in 1996, our then–prime minister, H. D. Deve Gowda, stood at the ramparts of Delhi's sixteenth-century red fort and delivered the traditional Independence Day address to the nation in Hindi, India's national language. Eight other prime ministers had done exactly the same thing forty-eight times before him, but what was unusual this time was that Deve Gowda, a southerner from the state of Karnataka, spoke to the country in a language of which he did not know a word. Tradition and politics required a speech in Hindi, so he gave one — the words having been written out for him in his native Kannada script, in which they, of course, made no sense.

Such an episode is almost inconceivable elsewhere, but it represents the best of the oddities that help make India India. Only in India could the country be ruled by a man who does not understand its national language; only in India, for that matter, is there a national language that half the population does not understand; and only in India could this particular solution have been found to enable the prime minister to address his people. One of Indian cinema's finest "playback singers," the Keralite K. J. Yesudas, sang his way to the top of the Hindi music charts with lyrics in that language written in the Malayalam script for him, but to see the same practice elevated to the prime ministerial address on Independence Day was a startling affirmation of Indian pluralism.

For the simple fact is that we are all minorities in India. There has never been an archetypal Indian to stand alongside the archetypal Englishman or Frenchman. A Hindi-speaking Hindu male from Uttar Pradesh may cherish the illusion that he represents the "majority community," an expression much favored by the less industrious of our journalists. But he does not. As a Hindu, he belongs to the faith adhered to by 81 percent of the population. But a majority of the country does not speak Hindi. A majority does not hail from Uttar Pradesh, though you could be forgiven for thinking otherwise when you go there. And, if he were visiting, say, my home state of Kerala, he would be surprised to discover that the majority there is not even male.

Even his Hinduism is no guarantee of his majority-hood, because his caste automatically puts him in a minority. If he is a Brahmin, 90 percent of his fellow Indians are not. If he is a Yadav, a "backward caste," 85 percent of his fellow Indians are not. And so on.

If caste and language complicate the notion of Indian identity, ethnicity makes it even more difficult. Most of the time, an Indian's name immediately reveals where he is from or what her mother tongue is: when we introduce ourselves, we are advertising our origins. Despite some intermarriage at the elite levels in our cities, Indians are still largely endogamous, and a Bengali is easily distinguished from a Punjabi. The difference this reflects is often more apparent than the elements of commonality. A Karnataka Brahmin shares his Hindu faith with a Bihari Kurmi, but they share little identity with each other in respect to their dress, customs, appearance, taste, language, or even, these days, their political objectives. At the same time, a Tamil Hindu would feel he has much more in common with a Tamil Christian or a Tamil Muslim than with, say, a Haryanvi Jat, with whom he formally shares the Hindu religion.

What makes India, then, a nation? What is an Indian's identity?

Let me risk the wrath of anti-Congress readers and take an Italian example. No, not that Italian example, but one from 140 years ago. Amid the popular ferment that made an Italian nation out of a congeries of principalities and statelets, the nineteenth-century novelist Massimo Taparelli d'Azeglio memorably wrote, "We have created Italy. Now all we need to do is to create Italians." Oddly enough, no Indian nationalist succumbed to the temptation to express the same thought — "We have created India; now all we need to do is to create Indians."

Such a sentiment would not, in any case, have occurred to the preeminent voice of Indian nationalism, Jawaharlal Nehru, because he believed India and Indians had existed for millennia before he gave words to their longings; he would never have spoken of "creating" India or Indians, merely of being the agent for the reassertion of what had always existed but had been long suppressed. Nonetheless, the India that was born in 1947 was in a very real sense a new creation: a state that had made fellow citizens of the Ladakhi and the Laccadivian for the first time, that divided Punjabi from Punjabi for the first time, that asked the Kerala peasant to feel allegiance to a Kashmiri Pandit ruling in Delhi, also for the first time. Nehru would not have written of the challenge of "creating" Indians, but creating Indians was what, in fact, our nationalist movement did.

Nations have been formed out of varying and different impulses. France and Thailand are the products of a once ruthless unifying monarchy, and Germany and the United States were created by sternly practical and yet visionary modernizing elites. Italy and Bangladesh are the results of mass movements led by messianic figures, Holland and Switzerland the creation of discrete cantons wishing to merge for their mutual protection. But it is only recently that race or ethnicity has again been seen as the basis of nationhood, as has become apparent in the prolonged breakup of the former Yugoslavia.

Most modern nations are the product of a fusion of population groups over the centuries, to the point where one element is indistinguishable from the next. The nineteenth-century French historian Ernest Renan pointed out, for instance, that "an Englishman is indeed a type within the whole of humanity. However, [he] is neither the Briton of Julius Caesar's time, nor the Anglo-Saxon of Hengist's time, nor the Dane of Canute's time, nor the Norman of William the Conqueror's time; [he] is rather the result of all these." We cannot yet say the same of an Indian, because we are not yet the product of the kind of fusion that Renan's Englishman represents.

So India cannot claim ethnicity as a uniting factor, since what we loosely have in common with each other as a generally recognizable "type" we also have in common with Pakistanis, Bangladeshis, Sri Lankans, Maldivians, and Nepalese, with whom we do not share a common political identity. (And further distinctions make matters worse — after all, Indian Bengalis and Punjabis have far more in common ethnically with Bangladeshis and Pakistanis than with

Bangaloreans and Poonawallahs.) Nor can we cite religion. Looking again at foreign models of the nation-state, many scholars have pointed out that the adoption of Christianity by both conquerors and the conquered helped the creation of the Western European nations, since it eliminated the distinction between ethnic groups in the society on the basis of their religion. But this is not a useful answer in India, for a Tamil Hindu can share a faith with a Haryanvi Jat and still feel he has little else in common with him. And equally important, over 200 million Indians do not share the faith of the majority, and would be excluded from any religiously defined community (as non-Christian minorities among immigrants in Europe feel excluded today from full acceptance into their new societies).

A third element that has, historically, served to unite nations in other parts of the world is language. In Europe, conquerors and the conquered rapidly came to speak the same language, usually that of the conquered. In India, attempts by Muslim conquerors to import Persian or Turkic languages never took root and, instead, the hybrid camp language called Urdu or Hindustani evolved as the language of both rulers and the ruled in most of North India. But Hindi today has made very limited inroads into the south, east, and northeast, so linguistic unity remains a distant prospect (all the more so given that languages like Bengali, Malayalam, and Tamil have a far richer cultural and literary tradition than the Hindi that seeks to supplant them).

No language enjoys majority status in India, though Hindi is coming perilously close. Thanks in part to the popularity of Mumbai's Bollywood cinema, Hindi is understood, if not always well spoken, by nearly half the population of India, but it cannot truly be considered the language of the majority; its locutions, gender rules, and script are still unfamiliar to most Indians in the south and the northeast. And if the proliferation of Hindi TV channels has made the spoken language more accessible to many non-native speakers, the fact that other languages too have captured their share of the TV audience means that our linguistic diversity is not going to disappear.

But my larger and more serious point is that the French speak

French, the Germans speak German, the Americans speak English (though Spanish is making inroads, especially in the Southwest and Southeast of the United States) — but Indians speak Punjabi, or Gujarati, or Malayalam, and it does not make us any less Indian. The idea of India is not based on language. It is no accident that Jawaharlal Nehru's classic volume of Indian nationalism, *The Discovery of India*, was written in English — and it is fair to say that Nehru discovered India in English. Indeed, when two Indians meet abroad, or two educated urban Indians meet in India, unless they have prior reason to believe they have an Indian language in common, the first language they speak to each other is English. It is in English that they establish each other's linguistic identity, and then they switch comfortably to another language, or a hybrid, depending on the link they have established. Language and religion are, in any case, an inadequate basis for nationhood. Over eighty countries profess Christianity, but they do not seek to merge with each other; the Organization of the Islamic Conference has more than fifty members, who agree on many issues but do not see themselves as a single nation. As for language, Arabic makes meetings of the Arab League more convenient, no doubt, but has hardly been a force for political unity; Spanish has not melted the political frontiers that vivisect Latin America; and England and the United States remain, in the famous phrase, two countries divided by a common language.

A more poetic suggestion made by the French historian Ernest Renan is that historical amnesia is an essential part of nation-building, that nations are those that have forgotten the price they have paid in the past for their unity. This is true of India, though the Babri Masjid tragedy reveals that we Indians are not very good at forgetting. We carry with us the weight of the past, and because we do not have a finely developed sense of historicism, it is a past that is still alive in our present. We wear the dust of history on our foreheads and the mud of the future on our feet.

So Indian nationalism is a rare animal indeed. It is not based on language (since there are at least twenty-three or thirty-five, depending on whether you follow the amended constitution or the ethnolinguists). Nor on religion, since India is a secular pluralist state that is home to every religion known to mankind, with the possible exception of Shintoism; and Hinduism — a faith without a national organization, no established church or ecclesiastical hierarchy, no uniform beliefs or modes of worship — exemplifies as much our diversity as it does our common cultural heritage. Not on geography, since the natural geography of the subcontinent — the mountains and the sea — was hacked by the Partition of 1947. And not even territory, since, by law, anyone with one grandparent born in pre-partition India is eligible for citizenship. Indian nationalism has therefore always been the nationalism of an idea.

To repeat the argument: we are all minorities in India. Indian nationalism is the nationalism of an idea, the idea of an ever-ever land — emerging from an ancient civilization, united by a shared history, sustained by pluralist democracy. India's democracy imposes no narrow conformities on its citizens. The Indian idea is the opposite of what Freudians call "the narcissism of minor differences"; in India we celebrate the commonality of major differences. The whole point of Indianness is its pluralism: you can be many things and one thing. You can be a good Muslim, a good Keralite, and a good Indian all at once. To borrow Michael Ignatieff's famous phrase, we are a land of belonging rather than of blood.

If America is a melting pot, then to me India is a *thali,* a selection of sumptuous dishes in different bowls. Each tastes different, and does not necessarily mix with the next, but they belong together on the same plate, and they complement each other in making the meal a satisfying repast. Indians are used to multiple identities and multiple loyalties, all coming together in allegiance to a larger idea of India, an India that safeguards the common space available to each identity.

That idea of India is of one land embracing many. It is the idea that a nation may endure differences of caste, creed, color, conviction, culture, cuisine, costume, and custom and still rally around a consensus. And that consensus is about the simple idea that in a democracy you don't really need to agree — except on the ground rules of how you will disagree.

Is such an idea sustainable in a land where 81 percent of the population adhere to one faith — Hinduism? There is no question but that the Indian ethos is infused by a pervasive and eclectic Hindu culture that draws richly from other traditions, notably Islamic ones. Recent news stories have chronicled the rise of an alternative strain in Indian politics, one that appeared to reject this consensus — that of an intolerant and destructive "Hindutva" movement that assaults India's minorities, especially its Muslims, that destroyed a well-known mosque in 1992, and conducted horrific attacks on Muslims in the state of Gujarat ten years later. The sectarian misuse of Hinduism for minority bashing is especially sad since Hinduism provides the basis for a shared sense of common culture within India that has little to do with religion. The inauguration of a public project, the laying of a foundation stone, or the launching of a ship usually starts with the ritual smashing of a coconut, an auspicious practice in Hinduism but one which most Indians of other faiths cheerfully accept in much the same spirit as a teetotaler acknowledges the role of champagne in a Western celebration. Hindu festivals, from Holi (when friends and strangers of all faiths are sprayed with colored water in a Dionysian ritual) to Deepavali (the festival of lights, firecrackers, and social gambling) have already gone beyond their religious origins to unite Indians of all faiths as a shared experience.

Festivals, *melas*, *lilas*, all "Hindu" in origin, have become occasions for the mingling of ordinary Indians of all backgrounds; indeed, for generations now, Muslim artisans in the Hindu holy city of Varanasi have made the traditional masks for the annual Ram Lila (the dance-drama depicting the tale of the divine god-king Rama). Hindu myths like the Ramayana and the Mahabharata provide a common idiom to all Indians, and it was not surprising that when national television broadcast a ninety-four-episode serialization of the Mahabharata, the script was written by a Muslim, Dr. Rahi

Masoom Raza. Both Hindus and Muslims throng the tombs and *dargahs* of Sufi Muslim saints. Hindu devotional songs are magnificently sung by the Muslim Dagar brothers. Hinduism and Islam are intertwined in Indian life. In the Indian context today, it is possible to say that there is no Hinduism without Islam: the saffron and the green both belong on the Indian flag.

A lovely story that illustrates the cultural synthesis of Hinduism and Islam in northern India was recounted by two American scholars. It seems an Indian Muslim girl was asked to participate in a small community drama about the life of Lord Krishna, the Hindu god adored by shepherdesses, who dance for his pleasure (and who exemplify through their passion the quest of the devout soul for the Lord). Her Muslim father forbade her to dance as a shepherdess with the other schoolgirls. In that case, said the drama's director, we will cast you as Krishna. All you have to do is stand there in the usual Krishna pose, a flute at your mouth. Her father consented, and so the Muslim girl played Krishna.

This is India's secularism, far removed from its French equivalent. Western dictionaries define *secularism* as the absence of religion, but Indian secularism means a profusion of religions, none of which is privileged by the state and all of which are open to participation by everybody. Secularism in India does not mean irreligiousness, which even avowedly atheist parties like the Communists or the DMK have found unpopular among their voters; indeed, in Calcutta's annual Durga Puja (the annual festival celebrating the goddess Durga, which is the Bengali Hindu's equivalent of Christmas), the youth wings of the Communist parties compete with each other to put up the most lavish Puja pandals or pavilions to the goddess. Rather, it means, in the Indian tradition, multi-religiousness. In the Calcutta neighborhood where I lived during my high school years, the wail of the muezzin calling the Islamic faithful to prayer blended with the tinkling bells and chanted mantras at the Hindu Shiva temple nearby and the crackling loudspeakers outside the Sikh *gurudwara* reciting verses from the Guru Granth Sahib. (And St. Paul's Cathedral was only minutes away.)

Hindus pride themselves on belonging to a religion of astonishing breadth and range of belief; a religion that acknowledges all ways of worshiping God as equally valid — indeed, the only major religion in the world that does not claim to be the only true religion. This eclectic and nondoctrinaire Hinduism — a faith without apostasy, where there are no heretics to cast out because there has never been any such thing as a Hindu heresy — is not the Hinduism that destroyed a mosque, nor the Hindutva spewed in hate-filled speeches by communal politicians. How can such a religion lend itself to "fundamentalism"? Hindu fundamentalism is a contradiction in terms, since Hinduism is a religion without fundamentals. To be an Indian Hindu is to be part of an elusive dream all Indians share, a dream that fills our minds with sounds, words, flavors from many sources that we cannot easily identify.

Of course it is true that, though Hinduism as a faith lends itself to eclecticism, this does not exempt all Hindus from the temptations of identity politics. Yet India's democracy helps to acknowledge and accommodate the various identities of its multifaceted population. No one identity can ever triumph in India: both the country's chronic pluralism and the logic of the electoral marketplace make this impossible. In leading a coalition government from 1998 to 2004, the Hindu-inclined Bharatiya Janata Party learned that any party ruling India has to reach out to other groups, other interests, other minorities. After all, there are too many diversities in our land for any one version of reality to be imposed on all of us.

India's national identity has long been built on the slogan "Unity in diversity." The "Indian" comes in such varieties that a woman who is fair-skinned, sari-wearing, and Italian-speaking, as Sonia Gandhi is, is not more foreign to my grandmother in Kerala than one who is "wheatish-complexioned," wears a *salwar kameez* and speaks Urdu. Our nation absorbs both these types of people; both are equally "foreign" to some of us, equally Indian to us all.

At a time when the Huntington thesis of a "clash of civilizations" has gained currency, it is intriguing to contemplate a civilization predicated upon such diversity, one which provides the framework to absorb these clashes within itself. Our founding fathers wrote a constitution for a dream; we continue to give passports to their ideals. Rushdie's "Overartist" finds his aural counterpart in the Muslim *ustads* playing Hindu devotional ragas and the Bollywood playback singers chanting Urdu lyrics. The music of India is the collective anthem of a hybrid civilization.

The sight in May 2004 of a Roman Catholic political leader (Sonia Gandhi) making way for a Sikh (Manmohan Singh) to be sworn in as prime minister by a Muslim (President Abdul Kalam) — in a country 81 percent Hindu — caught the world's imagination. That one simple moment of political change put to rest many of the arguments over Indian identity. India was never truer to itself than when celebrating its own diversity.

Ultimately, of course, what matters in determining the validity of a nation is the will of its inhabitants to live and strive together. Such a will may not be unanimous, for there will always be those who reject the common framework for narrow sectarian ends. But if the overwhelming majority of the people share the political will for unity, if they can look back to both a past and a future, and if they realize they are better off in Kozhikode or Kanpur dreaming the same dreams as those in Kohlapur or Kohima, a nation exists, celebrating diversity and freedom. That is the India that has emerged in the last sixty years, and it is well worth celebrating.

2

Hinduism and Hindutva:
Creed and Credo

THE QUESTIONS A CANDIDATE FOR PUBLIC OFFICE HAS to answer from the media can cover any subject, and intrusiveness is difficult to resist. Still, I was surprised with the frequency with which, when I was India's candidate for Secretary-General of the United Nations, journalists from Boston to Berlin expressed curiosity about my religious beliefs. I tend to think of faith as something intensely personal, not really a matter I feel any desire to parade before the world. But, in an era where religion has sadly become a source of division and conflict in so many places, I had to concede that the question was a legitimate one — especially after one of my rivals specifically appealed for support on the grounds of his religion.

It's true, in my view, that faith can influence one's conduct in one's career and life. For some, it's merely a question of faith in themselves; for others, including me, that sense of faith emerges from a faith in something larger than ourselves. Faith is, at some level, what gives you the courage to take the risks you must take, and enables you to make peace with yourself when you suffer the inevitable setbacks and calumnies that are the lot of those who try to make a difference in the world.

So I have had no difficulty in saying openly that I am a believing Hindu. But I am also quick to explain what that phrase means to me. We have an extraordinary diversity of religious practices within Hinduism, a faith with no single sacred book but many. Hinduism is, in many ways, predicated on the idea that the eternal wisdom of the ages about divinity cannot be confined to a single sacred book. We have no compulsory injunctions or obligations. We do not even have a Hindu Sunday, let alone a requirement to pray at specific times and frequencies.

What we have is a faith that allows each believer to reach out his or her hands to his or her notion of the Godhead. Hinduism is a faith that uniquely does not have any notion of heresy — you cannot be a Hindu heretic because there is no standard set of dogmas from which deviation would make you a heretic.

So Hinduism is a faith so unusual that it is the world's only major religion that does not claim only its set of beliefs to be true. I find that most congenial. For me, as a believing Hindu, it is wonderful to be able to meet people from other faiths without being burdened by the conviction that I have embarked upon a "right path" that they have somehow missed. I was brought up in the belief that all ways of worship are equally valid. My father prayed devoutly every day but never obliged me to join him: in the Hindu way, he wanted me to find my own truth. And that I believe I have. It is a truth that admits of the possibility that there might be other truths. I therefore bring to the world an attitude that is open, accommodating, and tolerant of others' beliefs. Mine is not a faith for those who seek certitudes, but there is no better belief system for an era of doubt and uncertainty than a religion that cheerfully accommodates both.

The misuse of religion for political purposes is a sad, sometimes tragic, aspect of our contemporary reality. As former UN Secretary-General Kofi Annan once said, the problem is never with the faith, but with the faithful. All faiths strive sincerely to animate the divine spark in each of us; but some of their followers, alas, use their faith as a club to beat others with, rather than a platform to raise themselves to the heavens. Since Hinduism believes that there are various ways of reaching the ultimate truth, the fact that adherents of my faith, in a perversion of its tenets, have chosen to destroy somebody else's sacred place, have attacked others because of the absence of foreskin or the mark on a forehead, is profoundly un-Hindu. I do not accept these fanatics' interpretation of the values and principles of my faith.

But what does it mean to me to be a practicing Hindu? I have never been particularly fond of visiting temples. I do believe in praying everyday, even if it is only for a couple of minutes. I have a little alcove at my home in Manhattan, where I try to reach out to the holy spirit. Yet I believe in the Upanishadic doctrine that the divine is essentially unknowable and unattainable by ordinary mortals; all prayer is an attempt to reach out to that which we cannot touch. Although I have occasionally visited temples, and I appreciate how important they are to my mother and most other devout Hindus, I don't really frequent them because I believe that one does not need any intermediaries between oneself and one's notion of the divine. "Build Ram in your hearts" is what Hinduism has always enjoined. If Ram is in your heart, it would matter very little what bricks or stones Ram can also be found in.

So I take pride in the openness, the diversity, the range, the lofty metaphysical aspirations of the Vedanta. I cherish the diversity, the lack of compulsion, and the richness of the various ways in which Hinduism is practiced eclectically. And I admire the civilizational heritage of tolerance that has made Hindu societies open their arms to people of every other faith, to come and practice their beliefs in peace amid Hindus. It is remarkable, for instance, that the only country on earth where the Jewish people have lived for centuries and never experienced a single episode of anti-Semitism is India. That is the Hinduism in which I gladly take pride. Openness is the essence of my faith. And that's the perspective from which I sought to serve in an office that must belong equally to people of all faiths, beliefs, and creeds around the world.

My avowal of my own Hinduism sits ill with those who assume that every believing Hindu automatically believes in the Hindutva project.* Yet it is hardly paradoxical to suggest that Hinduism, India's ancient homegrown faith, can help strengthen Indianness in ways that the proponents of Hindutva have not understood. In one sense Hinduism is almost the ideal faith for the twenty-first century: a faith that is eclectic and nondoctrinaire, one that responds ideally to the incertitudes of a postmodern world. Hinduism, with its openness, its respect for variety, its acceptance of all other faiths, is one religion that should be able to assert itself without threatening others. But this cannot be the so-called Hindu fundamentalism that has demonstrated such hateful intolerance toward other religious groups. It has to be the Hinduism of Swami Vivekananda, the great preacher and philosopher, who more than a century ago, at Chicago's World Parliament of Religions in 1893, articulated best the liberal humanism that lies at the heart of his (and my) creed:

> I am proud to belong to a religion which has taught the world both tolerance and universal acceptance. We believe not only in universal toleration, but we accept all religions as true. I am proud to belong to a country which has sheltered the persecuted and the refugees of all religions and all countries of the earth. I am proud to tell you that we have gathered in our bosom the purest remnant of the Israelites, who came to southern India and took refuge with us in the very year in which their holy temple was shattered to pieces by Roman tyranny. I am proud to belong to the religion which has sheltered and is still fostering the remnant of the grand Zoroastrian nation. I remember having repeated a hymn from my earliest boyhood, which is every day repeated by millions of human beings: "As the different streams having their sources in different places all mingle their water in the sea, so, O Lord, the different paths

---

* The purpose of which is to create a Hindu political identity for India.

which men take through different tendencies, various though they appear, crooked or straight, all lead to Thee." . . . The wonderful doctrine preached in the Gita [says]: "Whosoever comes to Me, through whatsoever form, I reach him; all men are struggling through paths which in the end lead to me."

Vivekananda went on to denounce that "sectarianism, bigotry, and its horrible descendant, fanaticism, have long possessed this beautiful earth." His confident belief that their death knell had sounded was sadly not to be borne out. But his vision — summarized in the Sanskrit credo "*Sarva Dharma Sambhava*, all religions are equally worthy of respect" — is the kind of Hinduism practiced by the vast majority of India's Hindus, whose instinctive acceptance of other faiths and forms of worship has long been the vital hallmark of Indianness. Vivekananda made no distinction between the actions of Hindus as a people (the grant of asylum, for instance) and their actions as a religious community (tolerance of other faiths): for him, the distinction was irrelevant because Hinduism was as much a civilization as a set of religious beliefs. In a different speech to the same Chicago convention, Swami Vivekananda set out his philosophy in simple terms:

Unity in variety is the plan of nature, and the Hindu has recognized it. Every other religion lays down certain fixed dogmas and tries to force society to adopt them. It places before society only one coat which must fit Jack and John and Henry, all alike. If it does not fit John or Henry, he must go without a coat to cover his body. The Hindus have discovered that the absolute can only be realized, or thought of, or stated through the relative, and the images, crosses, and crescents are simply so many symbols — so many pegs to hang spiritual ideas on. It is not that this help is necessary for everyone, but those that do not need it have no right to say that it is wrong. Nor is it compulsory in Hinduism. . . . The Hindus have their faults, but mark this, they are always for punishing their own bodies, and never for cutting the throats of their neighbors. If the Hindu fanatic burns himself on the pyre, he never lights the fire of Inquisition.

It is sad that this assertion of Vivekananda's is being contradicted in the streets by those who claim to be reviving his faith in his name. What this tells us is we should never assume that, even when religion is used as a mobilizing identity, all those so mobilized act in accordance with the tenets of their religion. Nonetheless it is ironic that even the Maratha warrior-king Shivaji, after whom the bigoted Shiv Sena is named, exemplified the tolerance of Hinduism. In the account of a critic, the Mughal historian Khafi Khan, Shivaji made it a rule that his followers should do no harm to mosques, the Koran, or to women. "Whenever a copy of the sacred Koran came into his hands," Khafi Khan wrote, Shivaji "treated it with respect, and gave it to some of his Mussulman followers."

Indians today have to find real answers to the dilemmas of running a plural nation. "A nation," wrote the Zionist visionary Theodor Herzl, "is a historical group of men of recognizable cohesion, held together by a common enemy." The common enemy of Indians is an internal one, but not the one identified by Mr. Togadia and his ilk. The common enemy lies in the forces of sectarian division that would, if unchecked, tear the country apart — or transform it into something that all self-respecting Hindus would refuse to recognize.

What Hinduism provides is a foundation that promotes a commonality among all religions and their beliefs. In fact, Muslim sociologists and anthropologists have argued that Islam in rural India is more Indian than Islamic, in the sense that the faith as practiced by the ordinary Muslim villagers reflects the considerable degree of cultural assimilation that has occurred between Hindus and Muslims in their daily lives. The Muslim reformist scholar Asghar Ali Engineer has written that "rural Islam . . . (is) almost indistinguishable from Hinduism except in the form of worship. . . . The degree may vary from one area to another; but cultural integration between the

Hindus and Muslims is a fact which no one, except victims of misinformation, can deny."

I once wrote that to some degree, India's other minorities have found it comfortable to take on elements of Hindu culture as proof of their own integration into the national mainstream. The tennis-playing brothers Anand, Vijay, and Ashok Amritraj all bear Hindu names, but they are Christian, the sons of Robert and Maggie Amritraj, and they played with prominent crosses dangling from their necks, which they were fond of kissing in supplication or gratitude at tense moments on court. But giving their children Hindu names must have seemed, to Robert and Maggie, more nationalist in these postcolonial times, and quite unrelated to which God they were brought up to worship. I would not wish to make too much of this, because Muslim Indians still feel obliged to adopt Arab names in deference to the roots of their faith, but the Amritraj case (repeated in many other Christian families I know) is merely an example of Hinduism serving as a framework for the voluntary cultural assimilation of minority groups, without either compulsion or conversion becoming an issue.

It is possible to a great extent to speak of Hinduism as culture rather than as religion (a distinction the votaries of Hindutva reject or blur). Interestingly, similar Hindu customs have survived in now-Muslim Java and now-Buddhist Thailand. Islamic Indonesians still cherish the Ramayana legend, now shorn (for them) of its religious associations. Javanese Muslims bear Sanskrit names. Hindu culture can easily be embraced by non-Hindus if it is separated from religious faith and treated as a heritage to which all may lay claim.

The economist Amartya Sen made a related point in regretting the neglect by the votaries of Hindutva of the great achievements of Hindu civilization in favor of its more dubious features.

As Sen wrote: "Not for them the sophistication of the Upanishads or Gita, or of Brahmagupta or Sankara, or of Kalidasa or Sudraka; they prefer the adoration of Rama's idol and Hanuman's image. Their nationalism also ignores the rationalist traditions of

India, a country in which some of the earliest steps in algebra, geometry, and astronomy were taken, where the decimal system emerged, where early philosophy — secular as well as religious — achieved exceptional sophistication, where people invented games like chess, pioneered sex education, and began the first systematic study of political economy. The Hindu militant chooses instead to present India — explicitly or implicitly — as a country of unquestioning idolaters, delirious fanatics, belligerent devotees, and religious murderers."

Sen is right to stress that Hinduism is not simply the Hindutva of Ayodhya or Gujarat; it has left all Indians a religious, philosophical, spiritual, and historical legacy that gives meaning to the civilizational content of secular Indian nationalism. In building an Indian nation that takes account of the country's true Hindu heritage, we have to return to the pluralism of the national movement. This must involve turning away from the strident calls for Hindutva that would privilege a doctrinaire view of Hinduism at the expense of the minorities, because such calls are a denial of the essence of the Hinduism of Vivekananda. I say this not as a godless secularist, but as a proud Hindu who is mortified at what his own faith is being reduced to in the hands of bigots — petty men who know little about the traditions in whose defense they claim to act.

3

The Politics of Identity

I 'LL TELL YOU WHAT YOUR PROBLEM IS IN INDIA," the American businessman said. "You have too much history. Far more than you can use peacefully. So you end up wielding history like a battle-ax, against each other."

The American businessman doesn't exist; he is a fictional character in my novel *Riot*, about a Hindu-Muslim riot that erupts in the course of the Ram Sila Poojan campaign, the forerunner of the agitation to construct a Ram Janmabhoomi temple on the site occupied for four and a half centuries by the Babri Masjid. As headlines in recent years have too often spoken of a renewed cycle of killings and mob violence over the same issue, I have received dozens of comments on the eerie similarity between art and life.

In the wake of the awful Gujarat riots — some might well call them a pogrom — in 2002, which took somewhere between a thousand and two thousand, overwhelmingly Muslim, lives, some callers pointed to the afterword of *Riot*, published just a few months earlier, in which I alerted readers to the threat by Hindu extremists to commence construction of their temple in defiance of court orders. I seek no credit for prescience. The tragedy in India is that even those who know history seem condemned to repeat it.

It is one of the ironies of India's muddled march into the

twenty-first century that it has a technologically inspired vision of the future and yet appears shackled to the dogmas of the past. The temple town of Ayodhya has no computer software labs; it is devoted to religion and old-fashioned industry. In 1992, a howling mob of Hindu extremists tore down the Babri Masjid, a disused sixteenth-century mosque that occupied a prominent spot in a town otherwise overflowing with temples. The mosque had been built in the 1520s by India's first Mughal emperor, Babur; the Hindu zealots vowed to replace it with a temple to Lord Ram, which, they say, had stood on the spot for millennia before the Mughal invader tore it down to make room for his mosque. In other words, they want to avenge history, to undo the shame of half a millennium ago with a reassertion of their glory today.

I remember vividly an American friend at a function in New York on December 6, 1992, telling me he had seen on the news that the Babri Masjid had been destroyed, and my simply refusing to believe it. "You must have heard it wrong," I asserted confidently. "That sort of thing simply wouldn't happen in India. And if some mob had actually tried to attack it, the police would have stopped them well before they destroyed the mosque. Maybe the TV reported it was damaged?" "It was destroyed," the American retorted. "I didn't just hear it on TV. I saw it. It was destroyed in full view of the cameras."

It took a while for my initial disbelief to dissipate. This couldn't have happened, I agonized, in the India I had grown up in. Of course, there had been riots in my youth, but they were spontaneous eruptions, and, for the most part, had been quickly brought under control. But an organized effort to pull down a mosque? The very thought was appalling — something I did not believe Indians, as a collectivity, were capable of contemplating.

And if they were, surely they wouldn't be allowed to complete the task? The destruction of a substantial building takes time, and I couldn't believe the authorities would have let the mob have the hours they needed to fulfill their malign intent. The India in which this could happen was an India that had changed immeasurably from the country in which I had reached adulthood. It was from a profound sense of loss and betrayal that I wrote, and spoke, of my anguish at the time.

Indians in New York were just as exercised as Indians in India. I recall two events in particular. That December I was invited, along with others, to speak at an event at Columbia University at which artists and writers responded to the tragedy. In the time allotted to me I chose to read three extracts from other writers — Tagore's immortal "Let My Country Awake," from his *Gitanjali;* a poignant short story by Saadat Hasan Manto about looters at the time of Partition who are helped and encouraged by a kind man who turns out to be the owner of the house being looted; and a brief passage from Salman Rushdie's *The Satanic Verses,* in which he talks about the Indian "Overartist," using art as a metaphor for the palimpsest that is the Indian identity. To my astonishment the organizers, an anticommunal group, came to me afterward to say that a number of Muslims in the audience had been outraged by my choice of the last passage. Did I not know that Rushdie was anathema to them? Could I disavow him and apologize? It was my turn to be outraged. I had not come to lend my voice to a denunciation of Hindu intolerance in order to condone Muslim intolerance.

There was nothing remotely offensive to anybody about the passage I had read; its content, its evocation of Hindu and Muslim artists painting over each other's work, was precisely what I had come to affirm. In choosing this passage by a great Indian Muslim writer I was seeking to uphold the idea of the pluralist, tolerant India that had been attacked along with the Masjid. I refused to apologize, let alone disavow what I had read. But it was a sobering reminder that intolerance comes in many shades.

The second episode at the time was an address I was invited to make to the Indian community at the consulate in New York. A number of Hindutva sympathizers turned up for the question-and-answer session that was to follow, prepared to denounce the "pseudo-secularism" that they expected would underlie my critique.

Instead I spoke as a believing Hindu — and I spoke passionately of my shame that this could have been done by people claiming to be acting in the name of my faith. How dare the *goondas* of Ayodhya reduce the soaring majesty of the Vedas and the Upanishads to the ignorant tub-thumping of their brand of identity politics? Why should any Hindu allow them to diminish Hinduism to the raucous self-glorification of the football hooligan, to take a religion of awe-inspiring tolerance and shrink it into a chauvinist slogan? My speech startled both the secular leftists in the audience and the acolytes of Hindutva. Some of the latter who had come to protest were chastened into silence; only one rose to question me, saying that he agreed with my vision of Hinduism but that such a faith could have only one logical outcome — support for the positions taken by Hindu political leaders. To which my response was simple: I was brought up by a strongly devout father in the Hindu belief that each of us had to find his own Truth. No true Hindu, I averred, would allow a politician to define his dharma for him.

But many Hindus have. India is a land where history, myth, and legend often overlap; sometimes Indians cannot tell the difference. Some Hindus claim, with more zeal than evidence, that the Babri Masjid stood on the exact spot of Lord Ram's birth, and had been placed there by the Mughal emperor as a reminder to a conquered people of their own subjugation. Historians — most of them Hindus — reply that there is no proof that Lord Ram ever existed in human form, let alone that he was born where the believers claim he was. More to the point, there is no proof that Babur actually demolished a Ram temple to build his mosque. To destroy the mosque and replace it with a temple would not, they say, be righting an old wrong but perpetrating a new one.

Of course, it does not matter what is historically verifiable when it comes to matters of faith. It is enough that millions of Hindus actually believe the *masjid* had occupied the site of a *mandir,* and indeed there is evidence of mosques having being built elsewhere in

India on the ruins of demolished temples. And yet, when to act on that belief causes deep hurt to innocents who had nothing to do with the original wrong — if there was one — do we not have a greater responsibility to the present than to the past?

One of my more thoughtful challengers from the Hindutva ranks, Mr. Ashok Chowgule of the Mahanagar Vishwa Hindu Parishad of Mumbai, believes in the notion that I previously mentioned, and wrote to me to argue that Babur's motive in constructing the *masjid* in 1528 was to establish a symbol that would remind the conquered people of India who was the master and who the slave. That may well have been the case — in 1528. But today? The symbol, if such it was, retained the offensive meaning imputed to it by Mr. Chowgule only as long as the reality it sought to symbolize. When Mughal rule disappeared, so too did the potency of that symbol. Western countries have lived for centuries among Roman monuments constructed for exactly the same purpose, which remained, after the fall of the Roman Empire, as monuments, nothing more.

By 1992 the only symbolic importance the Babri Masjid had lay in our minds — in the importance we chose to give it. The attack on it, however, symbolized something else to Muslims in India and around the world; which is why I wrote of my sense of shame and sorrow at what Hindus had done in the name of their faith. When Mr. Chowgule writes that "it is natural that a free people should recover their own symbols," he appears to exclude non-Hindus from his definition of the free Indian people. I admire Rana Pratap Singh, Chhatrapati Shivaji, and Rani Lakshmibai of Jhansi just as much as he does, but my admiration for Akbar, for Hyder Ali, and Tipoo Sultan is scarcely less. My sense of India's history embraces all their contributions (as well as those of a few South Indian figures the VHP never seems to mention, such as Krishna Deva Raya of Vijayanagar). I do not see Indian history as Hindu history, and the attainment of India's freedom means, to me, more than just the freedom of us Hindus.

There are some, like me, who are proud of *Hinduism*; there are others, including much of the VHP, who are proud of *being Hindu.* There is a world of difference between the two; the first base their pride on principle and belief, the second on identity and chauvinism. My Hindu pride does not depend on putting others down. Theirs, sadly, does.

To most Indian Muslims, the Ram Janmaboomi/Babri Masjid dispute is not about a specific mosque — which had in fact lain disused for half a century before its destruction, most of Ayodhya's Muslim minority having emigrated to Pakistan upon the Partition in 1947 — but about their place in Indian society. For decades after independence, successive Indian governments had guaranteed their security in a secular state, permitting the retention of Muslim Personal Law separate from the country's civil code and even financing Haj pilgrimages to Mecca. Two of India's first five presidents were Muslims, as were innumerable cabinet ministers, ambassadors, generals, and supreme court justices. Until at least the mid-1990s India's Muslim population exceeded Pakistan's. The destruction of the mosque seemed an appalling betrayal of the compact that had sustained the Muslim community as a vital part of India's pluralist democracy.

The Hindu fanatics who attacked the mosque had little faith in the institutions of Indian democracy. They saw the state as soft, pandering to minorities out of a misplaced and Westernized secularism. To them, an independent India, freed after nearly a thousand years of alien rule (first Muslim, then British), and rid of a sizable portion of its Muslim population by the Partition, had an obligation to assert its own identity, one that would be triumphantly and indigenously Hindu. They are not fundamentalists in any meaningful sense of the term; they are, instead, chauvinists, who root their Hinduism not in any of its soaring philosophical or spiritual underpinnings — and, unlike their Islamic counterparts, not in the theology of their faith — but rather in its role as a source of identity. They seek revenge in the name of Hinduism-as-badge, rather than Hinduism-as-doctrine.

The Hindu zealots of 2002 who chanted insultingly triumphalist slogans helped incite the worst elements on the Muslim side, who may have criminally set fire to a railway carriage carrying temple campaigners; in turn, Hindu mobs torched Muslim homes and killed innocents. As the courts deliberate on a solution to the dispute, the cycle of violence goes on, spawning new hostages to history, generating new victims on both sides, ensuring that future generations will be taught new wrongs to set right. We live, Octavio Paz once wrote, between oblivion and memory. Memory and oblivion: how one leads to the other, and back again, has been the concern of much of my fiction. As I pointed out in the last words of *Riot,* history is not a web woven with innocent hands.

*

My views have, over the years, earned me more than my fair share of belligerent e-mails and assorted Internet fulminations from the less reflective of the Hindutva brigade. I was excoriated as "anti-Hindu" and described by several as a "well-known leftist," which no doubt amused those of my friends who knew me in college thirty years ago as perhaps the sole supporter of Rajaji's pro-free-enterprise Swatantra Party in those consensually socialist times.

At least one correspondent, reminding me of the religion that has been mine from birth, succumbed to the temptation to urge me predictably to heed that well-worn slogan: "*Garv se kahon ki hum Hindu hain*" — Say with pride that we are Hindu.

I am indeed proud that I am a Hindu. But of what is it that I am, and am not, proud? I am not proud of my coreligionists attacking and destroying Muslim homes and shops. I am not proud of Hindus raping Muslim girls, or slitting the wombs of Muslim mothers.

I am not proud of those who assert the base bigotry of their own sense of identity in order to exclude, not embrace, others.

I am proud that Hinduism is a civilization, not a dogma. I am proud that India's pluralism is paradoxically sustained by the fact that the overwhelming majority of Indians are Hindus, because

Hinduism has taught them to live amid a variety of other identities.

I am proud to claim adherence to a religion without an established church or priestly papacy, a religion whose rituals and customs I am free to reject, a religion that does not oblige me to demonstrate my faith by any visible sign, by subsuming my identity in any collectivity, not even by a specific day or time or frequency of worship. As a Hindu I am proud to subscribe to a creed that is free of the restrictive dogmas of holy writ that refuses to be shackled to the limitations of a single holy book.

I am proud that I can honor the sanctity of other faiths without feeling I am betraying my own. I am proud that Hinduism understands that faith is a matter of hearts and minds, not of bricks and stone.

I am proud of those Hindus, like the Shankaracharya of Kanchi, who say that Hindus and Muslims must live like Ram and Lakshman in India. I am not proud of those Hindus, like "Sadhvi" Rithambhara, who say that Muslims are like sour lemons curdling the milk of Hindu India. I am not proud of those who suggest that only a Hindu, and only a certain kind of Hindu, can be an authentic Indian. I am not proud of those Hindus who say that people of other religions live in India only on their sufferance, and not because they belong on our soil.

I am proud of those Hindus who realize that an India that denies itself to some of us could end up being denied to all of us. I am proud of those Hindus who utterly reject Hindu communalism, conscious that the communalism of the majority is especially dangerous because it can present itself as nationalist. I am proud of those Hindus who respect the distinction between Hindu nationalism and Indian nationalism.

I am proud of those Hindus who recognize that the saffron and the green on the flag hold equal importance. The reduction of non-Hindus to second-class status in their own homeland is unthinkable. It would be a second Partition, and a partition in the Indian soul would be as bad as a partition in the Indian soil.

For Hindus like myself, the only possible idea of India is that of a nation greater than the sum of its parts. That is the only India that will allow us to call ourselves not Brahmins, not Bengalis, not Hindus, not Hindi-speakers, but simply Indians. How about another slogan for Hindus like me? *Garv se kahon ki hum Indian hain.*

4

Of Secularism and Conversions

I N ALL THE RECENT DISCUSSION ABOUT HINDUTVA, the bogeyman
has been the concept of secularism. Secularism is established in
India's constitution, but acolytes of Hindutva ask why India
should not, like so many other third world countries, find refuge in
the assertion of its own religious identity. It is a reasonable question,
which requires a reasonable answer — an Indian answer.

My generation grew up in an India that rejected the very idea
that religion should be a determinant of nationhood. That was the
basic premise of Indian nationalism. We never fell into the insidious
trap of agreeing that, since Partition had established a state for the
Muslims, what remained was a state for the Hindus. To accept the idea
of India you had to spurn the logic that had divided the country.

This was what that much-abused term, secularism, meant for us.
Religion is far too deeply rooted in all our communities to be wholly
absent from Indians' perceptions of themselves. So irreligion was not
the issue; every religion flourishes in India. In *The Great Indian Novel*
in 1989, I even argued the case for restoring dharma to its place in
Indian public life. One reader, the retired director-general of police
of Tripura state, Mr. B. J. K. Tampi, wrote to assert the broad meaning of dharma. "In Hindi," he writes, "*dharma* means only faith or

religion. But in Sanskrit the word has a preeminently secular meaning of social ethics covering law-abiding conduct."

Fair enough: in an afterword to my novel I had listed a whole series of meanings that have been ascribed to the term *dharma* — an untranslatable Sanskrit term that is, nonetheless, cheerfully defined as an unitalicized entry in many an English dictionary. (The *Chambers Twentieth-Century Dictionary* defines it as "the righteousness that underlies the law.") I agree with Mr. Tampi that no one-word translation ("faith," "religion," "law") can convey the full range of meaning implicit in the term. "English has no equivalent for dharma," writes P. Lal, defining it as a "code of good conduct, pattern of noble living, religious rules and observance." In his "The Speaking Tree," Richard Lannoy actually defines dharma in nine different ways in different contexts. These include moral law, spiritual order, sacred law, righteousness, and even the sweeping "the totality of social, ethical and spiritual harmony." Indeed, dharma in its classic sense embraces the total cosmic responsibility of both God and Man. My late friend Ansar Husain Khan, author of the polemical *Rediscovery of India,* suggested that dharma is most simply defined as "that by which we live." Yes — and "that" brings me to my point, and to Mr. Tampi's.

"In fact the four ends of human life," Mr. Tampi went on, "*dharma, artha, kama* and *moksha,* are always mentioned in that order. The purport is that the pursuit of wealth and pleasure should be within the parameters of *dharma* and *moksha* (the final emancipation of the soul from rebirth through religious practices)." Mr. Tampi adds, citing Swami Ranganathananda: "The excessive Indian fear of rebirth has led to the neglect of true worldly *dharma* for the sake of an otherworldly *moksha.* It has made men unfit both in the worldly (secular) and spiritual spheres." Now, I have never met the good Mr. Tampi, whose theological learning is all the more impressive in a policeman, but his analysis gladdens my secular heart. The fact is that, despite having done so much to attract the opprobrium of the Hindutva brigade, I do believe that dharma can be the key to bridging the present gap between the religious and the secular in India. The social scientist T. N. Madan has argued that the increasing secularization of modern Indian life is responsible for the rise of fundamentalism, since "it is the marginalization of faith, which is what secularism is, that permits the perversion of religion. There are no fundamentalists or revivalists in traditional society." The implication is that secularism has deprived Indians of their moral underpinnings — the meaning that faith gives to life — and religious extremism has risen as an almost inevitable antithesis to the secular project. The only way out of this dilemma is for Hindus to return to the tolerant, holistic, just, pluralist dharma articulated so effectively by Swami Vivekananda, which embraces both worldly and spiritual duty.

After all, as Mr. Tampi pointed out, the Hindu's secular pursuit of material happiness is not meant to be divorced from his obedience to the ethical and religious tenets of his faith. So the distinction between "religious" and "secular" is an artificial one: there is no such compartmentalization in Hinduism. The secularism avowed by successive Indian governments, as Professor R. S. Misra of Benares Hindu University has argued, is based on *dharma-nirpekshata* ("keeping apart from dharma"), whereas an authentically Indian ethic would ensure that secular objectives are infused with dharma.

I should stress that I find this view persuasive but incomplete. Yes, dharma is essential in the pursuit of material well-being, public order, and good governance; but this should not mean turning public policy over to *sants* — living "saints" — and *sadhus*, nor excluding any section of Indian society from its rightful place in the Indian sun. If we can bring dharma into our national life, it must be to uphold, rather than be at the expense of, our pluralist Indianness. Hinduism has always acknowledged the existence of opposites (and reconciled them): pain and pleasure, success and failure, creation and destruction, life and death are all manifestations of the duality inherent in human existence. These pairings are not contradictory but complementary; they are aspects of the same overarching reality. So also with the secular and the sacred: a Hindu's life must involve both. To acknowledge this would both absorb and deflect the Hindu resurgence.

Secularists are reproached not so much for their modernism as for their lack of a sense of their place in the grand Indian continuum, their lack of dharma. In my view, to live in dharma is to live in harmony with one's purposes on earth. This emerges from Hindu tradition, but it is not necessarily practiced in a traditional way. If I can be forgiven for quoting my own fictional character Yudhishtir in *The Great Indian Novel:*

India is eternal. But the dharma appropriate for it at different stages of its evolution has varied. If there is one thing that is true today, it is that there are no classical verities valid for all time. . . . For too many generations now we have allowed ourselves to believe India had all the answers, if only it applied them correctly. Now I realize that we don't even know all the questions. . . . No more certitudes. Accept doubt and diversity. Let each man live by his own code of conduct, so long as he has one. Derive your standards from the world around you and not from a heritage whose relevance must be constantly tested. Reject equally the sterility of ideologies and the passionate prescriptions of those who think themselves infallible. Uphold decency, worship humanity, affirm the basic values of our people — those which do not change — and leave the rest alone. Admit that there is more than one Truth, more than one Right, more than one dharma.

But secularism as an Indian political idea had, in any case, little to do with Western ideas privileging the temporal over the spiritual. Rather, it arose from the 1920s onward in explicit reaction to the communalist alternative. Secular politics within the nationalist movement rejected the belief that religion was the most important element in shaping political identity. Indian secularism lent itself to an India that had a wealth of religions, none of which should be more entitled by the state.

All the cant about "genuine" and "pseudo" secularism boils

down in the end to simply this: Professor Amartya Sen has put it rather well in declaring that political secularism involves merely "a basic symmetry of treatment of different religious communities." This kind of secularism is actually the opposite of classic Western notions of secularism, because, in effect, it actively helps religions to thrive by ensuring there is no discrimination in favor of or against any particular religion.

In a country like India, our secularism recognizes the diversity of our people and ensures their continued commitment to the nation by guaranteeing that religious affiliation will be neither a handicap nor an advantage. No Indian need feel that his birth into a particular faith automatically disqualifies him from any profession or office. That is how the political culture of our country reflected "secular" assumptions and attitudes. Though the Indian population was 81 percent Hindu and the country had been partitioned as a result of a demand for a separate Muslim homeland, of India's first five presidents, two were Muslims; so were many governors, cabinet ministers, chief ministers of states, ambassadors, generals, supreme court justices, and chief justices. During the 1971 Bangladesh war with Pakistan, the Indian air force in the northern sector was commanded by a Muslim (Air Marshal Lateef), the army commander was a Parsi (General Manekshaw), the general officer commanding the forces that marched into Bangladesh was a Sikh (Lieutenant-General Aurora), and the general flown in to negotiate the surrender of the Pakistani forces in East Bengal (Major-General Jacob) was Jewish. *That* is Indian secularism.

Do the critics of secularism want to end an India in which this kind of "secularism" is practiced? And if so, what is their alternative? Hindu chauvinism has tended to portray itself as qualitatively different from Muslim sectarianism. A. G. Noorani has reminded us that as far back as 1958, Prime Minister Jawaharlal Nehru had warned against the dangers of Hindu communalism in a speech to the All-India Congress Committee. Nehru's point was that the communalism of the majority was especially dangerous because it could present

41

itself as nationalist: since most of us are Hindus, the distinction between Hindu nationalism and Indian nationalism could be all too easily blurred.

Obviously, majorities are never seen as "separatist," since separatism is by definition pursued by a minority. But majority communalism is an extreme form of separatism, because it seeks to separate other Indians, integral parts of our country, from India itself.

This is not to suggest that secular Hindu liberals have got it entirely right. Among the most intriguing correspondence I received as a columnist was a pair of letters from a fellow Keralite, Mr. A. M. Pakkar Koya of Kozhikode, a Muslim with some decidedly perceptive and unconventional opinions.

Mr. Pakkar Koya believes that there is a threat to India from fundamentalism, but he sees it emerging from two kinds of fundamentalism: Hindu and Muslim. The main difference between the two, he argues, is that "the Muslim masses by and large agree with the aims of the fundamentalists and think this is something expected of them. In the name of Islam they are prepared to condone or live under the most retrogressive laws, especially when it comes to women's rights." The Hindu masses do not have so absolutist a view of their faith — as I too have argued in my own writings.

A more dangerous difference, Mr. Pakkar Koya writes, is that "once they come to power the Muslim fundamentalists will try to eliminate or silence the liberals in Muslim society and those who don't share their views." Hindu fundamentalists, he believes, are not quite as extremist; so Hindu liberals are in much less danger from them than Muslim liberals are from Muslim fundamentalists. But the problem with that understandable complacency, Mr. Pakkar Koya suggests, is that therefore "the Hindu liberals may not be as keen to prevent a [Hindu] fundamentalist takeover of India as were the secular government and liberals in Algeria to prevent a Muslim fundamentalist electoral victory."

"The most important difference," Mr. Pakkar Koya then avers, is that the fundamentalism of the Sangh Parivar "is mostly a reaction

blunders and missteps that led to the tragedy of Partition is one from which no side emerges unblemished, though obviously there is a difference between those who espoused communal politics and those who stood for secular pluralism. But putting Mr. Ahmed's "two assertions" aside, what we are left with is a more fundamental point: that Hindus do not understand Islam and Muslims, and do not try hard enough to look beyond their prejudices.

The intriguing point Mr. Ahmed makes is that Islam itself is misunderstood by the majority of Indians. Even I have been guilty of juxtaposing Hinduism's unique tolerance of all faiths against the teaching of the Semitic religions that each of them represents the only true path to God. Mr. Ahmed begs to differ, and he cites extensively from the Holy Quran to make the point that Islam is a tolerant faith. "Let there be no compulsion in religion. Truth stands out clear from Error; whoever rejects evil and believes in God hath grasped the most trustworthy hand-hold," says Sura 2, verse 256. "Invite all to the way of thy Lord with wisdom and beautiful preaching; and argue with them in ways that are best and most gracious; for thy Lord knoweth best, who have strayed from His path, and who receive guidance," says Sura 16, verse 125. On coexistence, the Quran declares, "O Mankind! We created you from a single pair of a male and a female, and made you into nations and tribes, that you may know each other and not despise each other" (Sura 49, verse 13). And the possibility of different attitudes to religion is explicitly spelled out in Sura 10, verse 47: "To every people was sent an Apostle; when their Apostle come before them, the matter will be judged between them with justice, and they will not be wronged."

I do not know which translation of the Quran Mr. Ahmed is quoting from, but I have no reason to doubt the accuracy of these extracts. The real issue is the way the faithful interpret the tenets of their faith. "The concept of dharma in Hinduism," Mr. Ahmed adds, referring to my writings on the subject, "is similar to that of *deen* in Islam, which connotes a way of life governed by the teachings of the Quran, the examples of the Prophet and the ever-present consciousness of accountability for all thoughts and actions, both open and secret, before God on the Day of Judgment." In other words, Hindus and Muslims have much more in common doctrinally than the fanatics of either faith would have us believe.

"Having lived together for centuries," Mr. Ahmed laments, "Hindus and Muslims in general have yet to learn and respect each other's way of life." He recalls that in 1962 Acharya Vinoba Bhave compiled a selection of verses from the Quran under the title "The Essentials of the Quran" and published it on the Prophet Muhammed's birthday. Another Hindu scholar, Professor K. S. Ramakrishna Rao, wrote a "simple yet erudite treatise on the life and message of the Prophet of Islam." These books were published, appropriately enough, in Varanasi under the auspices of the Akhil Bharat Sarva Sangh in Rajghat. Will an enterprising non-Muslim publisher today take on the challenge of getting Hindu thinkers to explain Islam, with empathy and understanding, to Hindus?

The fact is that there are too many diversities in our land for any one version of reality to be imposed on all of us. The version propagated by the proponents of Hindutva resembles nothing so much as the arguments for the creation of Pakistan, of which Indian nationalism is the living repudiation. The Hindutva movement is the mirror image of the Muslim communalism of 1947; its rhetoric echoes the bigotry that India was constructed to reject. Its triumph would mark the end of India, and that, I am convinced, Indians will not let happen.

*

In the late 1990s there was a spate of attacks on Christian churches and missionaries. I was outraged at the anti-Christian thuggery, and equally outraged that it was perpetrated in the name of Hinduism. Killers of children are not Hindus, even if they claim to be acting on behalf of their faith; it is as simple as that. Murder does not have a religion — even when it claims a religious excuse.

It is easy enough to condemn anti-Christian violence because it *is* violence, and because it represents a threat to law and order as well as to that nebulous entity we think of as India's "image." But one point that has not been sufficiently made has nothing to do with the violence itself. It is the great danger of admitting a religious justification for the thugs' actions — of seeing behind it an "understandable" Hindu resistance to Christian zealotry. The then prime minister, Atal Behari Vajpayee, even called for a national debate on religious conversions. Reasonable Hindutva sympathizers went around saying, "Look, of course the violence and the killing are inexcusable and should be dealt with. But do you know how much resentment these Christian conversions have provoked? They are going around cheating people into giving up their faith. Naturally some Hindus are angry."

That sort of line — which we have all heard, often embellished with anecdotal evidence of missionary "trickery" — comes perilously close to condoning the indefensible. Let us assume for a minute, for the purposes of argument, that Christian missionaries are indeed using a variety of inducements (development assistance, health care, education, sanitation, even chicanery) to win converts for their faith. So what? If a citizen of India feels that his faith has not helped him to find peace of mind and material fulfillment, why should he not have the option of trying a different item on the spiritual menu? Surely freedom of belief is his fundamental right, however ill founded his belief might be. And if Hindu zealots suspect that his conversion was fraudulently obtained, why do they not offer counterinducements rather than violence? Instead of destroying churches, perhaps a Hindu-financed sewage system or *paatshala* might reopen the blinkered eyes of the credulous. Better still, perhaps Christians and Hindus (and Muslims and Baha'is, for that matter) could all compete in our villages to offer material temptations for religious conversions. The development of our poor country might actually accelerate with this sort of spiritual competition.

Of course, I am being frivolous there, but my point is a serious one. The prime minister's call for a national debate may be unexceptionable, but the premise behind much of the criticism of conversions is troubling. It seems to accord legitimacy to the rhetoric of the Bajrang Dal and its cohorts — who declare openly that conversions are inherently antinational. Implicit in the challenge to conversions is the idea that to be Hindu is somehow more natural, more authentically Indian, than to be anything else, and that to lapse from Hinduism is to dilute one's identification with the motherland.

As a Hindu, I reject that notion utterly. As an Indian, I have always argued that the whole point about India is the rejection of the very idea that religion should be a determinant of nationhood. Our nationalist leaders never fell into the insidious trap of agreeing that, since Partition had established a state for the Muslims, what remained was a state for the Hindus. To accept the idea of India you had to spurn the logic that divided the country in 1947.

The danger of the communalism of the majority that Nehru had warned about in 1958 is that it might be seen as nationalist. And, to our detriment, this would cause the line between Hindu nationalism and Indian nationalism to be blurred. That is what is being done by those who argue against conversions: they are suggesting that an Indian Hindu who becomes Christian is somehow, subtly, turning antinational. This is not only an insult to the millions of patriotic Indians who trace their Christianity to more distant forebears, including the Kerala Christians who converted to the faith of Saint Thomas centuries before most Europeans became Christian. It is an insult, too, to the very idea of India. Indianness has nothing to do with which God you choose to worship, or not. Even if your adherence to a particular faith has been obtained by material inducements or chicanery.

I cheerfully tell Christian audiences that Hinduism asserts that all ways of belief are equally valid, and Hindus readily venerate the saints, and the sacred objects, of other faiths. Hinduism, I assert, is a civilization, not a dogma.

If a Hindu decides he wishes to be a Christian, how does it matter that he has found a different way of stretching his hands out toward God? Truth is one, the Hindu believes, but there are many ways of attaining it.

The fact that Hinduism has never claimed a monopoly on spiritual wisdom is what has made it so attractive to seekers from around the world. Its eclecticism is its strength. My late father was a devout Hindu who prayed faithfully twice a day, after his baths. He regularly went on pilgrimages to all the major temples and religious sites in our land. When a fire engulfed the Guruvayoor temple in the 1960s, he led a fund-raising drive in Bombay that saw much of his meager savings diverted to the rebuilding of that shrine. Yet, when a Christian friend presented him an amulet of the Virgin Mary that had personally been blessed by the pope, he accepted it with reverence and carried it around with him for years. That is the Hinduism most Hindus know: a faith that accords respect and reverence to the sanctified beliefs of others.

So the rejection of other forms of worship, other ways of seeking the Truth, is profoundly un-Hindu, as well as being un-Indian. Worse, the idea of Indianness rendered by those who are against religious conversion is one that mirrors that upon which Pakistan was created, of which the nationalism of Gandhi, Nehru, and Azad is the living repudiation. In many Muslim countries it is illegal for a Muslim to convert to any other faith; in some, such apostasy is even condemnable by death. Hindus have rightly sought for years to point out how different their faith is, how India has no room for such practices. There is no such thing as a Hindu heresy. Yet, ironically, it is the most chauvinist of the Hindutva brigade who want to emulate this Muslim convention.

*

The international outcry at the destruction of the Bamiyan Buddhas — the magnificent statues carved out of an Afghan mountainside by devout monks 1,400 years ago and described by the intrepid Chinese traveler Hsuen Tsang as among the greatest achievements of human civilization — did not take very long to die down. Within weeks, people around the world concluded that there was not much point to it anymore: the statues were gone, and the Afghan people were starving. Better attend to the living than to

49

mourn the destroyed, many said. And who can blame them?

But one of the saddest features of this outcry, to an Indian, must be the extent to which the world's critics and commentators linked the event to another act of destruction, this time on Indian soil. I refer, of course, to the tearing down of the Babri Masjid in Ayodhya in December 1992. Many foreign analysts drew a direct parallel between the two events. To take but one prominent example, the *New York Times* editorial observer Tina Rosenberg wrote of the Taliban's action that "such irreversible destruction of cultural and religious property has ample recent precedent." She cited Ayodhya and its blood-soaked aftermath as her principal example, and added, "Mobs often seek to destroy religious and ethnic sites, both to intimidate the people who hold them sacred and to send the message 'you do not belong here.'" Shamefully, that is just what an Indian mob did, and we who allowed it to happen will never be able to live it down.

Others, too, saw India's passionate denunciations of the Bamiyan destruction as tainted, if not undermined, by the fact that they issued from the lips of leaders who had condoned (and in some cases incited) a comparable act of cultural barbarism on their own soil. What have we come to that a land that has been a haven of tolerance for religious minorities throughout its history should have sunk so low in the eyes of the world? India's is a civilization that, over millennia, has offered refuge and, more important, religious and cultural freedom, to Jews, Parsis, several varieties of Christians, and, particularly in the south, to Muslims. Jews came to Kerala centuries before Christ, with the destruction by the Babylonians of their First Temple, and they knew no persecution on Indian soil until the Portuguese arrived in the sixteenth century to inflict it. In Kerala, where Islam came through traders, travelers, and missionaries rather than by the sword, the Zamorin of Calicut was so impressed by the seafaring skills of this community that he issued a decree obliging each fisherman's family to bring up one son as a Muslim to man his all-Muslim navy. The India where the singing of mantras routinely mixes with the cry of the muezzin, and where the chiming of church bells accompanies the *gurudwara*'s reading from the Guru Granth Sahib, is an India that is entitled to lament and to condemn what happened at Bamiyan. But that India must resist those Indians who pulled down the Babri Masjid.

The central battle in contemporary Indian civilization is between those who, to borrow from Whitman, acknowledge that we are vast, we contain multitudes, and those who have presumptuously taken it upon themselves to define (in increasingly narrower terms) what is "truly" Indian. The central tenet of tolerance is that the tolerant society accepts that which it does not understand and even that which it does not like, so long as it is not sought to be imposed upon the unwilling. Those who persecute young boys and girls trying to celebrate Valentine's Day have no right to claim they are doing so in the name of a culture that has long been a byword for tolerance. I cringe that an Indian state has self-righteously banned the Miss India contest, even if I believe that such contests enshrine a very limited aspect of Indian womanhood. I am appalled that a government minister intimidates a French television channel into altering its fashion programming because its models' attire is "contrary to Indian sensibilities," as if the minister is entitled to define what those sensibilities are, and when the only ones affected are those who voluntarily tune in to that channel. All this is being done in the name of *bharatiya sanskriti,* a notion of Indian culture whose assertion is both narrow-minded and profoundly antihistorical.

For where, in the Hindutva zealots' definition of *bharatiya sanskriti,* do the erotic sculptures of Khajuraho belong? Should their explicitly detailed couplings not be pulled down, as FTV's cable signals have been? What about the Kama Sutra, the tradition of the devadasis, the eros of the Krishna Leela — are they all un-Indian now? I wonder how many saw the irony at the recent Maha Kumbha Mela (the grand Hindu religious festival) of Naga sadhus parading their nakedness in front of women and children without anyone raising an eyebrow, while the police arrested a foreign tourist for similarly stripping and smearing herself with ash in an act she thought had been sanctified by millennial Indian tradition. When the late great Mexican poet Octavio Paz wrote his final ode to our civilization, *In Light of India,* he devoted an entire section to Sanskrit erotic poetry, basing himself, among other things, on the Buddhist monk Vidyakara's immortal eleventh-century compilation of 1,728 *kavya,* many of which are exquisitely profane. Are poets like Ladahachandra or Bha-vakadevi, who a thousand years ago wrote verse after verse describing and praising the female breast, to be expelled from the Swarajist canon of *bharatiya sanskriti?* Should we tell future Octavio Pazes seeking to appreciate the attainments of our culture that the Mahabhar-ata on Doordarshan is *bharatiya sanskriti,* but a classical portrayal of the erotic longings of the *gopis* for Krishna is not?

It may not seem to matter very much what some lumpen elements think of Valentine's Day. But if they are allowed to get away with their lawless acts of intolerance and intimidation, we are allowing them to do violence to something profoundly vital to our survival as a civilization. Pluralist India must, by definition, tolerate plural expressions of its many identities. To allow the self-appointed arbiters of *bharatiya sanskriti* to impose their hypocrisy and double standards on the rest of us is to permit them to define Indianness down until it ceases to be Indian. And when that happens we will have completely lost our right, in the eyes of the world, to condemn any future Bamiyans.

The real argument in our country is between those who believe in an India where differences of caste, creed, conviction, class, color, culture, cuisine, costume, and custom shouldn't determine your Indianness, and those who define Indianness along one or more of these divisions. In other words, the really important debate is not about conversions, but between the unifiers and the dividers — between those who think all Indians are "us," whichever God they choose to worship, and those who think that Indians can be divided into "us" and "them."

I too am proud of my Hinduism; I do not want to cede its verities to fanatics. To discriminate against another, to attack another, to kill another, to destroy another's place of worship on the basis of his faith is not part of Hindu dharma, as it was not part of the preacher and philosopher Vivekananda's. It is time to go back to these fundamentals of Hinduism. It is time to take Hinduism back from the fundamentalists.

5

On the Importance of Being Muslim and Indian

THE TEMPTATION TO SEE IN CRICKET LARGER METAPHORS for national issues has always proved difficult to resist.

One Sunday, while India was losing the 2003 World Cup final to Australia through a heartbreaking combination of ineptitude and ill luck, the *New York Times* treated its readers to an essay by a travel writer on his experience of being a "cricket heathen" in India. After mildly amusing descriptions of his discovery of the sport and the passions it stirred in the Indian soul, the author, Michael Y. Park, concluded with an anecdote: "Even when I tried to escape civilization deep into the Great Indian (Thar) Desert in the northwest, near the border with Pakistan, cricket dominated conversation. I was on a three-day camel trek, and my camel driver . . . played only camel polo and had never seen a professional cricket match because he'd never watched television. But . . . this man who had never been more than twenty miles from the fairy-tale fort of Jaisalmer and who had never heard of nuclear bombs or Uttar Pradesh, India's most populous state, rattled off statistics about the national team and details of the players' private lives. He even worked in a few disparaging remarks about the Pakistani team. [He] noted my astonishment.

'You have to understand,' [he] said, spitting out a gob of betel nut and saddling up his camel. 'Indians are crazy about this cricket.'"

It's a lovely story to illustrate the extent and reach of the passion for India's real national sport (despite all the General Knowledge quiz books that instruct students that India's national sport is hockey, the marketplace has voted decisively for cricket). But that was not the only reason I quoted it.

In reproducing the tale, I omitted the name of the cricket-chauvinist camel driver. Mr. Park does not make much of this, but it was Amin Khan. This committed fan of the national team, with his "disparaging remarks" about the players from across the border, is a Muslim.

It should hardly be worth mentioning. After all, 13 percent (perhaps 14) of our population follows both the Islamic faith and the fortunes of our national team. But it is a sad commentary on our times that the loyalty of Indian Muslims to India's cricketing success should have been questioned by certain elements in our country. It has long been one of the favorite complaints of the Hindutva brigade that Indian Muslims set off firecrackers whenever the Indian team loses to Pakistan. This is one of those "urban legends" that acquires mythic proportions in the retelling, even though the evidence for the charge is both sparse and anecdotal. Certainly some Muslims may have behaved in this way, but the percentage of the community they represent is minuscule. The camel driver, it is clear, would have been astonished at such conduct: even he, illiterate and poor, knows where his home is, and therefore where his loyalties lie.

But then those who identify the nation with a specific religion would themselves not expect devotees of other faiths to share their feelings. Their unseemly triumphalism after India's victory over Pakistan (a victory achieved by a team including two Muslims and a Sikh, and captained by a Hindu with a Christian wife) was unseemly precisely because it took on sectarian rather than nationalist overtones. And reports came in — perhaps exaggerated — of clashes between Hindu and Muslim groups within India in the aftermath of the defeat of Pakistan. What on earth, I wondered, would prompt petty bigots (on both sides) to reduce a moment of national sporting celebration into a communal conflict?

Cricket in independent India has always been exempt from the contagion of communalism. Despite the religious basis of Partition, Indian cricket teams always featured players of every religious persuasion. Three of the country's most distinguished and successful captains — Ghulam Ahmed, Mansur Ali Khan Pataudi, and Mohammed Azharuddin — were Muslims, as was our best-ever wicket-keeper, Syed Kirmani. Perhaps more important, so were two of the most popular cricketers ever to play for the country, Abbas Ali Baig and Salim Durrani. Who can forget the excitement stirred by Baig's dream debut in England in 1959, when he was conscripted out of Oxford University by an Indian team in the doldrums ("Don't be vague," an English commentator declared, "call for Baig!") and promptly hit a century both in his first tour match and on his Test debut? Or that magical moment when, as Baig walked back to the pavilion in Bombay after a brilliant 50 against Australia, an anonymous sari-clad lovely ran out and spontaneously greeted him with an admiring (and scandalously public) kiss? The episode is part of national lore; it has been immortalized in Salman Rushdie's novel *The Moor's Last Sigh*. Who cared, then, in those innocent 1960s, that Baig was Muslim and his admirer Hindu? Who in the screaming crowds that welcomed his appearance thought of Salim Durrani's religion when they cheered themselves hoarse over that green-eyed inconsistent genius with the brooding movie-star looks? I will never forget the outrage that swept the country when he was dropped from the national team during an England tour in 1972; signs declaring "No Durrani No Test" proliferated like nukes. I do not believe there have been two more beloved Indian cricketers in the last fifty years than Baig and Durrani — and their religion had nothing to do with it.

Which is as it should be. Apart from the great Muslim players I mentioned, India has been captained by Christians (Vijay Hazare and Chandu Borde), Parsis (Polly Umrigar and Nari Contractor), and a Sikh (Bishen Singh Bedi). Mohammad Kaif may be leading

India before the decade is over, just as he captained the national youth team to spectacular success a few years ago. Cricketing ability and sporting leadership have nothing to do with the image of your Maker you raise (or fold) your palms to in worship. When India wins (or loses), all of India wins (or loses).

The degradation of public discourse that has accompanied the rise of religious nativism in our country since the late 1980s must not be allowed to contaminate our national sport.

*

So it was with some trepidation that I declared, on the strength of his early performance in Test cricket, that Irfan Pathan was already well on the way to being my favorite player in what, in 2003–4, seemed an extraordinary Indian team. My enthusiasm might partly have been explained by being the father of twin sons who were then nineteen, and the sight of the nineteen-year-old Pathan bounding down to hurl his thunderbolts filled me with that mixture of pride and awe that I think of as typically paternal (admiration for what is being done, suffused by wonder that this youngster is doing it).

But that was not the whole story. After all, the Indian team was full of stars who deserve greater encomia. And yet — what had Pathan brought to the Indian team? Raw youth? We already had that in wicket-keeper Parthiv Patel, a year younger than Pathan; but Pathan's was a youthfulness raw only in its energy and enthusiasm. His conduct had a maturity that belied his nineteen years, and it was allied to a temperament his elders should value. Pathan was constantly striving, trying new angles, outthinking the batsmen, and he was always seeking to learn, to improve, to educate himself. Pathan had heart, and he also had a head. His English was not yet as ready-for-prime-time as his telegenic looks, but in his interviews he had already spoken of figuring out the difference between bowling in Australian conditions and in those of the subcontinent. Irfan Pathan was old enough to command a place in the team as a matter of right, and young enough to know that he still had a lot to learn.

But since I am not a sportswriter, there was another aspect that thrilled me about Irfan Pathan playing for India. And that lay in the simple fact that his very existence was a testament to the indestructible pluralism of our country. He hails from Gujarat, a state in which many — many with loud voices and great influence — have sought to redefine Indianness on their own terms. Neither his religion nor his ethnicity would have qualified him as Indian enough in their eyes. He is a Muslim, and not just a Muslim but the son of a muezzin, one whose waking hours are spent calling the faithful to prayer. Worse still, he is a Pathan, whose forebears belong to a slice of land that is no longer territorially part of India. To be a Gujarati Muslim Pathan might be thought of as a triple disqualification in this Age of Togadia. Irfan Pathan had not just shrugged off his treble burden, he had broken triumphantly through it.

And he had done so without apology for his identity, or his faith. Interviewed after his 3 for 32 in the last one-day international clinched India the series, Pathan told Dean Jones of his happiness that India had won "after" (not "because of") his bowling, and attributed this success to his Maker. "God is with me. I knew with God's help I'll bowl well. I had that confidence in God." So the muezzin's son had invoked Allah's blessings on his team, oblivious to the fact that its opponents were playing under the green banner of an Islamic Republic. What a wonderful reinvention of Indian secularism.

So when Irfan Pathan beamed that dazzling smile after taking yet another wicket for the India he so proudly represents, he filled my heart with more than cricketing pride. He reminded me that he represents a country where it is possible for a nineteen-year-old from a beleaguered minority to ascend to the peak of the nation's sporting pantheon; and even more, that he represents an idea, an immortal Indian idea, that our country is large enough and diverse enough to embrace everyone who chooses to belong to it. This is an idea that no one, however well-connected politically, has the right to deny. The pluralist palimpsest of Indianness can never be diminished by the killers of Gujarati Muslims and the evil men who incited them.

Irfan Pathan is their standing, leaping, glorious repudiation.

Or so I argued, and I was surprised by the reactions I received. I discounted the purely cricketing responses — including those from some who churlishly felt that the teenager's contribution to India's cricketing triumphs in Pakistan was not as great as my praise implied — on the grounds that they have somewhat missed the point. In bringing his vigor and his talent to the national cause, Irfan Pathan, a Gujarati Muslim of (to put it territorially) "Pakistani" ethnic origin, had repudiated those who had allowed themselves to forget (or who had consciously denied) an indestructible Indian idea.

A number of readers liked the piece — but of the many who disagreed with it, two, in my view, made strikingly interesting arguments that deserved attention on larger political grounds. One was passed on to me from an Internet discussion group that had reacted to my piece; the other was sent to me directly by an eminent Indian academician. One I disagreed with, the other I accepted.

The first, by a chat-room discussant called Saurabh, also objected to my "attempts to build up Pathan as the star of the Indian victory." He felt I was echoing Imran Khan's statements "downplaying India's team effort" and felt the problem lay in the Pakistanis' "inability to believe they can be beaten fair and square by India (unless of course it is Muslims who are responsible for their defeat)." Obviously, I did not share this piece of social psychology. But Saurabh then went on to hail Shiv Sena chief Bal Thackeray's comments reacting to what he called "Zaheer Khan's nice putdown of his Pakistani interviewer." (Zaheer had, I understand, retorted to a question about how he felt as a Muslim playing for India by pointing out that it was his country, he had grown up there, and it had made him who he was.) Thackeray, Saurabh explained, "immediately endorsed him as a 'true Indian Muslim.' That runs contrary to Tharoor's script of the Hindu Right as being unprepared to accept an Indian Muslim as Indian."

Now this took me a bit aback. I had thought Thackeray's comment nauseatingly patronizing, the equivalent of an anti-Semite bestowing the label of "good Jew." Are we now, in the enlightened first decade of the twenty-first century, to accept the notion that the leader of a Hindu-chauvinist political party is entitled to certify who is, or is not, a "true Indian Muslim"? The notion is as offensive as it is unsustainable. I admire Zaheer's forthright defense of his birthright no less than Thackeray does. But my point is precisely that an Indian Muslim should be free to define his Muslimness as he sees fit (in Irfan's case, with overt expressions of his piety, hardly surprising in a muezzin's son) without in any way diminishing his claim to Indianness. An Indian Muslim is simply that: an Indian and a Muslim. It is not for Mr. Thackeray and his ilk to determine what makes him a "true Indian Muslim."

The second notable critique came from Professor Syed Iqbal Hasnain, vice chancellor of the University of Calicut in Kerala. "As an educated Uttar Pradesh Muslim," Professor Hasnain wrote, "I felt humiliated that when some player or film actor performs for India, then the majority community feels that Muslims are patriotic Indians." I was again taken aback, since the last thing I had intended was to humiliate any Indian Muslim by my celebration of Irfan, but the good professor went on to explain: "There are hundreds and thousands of Muslims who are performing for India in various fields and nobody wants to acknowledge their contribution." In Kerala alone, Professor Hasnain argued, there are over 150 Muslim-funded institutions in the Malabar region providing medical education, and training nurses, paramedics, engineers, and teachers in fields as varied as arts and sciences, hospitality management, and costume and fashion design. These are "high-quality institutions," he explained, reflecting an estimated total investment of around 1,000 crore Indian rupees, entirely provided by individuals belonging to the Muslim community. And here's the rub: the students who attend these colleges, according to the professor, "are 90 percent non-Muslim boys and girls." There are, he adds, similar institutions in Tamil Nadu, Andhra Pradesh, and Karnataka. "In my view," Professor Hasnain concludes, "Irfan is not the standing, leaping, glorious repudiation of the killers of Muslims in Gujarat, but certainly the Muslim institution-builders of South India in general and Kerala in particular are the shining examples."

I accept the good professor's rebuke, but with one mild expression of self-defense. To celebrate one individual as representing a larger idea is not to deny that there are other examples that affirm the same idea. Irfan and cricket had captured the national imagination at the time; it was not unreasonable for a columnist to seize on them to make his point. No doubt there are worthier examples of Indian Muslims repudiating the assumptions of the murderous chauvinists of Gujarat and elsewhere.

*

This was not the first time, though, that I had unwittingly offended Indian Muslim readers in expatiating on the vexed subject of Indianness. "There is a certain kind of secularism which sometimes scares me even more than the militant fundamentalism of the mosque-bashers," began an e-mail I received in response to a series of columns on Hinduism and Indianness. "It wears a smiling face and speaks in a tender voice, asking Muslims to participate in Hindu 'culture' rather than 'religion.' 'Celebrate Deepavali with us,' these secularists say, and they perceive no irony in the way Deepavali takes over civil life in India the way Eid or Muharram can never aspire to. They are proud of the fact that rural Islam is almost indistinguishable from Hinduism, but they do not stop to wonder why it is not the other way around."

I sat up and took notice. I am used to criticism from all sides in our wretched national agonizing about secularism, but rarely in such terms from an Indian Muslim. The author of these words, Shahnaz Habib, went on:

> You write about the Amritraj family, "To give their children Hindu names must have seemed more 'nationalist.'" You have just equated Hindu with nationalist, a religion with the country,

the part with the whole. You go on to add that Muslim Indians
still "feel obliged to adopt Arab names in deference to the roots
of their faith." I wish I knew how you defined "obliged to." Is it
merely a compulsion of faith as you seem to see it or is it a joyous affirmation of being able to participate not only in a local
heritage but also in a culture that goes beyond national boundaries? Or could it be a political act? Could it be the insecurity of
living in a country where you walk into a nationalized bank to
be faced by a huge oil painting of goddess Lakshmi? Why are
there so few Muslim or Christian symbols in our public spaces if
cultural assimilation has been so successful?

And there was a particular poignancy to Ms. Habib's conclud-
ing paragraph: "I wish for you the knowledge of what it feels like to
be a minority. What it feels like to be on the wrong side of an accident of numbers. On one hand, the adventure of having more than
one culture to call mine. The magic of constantly challenging my
preconceptions. And [on the other,] the pain of wishing that my
Hindu friends knew as much about my Muslim festivals and customs
as I know about theirs, of wishing that I didn't have to explain my actions in my own country. And worse, feeling guilty for feeling this
pain."
    The e-mail gave me much to think about, both because of its
own thoughtfulness and because it is always salutary for a writer to
be reminded that one must never become too complacent in the belief that one's own good intentions are self-evident. I responded by
pointing out that certain cultural symbols are identified with a religious community but used by both — I mentioned the Hindu custom of the smashing of coconuts in my piece; I know Muslim women
who wear the *bindi* for decorative purposes, and Hindu men who
wear an *achkan*. Most Hindus do join in Muslim celebrations when
invited, though the *iftar* parties thrown during Ramadan by sundry
politicians suggest both tokenism and opportunism.
    In my column I had put the Hindu in "'Hindu' names" within
quotes because the names of the Amritraj trio are actually no more

Hindu than the names Bashir or Jamal are Muslim. Vijay and Anand are merely Sanksrit words connoting victory and bliss respectively, which have been used as names for millennia. Ashok is the name of a Buddhist king. They are indeed names with a hoary pedigree on Indian soil, which is why I suggested their use might have seemed more "nationalist." I believe my entire published work would demonstrate vividly that I have never identified Indianness with Hinduness, "a part with the whole."

Having said that, though, I was concerned by Muslims using Arab names as "a joyous affirmation of being able to participate not only in a local heritage but also in a culture that goes beyond national boundaries." First of all, what is this culture? It is not Islam, because Arab names are pre-Islamic and the same names are used by all Arabs, Christian, Muslim, or Druze. Should an Indian Muslim feel more affinity with Arab culture than with Indian? I hoped not, because then she would be giving ammunition to the worst bigots on the Hindutva side.

Ms. Habib's reply was impressive:

If we go back to the linguistic and geographical roots of "amrit" and "bashir," there is indeed nothing remotely religious about them. But to do so is to deny the cultural associations that have accrued to them over centuries of use. Most Indian Muslims naming their children are not trying to create a mini-Arabia.

But religion plays an important role in culture (and the cultural-identification process of naming). A name is not its original meaning; it is what it represents. Arab names may represent a geographical affiliation to Christian Arabs; to Indian Muslims, it represents the religion which originated in the Middle East. Piqued by your use of the phrase "obliged to," I was trying to point out that Indian Muslims have a dual heritage — that of the national culture encompassing the Ramayana and the freedom struggle as well as that of the Muslim civilization.

Fair enough — though I sense much room for further debate on this point. I was struck, nonetheless, by her observation about the paucity of Muslim or Christian symbols in our public spaces — of holidays being granted for Deepavali and not for Muharram in the Delhi publishing house in which she worked. These are, for the most part, unintentional slights. But her raising it is one more reminder that one can never fully put oneself in the shoes of another.

And yet, as I have often written, who in India is not a minority? A Keralite friend recently reminded me of the "southern discomfort" the journalist Madhavan Kutty wrote about in describing his experience of North India. In that case it's not being on the "wrong side of the accident of numbers"; it's being on the other side of the accident of geography and location. But if we were to remain perpetually on our own side, where would be the "magic of constantly challenging" not only our preconceptions, but our expectations of what Indianness can be?

That throwaway line observing that "Muslim Indians still feel obliged to adopt Arab names in deference to the roots of their faith" provoked a flurry of correspondence, many from other Christian readers who themselves do the same as the Amritrajes, a few from Hindus citing examples of friends of other faiths adopting Hindu names, and several from Muslims explaining to me why their names were as they should be.

The clearest explanation in the latter category came from my friend Professor Mohammed Ayoob, the eminent scholar from Orissa who currently teaches in Michigan. Ayoob-sahib pointed out that most Arabic names adopted by Indian Muslims are, in the perception of Muslims, Quranic (and therefore Islamic) rather than "Arabic." In other words, such names imply no extraterritorial allegiances, only loyalty to the wellsprings of the Holy Book. Some of the most common Muslim names, Professor Ayoob tells me, are names of prophets mentioned in the Quran. For example, Ibrahim (Abraham), Musa (Moses), Isa (Jesus), Yaqub (Jacob), Yusuf (Joseph), and Ayoob (Job). The same principle applies, naturally, to Muhammad and Ahmed (which is a variation of Muhammad — literally one who sings the praise of God).

There is a second set of Muslim names that have the prefix Abdul (literally servant or slave, the equivalent of Das in Hindu names). Abdul is prefixed to one of the ninety-nine names of God in the Quran that identify his various attributes, which gives us Abdul Rahim, Abdul Rahman, Abdul Karim, Abdul Latif, Abdul Qadir, and so on. "These are equivalent to Bhagwan Das or Ram Das among Hindu names," says Professor Ayoob. (Or, for that matter, "Jesudas" among Indian Christian names.)

The third set of names came from those of the Prophet's companions or from his family: Ali, Abu Bakr, Omar, Usman, Jaafar, Saad, Hassan, Hussein, Aisha, Fatima, etc. "These were adopted not because they were Arabic," writes Professor Ayoob, "but because these figures are held in high respect by Muslims all over the world." Fair enough.

These three sets make up the bulk of Arabic names among Muslim Indians, but there is also a fourth category. Professor Ayoob explains: "Non-Quranic Arabic names have been recently adopted especially as a result of the Gulf oil boom and the sizable number of Indian Muslims who have migrated to West Asia temporarily to find livelihood. They come into contact with Arabs who have non-Islamic Arab names, mistakenly think they are Islamic, and sometimes give such names to their children. Since the returnees from the Gulf are perceived as role models among low-middle-class and working-class Muslims because they have made money, the latter begin to name their children after those of the returnees and the contagion spreads." However, non-Quranic and non-Islamic Arab names, he stresses, are in a very small minority among Indian Muslims.

Why is this issue important at all? The question of the "foreign origin" of the names used by Indian minorities has become one element of the Hindutva assault on them for being insufficiently Indian. In one passage of his 1923 book, *Hindutva: Who Is a Hindu?* Veer Savarkar questions the patriotism of India's minority Muslim and Christian communities because "they do not look upon India as their holy land," he wrote. "Their holy land is far off in Arabia and

Palestine. Consequently their names and their outlook smack of foreign origin. Their love is divided." The implication is that the Muslims should seek inspiration in India's culture rather than Arabia's.

Professor Ayoob argues :

Arabic names are assumed by Indian Muslims not because of cultural affinity. Islam came to India (with the exception of Kerala) from the Turko-Persian lands of Central Asia. The cultural influence is, therefore, Persian more than Arab. Persian was the court language and the language of literature and of high culture. A cultured gentleman in north India until the turn of the twentieth century had to know Persian and had to be able to quote Persian couplets (this applied to both Hindu and Muslim old elites). Muslim elite families, therefore, adopted names of Persian origin for reasons of cultural and linguistic affinity. This had little to do with religion. Therefore, names like Parvez, Parveen, Firoz, Firoza, Shireen, Mehnaz, Mehjabeen, Shahnaz, Humayun, once adopted by elite families, also gradually became popular among the lower strata of society, although I would wager that Persian names are more common among the elite than they are among the "subalterns." Some Arabic names come through Persian because Arabic words, including names, have over time been adopted in Persian.

In other words, he concludes, these are "cultural" names, not religious ones. I do agree that the adoption of such Islamic/Quranic and Persian names is tied to the preservation of Muslim identity in India, but I do not think this should be a target of criticism. After all, one finds names like Kallicharan and Ramadhin among West Indian cricketers. This does not make them any less West Indian.

I should like to thank this eminent scholar and friend for his valuable contribution to the debate on this issue. More important, I agree that no Indian should feel obliged to take on elements of Hindu culture as "proof" of his or her own integration into the

THE *elephant,* THE *tiger,* AND THE *cell phone*

national mainstream. Equally, Hinduism can serve as a framework for the voluntary cultural assimilation of minority groups, if they want it. Yusuf Khan is no less Muslim because he chose the name Dilip Kumar to put on the marquee, and Shah Rukh Khan is no less Indian because he retained his Muslim name. In a country of such great cultural diversity, our names are, after all, one more tangible sign of the pluralism that is India's greatest strength.

Now if only Irfan Pathan, whose cricketing prowess fell away within a couple of years of his ascent to stardom, will recover his mojo for India. . . .

6

Making Bollywood's India a Reality

To me, Indian films, with all their limitations and outright idiocies, represent part of the hope for India's future. In a country that is still (whatever the official figures say) almost 40 percent illiterate, films represent the prime vehicle for the transmission of popular culture and values. Bollywood and its regional offshoots produce more than eight hundred films a year in nineteen languages and employ 2.5 million people, and their movies are watched over and over again by the Indian masses, especially those with few other affordable forms of entertainment.

In India, popular cinema emerges from, and has consistently reflected, the diversity of the pluralist community that makes this cinema. The stories they tell are often silly, the plots formulaic, the characterizations superficial, the action predictable, but they are made and watched by members of every community in India. Muslim actors play Hindu heroes, South Indian heroines are chased around trees by North Indian rogues. Representatives of some communities may be stereotyped (think of the number of alcoholic Christians portrayed on screen) but good and bad are always shown as being found in every community.

To take just one recent popular film: a Marathi-speaking "playback singer" records an Urdu poet's lyrics to the tune of a Tamil

Muslim's music; her voice is then lip-synched by a Telugu actress, swaying to the choreography of a Goan Christian dance director, as she is romanced by a Punjabi superstar; the resulting film, produced by a Gujarati and directed by a Bengali, is then promoted by a Jewish public relations executive and watched by Indians of every imaginable caste, creed, cuisine, costume and consonant, from all over the country. Bollywood embodies the very idea of India's diversity in the very way in which it is organized.

But that alone is not enough. India's diversity is under assault: the twentieth-century politics of deprivation has eroded the culture's confidence, and the politics of bigotry, which once partitioned the country, have again arisen. Hindu chauvinism and other forms of communalism has emerged from the competition for resources in a contentious democracy. Politicians seek to mobilize voters by appealing to narrow identities; by seeking votes in the name of religion, caste, and region, they have urged voters to define themselves along these lines. Indians have been made more conscious than ever before of what divides us. When caste and religion elevate sectarianism to the level of public policy, it becomes more important to be a Muslim, a Bodo, or a Yadav than to be an Indian.

In this situation, films can — and do — play a vital role in keeping alive an idea of India that enshrines its diversity. Film is a more potent weapon than that used by the advocates of hatred. To take one example: in the film *Zanjeer*, a megahit of 1971, the character actor Pran played Badshah Khan, a red-bearded Pathan Muslim who exemplified the values of strength, fearlessness, loyalty, and courage. This was just a year after the bloody birth of Bangladesh in a war in which most of the subcontinent's Pathans were on the other side. But far from demonizing the Pran figure, the filmmakers chose not to portray a strong Muslim character but to make him the most sympathetic presence in the film after the hero (Amitabh Bachhan himself).

Bombs and riots cannot destroy India, because Indians will pick their way through the rubble and carry on as they have done throughout history. But what *can* destroy India is a change in the spirit of its people. The central challenge of India as it enters the twenty-first century is not purely economic or simply political: it is the challenge of accommodating the aspirations of different groups in the national dream. The ethos of diversity — of an inclusionist, flexible, agglomerative India — helped the nation meet this challenge. The battle for India's soul will be between two visions of diversity, the secularist Indianism of the nationalist movement and the particularist fanaticism of the bigoted mob. The film world has a vested interest in the struggle because it too depends on the survival of the world from which it has emerged.

It is only through the Indian ethos of diversity, only by ensuring that all Indians find the same opportunity to fulfill their hopes and aspirations, that the nation can realize its potential. And even the trashiest film hit can embody loftier ideals: one megahit of the 1970s, *Amar Akbar Anthony*, was an action adventure film about three brothers separated in infancy who are brought up by different families — one a Christian, one a Hindu, and one a Muslim. As adults, one is a smuggler, one a street fighter, and one a policeman. How they rediscover each other and turn the tables on the villains is why the audience flocked to the film in their millions; but in the process they also received the clear message that Christians, Hindus, and Muslims are metaphorically brothers, too, seemingly different but united in their common endeavors for justice.

The Indian film industry is by far the largest in the world — making more films annually than Japan, and five times as many as Hollywood. Much of this is escapist entertainment, but it all reflects the understanding that the only possible idea of India is that of a nation greater than the sum of its parts. An India that denies itself to some Indians could end up being denied to all Indians; and so Indian films communicate the diversity that is the basis of the Indian heritage, by offering all of us a common world to which to escape, by allowing us to dream with our eyes open.

And what is the responsibility of the filmmaker in a developing society like India's? Even the most commercial filmmaker contributes toward, and helps articulate and give expression to, the cultural identity of the society. The vast majority of developing countries have emerged recently from the incubus of colonialism, which has in many ways fractured and distorted their cultural self-perceptions. Development will not occur without a reassertion of identity: that this is who we are, this is what we are proud of, this is the world we imagine when we want to entertain ourselves, even that this is what we want to be. In this process, culture and development, and films and national identity are fundamentally linked and interdependent. We have heard in the past that the world must be made safe for democracy. That goal is increasingly being realized; it is now time for all of us to work to make the world safe for diversity.

That is the popular Indian culture from which so many of us have emerged. Let us hope Bollywood always remains true to it, and that the self-appointed guardians of *bharatiya sanskriti* don't try to change it into something more "authentic" and less true.

7

Epic Interpretations

THE QUESTION OF EXCLUSIONIST INTERPRETATIONS of Indian authenticity keeps coming up. Some years ago, I found myself responding to a literary critic who wrote extensively about my clothing and (presumed) Hollywood haircut, essentially to make the point that I wasn't authentic enough an Indian writer for her taste (the episode is recounted in my *Bookless in Baghdad*). The notion of Indianness as something sanctified by a prescribed list of acceptable attributes is not just highly contestable, it is positively un-Indian.

Apropos of the way in which some authors have retold the works of others, I once remarked that a Ramayana from Ravana's perspective would bring the lumpen Hindu zealots of the Bajrang Dal onto the streets in protest. (Ravana, the demon-king of Lanka who kidnapped the virtuous Sita, Lord Rama's queen, is the traditional villain of the epic narrative.) To this suggestion, an erudite Indian ambassador, Shyamala Cowsik, then serving in Cyprus, wrote me to say that what I imagined had already been done, apparently before the Bajrang Dal was even a gleam in its founders' eyes. In the late 1960s, she informed me, the Ramayana was indeed retold from Ravana's point of view in a play called *Lankeswaran* by noted Tamil playwright and actor Manohar. I am informed that Manohar played

73

the hero Ravana himself, and *Lankeswaran* was staged literally hundreds of times in Tamil Nadu, to great applause, so much so that he was from then on known only as "Lankeswaran Manohar."

This is almost the equivalent of retelling the Bible from the point of view of Satan, but it is profoundly authentic to the Indian cultural heritage. Ambassador Cowsik went on to add: "Ravana, as you know, was the son of the Rishi Visravas and a great scholar, a much greater one than Rama, besides being a tremendous Shiva bhakta. In *Lankeswaran,* Sita was Ravana's daughter. Due to some curse that I do not now remember, having seen the play when I was just a little girl, she had to be put into a box and buried in a field in Janaka's kingdom, where of course she was found when the king was indulging in a spot of ceremonial plowing. Ravana actually carries his infant daughter, Sita, in that little box, underwater, all the way from Lanka to Mithila, and leaves her underground in the field where she is eventually found. The whole subsequent Rama-Ravana battle was interpreted by Manohar as an attempt by Ravana to get his beloved daughter back." Interestingly, Ravana was portrayed in *Lankeswaran* as a tragic hero, rather like the protagonists in Greek drama, which is more interesting than simply rewriting the Ramayana from the point of view of the traditional villainous Ravana.

Ambassador Cowsik's second point concerned the idea of the Ramayana as seen from Sita's perspective, which, I had warily suggested in my column, "might tremble on the brink of sacrilege to some." When she was ambassador to the Philippines from 1992–95, she told me, she was "astounded to find that in this ultra-Catholic corner of Southeast Asia, there was a local Tagalog [the main Filipino language] version of the Ramayana, the Radiya Mangandari. This version had traveled northward up from Indonesia, where of course it is very familiar, through the Muslim south of the Philippines to the main island of Luzon. In the process, it acquired various undertones and overtones, besides the very interesting concept of Rama's alter ego. Now this alter ego was stoppered up in a bottle, something like the djinn in the Arabic fairy tales. Deprived of his alter ego, Rama degenerates from a noble philosopher king to a rapacious, common or garden variety of conqueror. He stays so till the end of the play, which I sat through for three-and-a-half hours while the playwright translated it for me line by line into English, when he finally regains his alter ego and becomes once more the noble Rama. However, Sita remained unchanged throughout the play, and was a strong, self-reliant, highly principled, and fairly aggressive woman who does not indulge in any of the traditional husband-worship. The group that had staged the play wanted to take it to India and perform it at various small places besides the metros. I had to warn them that public reaction in the smaller towns (these days possibly also in the metros) might not be entirely favorable to such an interpretation of Rama's character, and so the idea was dropped."

As a footnote to this episode, Ambassador Cowsik added that she got hold of a detailed account of the Radiya Mangandari in English and sent it to Vinod C. Khanna, who was then our ambassador to Indonesia. He used it for a book on various versions of the Ramayana that he was writing, which has since been published. (What an outstanding example, if I might be permitted the digression, this pair is of the remarkable intellectual quality of our senior officialdom. Whatever unkind thoughts many of us may nurture about the Indian bureaucracy, ours is, clearly, a mandarinate of merit.)

I recount these stories at length because they remind us of how far we have traveled from the questing spirit of Indian epic tradition to the uncritical worship of today. When the Indo-British writer Aubrey Menen wrote a rationalist version of the Ramayana in 1956, *Rama Retold*, the book was promptly banned in India, and — deprived of its natural audience in our country — it has faded away without enriching our collective consciousness of the possibilities of the great epic. The Sahmat exhibition a few years ago of various depictions of Rama and Sita in art from around our country was attacked by intolerant Hindu fanatics outraged that some of the versions shown did not conform to their orthodoxy.

The Hindu tradition has always been a heterodox one: we have always believed there are versions of divinity for every taste, and uncountable ways of reaching out to the Unknowable. What a shame that the Hindu banner is now so visibly and volubly being waved by those who have shrunk the grandeur of the Hindu spiritual and philosophical heritage to the intolerant bigotry of their slogans. Our epics were constantly retold and reinvented for centuries; the Hindu imagination was not fettered by fear of experiment. Today, sadly, that is no longer the case. Writing about *Lankeswaran*, Ambassador Cowsik remarks that Manohar "faced absolutely no protest those days. Of course, I cannot say what would happen if this were to be tried out in North India these days." I am sure she would not recommend it.

2

India at Work and at Play

8

Hooray for Bollywood

THE NEWS THAT EMERGED IN EARLY 2007 that a leading political party, the Samajwadi Party (then in power in India's most populous state, Uttar Pradesh) wished to nominate the Bollywood superstar Amitabh Bachchan to India's highest office — that of the president of the Republic — should hardly have come as a surprise. Bachchan declared himself unworthy of the post, a view widely shared by the citizenry, who expected to see in the office a symbol of the state, usually of more advanced years than the sexagenarian heartthrob. But in India, the film world has proved a perfectly adequate stepping-stone to higher office.

This is, of course, not unknown in California, which has given the United States a president (Ronald Reagan), a senator (George Murphy), and a governor (Arnold Schwarzenegger). But Hollywood's muscle-bound hero has further to go than he thinks. He may have become governor, but he can't become God. That privilege is reserved for the Indian movie-star-turned-politician N. T. Rama Rao, who played so many mythological heroes in so many hit films that starstruck fans in his home state of Andhra Pradesh set up a temple to worship him. "NTR," as he was popularly known, traded his near-divine celebrity for the dross of office by founding his own political party, Telugu Desam, in 1980 and romping to victory in state elections. That made him chief minister of Andhra Pradesh, the equivalent of an American governor in a state of (then) some 50 million people.

NTR wasn't the first Indian movie star to assume control of the destinies of his fans. That distinction belongs to MGR, the actor M. G. Ramachandran of the adjoining state of Tamil Nadu. At about the time George Murphy was singing and dancing into the Senate from California in 1964, the Dravida Munnetra Kazhagam (DMK) Party in the (then) state of Madras was using the film world to bolster its burgeoning popularity. The party's leader, C. N. Annadurai ("Anna"), had long cultivated links with the Tamil film industry, and his principal lieutenant, M. Karunanidhi, was a prolific screenwriter. The DMK's biggest draw was the action hero MGR, a sort of Arnold without the pectorals, who brawled and romanced his way into the hearts of millions in blockbuster after blockbuster. Karunanidhi wrote films for MGR that contained stirring speeches about Dravidian pride, a major theme of the DMK, and barely veiled allusions to the rising sun, the party's electoral symbol. In 1967 the DMK rode into office on the votes of avid moviegoers, defeating the stately Congress Party (which sought in vain to counter MGR's appeal by enlisting the aging romantic hero Sivaji Ganesan). Annadurai became chief minister, and MGR stayed in the movies.

But when "Anna" died and Karunanidhi ascended to the top spot in the now renamed state of Tamil Nadu, MGR began to ask himself why he needed to play second fiddle in politics when he enjoyed top billing in the movies. The Congress Party, unable to defeat the DMK at the hustings, wooed him shamelessly; government interference was widely suspected in the decision to award him a national best actor award for a hokey performance as a rickshaw puller. In short order MGR split the DMK, founding the All-India Anna DMK (AIADMK) and winning a majority of seats in the state assembly at the next elections (with the support of the Congress Party). Though Karunanidhi's DMK and MGR's AIADMK briefly alternated in power in Tamil Nadu, MGR soon proved unchallengeable at the polls, demonstrating yet again that movie stars always trump screenwriters (even those on whom they used to depend for their best lines).

So great and so enduring was MGR's popularity as chief minister that when, toward the end of his career, he suffered a debilitating stroke, his party could not afford to let him relinquish office. At the mass rallies thronged by millions that were the AIADMK's principal means of mobilizing support, the speechless and nearly immobile movie star would be propped up on a high stage in his trademark wool cap and dark glasses, while recordings of his past speeches would be played on the sound system to fool the distant crowds into thinking he was addressing them. It worked for a while, but mortality took its course and the AIADMK itself split as MGR's wife and his close companion, both former leading ladies from his screen days, fought over his legacy. The wife won out briefly and succeeded him as chief minister, but her legitimacy was marital, not political. The Other Woman (in her day a far more popular movie star), Jayalalitha, wrested control of the AIADMK, using her fan clubs to bolster her appeal to the voters. She went on to win state elections and become chief minister in her own right.

India's is a federal system, and the appeal of politicians like NTR and MGR remains largely confined to their home states, which speak the language of the films they starred in (Telugu and Tamil, respectively). The closest India has to a nationwide film industry are the Hindi movies made by Bollywood, whose actors have also tried to translate box office appeal into votes. But none of them has sought to dislodge established political leaders in the northern states; they have, instead, aimed for seats in the national Parliament. Bollywood's biggest superstar, Amitabh Bachchan, was elected to Parliament at the peak of his career as a member of the Congress Party, but became rapidly disillusioned with political life and resigned his seat to return to the movies. Others have awaited the end of their movie careers before making the transition, and two even served in the country's Council of Ministers — the former "hero"

Vinod Khanna as a deputy minister for tourism and the former "villain" Shatrughan Sinha as a minister for health (which puts an on-screen sexual harasser in charge of India's battle against AIDS).

Movie appeal doesn't always work. In the highly literate state of Kerala, which boasts the sophisticated cinema of Adoor Gopalakrishnan and others, a box office hero, Prem Nazir, tried to enter the hustings and fared so badly he lost his security deposit. Cinematic popularity can get you elected, but it isn't enough to keep you in power. Jayalalitha's reputation for imperiousness and corruption has seen Karunanidhi defeat her twice, though she has bounced back each time (and is unlikely to have served her last term in power as chief minister of Tamil Nadu).

NTR, however, found his magic wearing thin during his first term and lost office comprehensively when he sought reelection. He fought back, augmenting his movie star appeal with populist calls for subsidized rice for the poor, and returned to power. But within months he faced a revolt within his own party, led by his technocratic and unglamorous son-in-law. NTR was unceremoniously ousted as chief minister, suffered a heart attack, and died soon after.

Unlike in his movies, there was no resurrection for NTR. The temple dedicated to him lies in ruins. No one worships there anymore.

9

Democracy and Demockery

SOCIOLOGISTS HAVE ANALYZED THE CLASS COMPOSITION of India's legislatures and traced an important change from a post-independence Parliament dominated by highly educated professionals to one more truly representative of the rural heartland of India. The typical member of Parliament today, the wry joke runs, is a lower-caste farmer with a law degree he's never used.

However, the fact that, particularly in the northern states, our voters elect people referred to openly in the press as "mafia dons," "dacoit leaders," and "antisocial elements" is a poor reflection on the way the electoral process has served Indian democracy. The resultant alienation of the educated middle class means that fewer and fewer of them go to the polls on election day.

The abstention of the highly educated from the ballot is only a symptom of a more debilitating loss of faith in the political process itself. Only 25 percent of Indians questioned in a Gallup poll in April 1996 expressed confidence in Parliament (whereas, in comparison, 77 percent said they trusted the judiciary). I have been unable to find more recent polls, but I would be surprised if the figures are much higher.

Defections and horse-trading are common, political principle rare. The spectacle of legislators in one state assembly after another being "'paraded'" before a Speaker or a governor to prove a contested majority, or — worse still — being "held hostage" in hotels by their leaders so they cannot be suborned by rivals until their claims to the majority are accepted, has done little to inspire confidence in the integrity of India's parliamentarians.

Don't get me wrong: I am not some elitist lamenting the country's takeover by the poor. The significant changes in the social composition of India's ruling class, both in politics and in the bureaucracy, since independence is indeed proof of democracy at work. But the poor quality of the country's political leadership in general offers less cause for celebration. Our rulers increasingly reflect the qualities required to acquire power rather than the skills to wield it for the common good.

Too many politicians are willing to use any means to obtain power. Even the time-honored device of the dodgy campaign promise has sunk to a record low: one leading politician, a former cabinet minister, became chief minister of India's most populous state by promising that, if elected, his first act would be to abolish an ordinance that prevented college students from cheating (the ordinance forbade outsiders from smuggling crib sheets into the exam halls, regulated the examinees' freedom to leave the exam hall and return to it, and so on). He won the youth vote, and the elections, in a landslide. He was as good as his word: within seconds of taking the oath of office, he withdrew the anti-cheating ordinance.

Sadly, this politician's willingness to elevate political expediency above societal responsibility is all too typical of his fellow politicians today. The profession of politics, for all the reasons described above, has to a great extent become dominated by the unprincipled, the inept, the corrupt, the criminal, and the undisciplined. As with the chief minister I described, their quest for power is unaccompanied by any larger vision of the common good. But they do get elected repeatedly, for one of the failures of Indian democracy has certainly lain in its inability to educate the mass of voters to expect, and demand, better of their elected representatives.

One minister I spoke to said that he had once made a proposal in the cabinet that every politician should attend and pass a course in basic Indian history and civics before being allowed to contest a seat. The proposal was immediately shot down; but patronizing as it sounds, there may be a case to revive it.

Far more dangerous to Indian democracy than the deficiencies of its guardians is the fact that the combination of expediency and corruption, flourishing with impunity under the protection of the democratic state, discredits democracy itself. The institutions of the Indian democracy must be able to deliver what all citizens of democratic states expect, namely national security and economic prosperity. If corruption, maladministration, and political failure results in a citizenry that feels insecure and deprived, the resultant disillusionment with the system can destroy Indians' belief in the very system that sustains India. And that is something every Indian needs to worry about.

My concern is more specifically to the faith in the system of what R. K. Laxman taught us to think of as the "common man" — the bedrock of Indian democracy. Whereas psephological studies in the United States have demonstrated that the poor do not vote in significant numbers during elections (the turnout in the largely poor and black district of Harlem during the last U.S. presidential elections was 23 percent), the opposite is true in India. Here it is the poor who take the time to queue up in the hot sun, believing their votes will make a difference, whereas the more privileged members of society, knowing their views and numbers will do little to influence the outcome, have been staying away from the hustings. Voter studies of Indian elections have consistently demonstrated that the lowest stratum of Indian society vote in numbers well above the national average while graduates turn out in numbers well below.

Yet they are the ones who also see how little they can expect from their leaders. It is not just the disgrace of fisticuffs, jostling, and the flinging of footwear in our state assemblies; not just the legion of unfulfilled campaign promises, crumbling foundation stones of bridges and roads "inaugurated" just before an election and never completed, fodder scams, and siphoned-off funds of development banks; not even the lordly air with which our elected representatives treat their masters — the people. It is, rather, that even the pretense of accountability is absent from the actions of so many of our politicians. They see themselves as having been elected not to serve but to exercise power and enjoy its benefits. But even this would be forgivable if the power was used to protect people from the vicissitudes of life. Instead the "common man" feels far more vulnerable than before.

Violence is an inescapable reality for the ordinary Indian; we cannot escape being sickened by the daily occurrence of riots, rapes in custody, murders by those who believe their power confers immunity, and rampant incidents of the powerful taking the law into their own hands. If that sounds like an exaggeration, one reads far too often of episodes of poor women in rural India being stripped naked and paraded through streets to humiliate them or members of their family into doing as they are told.

Though individual police officers, administrators, and judges have shown courage and commitment in the pursuit of justice, the democratic Indian state as a whole seems to be able to do little to end such occurrences. Indeed, the Marathi newspaper *Navakal* once compared the Indian state system to the drunken husband who contributes nothing to the household himself but beats his wife to obtain the money she has worked hard to earn — a telling image in a country where such domestic events are commonplace.

We simply cannot allow our politicians to continue to treat our people this way. There is no doubt that the combination of violence and corruption, flourishing with impunity under the protection of the democratic state, discredits democracy itself. I think it deeply sad that so many cynics see democracy in India as a process that has given free reign to criminals and corrupt cops, opportunists and fixers, murderous musclemen and grasping middlemen, kickback-making politicos and bribe-taking bureaucrats, mafia dons and private armies, caste groups and religious extremists. Worse, the danger is that ordinary people will themselves react by seeking solutions outside the democratic system.

The basis of democracy is, of course, the rule of the demos, the people; the rule, in other words, of all rather than few. Democracies uphold the right of the general body of citizens to decide matters of concern to society as a whole, including the question of who rules them in their name. We cannot let our politicians arrogate to themselves the rights of the demos. Churchill once described democracy as "the worst system of government except for all the others." It is the quality of our leaders that determines how bad that "worst" is. Our politicians will have to improve if India is to rise to the challenge. Let's send them to "democracy school" if we must.

10

The Bond That Threatens?

THE FAMILY, THAT QUINTESSENTIAL INDIAN SOCIAL institution, has made a modern comeback through a phenomenon that did not exist in the India I grew up in — that of the television soap opera.

Indeed, a major change has occurred in our entertainment habits. No longer do Indians merely throng to the melodramas of Bollywood (or should it now be Mollywood, in deference to "Mumbai"?), where aging superstars chase cavorting virgins around leafy trees, singing of love as the inevitable downpour drenches her blouse but not his ardor.

Instead, the faithful pining wives and drunken villains of Bollywood have given way to the multiple adulteries, serial bed-hopping, and steamy passions of Western-style soap operas. This has not escaped international attention. An august American literary journal publishes a picture, in riotous color, of the family at the heart of the television serial *Shanti*; a popular international newsmagazine reports that the septuagenarian wife of the then president of India, Shankar Dayal Sharma, instructs her servants to tape every episode of the afternoon serial *Swabhimaan* that her official duties oblige her to miss. Thanks to soap operas, a new vision of the Indian family, teeming with betrayals, infidelities, and rivalries of every sort, has gained entry into the living rooms of the middle class.

No doubt such dysfunctional television families reflect the changing mores of the new liberalizing India. But if they loom larger than life, they do so in only one sense of the term. In size and reach, soap opera families are smaller and less demanding than the families most Indians think of as our own.

The family, after all, is the bedrock Indian social unit. We Indians are as self-seeking as anyone else, but we are not individualists in the Western mode: India is not hospitable terrain for "atomic man," since India is not a society in which atomized individuals can accomplish very much. To get anything done in India we require other people — allies who see their interests as ours. Such allies are most readily found within the cocoon of a family unit, which generates our most vital support, practical, material, and psychological, as well as the most important of our social duties and obligations.

But we define family more liberally than the rest of the world. We are, after all, the only country in the world where even the taxman recognizes the extended joint family spanning several generations and several branches of the family tree, living together in an arrangement legally known as the "Hindu Undivided Family."

Sometimes the notion of "family" extends more broadly to a clan or a subcaste or even to distantly related neighbors in a village. I cannot remember a time growing up when there wasn't a young man from either of my parents' villages in Kerala, some related to us in ways I couldn't fully understand, living in our flat (and sharing my bedroom) while my father arranged for him to have some professional training and got him a job. That is in the nature of things in our society; it was expected that my father, as one who had done well, would help others get their start in life. India is not a welfare state in that the government provides little to our unfortunates, but it is a welfare society in which people constantly help each other out, provided they feel a connection that justifies their help.

Belonging to the family carries with it a complex web of entitlements and obligations, not least monetary. Our culture, with some exceptions, treats family income as commonly accessible, family expenditure as commonly undertaken, family meals as meant to be shared. The broader the definition of family, of course, the more the merry number who feel they have a right to partake of the family's assets.

This level of sharing does not, however, make India fertile ground for the idealistic ecumenism of the socialists. Despite the socialist rhetoric of our political class since independence, we are a society unfit for socialism. Very few Indians have a broader sense of community than that circumscribed by ties of blood, caste affiliation, or village. We take care of those we consider near and dear, and remain largely indifferent to the rest.

Which means that not everything about our family structures is innocent. Amid the many transformations of globalization overtaking our society today, I sometimes wonder if our traditions conspire with modernity against our general well-being. For instance, is the Indian commitment to family a threat to the environment? If the question seems preposterous, let me explain.

At a trivial level, it is common to find sumptuous luxury apartments in buildings that are filthy, rotting, and stained, whose common areas, walls, and staircases have not been cleaned or painted in generations. Each apartment owner is proud of his own immediate habitat but is unwilling to incur responsibility or expense for the areas shared with others, even in the same building. My mother once asked her "sweeper-woman" in Delhi to sweep the stairs of her building as well. The woman, who would have been paid extra for the chore, was astonished at the request. "But why should you, madam?" she asked. "The stairs don't belong to you."

This attitude is also visible in the lack of a civic culture in both rural and urban India, which leaves public spaces dirty and garbage-strewn, streets potholed and neglected, civic amenities vandalized or not functioning. The Indian wades through dirt and filth, past open sewers and fly-specked waste, to an immaculate home where he proudly bathes twice a day. An acute consciousness of personal hygiene coexists with an astonishing disregard for public sanitation.

Not surprisingly, India is home to many of the world's most polluted cities. The air in Kolkata or Delhi is all but unbreathable in winter, when car exhaust fumes, unchecked industrial emissions, and smoke from countless charcoal braziers in the street rise to be trapped by descending mist and fog. A French diplomat friend, undergoing a routine medical check after serving three years in Kolkata, was asked how many packs of cigarettes he smoked a day. When he protested that he had never smoked in his life, his doctor couldn't believe him: three years of breathing Kolkata's air had given him lungs resembling a habitual smoker's. Delhi is hardly better. When the Australian cricket team played there in November 1996, the manager said the air was so unfit to breathe that his players' performance was affected.

As a result of such unchecked pollution, respiratory diseases are rife in urban India. Factories belch forth noxious black clouds; effluents pour untreated into rivers; sewage systems reek and overflow. Despite the tree-huggers of the Chipko Andolan, deforestation and overcultivation take their own environmental toll of rural India. Environmental consciousness remains limited. Governments pass regulations, then regularly ignore them. Meanwhile, more and more cars reach the congested roads, more poisons and toxins flow into our water and air, and more small factories open up that do not meet pollution-control standards. But they will never be closed down, because unemployment is a greater political danger than lung cancer.

With respiratory illnesses, cardiovascular diseases, and lung ailments rife, the total health costs for the country resulting from illnesses caused by pollution are estimated at some 4.5 percent of India's gross domestic product. In other words, more than half our country's annual economic growth is being wiped out by pollution, and development is taking place largely at the expense of the environment.

This dismal picture, coupled with corrupt enforcement of environmental regulations, reflects the sad state of the Indian ecology in the first years of the twenty-first century. This does not, however, prevent politicians from making environmental issues an opportunistic excuse to delay major developmental projects. If the choice is between living poor in a "green society" and being prosperous in the midst of general pollution, I have no doubt that most Indians would be happy to choke and splutter all the way to the bank.

Which is why — to return to the beginning — the new soap opera families are both relevant and irrelevant to our real lives. For, given our basic social underpinnings, the triumphs and travails of a television family can seem both familiar enough to Indian viewers to engage us, and distant enough to entertain. Meanwhile, the real damage they do, in leaving Indians indifferent to the welfare of the broader environment in which their families function, takes place offscreen.

11

Cricket's True Spiritual Home

I HAVE OFTEN THOUGHT that cricket is really, in the sociologist Ashis Nandy's phrase, an Indian game accidentally discovered by the British.

This might seem a preposterous notion, in keeping with the characteristic acuminations of that mischievous scholar, whose wispy beard and twinkling eyes have revealed a capacity both to astonish and to provoke. And yet it is an entirely defensible idea: Nandy found the perfect words to express something I have been arguing since childhood. Everything about cricket seems to me ideally suited to the Indian national character: its rich complexity, the infinite possibilities and variations that could occur with each delivery, the dozen different ways of getting out, are all patterned for a society of infinite forms and varieties. Indeed, they are rather like Indian classical music, in which the basic laws are laid down but the performer then improvises gloriously, unshackled by anything so mundane as a written score.

If there is a cricket cliché drilled into fans' heads by generations of commentators, it must be that of relating to "the glorious uncertainties of the game." But that too echoes ancient Indian thought, as I have pointed out in *The Great Indian Novel*. Indian fatalists instinctively understand that it is precisely when you are seeing the ball

well and timing your fours off the sweet spot of the bat that the un-
playable shooter can come along and bowl you. A country where a
majority of the population still consults astrologers and believes in
the capricious influence of the planets can well appreciate a sport in
which an ill-timed cloudburst, a badly prepared pitch, a lost toss, or
the sun in the eyes of a fielder can transform the outcome of a game.
Even the possibility that five tense, exciting, hotly contested and occasionally meandering days of cricketing contest could still end in a
draw seems derived from ancient Indian philosophy, which accepts
profoundly that in life the journey is as important as the destination.

Interestingly enough, Indian expatriation is now becoming the
principal driver for the globalization of what used to be thought of as
a quintessentially English sport. A recent Indian visitor to New York
asked about cricket matches in the city and waxed eloquent about
the growth of the game in, of all places, Dubai. When I first heard of
the phenomenon, I had visions of Bedouins on camelback trying to
turn Chinamen upon the desert sands, and scorecards bearing the
regular notation "dust storm stopped play." Enlightenment soon followed, however: I duly learned about the lead taken in promoting
the game by the Air-India Sports Club, the success of the Dubai
cricket development program, and that many matches are played on
subkha grounds with sand outfields. And why not, indeed? After all,
there is a famous stadium in next-door Sharjah, and the United
Arab Emirates team would be a force to reckon with for the International Cricket Council (ICC) trophy if it were allowed to field some
of the subcontinental stalwarts who play the game around the Gulf.

The globalization of cricket is a phenomenon with which even
this chronically sedentary writer has some personal experience. In
the course of a peripatetic life I learned not only that Italians and Is-
raelis played cricket, but I ended up playing the game myself in two
less likely countries, Singapore and Switzerland.

If ever Singapore gets around to nominating a national sport,
you can be pretty sure it won't be cricket. Most Singaporeans appear
to believe that the term applies either to a noisy insect or a trademark cigarette lighter. So the fact that every Sunday I would dress up

like a poor relation of the Great Gatsby and venture hopefully into the drizzle clutching my bat invariably mystified my Singaporean friends. Bats, of course, they associated more with vampires than umpires. And the notion that anyone would spend the best part of his Sunday on an uneven field in undignified pursuit of five-and-a-half ounces of cork provoked widespread disbelief. "You mean they still play cricket here?" exclaimed one Singaporean. "I thought that ended with the Japanese occupation in 1941!"

In fact, there were twenty teams in the two Sunday Leagues run by the Singapore Cricket Association when I was there in the early 1980s, and innumerable others playing "friendly" matches on Saturdays. They ranged from the sometimes plebeian Patricians to the tavernless Tanglin Taverners, from NonBenders who chased every ball to Schoolboys who didn't, and from the two teams of the elite Singapore Cricket Club to the more esoteric acronyms of SAFSA and SPASA (known to the initiated as the Armed Forces and the Polytechnic respectively).

"I do not play cricket," Oscar Wilde once wrote, "because it requires me to assume such indecent postures." Most Singaporeans, a notoriously serious and straitlaced breed whose recreations are golf and economic growth, appeared to share his disdain. The Archbishop of Canterbury, who described cricket as "organized loafing," and the Nobel Prize–winning author (Kipling), who termed cricketers "flanneled fools," would have felt right at home in Singapore. Many a local utilitarian with the national devotion to statistics pointed out to me that cricket simply wasn't cost-efficient enough. The amount of space and time it took to give twenty-two players a game could, I was reliably informed, be more productively allocated to one hundred squash players, two hundred swimmers, or three hundred joggers. When I responded that eighty-eight cricketers could have more fun and exercise in the space taken up by the prime minister's daily game of golf, the silence that greeted me could have made central air conditioning obsolete.

Of course, neither Singaporeans nor Swiss, law-abiding citizens to a fault, can be expected to approve of any sport that is based on the principle of hit-and-run. So expatriates, especially Indians, tend to dominate the game in both countries.

But cricket has a surprisingly long pedigree in Switzerland. The Geneva Cricket Club's wine label (yes, they are a rather refined lot, these Swiss cricketers) bears an illustration of a cricket match being played on the city's Plainpalais field in 1817. Nearly two centuries later, the game continues to flourish in Geneva, having survived interruptions during the two world wars. The present Geneva Cricket Club (GCC), revived in 1955, plays in a well-equipped stadium that offers underground parking to sportsmen and the luxury of bowling (and fielding) on Astroturf.

The environs of this international city also house the cricketers of the Center Européen de la Récherche Nucléaire (CERN), where a hefty six might dent the casing of the world's biggest proton synchrotron accelerator. An amiable lot, the CERN cricketers tend to be at their best during the expansive tea breaks for which they (and their gifted if long-suffering spouses) are deservingly famous. (I played for them for four years, and apart from consuming more calories than I expended, I am pleased to report that I still feature in three places in the club records, which they have helpfully posted on the Internet.)

There is also an assortment of teams from the other major cities — Basel, Bern, Winterthur, Zug, and of course Zurich, which supports not one but two Sri Lankan elevens, neither of which is on speaking terms with the other. The Swiss teams are organized in an annual competition for the 40-over Brennan Cup, named for the former Australian ambassador who donated it, and they even boast an annual journal, named — what else? — *Swissden.*

Though neither the climate nor the quality of the cricket comes close to the ideal that every good Swiss would wish to aspire to, cricket in Switzerland — a country of diplomatic conferences — has found its own place in the scheme of international exchange. Here, British-educated Swiss returning from South Africa (and a few South African émigrés) field alongside Indians both east and west; Pakistani and Sri Lankan refugees shatter the stumps of Indian diplomats and United Nations officials; irrelevant Pommies hit sixes off irreverent Antipodeans. And they all retire to their convivial beers at the end of the game. Even if, in most cases, they don't have a pavilion to drink them in.

Cricket probably remains, along with the English language, one of the few colonial legacies in which imperialism gave more than it took. And in our postcolonial times, especially given the boost provided by the Indian Jagmohan Dalmiya's empire-strikes-back leadership of the International Cricket Conference, it is doing so far more successfully than during the days of the empire that invented the game.

But America remains the great challenge, despite an Indian population that now exceeds three million souls. Americans have about as much use for cricket as Lapps have for beachwear. Ever since Abner Doubleday, in the mid-nineteenth century, introduced a simplified version of the elemental sport in which bat contends with ball, Americans have been lost to the more demanding challenges — and pleasures — of cricket. Baseball is to cricket as simple addition is to calculus — the basic moves may be similar, but the former is easier, quicker, more straightforward, and requires a much shorter attention span. And so baseball has captured the American imagination in a way that leaves no room for its adult cousin. The notion that anyone would watch a game that could take five days and still not ensure a result provokes widespread disbelief among result-oriented Americans. "You mean people actually pay to watch this?" exclaimed one American I tried to interest in the game. "It's about as exciting as measuring global warming!"

"Yeah, and just as important to half the planet," I responded dryly.

To be a cricket fan in America while the ICC World Cup is going on is akin to being a Brazilian samba dancer quarantined at a Quaker prayer meeting during Carnival week. Sitting in New York, you could as well be in Timbuktu for all the awareness people around you have of what's happening. A billion people may be on tenterhooks around the world for the results of each match, but the august

New York Times, which likes to think of itself as a world-class newspaper, doesn't even report the scores.

In earlier days cricket fans in the United States built their schedules around trying to catch the static-ridden numbers squawked on the BBC World Service twice a day. Today, though none of the 103 channels on my Manhattan cable television set offer a glimpse of cricket, suburbanites with satellite dishes can buy a World Cup package hawked by Indian-American television entrepreneurs. During earlier World Cups, movie theaters in immigrant neighborhoods that normally screened Bollywood blockbusters aired telecasts of World Cup cricket matches instead. And now there's the Internet — willow.tv, named for the wood that cricket bats are made of, sells a package that video-streams all the matches onto your PC. So living in America is no longer cricketing purgatory.

But, except when matches are played in the Caribbean, the avid America-based fan desirous of watching world-class cricket has to contend with the tyranny of what the French like to call the *décalage horaire.* Cricket is played in the rest of the world when people in America are supposed to be asleep. So satellite television has spawned a curious subculture in New York City. On days of crucial matches, shadowy brown figures flit through the dark predawn streets, heading for the homes of the privileged few who own satellite dishes. They whisper into cell phones in an arcane code: "Who's at silly mid-on? Has Irfan bowled a maiden?"

One night, a grizzled New York doorman regarded my friend Nikhil and me with undisguised skepticism. It was 3:30 A.M. — not the usual hour for visitors to drop by, even in Manhattan. "They're expecting us," I told him firmly. "Buzz upstairs and see."

He did, and they were. But the grizzled guardian at the gates couldn't suppress a shake of his head as he directed my friend and me to the elevators. Our hostess, Neera, greeted us at her door and led us down a darkened hallway past a bedroom where one of her sons slept under a blanket. "He has an exam in the morning," she whispered. In the master bedroom a television flickered. Our host,

Sanjay, resplendent in white cotton pajamas and sitting propped up in bed, waved us to a sofa. "They won the toss," he announced in tones of doom. "We're getting clobbered."

Nikhil and I sat down heavily, after only three hours' sleep. "Maybe we shouldn't have got up for this," I said as raucous shouts arose from the TV, confirming a disastrous Indian showing. "Are you kidding?" Nikhil replied. "Would you have missed this for anything?"

I had to admit I wouldn't. After years of being denied the most sublime pleasure known to Subcontinental Man — watching an international cricket match — this was heaven. For fans like me, New York has long been a citadel of barbarism, where the world's greatest sport is neither played nor reported in the papers. For decades we had to get our news of important matches via shortwave radio. The Internet for the first time brought live scores on demand — manna from on high. But to actually see a match? So what if it was taking place nearly a dozen time zones away? Nothing could beat having a friend in Manhattan with a satellite dish who was (a) a cricket fan and (b) willing to let you into his home in the middle of the night to watch the Indian team in action.

So it was that recent Sunday morning. Roused by the hoots and whistles emanating from the TV, Neera and Sanjay's houseguest wandered in, bleary-eyed from sleep. A while later their elder son awoke; a recent recruit at a big-name Wall Street firm, he had gotten home from work after midnight but was determined to catch an hour or two of cricket before heading back to the office at 7 A.M. The younger son, with his accounting exam to take, joined us next. As the cricketers on screen trooped off to their stadium lunch, Neera whipped up a breakfast of eggs and bagels for the watchers. The match resumed, and as the Manhattan morning advanced, friends who had been obliged to keep more conventional hours began to drop in: a family with young children, another from Connecticut, a young couple who had eyes mainly for each other despite the magnetism of the match.

Conversation sparkled in the combination of Hindi and English that Indians know as Hinglish. A nephew of Sanjay's arrived with his baby; when he heard the score he almost dropped the infant. Relatives who couldn't make it called from assorted locations to ask for news. Masala chai flowed. By noon it was over. India had lost, half a world away. Nikhil and I headed back to reality.

"What's goin' on up there, anyways?" the doorman asked. I opened my mouth to explain, then shut it again. "You're American," I said with a sigh. "You wouldn't understand."

Like the other remnants of the colonial presence, cricket has been thoroughly Indianized without losing its essential British moorings. After producing Oxbridge-educated Test stars for England, Indian cricket now reaches deep into the subcontinental soil, sustaining innumerable grassroots tournaments, attracting the largest audiences for any spectator sport in the world and creating stars more comfortable in Marathi or Tamil than in the language of "silly mid-on," "sticky wicket," and "bowling a maiden over." Indeed, cricket is no longer what Americans imagine it is, a decorous sport played by effete Englishmen uttering polite inanities ("marvelous glance to fine leg, old chap") over cucumber sandwiches. World cricket now uses Hindi terms (the *doosra* trips off the tongues of Oxonian commentators). Cricket is now an Indian game; many who play it have no sense of owing it to England. Yet just as Indian nationalists used British traditions and institutions to overturn British rule, so also Indians have taken up an English sport and delight in beating the English literally at their own game. Today more than 80 percent of the game's global revenues come from India, as the vast television audience of a growing economic giant clamors for the sport.

So the cricketing cause in America may lie in the hands of Indian immigrants. Just as the growth in the Hispanic population made soccer a mainstream sport, the enthusiasm of subcontinentals might yet spill over to their American neighbors, just as Indians and Pakistanis have brought cricket stadia to the United Arab Emirates. It may be a long while before cricket acquires the worldwide following of soccer or even tennis, but thanks to the mobility of modern labor and the passion for the game shown by its émigrés, cricket is spreading around the world. Maybe, one day, America might even catch up.

12

Good Sports, Bad Sports

W AR, CLAUSEWITZ FAMOUSLY SAID, is nothing but the continuation of state policy by other means. All international sport is, in turn, nothing but an exercise in national chauvinism by other means. At some level we all pretend to tune in to the Olympics to admire human athleticism at its finest, but none of us can deny the special significance of the flags under which those athletes first enter the stadium, the anthem that is played when the winner mounts the podium — and, ultimately, that impossible-to-ignore, regularly updated medal tally, listing the gold, silver, and bronze awarded to each participating country, which makes up the Games' real honor roll.

Every Indian who follows the Olympics has known the cringe-making experience of scanning that list, the eyes traveling down past dozens of nations big and small before alighting on a solitary tennis or wrestling bronze that gives India, with its billion-strong population, its modest place on the tally. Even worse, we have all known the shame of waiting day after day for India to appear on the list at all, as countries, a hundredth our size, record gold upon gold while Indian athletes are barely mentioned among the also-rans. The experience has always brought chagrin. Indians like to think we can hold our own against the best in the world in any field: our Kalidasa can stand up to their Shakespeare, our Ramanujan to their Einstein, our Rukmini Devi to their Margot Fonteyn, our *K3G* to their *Titanic* and, these days, our Infosys to their Microsoft. In sport, however, it has been a different story. Our cricketers have twice (in 1971 and 1983) come close to being considered the best in the world, and though they seemed to be flirting with greatness again in 2003–4, they have fallen away again in 2007, eliminated humiliatingly with the minnows from the World Cup. Prakash Padukone in badminton and Vishwanathan Anand in chess almost, but not quite, attained the status of undisputed world champions. But that is all. In the Olympics, that domain of traditional sporting excellence since 776 B.C., our country's record has actually declined. The one gold medal we had become used to winning since the 1920s, in hockey, has proved elusive in recent Games, as our players have stumbled on Astroturf. In everything where simple human prowess is at stake — running, jumping, swimming, lifting, throwing — Indians simply don't count.

Poor Madhu Sapre was unjustly denied a Miss World title in the early 1990s because of her answer to the question, "What is the first thing you would do if you became the ruler of your country?" Her response — "I would build a sports stadium" — was considered dumb by the judges, and the almost-certain crown (she was the overwhelming favorite of the bookies) slipped from her grasp. Sapre's answer might not have been the brightest, but if the judges had any idea of how desperate Indians are for sporting success, they would have understood that it was not such an absurd priority for her to express after all.

Why is it that we do so badly? The explanations have ranged from the anthropological to the borderline racist. (Indians don't have the genes, the build, the stamina, the climate, whatever.) There are structural explanations and infrastructural ones: lack of training facilities, gymnasiums, running tracks, equipment, financial resources. We are a developing country, it is said; but other developing countries, from Jamaica to Ethiopia, regularly rake in the medals. Our talent pool isn't really a billion, some argue; it's only the well-off and middle class, maybe 300 million strong, who can afford to play sports.

But even that is a larger population base than a hundred countries that do better than us at the Olympics. Yet, it is true that the incentives for success are not great; the years of sacrifice and effort it takes to become a world-class athlete are simply not a realistic option to an Indian who needs to make a living, and sponsors are few and far between.

And then there's the usual Indian problem: sports administrative bodies and government departments are ridden with patronage and petty bossism, with officials more interested in protecting their turf than in promoting athletes. With all these factors, failure in the Olympics, it is suggested, is encoded in our national DNA.

And yet success or failure still depends on the individual athlete. Indian genes in a developing country did not prevent a Vijay Singh emerging from Fiji to rival Tiger Woods as the best golfer in the world. And if Indians can be better than Caucasians and Caribbeans on the cricket field, why can't they beat them in the Olympic stadium? My family's former domestic retainer, Dulal Chandra Dev, as passionate a sports fan as ever lived, had a typically Bengali-leftist analysis of the national predicament. The problem, he averred, was that we were drawing on a limited pool of effete city-bred athletes who were knowledgeable enough about a sport to try to take it up. What we needed to do, he asserted, was to go into the tribal areas, where people had never heard of the marathon or the javelin throw and had no idea what "Olympics" or even "Games" meant. Yet there we would find Santhals and Bhils who practiced these Olympic skills from birth in their daily lives. What's a 26-kilometer run, Dulal argued, to a tribal who runs twice that distance every day just to fetch water or wood? Archery and javelin throwing would be child's play to an aboriginal who hunts with bows and arrows and spears every day just to be able to eat.

It's a thought, and I am sure Dulal would be happy if the sports ministry took him up on it and sent talent scouts to Jharkhand immediately.

But I somehow doubt that the solution is quite that simple. It is one thing to have the skill, quite another to be able to use it in competition. The point about the Olympics is that you are measured against the world's best: it is not just your eye against his, your legs against hers, but what you can do against their trainer, their running shoe, their ergodynamic costume, their titanium archer's bow. And against that entire panoply of requirements, we seem chronically to fall short.

It doesn't have to be so. The newly globalized India of Wipro and Sania Mirza can find both the strength and the resources to compete. Some have seen in the embarrassment of our Olympic failures a metaphor of national decline. I am not so pessimistic myself. First of all, it was not as if India ever stood at the Olympian heights — we have no recorded history of global sporting accomplishment ever, so if we are starting at square one, it is not because we have fallen from square ninety-nine. Second, India always calls for more complex metaphors than most places, and ours is a country where a narrative of decline is never a sufficient explanation. In *The Great Indian Novel* I wrote that India was not a developing country but a highly developed one in an advanced state of decay. Such comments are the privilege of the satirist, but it is probably true to acknowledge that ours is a country where things are always getting both better and worse at the same time. That is also true in the sporting arena: we may not retain medals we have won in the past, but might gain ones in fields (boxing? weight lifting?) where Indian youngsters have acquired skills we always thought they lacked.

And then there is the final intangible, the vital ingredient of all sporting success, as important as skill, training, equipment, and discipline: heart. There is no national quota for the will to win, the determination to strive beyond oneself for the glory of the country. It is the quality that led Leander Paes, never a serious contender in any other singles tournament that ever mattered, to belie his ranking and battle his way to a bronze medal in tennis at the 1996 Olympics. He played above himself because he wanted that medal, and he wanted to stand on that podium and have "Jana Gana Mana" played before 300 million telespectators. That desire has to come from within, but it costs nothing. The next Paes might be an archer, a swimmer, a wrestler. It might even (if he and Mahesh Bhupathi can put their differences aside to combine for the sake of the country) be Paes himself.

13

Bad Sports, Bad Spots

I HAVE TO CONFESS TO DECIDEDLY MIXED EMOTIONS on hearing the news that the private broadcaster Nimbus Communications has got into trouble with the government for allegedly broadcasting racist ads on its Neo Sports channel.

The mixed emotions come, first, from the fact that this is a channel I both love and hate. Whenever I visit India, I morph into a Neo Sports addict. After decades living in countries where I was deprived of the possibility of watching cricket on television, I seize every guilty opportunity to cancel appointments and turn off my phone, so that I can sit goggle-eyed before the tube, soaking in the goings-on on the greensward. And no one offers quite the range of cricket that Neo does — live and recorded, from home and abroad, Test matches and one-dayers and Ranji trophy games. Rare is the moment when the cricket-starved soul cannot find some balm on Neo Sports.

At the same time, the channel infuriates me. It possesses, for one thing, the single most irritating voice on the planet, an androgynous sloganeer with a gratingly self-satisfied accent who informs listeners with teeth-grinding regularity of the name of the channel they are watching. Fortunately for him or her, this occurs offscreen, so that viewers never learn who they can throw rotten eggs at. The executives of Nimbus appear blissfully unaware that this creature's mere enunciation of the words *Neo Sports* has done more than any rival or enemy can to incite sheer hatred toward the brand name among the most Gandhian of cricket fans.

And then there are the ads. One can't blame Neo, which is still a fledgling channel, for filling its commercial spaces with advertisements for itself (after all, how many repeats of Airtel's "Songcatcher" ads can any station inflict on its viewers without being accused of cruel and unusual punishment?). But who on earth conceives and approves these excrescences on the national psyche? I was in India when the West Indies team was touring, and watched in mounting horror as Neo ran a pair of promos in appalling taste about the visitors. One showed a West Indian at a *dhaba,* his mouth aflame after being served a deliberately overspicy meal, running from person to person looking for water, only to have the Indians there stick their fingers into their glasses, throw dentures into their water, and so on, until he finally flings himself at a tap and discovers it has run dry. The tag line: "It's tough to be a West Indian in India." Bad enough, but far worse was a second ad, in which a romantic black couple is rowed out to the middle of a lake by a boatman who abruptly stops, glowers at them, and proceeds to strip off his clothes. The audience is clearly meant to expect that he will assault the girl — but once he is down to his shorts he jumps into the water, leaving the couple moored mid-lake without an oar. Repeat tag line: "It's tough to be a West Indian in India."

Of course, I can figure out from deep mid-wicket what the advertisers thought they were doing. First, they thought the ads were funny. Now, humor is the most subjective of qualities, and though I can't for the life of me find anything remotely funny in these two ads, I imagine somewhere in this vast subcontinent of ours there may well have been a few people who actually laughed, though I can only imagine they must have been hit by a bouncer on the back of the head when they were young. Second, the bosses at Neo Sports probably imagined that this was a clever way of promoting the cricketing contest and in so doing, drawing attention to themselves in the hope of expanding their viewer base.

It doesn't take an exceptional intelligence to point out that an ad that demonizes a group of people, whether identified by nationality or color, as "Others" to be mistreated is inherently offensive. And that a story line that mocks people of that group, and depicts people denying them basic human courtesies, is not funny. Nor that depicting Indians, who as a people must rank among the most hospitable on earth to foreigners of any kind, as being neither welcoming nor courteous but positively nasty to strangers, is unfair and untrue: it both promotes xenophobia and denies our true national character. In other words, the ad campaign was fundamentally misconceived, ill thought out, and disastrously executed, and those responsible should be spanked with the business end of an extra-heavy Tendulkar bat.

But should there be more? This is where I get conflicted again. I detested the ads, but I was not happy to read in mid-February that the government "slapped a notice on Nimbus, asking for an explanation." And worse still, that Neo Sports faces a minimum thirty-day ban if charges of violating the advertising code are proven. Not only does that seem unnecessarily harsh toward the company, it will punish an entire class of innocents, the cricket fans who would have been deprived of their channel during the World Cup. Far more worrying, it allows the heavy hand of government to intrude into the space for public discourse that is so essential a part of any functioning democracy. An official of the Information and Broadcasting Ministry was quoted as saying: "The ads were in bad taste and perceived to be derogatory against [foreign] citizens." Bad taste is a matter for individuals to determine, not bureaucrats or even judges. And if Indians are to be punished for being derogatory toward foreigners, it will not be long before we return to the bad old days when the avatars of Indo-Soviet friendship banned James Bond's *From Russia with Love* and later only allowed its release under the title *From 007 with Love*. In a free society, when the media errs, viewers should make their views known, advertisers should protest, and the company should be forced to think twice about its reputation. But let's get the government's unimaginative fingers off our remote controls.

14

Salad Daze

I T'S NOT OFTEN THAT A MAGAZINE generates an entire subculture, especially when it lasted just a decade and aimed itself at people who are now reaching the age of looking fondly back at their salad days. Yet if anything constituted the lip-smacking dressing of my salad days, it would have been the first "youth magazine" India ever had, the *Junior Statesman* (soon reduced, in popular discourse, and then officially, after a readers' contest that confirmed fans' fondness for the initials, to *JS*).

It may seem a bit odd today to praise a publication that has already been buried for three decades. But anyone who was a teenager in India between 1967 and 1976 will not need persuading about the extraordinary impact that *JS* had on their generation. I still meet middle-aged matrons who wax eloquently nostalgic about the magazine, including people who can quote back at me from memory things I'd forgotten I'd written.

With the plethora of entertainment choices available to young Indians today, it's easy to underestimate the impact that a single magazine can have on the consciousness of a generation (of course, a largely urban, English-speaking, and moderately affluent generation). When *JS* appeared, there was no TV in India (except for a single black-and-white channel in Delhi, largely devoted to agricultural programming, and nothing anywhere else), computers didn't exist, and PlayStation wasn't even a gleam in an inventor's eye. Young people could read books or listen to music; the magazines available were by and large turgid, unimaginative masses of dense text, largely devoted to the increasingly unconvincing utterances of politicians. (No Indian versions of *Cosmo* or *Maxim* in those days!) And then *JS* appeared, with Pop Art graphics, wildly kaleidoscopic illustrations, a foldout larger-than-life blowup of some teen icon, and articles whose sensibility alternated between *Seventeen* magazine and Hunter S. Thompson on a (relatively) sober day. It rapidly became the must-read mag for Indian teens everywhere.

And it wasn't just importing recycled PR handouts of Western celebrities. *JS* didn't just make space for, it *created* a dizzying number of Indian artists and writers.

M. J. Akbar and I made our debuts as writers in the same issue of *JS* back in 1967. Writing for *JS* meant sharing space with the likes of editor Desmond Doig, journalist, mountaineer, and dandy; Dubby Bhagat, a general's son who delighted in knocking down every stereotype you might have been tempted to assume about him; Bhaskar "Papa" Menon, who wrote a brilliant column called "Bounder" and became the first *JS* contributor to go off to New York to work (and write) for the United Nations; Anurag Mathur, who wrote very serious short stories that didn't prefigure the hilarity of *The Inscrutable Americans;* Sunil Sethi, who reported from and on Delhi with the easy sophistication later known to legions of television viewers; or C. Y. Gopinath, earnest, bespectacled, and erudite, an editor's and reader's favorite. And, of course, the remarkable Jug Suraiya, who in those days had to be read with dictionary in hand, since he loved words nobody else had been inclined to use in print before, and who acquired a fan following nationwide that has since grown (and grown up) with him.

And *JS*'s eclectic subject matter was similarly nurturing of *desi* talent. The singer-actress Asha Puthli was first hyped in the pages of *JS;* so were tabla maestro Zakir Hussain, dancer Swapna Sundari, cineaste Shyam Benegal, and the model-turned-beauty-queen-turned-movie-star Zeenat Aman. Simi Garewal wrote an advice column; Raghu Rai and Sondeep Shankar took pictures of everything; the wonderfully named sisters Papiya and Tuk Tuk Ghosh offered witty insights into all sorts of subjects (they were so prolific that many readers suspected they were the figments of the JS staff's fevered imaginations, until in 2006 came the tragic news that Papiya, by then an eminent historian at Patna University, had been murdered in her home in that lawless city). They rubbed shoulders (or at least column inches) with the likes of Jatin Das, whose paintings JS vividly depicted well before he went on to national prominence as one of our great modern artists (not to mention father of the lovely and talented Nandita). Or King Jigme Singye Wangchuk of Bhutan, who, as a teenage monarch, gave JS the exclusive scoop on his coronation (accompanied by the lush photography JS was known for and which was not yet widely practiced in the country outside the somewhat stodgy pages of *the Illustrated Weekly of India*).

Nostalgia is a middle-aged affliction; it attaches importance to the memory of experiences that mean little to the majority who did not share them. So writing about JS is a little self-indulgent. The magazine died young, folded while still profitable by the *Statesman*'s chief honcho C. R. Irani after a quarrel with Doig, who passed away soon after of a heart attack. It barely lasted a decade, and anyone leafing through a back copy today (if one can be found) is bound to find it quaint, with its dated 1960s lingo and its calibrated air of cautious rebelliousness, celebrating youthful freedom but within sensible bounds.

And yet JS's achievement lay in giving a generation of young Indians the sense that they mattered; that their concerns, interests, fantasies, and creative outpourings had a place in our society; and that they could, through the simple fact of the circulation of a magazine, link themselves to a network of other young Indians across the country who shared these concerns and interests. In so doing, JS expanded, for many of us, the world of the possible. And it encouraged us to go out and make those new possibilities happen. There has never been a substitute for JS, and amid today's plethora of diversions for India's young, there probably never will be.

15

Wholly Holidays

I WROTE THESE WORDS IN NEW YORK ON A GOOD FRIDAY, when, I
am pleased to say, most employers observe a holiday. But I had
just come across the postman downstairs and retrieved my mail.
"You don't have the day off?" I asked somewhat incredulously. He
shook his head. "What about Easter Monday?" Not that either, he
responded. As a postman he gets just six days off a year, mainly on
secular occasions like Presidents Day, and two weeks' leave. I thanked
him and retreated to my apartment, suitably humbled by the Protestant work ethic.

*

Of all the various ways of measuring the relative underdevelopment of
nations, from GNP tables to the Human Development Index, I once
suggested that the most useful one that I could imagine constructing
would be the Holiday Index. Whereas America, with its paucity of
holidays, would score poorly on the Index, I think we in India would
do pretty well on it. But that's not necessarily a good thing.

Festivals and *melas* — mass gatherings of people united around
a common event — define our need for escape, and I sometimes suspect that India has more of them than any other country. A look at

the government of India's official list of holidays also suggests that we are also entitled to take more time off than any other country in the world. Indians contemplate a calendar that offers a choice of forty-four official holidays for a variety of religious and secular occasions, ranging from Independence and Republic Days to *Id-e-Milad,* the birthday of the Prophet Mohammed. Whereas Western dictionaries describe secularism as the absence of religion, our secularism favors a multitude of religions: the birthdays of Guru Gobind Singh, Guru Ravidas, and even Maharishi Valmiki are legitimate excuses to have a day off, as are the ascensions of Buddha, Christ, and Mahavira of the Jains. Going a step further, we have the Hindu festivals of Mahashivaratri and Ganesh Chathurthi, in honor of the gods Shiva and Ganesh, respectively. Throw in the Parsi New Year and the Shia Muharram, and you can see how secularism has deferred to religion, to the benefit of the indolent of all faiths.

But the secular harvest festivals of Dussehra, Onam, and Vaisakhi are celebrated, too. And the birthday of that eclectic spiritualist Mahatma Gandhi. Deepavali, our festival of lights, may not be entirely secular, despite all the godless gambling it encourages, but Holi is just a Dionysian spring festival and Raksha Bandhan a nondenominational day of brotherhood: we can take them off, too. We flock in our millions to the Kumbh *mela* and other religious gatherings; we overflow the *maidans* for our regular Ram-*lilas* in every little town.

And when it comes to holidays, who needs an occasion? Add to all these official tamashas the 104 weekend days, annual leave, casual leave, compassionate leave, and sick leave, and it is perfectly possible for a government employee to work just one-third of the days on the calendar and legitimately collect a full year's salary. And I have not even counted days lost due to strikes, hartals, bandhs, lockouts, and the like. Or the "unofficial holidays" that are taken in every office around the country when there is a cricket Test match or one-day international on television, and people report to work in body but focus their minds, and as far as possible their eyes, on the distant pitch.

Shakespeare, who had a thought for every issue and an epigram for every thought, pointed out, "If all the year were playing holidays/ To sport would be as tedious as to work." (*Henry IV*, Part I, Act 1, sc. 2, for pedantic readers). But he hadn't met the Indian holidaymaker: our capacity for celebration is truly undimmed by repetition. Had old William seen the enthusiasm with which our youths spray colored water on female strangers or the *lakhs* thronging our *melas* from Pushkar to Prayag, he would undoubtedly have agreed that age cannot wither, nor custom stale, the infinite variety of our holidays.

So India, I suspect, would ride high on the Holiday Index. I wonder how Bangladesh or Burkina Faso would fare. My wholly unscientific theory is that the poorer the country, the more holidays it gives itself, and the more festivals it conducts. Productivity might suffer from so many absences, but part of the problem is that we are not producing all that much anyway when we work, so that we don't lose all that much when we don't.

But wait a minute — perhaps I am being too materialist here. Is it that we are poor because we have so many holidays, or that we have so many holidays because we are poor?

Festivals and *melas* are the holiday events of the poor. The rich have no shortage of opportunities to enjoy themselves by themselves, whereas the poor have few outlets and pleasures other than communal ones. For an Indian villager, a day at the local *mela* is his opera ticket, tennis tourney, and beach vacation rolled into one — and in celebrating it he experiences some of the happiness that Thomas Jefferson told rich Americans it was the duty of government to allow him to pursue.

So poor countries — or at least countries with poor people — need more holidays and public festivals to give people the chance to amuse themselves than the rich ones do. Perhaps we should leave our holidays intact, after all.

16

Memories of a Bombay Childhood

I F THERE IS ONE INDIAN CITY that epitomizes much of what I'd like to think I stand for, it is Bombay (Mumbai, as it has recently been renamed), which used to offer a hospitable home for the kinds of ideas and initiatives (though not always the politics) that I value. Thriving, energetic, and resourceful, it was an advertisement for the free enterprise culture I advocated from my schooldays; its citizens rubbed shoulders with one another in an environment that largely transcended the man-made divisions of caste and religion that I despise; and the air was redolent of a cosmopolitanism more eclectic than anywhere else in the land. My own recollections of the city, *urbs prima in Indis,* involve these very issues.

I spent more of my childhood in Bombay than anywhere else. We moved to the city not long after my second birthday and left it (for Calcutta) just before my thirteenth, so my memories of Bombay are inevitably tied up with my schooling there. This took place in the squat red-white-and-blue building, opposite the Cooperage Stadium, which housed Campion School.

Campion was, like its eponymous Elizabethan martyr, a Catholic institution, one of many through which the Jesuits fulfilled their considerable talent for educating the privileged of the third world. It was a not wholly successful vocation, for the Jesuits were uncomfortably elitist and the elites enthusiastically Jesuitical. But perhaps because of its academic limitations, Campion encouraged the idea that there was more to school than studies. It offered a variety of extracurricular activities that helped you to find yourself outside the classroom even if you had lost yourself inside it.

So it was in Bombay and at Campion that I first acquired a healthy regard for imagination and innovation, and for the hard work that went into developing both. There was a flourishing school magazine to which any wielder of words, however young, was encouraged to contribute. Campion also got its students quickly involved in the pleasures of debating and speech making: we were all taught to elocute, with excruciating precision, from an early age, and one of my earliest experiences of an interschool debate was of being primed, at the age of seven, to interject from the floor in a contest of my seniors with their insufferably superior counterparts from Cathedral.

Above all, Campion instilled in its boys a love of the theater. There were frequent opportunities for participating in what was called (with no pun intended) interclass dramatics; and the school offered, in an inspired and wholly unprecedented coup, optional after-class instruction in drama from one of the most talented, vibrant, and experienced figures of the Bombay stage, Pearl Padamsee — a small, bouncing bundle of barely repressed energy who transformed several classloads of self-conscious, awkward schoolboys into confident, compelling actors and directors. Pearl's classes were great fun, but they also led to bigger things — not just drama competitions at school but to extravagant public productions in overflowing Bombay theaters where people with no connection to Campion paid for standing-room-only tickets to watch us perform.

I loved my theater years at Campion, which sometimes taught me about matters that had nothing to do with the theater. One of the more memorable footnotes to my experiences on the school stage occurred early in my career as a Pearl protégé. I was a ten-year-old representing the sixth grade in an interclass theatrical event at which the eighth grade's sketch featured Chintu (Rishi) Kapoor, younger son of the matinee idol and producer Raj Kapoor and later to become a successful screen heartthrob in his own right. I had acted, elocuted a humorous poem and MC'd my class's efforts to generous applause, and the younger Kapoor was either intrigued or disconcerted, for he sought me out the next morning at school.

"Tharoor," he asked me at the head of the steps near the toilet, "what caste are you?"

I blinked my nervousness at the Great Man. "I — I don't know," I stammered. My father, who had shed his caste name for nationalist reasons in his student days and never mentioned anyone's religion, let alone caste, had not bothered to enlighten me on such matters.

"You don't know?" the actor's son demanded in astonishment. "What do you mean, you don't know? Everybody knows their own caste."

I shamefacedly confessed I didn't.

"You mean you're not a Brahmin or something?"

I couldn't even avow I was a something. Chintu Kapoor never spoke to me again. But I went home that evening and extracted an explanation from my parents, whose eclectic liberality had left me in such ignorance. They told me, in simplified terms, about the Nair caste, to which we belonged; and so it is to Chintu Kapoor, celluloid hero of the future, that I owe my first lesson about my genealogical past.

The other incident connected with my Campion acting career that has remained in my memory is of performing in a Christmas play. It was called *The Boy Who Wouldn't Play Jesus* and had been written by an American with a social conscience, Bernard Kops. The play was unusual in several respects, including that it was meant to be performed by schoolchildren; the cast were to portray themselves rehearsing a Christmas play. All is good-natured chaos until the hero, a good hamburgers-and-root-beer American kid, decides that, as long as there's so much suffering and injustice in the world, he won't play Jesus. So he leads the cast off the stage and into the audience, collecting funds for — remember this was a 1960s American play — the hungry children of Bombay.

So here we were, privileged Bombay kids, performing *The Boy*

Who Wouldn't Play Jesus (with me in the title role). The play was written to be easily adapted to any group of children, for they were all to use their own names and "be themselves," but Pearl took the adaptation process a stage further. We too would protest injustice and suffering by refusing to play Jesus; but the issue that roused the Indian cast of Campion's Christmas play, that prompted them to walk into the aisles shouting slogans, would not be India's starving but Vietnam's.

This was 1967, and the Vietnam War was a favorite theme of the anti-American left, but Pearl was no radical, and Campion no training ground for revolutionaries. She had no political message to deliver to the audience of parents, teachers, and VIP invitees in our seething hotbed of social rest. All she was trying to do in changing the script was not to offend Bombayites.

At the time, aged eleven, I gave it no more than a passing thought. We were all aware of the change from our cyclostyled scripts and I believe we all thought it was justified: after all, *we* were the children of Bombay and we weren't starving, were we? It was only very much later that I realized what I had lent my innocence to. It was the Christmas after the Bihar famine, when thousands had lost their lives to hunger less than a day's train ride from Bombay, and massive infusions of food aid were being shipped in to keep Indian children alive. But we, insulated in the security of our Campion existence, and too young to pay attention to the front pages of our parents' papers, remained unaware of our own people's plight. We could have changed "Bombay" in the script to "Bihar" or "Calcutta," and the play might have had a startling relevance to its audience. But a pointed reminder of the reality outside our ivoried bower would only have proved embarrassing to our distinguished well-wishers. We needed an alien cause — popular with the educated class we were being trained to join, but far enough from our daily lives to cause no discomfort — to provoke our carefully rehearsed outrage.

And yet that too was Bombay: cosmopolitan yet conventional, both creative and conformist. It was a remarkable city to grow up in.

17

Nothing to Laugh About

THERE IS, SADLY, VERY LITTLE EVIDENCE TODAY that Mahatma Gandhi's puckish sense of humor has been inherited by his political heirs. Asked once what he thought of Western civilization, the Mahatma replied, "It would be a good idea." Upbraided for going to Buckingham Palace in his loincloth for an audience with the king-emperor, Gandhi retorted, "His Majesty had on enough clothes for the both of us."

Gandhiji was an exception: the Indian nationalist leaders and the politicians who followed them were in general a pretty humorless lot. I yield to no one, except perhaps Dr. Sarvepalli Gopal, in my admiration for the extraordinary intellect of Jawaharlal Nehru, but dig deep into his writings and speeches and you would be hard-pressed to come up with a good joke. The best might be the one classic epigram he uttered. Reacting with undisguised culture shock to his discovery of America after a trip there in 1949, Nehru said: "One should never visit America for the first time."

Nehru's daughter Indira Gandhi was no better. While researching my doctoral dissertation on her foreign policy, I read practically everything she ever said between 1966 and 1977. I can honestly say I came across only one line that was remotely witty. "In India," she remarked once, "our private enterprise is usually more private than enterprising." But from what one knows of the lady, the comment had probably been scripted for her. Sharp, if not particularly amusing, was her answer to an American journalist in 1971 about why she had refused to meet with Pakistan's General Yahya Khan: "You cannot shake hands with a clenched fist." Both these remarks have the merit of provoking thought beyond the immediate reaction to their cleverness.

But neither, alas, was typical. In his shoddy *Reminiscences of the Nehru Age*, the former secretary to our first prime minister, M. O. Mathai, cited only one remark of either father or daughter that he found witty. When Nehru and Indira expressed astonishment that Mathai had slept so soundly after the death of his mother, he apparently replied, "That shows I have a clear conscience." To which Indira retorted, "It can also mean that you have none." Sharp enough, but hardly an example of great wit.

As for the other remarkable figures who have marched the national stage, as far as political humor is concerned, our national cupboard is bare. During the national movement, the poetess Sarojini Naidu, "the nightingale of India," came up with a couple of good cracks: her classic comment about Mahatma Gandhi's frugal lifestyle and his army of aides — "If only he knew how much it costs us to keep him in poverty" — is of course one of the great one-liners of the independence struggle. Some also ascribe to her a crack about Sardar Patel: "The only culture he knows is agriculture." I had heard the line before, but was unaware it had been spoken in a political context, nor indeed that Sardar was its intended victim, so full marks to Sarojini Naidu there.

We have had our share of political buffoons (does anyone still remember the egregious Raj Narain?), but buffoonery does not count as humor, any more than slapstick can pass for wit.

But where are the Indian equivalents of the great political wisecracks of other democracies? British parliamentary tradition is replete with examples of often savagely cutting humor. In 1957, Labor leader Aneurin Bevan was attacking Foreign Secretary Selwyn Lloyd in the House of Commons when Prime Minister Harold Macmillan walked in. He promptly interrupted himself: "There is no reason to attack the monkey," he said, "when the organ grinder is present." Bevan is still worshiped by misty-eyed old Laborites, but he was not universally loved within his own party. The most famous put-down of him came from his near-namesake, the Labor Party's postwar Foreign Secretary Ernest Bevin. Someone remarked to Bevin that "Nye [Aneurin Bevan's nickname] is his own worst enemy." Bevin snapped back: "Not while I'm alive he isn't."

Of course, a lot of political humor involves invective, which the rules of decorum oblige politicians to embroider creatively. In 1978, Britain's then Chancellor of the Exchequer, Denis Healey, reacted to criticism from the Tory who would succeed him, Sir Geoffrey Howe, by dismissing it as "like being savaged by a dead sheep." The remark is still recalled fondly by political observers nearly three decades later, though both protagonists have long since ended their careers. Decades earlier, Winston Churchill had scornfully described the mild-mannered Labor Prime Minister Ramsay MacDonald as "a sheep in sheep's clothing." This was kinder than his most famous assault on the same prime minister. In a 1931 speech about MacDonald, Churchill described going to the circus as a child, for "an exhibition of freaks and monstrosities." He had, he said, most wanted to see "the boneless wonder, but my parents judged that the spectacle would be too revolting and demoralizing for my youthful eyes. I have waited fifty years to see the boneless wonder sitting on the Treasury Bench."

The British are also fond of showing erudition in their humor. Churchill was echoing a famous line of the sixteenth-century thinker John Bradford when he commented about Sir Stafford Cripps, "there, but for the grace of God, goes God." Few could have escaped the allusion to Helen of Troy when a left-wing parliamentarian in the 1960s called a female education secretary, Barbara Castle, "the face that had sunk a thousand scholarships."

Indian literature and mythology offer plenty of material for similar humor, but few have taken up the challenge. When in the early 1970s Karan Singh, as minister for health, proved slow to act during a junior doctors' strike in New Delhi, posters went up on the streets asking, "Are you Karan or Kumbhakaran [the mythological figure who slept six months a year]?" But no MP thought of expressing such an idea in the Lok Sabha.

From what we know of them, our politicians have less reason than most to take themselves seriously. Fearing that perhaps it was I who was uninformed, I asked the readers of one of India's more literate newspapers to send me examples of great Indian political humor that I might have overlooked. The results offered slim pickings indeed. The sharp-tongued Krishna Menon proved a particular favorite of Malayali readers. Advocate P. S. Leelakrishnan of Quilandy in Kerala reminded me of Menon's cutting comment when American arms aid to Pakistan was described as not being directed at India: "I am yet to come across a vegetarian tiger."

Getting back to parliamentary humor, V. Ramachandran of Kancheepuram offered me a line whose author he could not recall. During a debate on the Indian automobile industry, an opposition member declared, "The only part of an Indian car which does not make a noise is the horn." Full marks for wit but not, I believe (given the deafening klaxons that were always an integral part of Indian traffic jams) for accuracy.

As for the Indian equivalents of the great political wisecracks of other democracies, Mr. Leelakrishnan again offered me the only example worth citing. When Panampilly Govinda Menon was chief minister of Travancore-Kochi (the forerunner of Kerala state) in the early 1950s, he pointed to the chief minister's chair in the assembly and told the ambitious leader of the opposition, T. V. Thomas, "For you to sit in this chair you will have to be reborn as a bug."

And for Indians to laugh about the sense of humor of their political leaders, they will need to be reborn as hyenas.

18

The Sari Saga

EARLY IN 2007 I FOUND MYSELF unwittingly caught up in a row over sexism (mine) and feminism (others'). It all began with a casual observation in one of my columns, prompted by my last few visits to my homeland: Whatever became of the sari?

For centuries, if not millennia, the alluring garment, all five or six or nine yards of it, has been the defining drape of Indian womanhood. Cotton or silk, Banarasi or Pochampalli, shimmering Kanjeevaram or multicolored *bandhani*, with the *pallav* draped front to back over the left shoulder or in the Gujarati style, back to front over the right, the sari has stood the test of time, climate, and body shape. Of all the garments yet invented by man (or, not to be too sexist about it, mankind) the sari did most to flatter the wearer. Unlike every other female dress on the planet, the sari could be worn with elegance by women of any age, size, or shape; you could never be too fat, too short, or too ungainly to look good in a sari. Indeed, if you were stout, or bowlegged, or thick-waisted, nothing concealed those handicaps of nature better than the sari. Women looked good in a sari who could never have got away with appearing in public in a skirt.

So why has this masterpiece of feminine attire begun fading from our streets? On recent visits home to India I have noticed fewer and fewer saris in our public places, and practically none in the workplace. The salwar kameez, the trouser, and even the Western dress suit have begun to supplant it everywhere. And this is not just a northern phenomenon, the result of the increasing dominance of our culture by Punjabi-ized folk who think nothing of giving masculine names to their daughters. At a recent press conference I addressed in Trivandrum, the state capital of Kerala, there were perhaps a dozen women journalists present. Only one was wearing a sari; the rest, all Keralites without exception, were in salwar kameezes. And when I was crass enough to ask why none of the "young ladies" present wore saris, the one who did modestly suggested that she was no longer very young.

Youth clearly has something to do with it; very few of today's under-thirty women seem to have the patience for draping a sari, and few of them seem to think it suitable for the speed with which they scurry through their lives. ("Try rushing to catch a bus in a sari," one young lady pointedly remarked, "and you'll switch to jeans the next day.") But there's also something less utilitarian about their rejection of the sari for daily wear. Today's younger generation of Indian women seem to associate the garment with an earlier era, a more traditional time when women did not compete on equal terms in a man's world. Putting on pants, or a Western woman's suit, or even *desi* leggings in the form of a *salwar,* strikes them as more modern. Freeing their legs to move more briskly than the sari permits is, it seems, a form of liberation; it removes a self-imposed handicap, releasing the wearer from all the cultural assumptions associated with the traditional attire.

I think this is actually a great pity. One of the remarkable aspects of Indian modernity has always been its unwillingness to disown the past; from our nationalists and reformers onward, we have always asserted that Indians can be modern in ancient garb. Political ideas derived from nineteenth- and twentieth-century thinkers have been articulated by men in *mundus* and dhotis that have not essentially changed since they were first worn two or three thousand years ago. (Statuary from the days of the Indus Valley Civilization more than four thousand years ago show men draped in waistcloths that

Mr. Karunanidhi would still be happy to don.) Gandhiji demonstrated that one did not have to put on a Western suit to challenge the British Empire. Where a Kemal Ataturk in Turkey banned his menfolk's traditional fez as a symbol of backwardness and insisted that his compatriots don Western hats, India's nationalist leaders not only retained their customary headgear, they added the defiantly *desi* "Gandhi cap" (oddly named, since Gandhiji himself never wore one). Our clothing has always been part of our sense of authenticity.

I remember being struck, on my first visit to Japan some fifteen years ago, by the ubiquitousness of Western clothing in that Asian country. Every Japanese man and woman in the street, on the subway, or in the offices I visited wore suits and skirts and dresses; the kimono and its male equivalent were preserved at home, and brought out only for ceremonial occasions. An Asian ambassador told me that envoys were expected to present their credentials to the emperor in a top hat and tails. This thoroughgoing Westernization was the result of a conscious choice by the modernizing Meiji Emperor in 1868. One sees something similar in China today; though the transformation is not nearly as complete as in Japan, the streets of Beijing and Shanghai are more and more thronged with Chinese people in Western clothes. In both Japan and China, I allowed myself to feel a perverse pride that we in India were different: we had entered the twenty-first century in clothes that our ancestors had sported for much of the preceding twenty.

Today, I wonder if I've been too complacent. What will happen once the generation of women who grew up routinely wearing a sari every day dies out? The warning signs are all around us now. It would be sad indeed if, like the Japanese kimono, the sari becomes a rare and exotic garment in its own land, worn only to temples and weddings.

Saying which, I went on to appeal to the women of India to save the sari from a sorry fate.

Feedback is, of course, the lifeblood of the writer, but sometimes you get so much feedback it amounts to a transfusion. Practically every woman in India with access to a keyboard rose up to deliver the equivalent of a smack across the face with the wet end of a *pallu*. E-mails flooded in to all my known addresses, including to my publishers and agents; the blogosphere erupted with catcalls, many of which were duly forwarded to me by well-meaning friends. Having digested as many of them as I could take, the only fashion statement I was left in a condition to make would have been to don sackcloth and ashes.

So where did I go wrong? It seems my innocent expression of concern at the dwindling appearance of the sari on Indian streets and offices was offensively patriarchal. It reflected the male gaze, demanding of the female half of the population that they dress in order to be alluring to the masculine eye. Worse, by speaking of the declining preference for the sari among today's young women in terms of a loss for the nation, it placed upon women alone the burden of transmitting our society's culture to the next generation. And this was unacceptably sexist: after all, I had only called for the sari's survival, never demanding that Indian men preserve the dhoti or *mundu*. These arguments were made, with varying degrees of emphasis, by a variety of critics, most notably in a lengthy e-mail from Vinutha Mallya and in an "Open Letter" addressed to me by a blogger who signed herself Emma.

I admitted right away that all these points were valid ones, as far as they go. Yes, I wrote as a man, because that is what I happen to be. If columnists were all obliged to be Ardhanarishwaras (the half-man, half-woman figure of Hindu mythology), we might be more evenhanded in our judgments, but I doubt very much that all our columns would be worth reading. The purpose of a column is to offer an individual perspective — with which the reader is not only free to disagree, but encouraged, even invited, to disagree. If my point of view offended any of my female readers, I apologize, but I do not apologize for having expressed my point of view on this subject, as on any other. If a female columnist were to expatiate on the merits of tight jeans on male hips, I may not agree with her, but I would not excoriate her for taking a female view of male attire. What other view could she take but her own?

What about my unreasonable demand that women preserve and transmit Indian culture? I have to concede that Indian men have abandoned traditional clothing in even larger numbers than women have put aside the sari. For every Karunanidhi or Chidambaram who adorn our public life in spotless white *mundus*, there are ten others in trousers. And, as several of my critics pointed out, my argument was a bit rich coming from someone who spends his working days in a Western suit and tie.

Point conceded, but I should hasten to add that this is not a result of my own preference, but of the norms of international officialdom. Early in my UN career I turned up at work in an elegant cream kurta, only to have my Danish boss ask disparagingly, "Who do you think you are — a surgeon?" I still wear kurtas all the time after hours, at least when the climate permits it, and *mundus* in Kerala; but it was clear to me that if I was to represent the United Nations to the world, I was expected to do it in a suit and tie. Indian women in India, on the other hand, would face no disdain for sporting the sari: if they choose not to, it is because they choose not to, not because their employment obliges them not to.

And let's face it — whatever the aesthetic merits of the dhoti or *mundu*, they pale in comparison with those of the sari. It's fatuous to suggest, as several of my critics did, that the two are equivalent. Ask a fair-minded jury of women and they'll agree that the beauty of a well-crafted sari is a source of nonsexist pleasure — to them, not just to men — in a way that no dhoti can possibly match.

Saris may well be a hassle to wear, and less convenient to get around in, but those are points I had already conceded. What they are, though, is special — and to my relief a handful of Indian women wrote to say they agreed with me. Shreyasi Deb sent me a blog post in which she declared, "I know that the ultimate weapon in my kitty is the saree. . . . This Sunday I have taken down my Ikat, Chanderi, Puneri, Laheriya, Bandhej, Bomkai, Gadwal, Narayanpet, Maheshwari, Kantha, and Kanjeevaram sarees and stroked them in the reflecting sunlight." (I guarantee no man would ever think of doing anything similar with his dhoti collection.) And Sindhu Sheth wrote that she would heed my appeal: "I have decided to wear a sari (instead of my regular churidar-kurta) — once a week, to begin with." In that "to begin with" lies the hope that my original appeal will not have been entirely in vain.

19

The Challenge of Literacy

For those who care about illiteracy, India is the largest country in a subcontinent that gives great cause for concern. South Asia has emerged as the poorest, the most illiterate, the most malnourished, and the least gender-sensitive region in the world, with over half the world's illiterate adults and 40 percent of the world's out-of-school children. South Asia has by now the lowest adult literacy rate (49 percent) in the world. It has fallen behind Sub-Saharan Africa (at 57 percent), even though in 1970 South Asia was ahead. Thirty-seven percent of all Indian primary school children drop out before reaching the fifth grade. We have a shortage of schools and a shortage of teachers, and the problem gets worse every year because of population growth. Our subcontinent has the worst teacher-pupil ratio in the world. The illiterate population of India exceeds the total combined population of the North American continent and Japan.

India has made only uneven progress in educating its population. Whereas most districts in Kerala, following the introduction of free and compulsory education by an elected Communist government in 1957, have attained 100 percent literacy, the national literacy level still hovers around the halfway mark; the current figure is 62 percent. Kerala has a literacy rate of nearly 100 percent while

Bihar is at only 44 percent. And Bihar has a female literacy rate of only 29 percent.

The traditional explanation for the failure to attain mass education is two-pronged: the lack of resources to cope with the dramatic growth in population (we would need to build a new school every day for the next ten years just to educate the children already born) and the tendency of families to take their children out of school early to serve as breadwinners or at least as help at home or on the farm. Thus, though universal primary education is available in theory, fewer than half of India's children between the ages of six and fourteen attend school at all.

But official national policy is undoubtedly in favor of promoting literacy. As a schoolchild I remember being exhorted to impart the alphabet to our servants under the Gandhian "each one teach one" program; and many of us were brought up on Swami Vivekananda's writings about the importance of education for the poor as the key to their uplift. But it is true that, fifty-nine years after independence, progress has still been inexcusably slow, and that Indian politicians are all too quick, as Mrs. Indira Gandhi once was, to take refuge in sharp rejoinders about not drawing the wrong conclusions from the illiteracy figures. Education, Mrs. Gandhi would often say, was not always relevant to the real lives of village Indians, that India's illiterates were still smart, and illiteracy was not a reflection of their intelligence or shrewdness (which they demonstrated, of course, by voting for her). Fair enough, but Kerala's literate villagers are smart, too.

Now, there *has* been good news. The adult literacy rate has more than tripled since 1951, from 18 percent in 1951 to 62 in 2001. (But one must be wary of these figures. UNESCO defines an illiterate person as one who cannot, with understanding, both read and write a short, simple statement on their everyday life. By that definition, I suspect fewer than half our population would really qualify as literate.) The increase is even more dramatic for female literacy, from 9 percent to 43 percent. The gender gaps have been closing as female literacy increased much faster than male literacy.

The task of providing elementary education to all children is massive. India is making a major effort now to expand primary edu-cation. Our primary school system has become one of the largest in the world, with 150 million children enrolled. But it's not enough.

We hear more and more from progressive economists about the importance of what they call "human capital." Human capital is de-fined as the stock of useful, valuable, and relevant knowledge built up in the process of education and training.

Literacy is the key to building human capital and human capi-tal is the vital ingredient in building a nation. There is no industrial society today with an adult literacy rate of less than 80 percent. No illiterate society has ever become an industrial tiger of any stripe.

A key strategy for creating sufficient and appropriate human capital is to focus on basic education for all children. As Gabriela Mistral has so poignantly said, "We are guilty of many crimes, but our worst sin is abandoning the child; neglecting the foundation of life. Many of the things we need can wait; the child cannot. We can-not answer Tomorrow. Her name is Today."

But it's not enough to inveigh against the lamentable state of our country's literacy. What is striking from the international expe-rience is that whenever and wherever basic education was spread, the social and economic benefits have been quite impressive and vis-ible. The development strategies followed in recent decades by Japan, the East Asian industrializing tigers, and China laid a firm ba-sis for equitable growth by massive investment in basic education for all. Literacy was fundamental not only to accelerating the economic growth of these countries but to distributing resources more equi-tably and thereby to empowering more people.

It is a truism today that economic success everywhere is based on educational success. And literacy is the basic building block of education. It is not just an end in itself: literacy leads to many social benefits, including improvements in standards of hygiene, reduction in infant and child mortality rates, decline in population growth rates, increase in labor productivity, rise in civic consciousness, greater po-litical empowerment and democratization — and even an improved sense of national unity, as people become more aware than before of the country they belong to and the opportunities beyond their immediate horizons.

Literacy is also a basic component of social cohesion and national identity. The foundations for a conscious and active citizenship are often laid in school. Literacy plays a key role in the building of democracy; Kerala provides a striking example of how higher levels of literacy lead to a more aware and informed public. Adult literacy in Kerala is nearly 100 percent, compared to the Indian average of 62 percent. As a result, nearly half of the adult population in Kerala reads a daily newspaper, compared to less than 20 percent elsewhere in India. One out of every four rural laborers reads a newspaper regularly compared to less than 2 percent of agricultural workers in the rest of the country. So literacy leads directly to an improvement in the depth and quality of public opinion, as well as to more active participation of the poor in the democratic process.

Amartya Sen, the polymath Nobel laureate in economics, has reminded us that "the elimination of ignorance, of illiteracy, and of needless inequalities in opportunities [are] objectives that are valued for their own sake. They expand our freedom to lead the lives we have reason to value." We sometimes forget that in his most famous poem, the other Nobel Prize–winning Bengali, the immortal poet Rabindranath Tagore, implicitly spoke of education as fundamental to his dream for India. It was in a place "where the mind is without fear and the head is held high; where knowledge is free" and "where the mind is led forward . . . into ever-widening thought and action" that Tagore hoped his India would awake to freedom. Such a mind is, of course, one that can only be developed and shaped by literacy.

But more prosaically, illiteracy must be fought for practical reasons. How are we going to cope with the twenty-first century, the information age, if half our population cannot sign their name or read a newspaper, let alone use a computer keyboard or surf the Net? Tomorrow's is the information age: the world will be able to tell the rich from the poor not by GNP figures but by their Internet connections. Illiteracy is a self-imposed handicap in a race we have no choice but to run.

But it is also essential to focus on one specific aspect of the literacy challenge in our country today. The saddest aspect of India's literacy statistics is the disproportionate percentage of women who remain illiterate. Sixty percent of India's illiterates are women. Female literacy (43 percent) was 26 percentage points below the male literacy (69 percent). No society has ever liberated itself economically, politically, or socially without a sound base of educated women.

One of the more difficult questions I used to find myself being asked as a United Nations official, especially when I had been addressing a generalist audience, was: What is the single most important thing that can be done to improve the world? It's the kind of question that tends to bring out the bureaucrat in the most direct of communicators, as one feels obliged to explain how complex the challenges confronting humanity are; how no one task alone can be singled out over other goals; how the struggle for peace, the fight against poverty, the battle to eradicate disease, must all be waged side by side — and so mind-numbingly on. But of late I have cast my caution to the winds and ventured an answer to this most impossible of questions. If I had to pick the one thing we must do above all else, I now offer a two-word mantra: "Educate girls."

It really is that simple. There is no action proven to do more for the human race than the education of the female child. Scholarly studies and research projects have established what common sense might already have told us: if you educate a boy, you educate a person, but if you educate a girl, you educate a family and benefit an entire community.

The evidence is striking. Increased schooling of mothers has a measurable impact on the health of their children, on the future schooling of the child, and on the child's adult productivity. The children of educated mothers consistently outperform children with educated fathers and illiterate mothers. Given that they spend most of their time with their mothers, this is hardly surprising.

A girl who has had more than six years of education is better equipped to seek and use medical and health care advice, to immunize her children, to be aware of sanitary practices from boiling water to the importance of washing hands. A World Bank project in Africa established that the children of women with just five years of school had a 40 percent better survival rate than the children of women who had less than five years in class. A Yale University study showed that the heights and weights for newborn children of women with a basic education were consistently higher than those of babies born to uneducated women. A UNESCO study demonstrated that giving women just a primary school education decreases child mortality by 5 to 10 percent.

The health advantages of education extend beyond childbirth. The dreaded disease AIDS spreads twice as fast, a Zambian study shows, among uneducated girls than among those who have been to school. Educated girls marry later, and are less susceptible to abuse by older men. And educated women tend to have fewer children, space them more wisely, and so look after them better; women with seven years' education, according to one study, had two or three fewer children than women with no schooling. The World Bank, with the mathematical precision for which they are so famous, has estimated that for every four years of education, fertility is reduced by about one birth per mother.

The more girls that go to secondary school, the Bank adds, the higher the country's per capita income growth. And when girls work in the fields, as so many have to do across the developing world, their schooling translates directly to increased agricultural productivity, which in turn leads to a decline in malnutrition. The marvelous thing about women is that they like to learn from other women, so the success of educated women is usually quickly emulated by their uneducated sisters. And women spend increased income on their families, which men do not necessarily do (rural toddy shops in India, after all, thrive on the self-indulgent spending habits of men). Educate a girl, and you benefit a community: QED.

As my former colleague Catherine Bertini of the World Food Program once put it: "If someone told you that, with just twelve years of investment of about $1 billion a year, you could, across the developing world, increase economic growth, decrease infant mortality, increase agricultural yields, improve maternal health, improve children's health and nutrition, increase the numbers of children — girls and boys — in school, slow down population growth, increase the number of men and women who can read and write, decrease the spread of AIDS, add new people to the workforce and be able to improve their wages without pushing others out of the workforce — what would you say? Such a deal! What is it? How can I sign up?"

Sadly, the world is not yet rushing to "sign up" to the challenge of educating girls, who lag consistently behind boys in access to education throughout India, with the honorable exception of Kerala. Indeed, we have a long way to go: we boast one state, Bihar, which even enthroned an illiterate woman as chief minister — as if to showcase its abysmal figure of a 23 percent female literacy rate, one of the worst on the planet. But her seven daughters did indeed receive an education — so perhaps, after all, there are grounds for hope.

Certainly, there is no better answer. India must educate itself — achieve 100 percent literacy nationwide — if we are to fulfill the aspirations we have begun to dare to articulate and rise to the development challenges of the twenty-first century.

20

Reconstructing Nalanda

OR THOSE WHO CARE ABOUT INDIAN EDUCATION, 2006 was a curious year. It began with the eruption of the hugely divisive reservation controversy (following a political decision to increase quotas for "backward classes" in India's top universities, regardless of merit) and ended with the impetus being given, inspired by President Abdul Kalam himself, to the endeavor of reconstructing the oldest and greatest of India's meritocratic universities, Nalanda.

Founded in 427 by Buddhist monks at the time of Kumaragupta I (415–455), Nalanda was an extraordinary center of learning for seven centuries. The name probably comes from a combination of *nalam* (lotus, the symbol of knowledge) and *da*, meaning "to give," so Nalanda means "Giver of Knowledge." And that is exactly what the university did, attracting prize students from all over India, as well as from China, Indonesia, Japan, Korea, Persia, Sri Lanka, Tibet, and Turkey. At its peak, Nalanda played host to more than ten thousand students — not just Buddhists, but of various religious traditions — and its education, provided in its heyday by two thousand world-renowned professors, was completely free.

The Chinese scholar Hsuen-Tsiang (Xuanzang in today's Pinyin spelling), who visited India in 630 under the Guptas and stayed for some time at Nalanda, has left us a vivid description of the university.

He wrote of "richly adorned towers" with observatories "lost in the vapors of the morning." The university's architecture was remarkable, with nine-story buildings, eight separate compounds, ten temples, several meditation halls, a great library, and dozens of classrooms. Its setting, too, was full of beauty, dotted with lakes and parks. Most important, its finances were secure, since the monarch "has remitted the revenues of about one hundred villages for the endowment of the convent." In addition, the villagers supplied food to the students, whose material needs were entirely met by the university so that they could concentrate on "the perfection of their studies."

The accounts of foreign travelers portray a university throbbing with intellectual excitement, a center of learning devoted not only to the study of Buddhist texts but to Hindu philosophy, the Vedas, and theology in general; logic, grammar, and linguistics; the practice of medicine and the study of other sciences, notably mathematics and astronomy; and more down-to-earth subjects like politics, the art of war, and even handicrafts. Contemporary visitors speak of a system of education that went well beyond the oral recitation and rote learning normally practiced in monasteries. Nalanda's teachers practiced a variety of instructional methods: exposition was followed by debate and discussion, lectures featured lengthy question-and-answer sessions, and ideas were illuminated by extensive resort to parables and stories. Admission required a strict oral examination; literally so, since strangers were not permitted to enter unless they could satisfactorily answer a number of questions from the gatekeeper testifying to their basic level of educational attainment.

The university was an Indian invention. In Hindu tradition, education emerged from the *gurukul*, the teacher's home, where students went to acquire learning. The Buddhists, however, congregated in monasteries, which became centers of learning in their own right, supplanting the home of the teacher. Nalanda was not alone as a prominent Indian university. Kasi (Varanasi) and Kanchi were particularly renowned for their religious teaching, and Taksasila (Taxila in today's Pakistan) placed greater emphasis on secular studies; but Nalanda combined the religious and the secular, a Buddhist university offering a nonsectarian education to young men from near and far. These were the Oxfords and Harvards of their time, centuries before either of those universities was founded. Today our universities, barring an IIT here and a St. Stephen's there, are a long way short of world-class. Rebuilding Nalanda must be more than an exercise in constructive nostalgia. It must involve a new level of ambition, or it will be a futile exercise.

The Yale scholar Jeffrey Garten, writing in the *New York Times*, argued that "Nalanda represents much of what Asia could use today — a great global university that reaches deep into the region's underlying cultural heritage, restores many of the peaceful links among peoples and cultures that once existed, and gives Asia the kind of soft power of influence and attraction that it doesn't have now. The West has a long tradition of rediscovering its ancient Greek and Roman roots, and is much stronger for that. Asia could and should do the same, using the Nalanda project as a springboard but creating a modern, future-oriented context for a new university."

Nalanda was destroyed three times by invaders, but rebuilt only twice. The first time was when the Huns under Mihirakula laid waste to the campus during the reign of Skandagupta (455–467), when Nalanda was only a few decades old. Skanda's successors Puragupta and Narasimhagupta promptly undertook the restoration of the university, improving it with the construction of even grander buildings and endowing it with enough resources so that the university could be self-sustaining in the longer term. The second destruction came a century and a half later, with an assault by the Gaudas in the early seventh century. This time the great Hindu king Harshavardhana (606–648) restored the Buddhist university, once again upgrading the buildings and facilities.

But nearly eight hundred years after its founding, Nalanda was destroyed a third time and burned by Turkish Muslim invaders under Bakhtiyar Khilji in 1197. This time there was to be no reconstruction: not only were there no equivalent of the Gupta kings or Harsha to rebuild it, but the university had already been decayed from within by the cancer of corruption on the part of its administrators and by declining enthusiasm for Buddhist-led learning. If we are to rebuild it eight hundred years later, we will need not just money but the will to excellence, not just a physical plant but a determined spirit. A great university is the finest advertisement for the society that sustains it. If we re-create Nalanda, it must be as a university worthy of the name — and we must be a society worthy of a twenty-first-century Nalanda.

21

Cops and Jobbers

I T's NOT A GREAT TIME TO BE A POLICEMAN in India these days. In 2006 came revelations of the brutal killings of young migrant workers and their children in the Delhi suburb of Nithari (and the fact that the police took no notice of the reports of missing children for over twenty months). This was hard on the heels of public outrage over the shoddy police work in the original prosecution of the Jessica Lall case (when a model tending bar at a private party was cold-bloodedly shot dead by a politician's son, and the killer's influential political connections seemed inversely proportional to the competence with which the charges were documented). And not long after, the police were revealed to have failed to act on the murder of teenager Priyanka Bhotmange and her Dalit family, apparently because her "untouchable" status made hers a low-priority dossier. Then came the unconvincing official explanations for the death of a British tourist in a Goa village in 2006, which suggested the police had something to hide, not least their own incompetence. All of these, taken together with the lingering memories of the complicity of the Gujarat police in the massacres in that state in 2002, have contributed to a sense that the nation is ill served by its policemen. The image of the police is largely of a force besmirched by inefficiency, corruption, politicization, and lack of anything resembling devotion to duty.

If the news pages offer little consolation to the khaki-clad upholders of the law, perhaps it's time to turn to fiction. For the best antidote to negativism about the police must surely be the richly evocative, warmly sympathetic account of the force provided by Vikram Chandra in his monumental novel *Sacred Games.* (But let me hasten to assure nonliterary readers that this isn't a book review.)

Vikram Chandra's meticulously researched, deeply felt novel is (among other things) a warts-and-all portrait of the police at work in the city he still calls Bombay. His protagonist, the battle-weary, divorced Sikh inspector Sartaj Singh, is a wonderfully imagined and carefully drawn three-dimensional human being, vulnerable to the petty temptations that policing offers in our society, prone to cutting a few corners and bending a few rules, but fundamentally committed to the right values. Sartaj's essential decency is a constant, and it is mirrored in the faith of his constable, Katekar. Both men take seriously the duty to serve the public: "*Sadrakshanaay Khalnigrahaniya*" is the motto of the Bombay police, "Protect the virtuous, punish the wicked." As Vikram Chandra writes: "Katekar knew he could never confess this urge to anyone, because fancy talk of protecting the good and destroying evil and seva and service would elicit only laughter. Even among colleagues, this was never to be spoken about. But it was there, however buried it may be under grimy layers of cynicism." In doing a job that the novel describes elsewhere as mired in "its unspeakable hours, its monotony, its political complications, its thanklessness, its exhaustion," Sartaj occasionally reveals "a senseless, embarrassing idealism." Once, after rescuing "a trembling ten-year-old girl" from her kidnappers, he mutters, "Today we did good work."

Sacred Games depicts cops on the take, but almost never out of sheer greed and absolutely never at the expense of the job itself. Sartaj is a basically honest man who discovers that his monthly transportation allowance barely covers three days of fuel for his motorcycle. And "of the many notes he dropped into the hands of informants every day, maybe one or two came from his minuscule *khabari* allowance." So the proceeds of corruption are often spent in the cause of duty — an indictment of our society, that we underpay and underequip our police, rather than of the policemen themselves.

Of course, a novel is not a work of public policy, nor a substitute for investigative journalism. But Vikram Chandra did his research thoroughly, spending many years closely observing the working lives of Bombay policemen. And there is no reason why a good novel can't be as valuable in its insights as serious sociology. Sure, the policemen in *Sacred Games* are not depicted fabricating cases to frame innocents, or extorting money from law-abiding citizens, or discriminating against Muslims or other minorities — all offenses that our police have, at one time or another, been accused of. They beat suspects, hardly an approved method of investigation, but at least in this novel they never beat anyone who doesn't deserve a good hiding, or anyone you actually feel sorry for. And though the presence of politicians is never absent from their lives — especially that of senior policemen, who are portrayed as unavoidably in thrall to political leaders — Vikram Chandra doesn't show his policemen as to be so politicized as to suborn justice for political ends.

In that he may be kinder to our agents of law enforcement than they entirely deserve: both in Gujarat and, as the Srikrishna Commission so graphically demonstrated, in Bombay itself during the 1992 riots, the police were partisan, and they were partisan because their political overlords wished them to be. The great danger in a democracy is that the police imagine their duty is to the elected rulers of the day rather than to the Constitution and the society that has entrusted them with its safety. Of course, the police are unlikely to be immune to the pressures of political reality in a country where politics infects every activity like a virus. But it is the absence of a self-correcting mechanism when this happens that should worry us all.

Still, I'm pleased that Vikram Chandra's book gives us a more nuanced portrait of the Indian police than we might glean from popular stereotype. Good news stories about the Indian police (like the recent arrival of an all-women's police contingent to help the UN keep the peace in Liberia) are all too rare.

22

Becoming Bengaloorued

ONE INDIAN PHENOMENON THAT NEVER CEASES TO SURPRISE, and often confuse, foreigners is India's penchant for renaming its cities. An American businessman who was planning a visit to India after a long absence told me that his associate there "used to live in Madras, but he seems to have moved to some place called Chennai." When told that his friend hadn't moved at all but that Madras had become Chennai, his jaw dropped. "But cities don't do that," he said weakly.

Well, in India they do. The victorious Indian nationalists of 1947 were at first careful not to upend the familiar verities of Indian life when the British left, so the cities of the Raj kept their names for decades, even while streets named for British imperialists were gradually renamed for those who had resisted them. In the first decades after independence, practically the only city that changed the spelling of its name was Kanpur, which the British had absurdly spelled Cawnpore, a form that sounded affected to every Indian ear. The Anglicized "Poona" also became Puné to reflect the way the name was actually pronounced, and Mysore state was renamed Karnataka to resurrect the proud tradition of what the British had called the "Carnatic" region. But the big metropolises of the land — Bombay, Calcutta, Delhi, and Madras, the four best-known Indian cities internationally (until they were joined by Bangalore) — stayed what they had always been for the first fifty years of India's independence.

Then change came. The self-appointed guardians of Indian-ness — politicians looking for new postures to affect, and new issues on which to assert themselves — finally came into their own in the 1990s. They proclaimed their determination to reverse the coloniza-tion of the Indian sensibility by "restoring" the "original" names of cities that had allegedly been mangled by the foreign conquerors. So the government of Maharashtra, led at the time by the chauvinist re-gional party the Shiv Sena, renamed the state capital Mumbai, pro-scribing the use of the word *Bombay* for any official purposes. The city of Bombay (whose name came from the Portuguese Bom Bahia, or "good bay") had never existed before the colonial era created it, but it had developed from a number of fishing villages, one of which may (and I use the word advisedly) have been called Mumbai. So Mumbai's claims were at least debatable, but even if the case for it could be sustained, what was worse was the decision to abandon a name with nearly four centuries of global resonance. This struck me at the time as the equivalent of a company jettisoning a well-known brand in favor of an inelegant patronymic — as if McDonald's had renamed itself Kroc's in honor of its inventor. "Bombay" had entered global discourse; it conjured up associations of cosmopolitan bustle; it is still attached around the world to products like Bombay gin, Bombay duck, and the overpriced colonial furniture sold by "The Bombay Company"; in short, it enjoyed name recognition that many cities around the world would spend millions in publicity to acquire. "Mumbai" was already the city's name in Marathi, but what has been gained by insisting on its adoption in English, aside from a nativist reassertion that benefited only sign painters and letterhead printers? (The Shiv Sena went one step further and renamed the city's main railway station, Victoria Terminus, an Indo-Gothic-Saracenic excres-cence universally known as V.T. and completely devoid, in everyone's imagination, of any association with the late Queen-Empress. V.T. is henceforth to be known as Chhatrapati Shivaji Maharaj Terminus: try telling that to a Bombay taxi driver.)

Not to be outdone, another regional party heading the government in Madras, the DMK — which had, in an earlier spell in office, renamed the state of Madras as Tamil Nadu ("homeland of the Tamils") — decided that the city of Madras also would be rebaptized. The chief minister had been informed that "Madras," like Bombay, was actually a Portuguese coinage, derived either from a trader named Madeiros or a prince called Madrie. "Madras is not a Tamil name," announced the chief chauvinist to justify his decision to rename the city Chennai, the word used (though not always) by Tamil speakers. Once again, name recognition — Madras kerchiefs, Madras jackets, Bleeding Madras, the Madras monitoring system — went by the board as Chennai was adopted without serious debate. More unfortunately, the chief minister had overlooked the weight of evidence that Madras was indeed a Tamil name (derived, alternative theories go, from the name of a local fisherman, Madarasan; or from the local Muslim religious schools, *madarasas*; or from *madhuras*, from the Sanksrit and Tamil words for honey). Worse, he had also overlooked the embarrassing fact that Chennai was not, as he had asserted, of Tamil origin. It came from the name of Chennappa Naicker, the Raja of Chandragiri, who granted the British the right to trade on the Coromandel Coast — and who was a Telugu speaker from what is today Andhra Pradesh.

So bad history was worse lexicology, but in India-that-is-Bharat it is good politics. The Communist government in Bengal soon followed: "Calcutta" would henceforth become Kolkata, which was the way Bengalis pronounced it in their native tongue. (The International Air Transport Association, however, resolutely insists that airlines still tag your bags to CCU, not KKT, which belongs to Kentland Airport in the USA. In Tamil Nadu, the state government has allegedly instructed postmen not to deliver mail addressed to "Madras" — compelling evidence of the pettiness that underlies the directive — but baggage tagged to CHN rather than MAA will end up in Jeonju, South Korea). The habit proved catching: Kolkata's Kommunist kousins in Kerala decided that Cochin — a name that had stood for centuries and even been exported (to Southeast Asia's

155

Cochin-China) — would henceforth be Kochi. And as the twenty-first century dawned with computer professionals in the West discovering Bangalore — and even beginning to fear their jobs would be "Bangalored," outsourced to India — the politicians of Karnataka decided that their capital's newfound fame more properly belonged to "Bengalooru," the "city of boiled beans" rather than of India's burgeoning Silicon Plateau.

So can we now buy railway tickets to Bengalooru? I remember how my teammate and I, heading off to represent St. Stephen's College at a debating competition in what was still Calcutta, got our student concession forms made out to "Haora," as the newspapers had informed us that Howrah, Calcutta's grand colonial-era station, had been renamed. It was only after queuing for two hours that we discovered that, whatever the Bengali Babus of Writers' Building may have decreed, the Indian Railways had not yet digested the new reality. We were sent back to college with the proverbial flea in our ear — for having attempted to buy tickets to a station that didn't (yet) exist.

It took years for "Haora" to catch on. "Bengalooru" may happen faster. But who on earth benefits from all this? Was it really necessary for Keralites, who had gotten used to calling their capital Trivandrum in English and Thiruvandooram in Malayalam, to jettison both abbreviated forms for the glory of "Thiruvananthapuram," a word I have never heard anyone actually use? Or to insist that "Trichur," which is in fact a close approximation of the popular local pronunciation, be respelled "Trissur," which must have been dreamt up by Kerala's last surviving illiterate? And after sixty years of independence, isn't it time to start drawing the line somewhere? Isn't it time to say we are what we are, the product of a history we cannot deny, and the names of our towns and cities will reflect the centuries of influence from various quarters that have gone into making the India of today?

So far the rulers of Delhi have remained immune to the contagion, even though the name itself is a British misspelling: it should have been either "Dehli" or, more colloquially, "Dilli," but none of the local languages puts an h sound after the l in the capital's name. Clearly, the people in power in Delhi (both Old and New) have more important things to do than to obsess about the spelling of the city's name. But given the quality of many of the politicians aspiring to national office, it would not entirely surprise me if someone started a clamor to rename India's capital as well. After all, there is something marvelously anti-elitist about being able to oblige English speakers to accept such changes: it is a reminder that, in independent India, power over the English labels of places has passed to those who were never comfortable in that language.

What's in a name, Shakespeare asked, and of course the trains will be just as crowded at Chhatrapati Shivaji Maharaj Terminus as they were at V.T. But are we so insecure in our independence that we still need to prove to ourselves, in this childish manner, that we are free? Is there no comfort, after all, in being able to take places for granted, without the continuing sense that they are still susceptible to being renamed? And where do we stop? British spellings may have been quaint or even inaccurate, but they had the familiarity of long usage. If they are to be expunged, will our politicians next move from orthography to religious orthodoxy? After all, the city of Allahabad, on the confluence of the holy Ganga and Jamuna rivers, was known as Prayag for millennia before Muslim rulers renamed it in honor of their God. Will it be renamed, too, on the basis of a far stronger case than Mumbai or Chennai — and if so, what signal would that send to India's Muslims? When will we decide, for pity's sake, that we have disrupted enough of our historical legacy, and that the time has come to leave well enough alone?

In some parts of India, it is customary for a bride, upon marriage, to take on a new name — not just a surname, but a first name — chosen by her husband's family. It's a signal that her old life is over, and that she now belongs completely to another. This is the kind of thinking that underlies India's renaming mania. It is as if the rulers of Bombay and Madras, men of dubious credentials and modest achievement, wanted to show that they were now the lords and masters of these cities — and to demonstrate the change by conferring a new name upon them. For what these aggressive nativists are doing is to demonstrate that they are now in charge, that the old days are over. They are asserting their power, the power to decide what a thing will be, the power to name — for if one does not have the ability to create, one can at least claim the right to define.

23

India's Lost Urban Heritage

WHEN EVEN A BOOSTER OF THE NEW INDIA like myself looks around the decay and dilapidation of some of our cities — our rutted roads, uncollected garbage, choked drains, corroded water pipes, peeling paint, and plentiful potholes — one is tempted to think back to the great Indian cities of antiquity and wonder what went wrong.

Evidence of human habitation in India goes back to the Second Interglacial Period, between 400,000 and 200,000 B.C. Whereas some relics and implements of the prehistoric period have been found, there is no substantial body of information available from archaeological or other sources for the years before 3000 B.C. But Indian religious philosophy and myth describe cycles of existence that are dated precisely back into prehistory. There are continuities in Indian life that suggest a closer connection to the formally "unknowable" past than we might otherwise dare imagine. Historians have seen many of today's rural Indians as virtually a living archive of the country's ethno-history. But what of our city dwellers? Can we trace the heritage of Howrah back to the halls of Harappa?

I'm not being facetious here. The first proof of early Indian civilization, after all, dates back to about 3250 B.C., in the valley of the river that has given our country its name. The discovery of the Indus

159

Valley Civilization occurred by accident, when a pair of enterprising contractors in Sind in the late nineteenth century supplied the builders of a major road with bricks from a desert trove. The bricks turned out to be more than 4,000 years old. This got the Archaeological Survey of India interested, and in 1922 British and Indian archaeologists dug up the source of the bricks — not just one but two complete cities buried in the sand some four hundred miles apart. The bigger city was at Mohenjodaro on the Indus, the smaller at Harappa on the banks of its tributary, the Ravi. Subsequent excavations — within a region some five hundred miles on either side of the Indus and about one thousand miles along its course — unearthed remains of other ancient cities, all contemporaneous with the other great valley civilizations of the world, the Nile and the Tigris-Euphrates.

At Mohenjodaro no fewer than nine layers of buildings were excavated, evidence of a city that had been built and rebuilt for centuries. Archaeologists' finds — jewelry, terra-cotta figurines and seals, statuary, and earthenware — speak of a rich and well-developed culture, well in advance of its time (the Chalcolithic Age, when stone implements coexisted with those of copper and bronze). The cities were well planned, with broad avenues intersecting at right angles, advanced sewage and drainage systems (including septic tanks), spacious two-story homes, and hypocaustically regulated public baths. (Today few Indian towns boast a public swimming pool, but water was clearly important to our civilization in those days, and the remarkable "Great Bath" of Mohenjodaro may have had a ritual significance.) Wheat, barley, and dates were cultivated; several animals, from the camel to the humped zebu, were domesticated (though the cat was apparently unknown); they had already invented the wheel, and probably yoked buffalo or oxen to their carts. Gold, silver, copper, bronze, and lead were used, and garments of cotton spun and woven some two to three thousand years before Westerners wore them.

Somehow our modern cities never quite lived up to this heritage. Perhaps in other aspects they did: historians believe the society of the Indus Valley Civilization to have been a patriarchal and hierarchical one, probably ruled by a dominant priestly class, refined (with much personal ornamentation), religious (worshiping Pashupati, Lord of the Beasts, a precursor of later Hindu gods), and not particularly warlike — for they had no swords or defensive armor. Some historians have deduced a king who was worshiped as divine; others see a bureaucratic system at work in the meticulous organization and professional urban planning. Some of the art that has survived is simply magnificent, with one famous figure of a dancing girl reflecting considerable creative and casting skill. Despite its patriarchy, the Indus society was far more egalitarian, apparently, than its contemporaries, with ordinary citizens living far better than in Egypt or Mesopotamia, even enjoying a degree of comfort and luxury then unknown in the civilized world.

Some of these conclusions are speculative, since the pictographic script found on the seals has not been conclusively deciphered, but most are widely accepted. The cities were obviously connected by trade, and recent evidence suggests their commerce was international, for similar seals have been found as far away as Sumer in Iraq, with which trade could have been conducted along the Makran Coast. Here, too, is the earliest evidence of Indian pluralism, for the Indus society was apparently multiracial: the human beings depicted on Indus Valley artifacts are of several ethnic types, as are the skulls found in the excavations.

In other words, in these cities of the distant past, our forebears created a society not unlike our own — and arguably superior to ours in many respects. For over a thousand years, till about 1750 B.C., the Indus Valley Civilization flourished and prospered. It was then snuffed out abruptly. The archaeological evidence — heaps of skeletons, signs of disarray and sudden death — suggests some sort of catastrophe: perhaps a natural disaster, perhaps a brutal invasion. A great flood from the Indus itself, possibly triggered by an earthquake, is one possibility. Another is the advent of a horde of nomads who would

one day give our country the foundations of its present civilization —
the Aryans. The destruction of the Indus Valley Civilization snapped
the umbilical cord that linked its way of life to those of later generations of Indians. Dare one suggest that as we look to the twenty-first
century, we might do well to be inspired by an Indian example —
one that flourished in the twenty-first century before Christ?

3

Indians Who Made My India

24

The Legacy of Gandhi and Nehru

THE TUMULTUOUS TWENTIETH CENTURY produced many remarkable leaders, but few nations were blessed with a pair
quite like India's Mahatma Gandhi and his protégé Pandit
Jawaharlal Nehru. Gandhi was idealistic, quirky, quixotic, and determined, a cross between a saint and a ward politician; like the best
crossbreeds, he managed to distill the qualities of both and yet transcend their contradictions. Nehru was a moody, idealist intellectual
who felt an almost mystical empathy with the toiling peasant masses;
an aristocrat, accustomed to privilege, who had passionate socialist
convictions; an Anglicized product of Harrow and Cambridge who
spent over ten years in British jails; an agnostic radical who became
an unlikely protégé of the saintly Mahatma. Together they brought a
nation to freedom and laid the underpinnings for the world's largest
democracy.

Gandhi's life was, of course, his lesson. He was unique among
the statesmen of the twentieth century in his determination not just
to live his beliefs but to reject any separation between beliefs and action. In his life, religion flowed into politics; his public persona meshed
seamlessly with his private conduct.

Gandhi was the extraordinary leader of the world's first successful nonviolent movement for independence from colonial rule. At

the same time he was a philosopher who was constantly seeking to live out his own ideas, whether they applied to individual self-improvement or social change: his autobiography was typically subtitled *The Story of My Experiments with Truth*.

No dictionary imbues "truth" with the depth of meaning Gandhi gave it. His truth emerged from his convictions: it meant not only what was accurate, but what was just and therefore right. Truth could not be obtained by "untruthful" or unjust means, which included inflicting violence upon one's opponent. For Gandhi, the way to truth was not by the infliction of suffering on one's opponent, but on one's self. It was essential to willingly accept punishment in order to demonstrate the strength of one's convictions.

To describe his method, Gandhi coined the expression *satyagraha* — literally, "holding on to truth" or, as he variously described it, truth force, love force, or soul force. He disliked the English term "passive resistance" because satyagraha required activism, not passivity. If you believed in truth and cared enough to obtain it, Gandhi felt, you could not afford to be passive: you had to be prepared actively to suffer for truth.

It was satyagraha that first bound Nehru to Gandhi, soon after the latter's return to India in 1915 from a long sojourn in South Africa, where his morally charged leadership of the Indian community against racial discrimination had earned him the sobriquet of Mahatma ("Great Soul," a term he detested). Gandhi's unique method of resistance through civil disobedience, allied to a talent for organization gave the Indian nationalist movement both a saint and a strategist.

Gandhi's singular insight was that self-government would never be achieved by the resolutions passed by a self-regarding and unelected elite pursuing the politics of the drawing room. To him, self-government had to involve the empowerment of the masses, the toiling multitudes of India in whose name the upper classes were clamoring for Home Rule. This position did not go over well with India's political class, which consisted in those days largely of maharajahs and lawyers, men of means who discoursed in English and demanded the rights of Englishmen. Nor did Gandhi's insistence that the masses be mobilized not by the methods of "princes and potentates" but by moral values derived from ancient tradition and embodied in *swadeshi* (self-reliance on indigenous products) and satyagraha.

To put his principles into practice, the Mahatma lived a simple life of near-absolute poverty in an ashram and traveled across the land in third-class railway compartments, campaigning against untouchability, poor sanitation, and child marriage, and preaching an eclectic set of virtues from sexual abstinence to the weaving of *khadi* and the beneficial effects of frequent enemas. That he was an eccentric seemed beyond doubt; that he had touched a chord among the masses was equally apparent; that he was a potent political force soon became clear. He captured the imagination of the nation by publicly breaking English law in the name of a higher law ("the voice of conscience") and challenging the British to imprison him.

It was when the British passed the Rowlatt Act in March 1919, suspending the rights of defendants in sedition trials, that Jawaharlal Nehru became a serious follower of Gandhi, signing the "satyagraha pledge." Despite the initial reluctance of his father, the redoubtable lawyer Motilal Nehru, Jawaharlal soon followed Gandhi into the streets and into jail. Within a decade Motilal suggested to the Mahatma that "the need of the hour is the head of Gandhi and the voice of Jawahar."

Gandhi did not need persuading: he pushed and promoted the younger man, winning him the presidency of the Indian National Congress in 1929, two months before his fortieth birthday. Despite differences over both tactics (the younger, more impatient Nehru wanted independence immediately whereas Gandhi believed Indians had to be made ready for their own freedom) and philosophy (the agnostic Nehru had little patience for the Mahatma's spirituality), the two men proved a formidable combination. Gandhi guided Jawaharlal to the political pinnacle; Nehru in turn proved an inspirational campaigner as president of the party, electrifying the nation with his speeches and tireless travel.

Where sporadic terrorism and moderate constitutionalism had both proved ineffective, Gandhi took the issue of freedom to the masses as one of simple right and wrong and gave them a technique to which the British had no response. By abstaining from violence Gandhi wrested the moral advantage. By breaking the law nonviolently he showed up the injustice of the law. By accepting the punishments imposed on him he confronted his captors with their own brutalization. By voluntarily imposing suffering upon himself in his hunger strikes he demonstrated the lengths to which he was prepared to go in defense of what he considered to be right. In the end, his moral rectitude and Nehru's political passion made the perpetuation of British rule an impossibility.

But neither could stave off the demand of the Muslim League for the creation of Pakistan as a Muslim homeland on the subcontinent, and the partition of India amid bloody communal rioting. When independence came amid tragedy, Gandhi felt he had failed.

Of course, there was much more to Gandhism — physical self-denial and discipline, spiritual faith, a belief in humanity and in the human capacity for selfless love, the self-reliance symbolized by the spinning wheel, religious ecumenism, idealistic internationalism, and a passionate commitment to human equality and social justice (no mean conviction in a caste-ridden society). The improvement of his fellow human beings was arguably more important to him than the political goal of ridding India of the British. But it is his central tenet of nonviolence in the pursuit of these ends that represents his most significant original contribution to the world. Though the Mahatma never won the Nobel Peace Prize, several who did — Martin Luther King Jr. in the United States, Adolfo Perez Esquivel in Argentina, Nelson Mandela in South Africa, and Aung San Suu Kyi in Burma — all sought inspiration from his teachings.

Upon the Mahatma's assassination in 1948, Nehru became the keeper of the national flame, the most visible embodiment of India's struggle for freedom. Incorruptible, visionary, ecumenical, a politician above politics, Nehru's stature was so great that the country he led seemed inconceivable without him. Gandhi's death could have led Nehru to assume untrammeled power, but he did not. Instead he spent a political lifetime trying to instill the habits of democracy in his people — a disdain for dictators, a respect for parliamentary procedures, an abiding faith in the constitutional system. He himself was such a convinced democrat, profoundly wary of the risks of autocracy, that, at the crest of his rise, he authored an anonymous article warning Indians of the dangers of giving dictatorial temptations to Jawaharlal Nehru. "He must be checked," he wrote of himself. "We want no Caesars." And indeed, his practice when challenged within his own party was to offer his resignation; he usually got his way, but it was hardly the instinct of a Caesar.

As prime minister, Nehru carefully nurtured the country's infant democratic institutions. He paid deference to the country's ceremonial presidency and even to its largely otiose vice presidency; he never let the public forget that these notables outranked him in protocol terms. He wrote regular letters to the chief ministers of the states, explaining his policies and seeking their feedback. He subjected himself and his government to cross-examination in Parliament by the small, fractious but undoubtedly talented opposition, allowing them an importance out of all proportion to their numerical strength, because he was convinced that a strong opposition was essential for a healthy democracy. He took care not to interfere with the judicial system; on the one occasion he publicly criticized a judge, he apologized the next day and wrote an abject letter to the chief justice, regretting having slighted the judiciary. And he never forgot that he derived his authority from the people of India; not only was he astonishingly accessible for a person in his position, but he started the practice of offering a daily *darshan* at home for an hour each morning to anyone coming in off the street without an appointment, a practice that continued until the dictates of security finally overcame the populism of his successors.

On May 27, 1964, Jawaharlal Nehru died at the age of seventy-four. Just five days earlier, the prime minister had told a press conference, in reply to a question about whether he should not settle the issue of a successor in his own lifetime: "My life is not coming to an end so soon." When he died, Robert Frost's immortal lines were found on his bedside table, written out by him in his own hand: "The woods are lovely, dark and deep/But I have promises to keep/And miles to go before I sleep./And miles to go before I sleep."

An earthquake rocked New Delhi on the day of Nehru's death, and many saw this as a portentous omen. Cynics (at home and abroad) waited for his survivors to fight over the spoils; few predicted the democracy that Nehru had been so proud of would survive. But it did. India kept Nehru's "promises." There were no succession squabbles around Nehru's funeral pyre. Lal Bahadur Shastri, a modest figure of unimpeachable integrity and considerable political and administrative acumen, was elected India's second prime minister. The Indian people wept, and moved on.

Nehru never doubted that they would. During his seventeen years as prime minister, by his speeches, exhortations, and, above all, by his own personal example, Jawaharlal imparted to the institutions and processes of democracy a dignity that placed it above challenge from would-be tyrants. Democratic values became so entrenched that when his own daughter Indira suspended India's freedoms with a state of emergency for twenty months, she felt compelled to return to the Indian people for vindication, held a free election, and comprehensively lost it.

In 2004, forty years after Nehru's death, another confident government, secure in its assumption of popularity and increasingly accustomed to seeing itself as a natural party of governance, bit the dust. But the graciousness with which Prime Minister Atal Behari Vajpayee immediately accepted the electorate's verdict and used it as an opportunity to affirm the transcendent values of democracy was itself an advertisement of India's democratic maturity. Nothing so much became the Bharatiya Janata Party in office as its leaving of it.

The legacies of the two men marked India's twentieth century. While the world disintegrated into fascism, violence, and war, Gandhi taught the virtues of truth, nonviolence, and peace. He destroyed the credibility of colonialism by opposing principle to force. And he set and attained personal standards of conviction and courage that few will ever match. The principal pillars of Nehru's legacy to India — democratic institution-building, staunch pan-Indian secularism, socialist economics at home, and a foreign policy of nonalignment — were all integral to a vision of Indianness that sustained the nation for decades. Today, both legacies are fundamentally contested, and many Indians have strayed from the ideals bequeathed to them by the Mahatma and the Pandit. Yet Gandhi and Nehru, in their very different ways, each represented that rare kind of leader who is not diminished by the inadequacies of his followers.

The American editor Norman Cousins once asked Jawaharlal Nehru what he hoped his legacy to India would be. "Four hundred million people capable of governing themselves," Nehru replied. The numbers have grown, but the very fact that each day over a billion Indians govern themselves in a pluralist democracy is testimony to the legacy of these two men.

25

The Man Who Saved India

AS A RECENT BIOGRAPHER OF JAWAHARLAL NEHRU, I have been somewhat disconcerted to discover that my admiration for my subject immediately prompts people to assume that I must dislike his formidable deputy, Sardar Vallabhbhai Patel. In fact, I count myself among the doughty Sardar's fans, and am at somewhat of a loss to account for the presumed incompatibility of these two inclinations.

It is true that the two men had their differences, which neither kept particularly secret. Just before independence Patel was privately scathing about Jawaharlal's "acts of emotional insanity" and "child-like innocence, which puts us all in great difficulties quite unexpectedly." Nehru, in turn, could not have been unconscious of the fact that the older man (Patel was fourteen years his senior) was seen by many congressmen as more deserving of the country's leadership than the mercurial Jawaharlal. But it was not true, scurrilous rumors notwithstanding, that Nehru had initially omitted Patel from the cabinet list and had been obliged by Mountbatten to include him. Nehru, in inviting Patel to serve as his deputy, called him "the strongest pillar of the cabinet." Patel replied: "My services will be at your disposal, I hope, for the rest of my life and you will have unquestioned loyalty and devotion from me in the cause for which no man in India has sacrificed as much as you have done. Our combination is unbreakable and therein lies our strength." The Sardar's assurances were sincere and their "combination" was indispensable as independent India consolidated its unity and found its feet. (Sadly, "the rest of my life" Patel alluded to would extend no more than another three years.)

Vallabhbhai Jhaverbhai Patel was the humble fourth son of an impoverished farmer who had fought in the armed forces of the Rani of Jhansi. He had revealed a capacity for hard work at school and also for political organization when, as a high school student, he successfully conducted the election campaign of one of his teachers for a seat on the municipal council, defeating the overwhelming favorite, a rich businessman. Married at sixteen, he worked to support his family, including his elder brother's legal studies in England. Patel was self-employed from the start, working as a largely self-taught lawyer in Godhra, a town that was to assume tragic importance at a later stage of our history. But when his wife died sadly young in 1909 (while Patel was arguing a case), he too traveled to England to study law, financing his education entirely out of his own savings. Patel did well; he was admitted to the bar in 1913 and returned immediately to Ahmedabad to set up what soon became a flourishing and highly lucrative legal practice. England had Westernized him. Vallabhbhai Patel came back a bit of a dandy, fond of Savile Row suits and comfortable living, exemplified in his joining the Gujarat Club, a bastion of Anglicized attitudes. In 1916, when Mahatma Gandhi returned to India, both Nehru and Patel were living well, practicing law, and well on the way to becoming top-of-the-line brown sahibs.

It was satyagraha that first bound Patel and Nehru to Gandhi. Patel first became impressed with the Mahatma on hearing him speak particularly about the principles of truth that lay behind satyagraha. In late 1917 Gandhi was elected president of the Gujarat Sabha and Patel was elected secretary, marking the first formal association between the two men, which would last their lifetimes. Patel, a fellow Gujarati lawyer, was among Gandhi's first and most devoted followers, working closely with him on his efforts to obtain decent wages for Ahmedabad's mill workers. The Savile Row suits went onto a bonfire as he took to the Mahatma's taste for simpler dressing, though he wore a bit more than Gandhi, donning dhoti and kurta.

In those days Patel was constantly by Gandhi's side. He was the Mahatma's chief lieutenant in the Kheda agitation in 1918 (a no-tax campaign in which the peasants refused to pay revenues demanded by the British despite famine and crop failure following heavy rains and flooding). The British tried to crack down by confiscating the farmers' land, cattle, and even what little crops they had grown. Patel exhorted them not to give in. When Gandhi went to Delhi for talks with the viceroy, Lord Chelmsford, he left Patel in charge of the struggle on the ground. In the end the government relented, the taxes were lifted on the poorest cultivators, and the confiscated property returned. It was the first of many organizational triumphs for Patel.

In 1920 Patel resigned from the Viceroy's Council, on which he served alongside the likes of Jinnah, to support the Mahatma's non-cooperation movement. In 1927, when Nadiad and other districts of Gujarat were flooded and Gandhi was traveling in South India, Patel led the relief work, keeping the Mahatma informed and acting as his surrogate in the region. In 1928 he led the Bardoli satyagraha campaign and proved himself a champion of nonviolent resistance. Once again the British hiked the tax on land and Patel led their resistance to the new and unjust charges. Once again the British reacted by confiscating land, cattle, and crops; they went further than they had in Kheda by arresting hundreds of farmers and provoking an exodus of the dispossessed. Patel rallied the remnants, vowing not to give in. He devised a system whereby the farmers only sold milk, vegetables, and other essentials to purchasers bearing a chit from the local satyagraha committee. The struggle raged for six months, before it ended with the government agreeing to hold an inquiry into the merits of the tax increase, to return all the confiscated items, and to release the arrested farmers. With Bardoli, a city in Gujarat, Patel acquired the stature of a hero in the eyes of Congress leaders; the Mahatma bestowed upon him the title of "Sardar," or leader, and hailed him publicly as "my right hand." Many thought he might be made president of the Congress Party in Calcutta at the end of 1928 as a reward, but Gandhi asked Motilal Nehru to take on that role once more, and Patel bided his time.

The following year Gandhi prepared the ground for a political earthquake: he wanted Motilal to be succeeded as president of the Congress Party by his son. Jawaharlal, a stirring and radical leader who had done his own share to organize the peasantry in Uttar Pradesh and had gone to jail several times, had acquired great popularity as the glamorous face of Indian nationalism, his appeal differing greatly from that of the spiritual Mahatma and the doughty Patel. Though his writings and speeches and his international standing had made him a national figure, Nehru was conscious that he would not yet be the genuinely democratic choice of the party. But Gandhi would not be deterred. He cajoled and cudgeled Jawaharlal into submission, overcoming the objections even of Motilal himself, who feared that imposing his son on the party would not be fair either to the party or to Jawaharlal. (Ironically, it was Motilal who had first suggested to the Mahatma that "the need of the hour is the head of Gandhi and the voice of Jawahar.") Sardar Patel, fifteen years older than Jawaharlal and a valiant organizer who was already being thought of as the "Iron Man" of the Congress Party, had more support than Nehru for the top job. But though the All-India Congress Committee (AICC) was not enthusiastic about Gandhi's announcement that Jawaharlal would lead it, the party could not repudiate the Mahatma. On September 29, 1929, two months before his fortieth birthday, Jawaharlal Nehru was elected to preside over the Congress Party at its December session in Lahore.

Sardar Patel it was, though, who conducted talks with Jinnah in the hope of forging a common front for the Round Table Conference convened by the British. He was the cool-headed, calm lawyer; Nehru the impatient, mercurial, hothead whom Patel sought to exclude from the process. Nonetheless, this attempt at peacemaking with the Muslim League failed. Patel was a leading light of Gandhi's Salt March to Dandi, in the course of which he earned his first prison sentence. A year later, having been released from prison as a result of the Gandhi-Irwin Pact, Patel succeeded Nehru as Congress president. He succeeded in steering the Karachi Congress session toward moderation, despite the passions aroused by the British execution of the unsuccessful insurrectionist Bhagat Singh and other revolutionaries.

It was to be of no avail. Gandhi, Patel, and Nehru were all arrested following the failure of the Round Table Conference. Gandhi and Patel spent sixteen months together in Yeravada prison in Pune. Gandhi, Nehru, and Patel all spent much of the early 1930s in prison. While the Sardar was in jail his mother and brother both died; on each occasion he refused to accept a conditional release to attend their funerals.

In 1937 the British called elections based on the Government of India Act, which offered only a limited franchise to Indians and did so under the iniquitous system of "communal awards," which entitled voters only to vote for candidates of their own religious persuasion. Nehru wanted to boycott these elections, but Patel felt that half a loaf was better than no bread. This time the Patel view (which was also that of Rajagopalachari and others) prevailed. Gandhi persuaded Nehru to lead the Congress election campaign. Patel was in charge of selecting the candidates and the overall organizational effort. It was a great success for both of them: Congress won 62 percent of the seats it contested, emerging as the largest single party in nine of the eleven provinces and winning an outright majority in six of them.

In 1937 Patel hoped to succeed Nehru again as party president, but the Mahatma nominated Nehru for a second successive term and Patel, ever the loyalist, withdrew his candidature. After Congress resigned office in protest against the viceroy's unilateral declaration of war against Germany in 1939, Maulana Azad assumed the party presidency. Both Nehru and Patel wasted the war years in jail, having been arrested for their role in the "Quit India" movement. After their release, both Nehru and Patel assumed key leadership roles in the waning days of British rule. In February 1946, when the famous Indian naval mutiny occurred in Bombay and Indian sailors on board the cruiser INS *Talwar* took command, hauled down the Union Jack and raised the tricolor instead, training their guns on the city, it was Patel who rushed to the port and firmly persuaded the young men to surrender.

In April 1946 Maulana Azad, after an unprecedented six years as Congress president, announced that he would be resigning and handing the reins to Jawaharlal. Sardar Patel and Acharya Kripalani, Congress's general secretary, announced their candidacies as well, but the Mahatma intervened swiftly and decisively, and both men withdrew. On May 9, Kripalani announced that Jawaharlal Nehru had been elected unopposed as president of the Congress Party — leading inevitably to his becoming the first prime minister, initially of an interim government, and then, a year later, of independent India.

In Nehru's first cabinet, Patel was named his deputy and in charge of home affairs, bringing his considerable organizational skills to the calamitous law-and-order situation and to the integration of the princely states. The new prime minister of India and his deputy had to deal with the consequences of the carnage sweeping the country; preside over the integration of the princely states into the Indian Union; settle disputes with Pakistan on issues involving the division of finances, of the army, and of territory; cope with massive internal displacement, as refugees thronged Delhi and other cities; keep a fractious and divided nation together; and define both a national and an international agenda. On all issues but that of foreign policy, Nehru relied heavily on Patel, who welded the new country into one with formidable political and administrative skills and a will of iron.

As prime minister, Jawaharlal had ultimate responsibility for many of the decisions taken during the tense period 1947–49, but it is true to say he was still finding his feet as a governmental leader and that on many key issues he simply went along with what Patel and Mountbatten wanted. Nehru was the uncontested voice of Indian nationalism, the man who had "discovered" India in his own imagination, but he could not build the India of his vision without help. When the Muslim rulers of Hindu-majority Junagadh and Hyderabad, both principalities surrounded by Indian territory, flirted with independence (in Hyderabad's case) and accession to Pakistan (in Junagadh's), the Indian army marched in and took over with scarcely a shot being fired. In both cases the decision was Patel's, with acquiescence from Nehru. It was Patel who managed the integration of the princely states into the Union with a combination of firmness and generosity: "We are all knit together by bonds of blood and feelings. . . . Therefore, let us sit together as friends." What could have been messy and administratively a nightmare was managed with remarkable smoothness and efficiency under Patel's firm hand.

There were clashes in the cabinet on some of these issues, and in late 1947 Patel even told Mahatma Gandhi that he was seriously contemplating resignation. But the Mahatma persuaded his two disciples to try to work together. This they did; it was then the Mahatma turned against both of them when funds due as part of the national division of assets were not released to Pakistan by India because Patel (backed by Nehru) feared the money would be used to buy arms for war against India in Kashmir. Gandhi fasted against his own government; Patel offered to resign, but the Mahatma ended his fast only when his government gave in to his demands.

In the philosophical differences between Gandhi and Nehru, Patel occupied the middle ground. On economics, he was Gandhian in his desire to promote self-sufficiency and Nehruvian in his respect for industry, but he set far greater store by private enterprise. The Nehruvian vision of the country's foreign policy as an emanation of the nation's self-respect would have appealed to Patel, but he was far too much of a hardheaded realist to accept what he saw as the more woolly-minded of Nehru's international ideas. Patel was not in favor of India joining the Commonwealth, and he was severely critical, in private and directly in writing to the prime minister, of Nehru's Tibet and China policy.

In political style, Patel was much more of a pragmatist than Nehru; ever the hard-boiled realist, he was not easily swayed by passion, emotion, or ideology. A superb organizer and fund-raiser during the struggle for freedom, Patel proved an excellent administrator in government. His strong support for the civil servants, whose loyalty

was initially suspect because of their service to the British Raj, preserved India's "steel frame." It was Patel who, in the teeth of opposition from nationalist politicians who had been jailed (and worse) by
Indian civil servants in the service of the Raj, insisted upon incorporating into free India's Constitution two articles protecting the positions, the independence, and the privileges of the Indian civil service.
Without this the administration might have disintegrated. Patel ran
his Home Ministry as firmly as he administered the country as a
whole, and he brooked little interference from Nehru. He was firm
and decisive in integrating the princely states, and his political
toughness was never better seen than in his determination to pursue
the use of force on Hyderabad and Junagadh, actions he executed
swiftly and brilliantly.

Patel was, of course, far more conservative than Nehru, even if
he was not the "Tory" of the Congress Party (a distinction even the
British privately conferred upon Rajaji). Nehru gave in to his insistence on the maharajahs' privy purses being guaranteed in perpetuity (a policy that would be undone two decades later by Nehru's
daughter, Indira Gandhi). Yet Patel was hardly a monarchist: in 1939
he had personally led a popular movement against the Thakore of
Rajkot, declaring that a "state cannot survive whose raja wastes
money on dances while the peasants die of starvation." It was rather
his sense of what it would take to persuade the princes to join the republic, as well as his own integrity that was at stake: Patel was always
known as a man who, once he gave his word, never failed to keep it.
Patel also differed with Nehru on the question of the right to property and fair compensation for the expropriation of land, an issue on
which his views initially prevailed. As the historian Sarvepalli Gopal
put it, "The differences between Nehru and Patel derived from a
conflict between two different systems of thinking and feeling; what
enabled an avoidance of open rupture was mutual regard and Patel's
stoic decency."

Political clashes were, however, inevitable. When the time came
for the position of governor general of India to be converted to that
of president of the republic (upon the adoption of independent

India's new Constitution on the symbolic date of January 26, 1950, the old Independence Day becoming the new Republic Day), Patel engineered the election of his crony Rajendra Prasad as the Congress candidate at the expense of the incumbent governor general, Rajaji. Jawaharlal had been completely bypassed; he was so surprised that he actually asked Prasad to withdraw and propose Rajagopalachari's name himself. Prasad cleverly suggested that he would do whatever Nehru and Patel agreed upon, at which point Nehru understood and threw in the towel. One of Prasad's first acts upon election was to ask that January 26 be changed to a date deemed more auspicious by his astrologers. Jawaharlal flatly turned him down, declaring that India would not be run by astrologers if he had anything to do with it. This time, Nehru won.

But it is true that a key area that divided Nehru from Patel was the issue of the treatment of India's Muslim minority, and this may be where the two men's admirers diverge irreconcilably. Both Nehru and Patel strove, like their mentor Mahatma Gandhi, to keep the country united. But once Partition had occurred, Patel was inclined to see India as a state that symbolized the interests of the Hindu majority, while Nehru's idea of India explicitly rejected the two-nation theory; having spurned the logic that had created a state for Muslims, he was not about to succumb to the temptation of mirroring that logic by allowing India to become a state for Hindus. "So long as I am prime minister," he declared in 1950, "I shall not allow communalism to shape our policy." Patel, on the other hand, was suspicious of the loyalties of Muslims who remained in India and felt those loyalties had to be proven. On one occasion, he proposed that Muslim officials should seek permission from the government before visiting Pakistan; Nehru objected to any double standard (other officials required no such permission in those days), and the prime minister prevailed.

And yet, this does not mean that Patel was communalist in his approach to India's Muslims. As home minister, Patel dealt with the communal disturbances that accompanied Partition firmly and evenhandedly; he transferred army units from Poona and Madras to restore order in Delhi, and asked the army to move ten thousand homeless Muslims into the Red Fort to protect them from Hindu rioters. But he saw Muslims in India, in the words of the historian Sarvepalli Gopal, as "hostages to be held in security for the fair treatment of Hindus in Pakistan." Temperamentally, the Sardar was more inclined to draw the conclusion from Partition that an entire community had in effect seceded; he once suggested in 1948 that if Hindus were expelled from Pakistan, an equal number of Muslims should be expelled from India, an idea that appalled Nehru, who slapped it down immediately.

No wonder, then, that readers aware of my views on communal bigotry should presume my hostility to Patel. But one must make allowances for the temper of the times; and more important, Patel's fundamental decency became apparent on a communal issue on which he and Nehru in fact disagreed.

This was in 1950, with the government under pressure from the right to intervene militarily in East Pakistan, where a massacre of Hindus had begun. Jawaharlal first tried to work with his Pakistani counterpart, Liaquat Ali Khan, on a joint approach to communal disturbances and then, when this had been ignored, offered President Rajendra Prasad (a Patel ally) his resignation. But when Patel called a meeting of Congress Party members at his home to criticize Jawaharlal's weakness on the issue, Nehru fought back, withdrawing his offer of resignation, challenging Patel to a public debate on Pakistan policy and even writing to express doubt as to whether the two of them could work together anymore. The counterassault was so ferocious that Patel backed off and affirmed his loyalty to Jawaharlal, supporting the pact Nehru signed with his Pakistani counterpart.

Yet Patel did so not because he could not have defeated Nehru politically, but because he felt Nehru deserved his support on an issue of principle. Whereas the Hindu Mahasabha sympathizers in the cabinet, Shyama Prasad Mookherjee and K. C. Neogi, resigned over the Nehru-Liaquat Pact, Patel not only urged them to stay, he committed himself to the pact's implementation. His logic was Gandhian: the problem may have started with the mistreatment of

Hindus in East Pakistan, but the moment retaliatory measures were taken against Muslims in West Bengal, India, in his view, lost the moral authority to put itself on a different plane than Pakistan or to take military action against it. Those who saw Patel as a hard-liner and a Rashtriya Swayamsevak Sangh (RSS) sympathizer were surprised, but those who knew him as a lifetime Gandhian — and a man of his word who had been trained to respect and believe in the law — were not.

The Nehru-Patel partnership lasted only three years beyond independence. Sardar Patel had suffered a heart attack a few months after the Mahatma's assassination; then stomach cancer struck, and in December 1950, having fulfilled his historic role of consolidating India's fragile freedom, he passed away, age seventy-five. Patel and Nehru had also served as a check upon each other, and his passing left Jawaharlal unchallenged.

And yet, it must not be forgotten that Mahatma Gandhi's assassination by a Hindu fanatic strengthened the fundamental unity of the two men. The Mahatma's last conversation was with Patel; it is believed that the Sardar had been describing his differences with Nehru and seeking permission to quit the cabinet. Gandhiji again advised them to work together, and his death minutes later made that request a binding obligation upon the Sardar. Nehru (who had been scheduled to meet with the Mahatma on the same subject immediately after that fateful prayer meeting) saw it the same way. Gandhi's death brought the two together again; in their grief they put their differences behind them. It is time that their followers do the same. The heritage of all Indians is richer for having both Nehru and Patel to honor.

26

The Man Who Stayed Behind

I T IS ONE OF THE MORE INTRIGUING PARADOXES of Indian nationalism that the man who led the Congress Party for most of the
crucial years before independence — at a time when the struggle
was increasingly seen as being not just between Indians and British
but between advocates of a united India and followers of Muslim
separatism — was himself a Muslim.

Maulana Abul Kalam Muhiyuddin Ahmed — Maulana "Azad"
(free) as he had baptized himself in his twenties — was president of
the Indian National Congress from 1940 to 1945, leader of the Quit
India movement and head of Congress Party delegations in crucial
meetings during this period. As a Muslim divine, steeped in the erudition of his faith, and as a committed nationalist unalterably opposed to the proposed partition of his country, Azad symbolized the
all-inclusive aspirations of the nationalist movement. The Muslim
League leader Mohammed Ali Jinnah disparaged him as the "Muslim Lord Haw-Haw" (a reference to the British traitor who made
propaganda broadcasts for the Nazis during World War II) and a
"Congress Showboy," a token elected by the Congress Party in 1940
to advertise its secular credentials. Maulana was too dignified a figure to respond to these insults. But at the All-India Congress Committee session in July 1947 that debated the Partition plan, Azad

stayed silent throughout, and finally abstained from voting on the resolution. He could not vote against it because he knew that the League's appeal had now captured most of the Muslim masses, and he had learned through bitter experience how intractable the League's leaders were and how illusory the prospects of cooperation with them in a national government. So Partition, the very idea of which he found abhorrent, had become inevitable, and Maulana Azad was too intelligent a man not to acknowledge reality. His silence was the silence of a man who had nothing left to say; no words could have been adequate in the face of this transcendent political failure.

The irony was that he was ten times the Muslim that the secular, bacon-and-sausage-eating, English-educated, and Westernized Jinnah was. Born in Mecca and raised in Calcutta, Maulana Azad was a brilliant Islamic scholar, completing his religious studies at the astonishingly young age of sixteen, some nine years younger than the norm. He was a linguist, mastering Persian and Arabic in addition to Urdu and Hindi; an internationalist, who traveled extensively in the Arab and Muslim worlds acquiring a deep understanding of the main currents in those societies; a scholar, who read widely and retained a profound, even enyclopedic, knowledge of political and social issues; an educationist, who founded the Jamia Millia Islamia University in Delhi; a journalist and writer, who started, edited, and wrote India's first nationalist newspapers in Urdu; and a man of action, who led the Khilafat movement and the Dharasana agitation, and who remains the youngest-ever president of the Indian National Congress, having been first elected to that position in 1923 at the age of barely thirty-five.

And in the midst of all this he was a deeply humane and reflective Islamic thinker. Where Jinnah's was an Islam of identity, Azad's was an Islam of faith and conviction, the source of his intellectual worldview. As a follower of the Ahl-i-Hadith school of Islamic theology, he took a broad and all-encompassing view of his faith, reflected in several treatises liberally reinterpreting the holy texts and principles of Islam. Within the grand debate in Islamic jurisprudence between votaries of Taqlid, or strict adherence to conformity, and

186

Tajdid, or constructive reinterpretation of doctrine in the light of contemporary social needs, the Maulana stood uncompromisingly for innovation. Muslim scholars counted him among the most gifted exponents of *wahdat-i-deen,* the Islamic equivalent of "Sarva Deva Samabhavaha," or the essential oneness of all religions, and his unfinished *Tarjuman-al-Quran* is a remarkable exposition of the Koran as a vehicle for pluralism, intercommunal harmony and coexistence.

After Partition, Azad understood his historic role as the country's most important Muslim leader; in his person he symbolized the new democracy's guarantee that his co-religionists could remain in their homeland in security and dignity. In the wake of Partition he traveled extensively in the regions rent by communal carnage, directing the organization of relief work and setting up refugee camps, making powerful speeches to large audiences to promote peace in the newly drawn border areas and encouraging his fellow Muslims throughout India to remain loyal to their homeland, without fear for their safety and well-being. His devotion to this role sometimes involved him in clashes in the cabinet, notably with Deputy Prime Minister and Home Minister Sardar Vallabhbhai Patel over security issues in Delhi and Punjab, as well as over the allocation of resources to displaced Muslims for relief and rehabilitation. "If you want to see Pakistan, go to the Education Ministry," one politician darkly growled about the Maulana's appointment of Muslim officials to positions in his own department.

Nothing could have been less fair to Azad's ecumenical spirit: this was a man who fought hard in the Constituent Assembly to end separate electorates for Muslims, and who devoted his life to the protection of religious freedom and the equal treatment of all Indians irrespective of faith. As education minister he began the process of tackling the gigantic challenges of educating a populace which, at the time of independence, was only 18 percent literate. As a deeply religious man himself, Azad saw the use of religion in political life as sheer manipulative opportunism: the real problems of all Indians, in his view, were economic, not religious. It little mattered what God you prayed to, or how, if you did not have enough to eat or a school to send your child to. So he was a man of religion and, counterintuitively, a strong supporter of Nehruvian socialism. For Azad, Nehru's economic and industrial policies would bring to his people the justice on earth that, in spiritual terms, only Allah could dispense in heaven. Nehru, never a great fan of religious thinking, hailed Azad's "razor-sharp mind" that cut through the fog of theological disputes: he wrote of how much he had learned from his conversations with Azad when they were both imprisoned by the British.

But it is above all as a visionary of the place of Muslims in India's civilizational history — and therefore in its present and its future — that Azad must be remembered. When he became president of the Indian National Congress at Ramgarh in 1940, Azad delivered perhaps the greatest testament of the faith of a religious Muslim in a united India. He declared that "every fiber of my being revolted" against the thought of dividing India on communal lines. "I could not conceive it possible for a Mussulman to tolerate this," he declared, "unless he has rooted out the spirit of Islam from every corner of his being." It galled him that the secularized Jinnah claimed to speak for India's Muslims and to assert their claims to being a separate nation, while Maulana was both a deeply committed Muslim and a passionate Indian. "I am a Mussulman and proud of the fact," he said to his majority non-Muslim Congress audience. "Islam's splendid traditions of thirteen hundred years are my inheritance. I am unwilling to lose even the smallest part of this inheritance. In addition, I am proud of being an Indian. I am part of that indivisible unity that is Indian nationality." And then he added — this is the key part — "I am indispensable to this noble edifice. Without me this splendid structure of India is incomplete. I am an essential element which has gone to build India. I can never surrender this claim. It was India's historic destiny that many human races and cultures and religions should flow to her, and that many a caravan should rest here. . . . One of the last of these caravans was that of the followers of Islam. They came here and settled for good. We brought our treasures with us, and India too was full of the riches of her own precious heritage. We gave her what she needed most, the most precious of gifts from Islam's treasury, the message of human equality. Full eleven centuries have passed by since then. Islam has now as great a claim on the soil of India as Hinduism."

It took courage to say this. The Maulana was not immersing his Islam in any soft and fuzzy notion of Indian secularism, still less was he uncritically swallowing Hindu professions of tolerance and inclusiveness. He was instead asserting his pride in his religious identity, in the majesty and richness of Islam, while laying claim to India for India's Muslims. He dismissed talk of Partition by arguing that he was entitled — just as any Hindu was — to a stake in all of India, from Kashmir to Kanyakumari, from the Khyber Pass to Khulna; why should he accept the Pakistani idea of a narrower notion of Muslim nationhood that confined Indian Muslims to a truncated share of the heritage of their entire land? He was a far more authentic representative of Indian Islam than Jinnah, and it is part of the great tragedy of 1947 that it was Jinnah who triumphed and not Azad.

Partition was, of course, less a triumph for Indian Muslims than an abdication. Azad realized this, and among those Muslims who opposed Partition, he represented a key bridge between secularists like Rafi Ahmed Kidwai and Saifuddin Kichlew, on the one hand, and Deobandi Muslim fundamentalists like Maulana Maudoodi (who felt that Islam should prevail over the world at large and certainly over India as a whole, and believed it to be treasonous — both to India and to Islam itself — to advocate that the religion be territorially circumscribed as Jinnah and the Muslim Leaguers did). Critics like Keonraad Elst have associated Azad with the latter view, seeing him as a surrogate fifth columnist for an eventual Islamicization of the whole of India. Though there is no denying that in some of his appeals to Muslim supporters Azad may have given grounds for such beliefs, Elst and others overlook the profundity of Azad's lifelong engagement with the multireligious civilizational heritage of his homeland. "Islam," Azad averred, "has now as great a claim on the soil of India as Hinduism. If Hinduism has been the religion of the people here for several thousands of years, Islam also has been their religion for a thousand years. Just as a Hindu can say with pride that he is an

Indian and follows Hinduism, so also we can say with equal pride that we are Indians and follow Islam. I shall enlarge this orbit still further. The Indian Christian is equally entitled to say with pride that he is an Indian and is following a religion of India, namely Christianity." What became the great cliché of "unity in diversity" emerged from Azad as an affirmation of the equality of the rights of all of India's communities to be themselves.

Today, Maulana Azad is largely forgotten. To Pakistanis, he was a pathetic figure on the wrong side of history; to Indian Muslims, a symbol still, but little more; to other Indians, a name associated with medical colleges and other institutions rather than the progenitor of a legacy either to cherish or contest. His tomb lies largely neglected in Delhi. In the history of nations, the great rewards go to the winners, and Azad, by his own lights, failed in the most important cause of his life. But in the history of the ideas that make up the intellectual underpinnings of any country, there must be an honored place for those who, whether they won or lost, had the great merit of being right. Maulana Azad was right. That is his legacy — and ours.

27

The Man Who Wanted More

IT IS DIFFICULT TODAY TO IMAGINE THE SCALE of what Babasaheb Bhimji Rao Ambedkar accomplished. To be born into an "untouchable" family in 1891, and as the fourteenth and last child of a poor Mahar *subedar*, or corporal, in an army cantonment, would normally have guaranteed a life of neglect, poverty, and discrimination. Not only did Ambedkar rise above the circumstances of his birth, but he achieved a level of success that would have been spectacular for a child of privilege. One of the first untouchables ever to enter an Indian college, he became a professor (at the prestigious Sydenham College) and a principal (of no less an institution than Bombay's government law college). One of the earliest Indian students in the United States (on a merit scholarship paid for by the Gaekwar of Baroda), he earned multiple doctorates from Columbia University and the University of London, in economics, politics, and law. An heir to millennia of discrimination, he was admitted to the bar in London and became India's James Madison as the Chair of the Constitution Drafting Committee. The son of illiterates, he wrote a remarkable number of books, whose content and range testify to an eclectic mind and a sharp, if provocative, intellect. An insignificant infant scrabbling in the dust of Mhow in 1891 became the first law minister of a free India, in the most impressive cabinet ever assembled in New Delhi. When he died, aged only sixty-five, he had accumulated a set of distinctions few have matched; only one remained. In belated recognition of that omission, he was conferred posthumously in 1990 the highest award his country has to offer — the Bharat Ratna.

Ambedkar was a self-made man in the profoundest sense of that term. Even his name was his own creation, for he was born a Sakpal, but decided to take a name based on that of his village (Ambavade) as Maharashtrian Brahmins did. He was born a Hindu Mahar, but died a Buddhist, converting with hundreds of thousands of his followers at a public ceremony months before his death. Once a child who was refused water in school because his touch would "pollute" the caste of the person serving it to him, he married a Brahmin. He wore Western suits in rejection of the traditional trappings of a society that had for so long enslaved his people. And he raged against the injustice of social discrimination. Not for him the mealy-mouthed platitudes of the well-meaning: he was prepared to call a spade a bloody shovel, and to do so in print. It was an attitude that Indian society was not prepared for, but at a time when Indians were fighting for their freedom from foreign rule, it was both appropriate and necessary that Indians should fight equally against domestic oppression.

Ambedkar rejected what he saw as the patronizing indulgence of the Gandhian approach to untouchability. The Mahtama called them "Harijans" — children of God. Arrant nonsense, said Ambedkar, aren't we all children of God? He used, instead, Marathi and Hindi words for the "excluded" (*Bahishkrit*), the "oppressed" (*Dalit*), and the "silent." He publicly burned the *Manusmriti*, the ancient lawbook of the caste Hindus. He was an equal opportunity offender, condemning caste consciousness in the Muslim community with as much vehemence as he savaged the Hindus. Ambedkar fought for his people, and he fought against injustice and oppression by whomever it was practiced. He was an enemy of cant and superstition, an iconoclast who had contempt for traditions that he felt deserved no sanctity.

It wasn't easy. As a nationalist, he was sensitive to the charge that he was dividing Indians at a time when they needed to be united against the British. When he demanded separate electorates for his people, Mahatma Gandhi undertook a fast unto death until an unconvinced Ambedkar, fearing mass reprisals if the Mahatma died, caved in. Gandhi, who abhorred untouchability, believed that the answer lay in the social awakening of caste Hindus rather than in building walls of separation. Ambedkar, who lived with the daily reality of caste discrimination, was not convinced that the entrenched practices of traditional Hinduism could ever disappear. In the end he opted out of the religion altogether, embracing the ethics of equality that Buddhism embodied.

Buddhism also inspired his faith in democracy, which infused his role as the Father of India's Constitution. Whereas some saw Ambedkar, with his three-piece suit and formal English, as a Westernized exponent of Occidental constitutional systems, he was inspired far more by the democratic practices of ancient India, in particular the Buddhist *sanghas. Sangha* practice had incorporated democratic voting by ballot, formal rules of precedence and structured debates, and parliamentary practices like committees, agreed agendas, and the tabling of proposals for the conduct of business. This in turn had its precedence in the system of governance that prevailed in the ancient Indian tribal republics like those of the Lichchavis and the Shakyas. "This democratic system," Ambedkar told the Constituent Assembly, "India lost. Will we lose it again?"

His skepticism was not cynical: he saw in the institutions of Indian democracy that he was helping to create the best guarantee for the future development and welfare of his own people, the oppressed and marginalized of India. He fought hard to introduce into the Constitution fundamental protections and guarantees of civil liberties for individual citizens, including freedom of religion and speech, economic and social rights for women, and the outlawing of all forms of discrimination. Ambedkar also convinced the Constituent Assembly that it was not enough to abolish untouchability: what was needed to undo millennia of discrimination and exploitation was a system of affirmative action to uplift the oppressed, including reservations of jobs in the civil service, schools, and universities. When the Constitution was adopted, Ambedkar rather typically remarked: "If things go wrong under the new Constitution the reason will not be that we had a bad Constitution. What we will have to say is that Man was vile."

The comment suggests a deep pessimism about human nature for which he can scarcely be blamed, after witnessing the humiliations heaped upon millions for no reason other than their accident of birth. But if there is one failure that can be ascribed to him, it lay in his impatience with established political structures as instruments of change. After independence, as a minister in Nehru's first cabinet, he might have got a great deal done through the Congress Party, but he denounced it as a dharamsala, or rest home, devoid of principle or policy, "open to all, fools and knaves, friends and foes, communists and secularists, reformers and orthodox, and capitalists and anticapitalists." In his own quest for political rigor he founded no fewer than three parties, each of which faded away. He was better at articulating powerful ideas than in creating the structures to see them through. But the Constitution of which he was the principal author remains the best instrument for pursuing his ideas. The leader and spokesman of a community left his greatest gift to all communities — a legacy that belongs to all of us, and one of which we are yet to prove ourselves wholly worthy.

28

Anchored in Himself

HEN K. R. NARAYANAN WAS ELECTED AS PRESIDENT of India in 1997, there was a great deal of self-congratulation in the air. What was hailed most widely by politicians and pundits was not merely the triumph of a unifying figure at the helm of a fissiparous polity but that a Dalit — an "untouchable" outcaste — should ascend to the highest office in the land four weeks before the fiftieth anniversary of India's independence. I was just as proud as the next man to see Mahatma Gandhi's wishes being fulfilled at this auspicious time, but I thought (and wrote at the time) that it did a disservice to President Narayanan to reduce him to a symbol of his caste, or lack thereof. The nation had much to congratulate itself about in his election — not because Narayanan was a Dalit, but because he possessed one of the finest minds to have been exercised in high office in our country.

Like many others who have followed our affairs of state, I too have a Narayanan story. It goes back to 1984, when a leading national journal asked me to review his book *India and America*, published at the end of his tenure as ambassador to the United States. I am normally allergic, both as a reader and as a reviewer, to collections of official speeches; I find them usually drab and unilluminating, the self-promotional attempts of functionaries to accord their routine reflections an unmerited permanence. But Narayanan's was a worthy exception to this rule, and I engaged with it at some length, finding much to praise and a few things to criticize.

I had never met Narayanan, and my review was pseudonymous. So I was all the more surprised when the editor of the magazine forwarded to me a letter received in the name of my alias, from none other than K. R. Narayanan himself. It was an uncommonly gracious letter, thanking me not merely for my kinder words but for my criticisms, saying how much he had learned from my comments and expressing a desire to meet me. This was so exceptional an experience for me as a reviewer that I shed my anonymity and wrote back to the author — by then vice chancellor of Jawaharlal Nehru University, a fitting position for an individual of such intellectual integrity. Our first meeting occurred a year or so later, when K. R. Narayanan, by then minister of state for science and technology, was visiting Geneva, where I was living and working at the time. The minister was as disarming in person as he had been in his correspondence: kind, soft-spoken, intellectually curious, morally engaging. A lifelong friendship was born.

Thereafter I made it a point to call on him on all my visits to Delhi. I was then privileged to see him, on and off, for eighteen more years, through spells in office and out of it. I saw him as minister in two different ministries, as vice president, and finally as president. The surroundings changed, but as each receiving room became grander and more awe inspiring, the man himself did not change. It was as if his own humanity was so genuine that it could not be affected by its external trappings. Few people who have held high office are so profoundly anchored in themselves that they are immune to being swayed by the tall waves and high winds that buffet the ship of state. K. R. Narayanan was an exception. Through all the positions he held, it could truly be said of our tenth president, as it can of few others, that he remained himself.

Whenever we met, we conversed and argued; I was bowled over not only by the range and depth of his engaging intellect but by his humility and modesty, qualities that are so uncharacteristic of highly placed Indians. He was never a "typical politician," but he survived politics while managing to stay above its worst aspects. That is what made him a worthy successor to the likes of Dr. Sarvepalli Radhakrishnan and Dr. Zakir Hussain.

President Narayanan had written and spoken enough — especially before his ascent to the rarefied levels where speechwriters churn out his words — for us to have a sense of where he stood on the vital issues confronting the nation. His vision of a multireligious and multilingual India was the national counterpart of his view of a multi-ideological, multicultural world. Behind the mild manner and the invariably courteous smile, his was an unusual and eclectic spirit, forthright and remarkably free of cant. Narayanan's writings and speeches revealed the unusual mind of a man who, despite spending most of his adult life in government — and an awful lot of it as a career diplomat — could cheerfully whisk the tail of many an officially blessed sacred cow. He once described the sanctified Belgrade nonaligned summit of 1961 as "a very decorous, high level, and rather unsuccessful attempt to run away with some of Nehru's clothes." Krishna Menon he portrayed as a man thriving on "tea and antipathy." After forty years of international experience he wrote that even the consensual national dogma of continuity in India's foreign policy was often based on no more than "easy and inglorious routine." Even at the peak of our adherence to nonalignment as the be-all and end-all of our foreign policy, Narayanan was one of the few senior diplomats capable of rising above the usual official tendency to treat it as some sort of magic mantra which needed only to be incanted to be understood.

Narayanan's view of the world was rooted very firmly in a vision of India. Not an idealized, propagandist's vision, but a vision of an India whose injustices and inequalities the president himself had keenly felt as a member of an underprivileged community; yet an India that offered, through a constitutional system of democracy authored principally by a member of that same community, the possibility of overcoming these injustices. As a Keralite, Narayanan hailed from the state that had done most to fulfill the human potential of its people, a state whose record of literacy, communal tolerance, gender equality, workers' rights, and integrity in public life should be a model for the rest of the country. As a human being, he brought to the helm of our ship of state a rare intelligence, a broad education, and an identification with the downtrodden that both Ambedkar and Gandhiji would have been proud to see in the Rashtrapati Bhavan.

It was particularly fitting that, on the fiftieth year of our political independence, the presidency was won by one whose life had been shaped by the iniquities *and* the opportunities of India, and whose mind reflected this appreciation. India was lucky, for five years, that the highest office in the land was occupied by someone who was born among the lowest of the low: a man who was not only a Dalit but one born in a thatched hut with no running water, whose university refused to award him his degree at the same ceremony as his upper-caste classmates, and yet who rose above his lot to triumph without bitterness. The country learned about his Tata scholarship to England, the letter from Professor Harold Laski to Prime Minister Jawaharlal Nehru urging him to take the young man into the Foreign Service, the illustrious career that followed in diplomacy, education, and politics, culminating in his assumption of the highest position his country could offer. Obituarists better qualified than I have written of his principled positions on political issues, his memorable assertion of his independent convictions at the state dinner for President Clinton, his courage in sending improper decisions back to the cabinet for reconsideration.

And yet none of that tells the whole story about K. R. Narayanan, about why he will be missed by those who had the privilege of encountering him in person. I salute K. R. Narayanan for what he did, but I write now to praise him for who he was. Decent, learned, unaffected, a gentleman through and through in a land — and a profession — where gentlemen seem a vanishing breed, K. R. Narayanan stood for an idea of India that appealed to the better angels in all of us Indians. As president he led an India whose injustices he had keenly felt but an India that offered, through its brave but flawed experiment in political democracy, the real prospect of change through affirmative action and the ballot box. In his five years as our *rashtrapati*, the man who did not change embodied the enduring values of a country that has changed profoundly. That is what we have lost with his passing, and it is a loss that touches every one of us.

29

Tea and Antipathy

I ONLY MET THE LEGENDARY V. K. KRISHNA MENON ONCE, and in hardly the most propitious of circumstances. My father, then only thirty-eight, had been hospitalized with a heart attack and I was in the ward, an anxious child of twelve, when his old friend came calling. Krishna Menon was out of office at the time, having been defeated the previous year in his attempt to be reelected to his seat in Parliament, and I did not quite know what to make of him. He arrived in his white *mundu* and shirt, the unruly shock of white hair distinctive above his hawklike nose, trailing a couple of hangers-on, and greeted my father with a bluff comment: "What's this about a heart attack? Chandran, I didn't know you had a heart." That is all I remember about the great man, though I also recall being childishly offended by his remark, then growing up to think that his was a very witty comment, only to conclude a few years later that it was not witty enough. (My father was famed for his generosity of spirit, so Menon could easily have said, instead: "Chandran, we all know you have a heart. You didn't have to prove it this way.")

Four years later, when I went to college in Delhi, Krishna Menon was back in Parliament and my father urged me to call on him. I never did, for reasons I can no longer explain; and before I had graduated, he had passed away. My father had helped him establish the India Club in London's The Strand, where *masala dosas* and tea could always be had at prices affordable to young Indian newsmen. I never learned whether Menon had been partial to *dosas,* but of tea he was a notorious addict, admitting to consuming thirty-eight cups a day. I will always regret never sharing one of those with him.

On May 3, 2007, the handful of people who still care marked V. K. Krishna Menon's 110th birthday. Or maybe it was his 111th; even on the subject of his date of birth, Menon could not shake off controversy. He was an extraordinary figure, one who attracted more opprobrium in his lifetime than any other Indian leader, certainly in the West, where the choice epithets about him ranged from "Mephistopheles in a Savile Row suit" to "the snake charmer with hooded eyes" and even, unimaginatively, "the devil incarnate." *Time* put him on its cover, a snake hissing behind his head: it was an honor the magazine had been slow to accord the Mahatma, but Menon was a foreigner most Americans loved to hate.

He has also, paradoxically, been unjustly treated by the guardians of our historical memory. Krishna Menon is remembered in India largely for two things: delivering a record-setting marathon seven-hour-and-fifty-eight-minute speech on Kashmir in the Security Council fifty years ago, during the course of which he fainted, had to be revived, and carried on; and presiding over a Defense Ministry whose lack of preparedness for war in 1962 led to the humiliation of military defeat by China, a humiliation seen as having been brought about by Menon's own leftist illusions about the Communist giant. His abrasive personality, his reluctance to suffer fools gladly, his bluntness to those he did not judge intellectually worthy of his time — even Nehru's sister Vijaylakshmi Pandit, the first female president of the United Nations General Assembly, fell short of his standards and complained to the prime minister of his "rudeness" to her — meant that he had few genuine loyalists. In good times, his brilliance, his restless energy, his eloquence, and his astonishing reserves of stamina carried the day and won him admirers, if not fans; but when disaster came, he was left friendless and alone, abandoned by the party he had served without pay or thanks in the best years of his life. He died a forgotten backbencher, without even a political party to call his own.

His had been an unusual life. Much of it had been spent in London, where he devoted himself to fighting the battle for India's independence on Britain's home turf, against men "who draw their incomes from India and spend the evenings of their life in maligning India and her people." He enjoyed the cut and thrust of debate, serving as a Labor Party councillor for the London borough of St. Pancras, where he established libraries and started a literary festival (Menon had been an early consulting editor for Penguin Books, tricking Allen Lane into publishing A *Passage to India* by implying it was a travel book). Nehru, who had admired Menon's record in the U.K., rewarded him by making him independent India's first High Commissioner in London, a position he used to put the former colonial masters firmly in their place. That acerbic wit rarely failed him: when the hapless Brigid Brophy complimented him on his English, Menon retorted scathingly, "My English, Madam, is much better than yours. You merely picked it up; I learned it."

It was not an approach calculated to win friends, but it did influence people. I have read no more remarkable exposition of the mind-set of the first generation of India's nationalist leaders than Krishna Menon's magisterial interviews with the Canadian political scientist Michael Brecher, published in 1968 as a book titled *India and World Politics: Krishna Menon's View of the World*. It is difficult to think of an Indian leader other than Nehru who would have been capable of the extensive discourse on world affairs, human history, and international politics that Menon so magisterially managed.

I did not agree with most of Krishna Menon's views — his socialism was imbibed directly from Harold Laski at the London School of Economics, and his anti-Americanism was visceral rather than rational — but I admired the way he expressed them. Unlike my father, Krishna Menon may not have had a heart, but he had a brain, and a tongue. In this golden jubilee year of his historic UN speech, they're both worth raising a toast to.

30

Smother India

Of the dozen prime ministers who have ruled India, the world's most populous democracy, since independence from Britain in 1947, none evokes the extremes of adulation and hatred that Indira Gandhi does. Shrewd politician, two-time prime minister (with a total of fifteen years in office), and autocrat, she is deified and despised in equal measure: like India herself, Indira leaves no one indifferent.

Her life can clearly be divided into two phases: a modest, even unremarkable youth and early adulthood, followed by a formidable middle age. Surviving childhood frailty and a brush with the tuberculosis that had killed her mother, Indira was a sickly and often bedridden young woman with a penchant for silence. Even her famous childhood identification with Joan of Arc was a fabricated piece of adult self-mythologizing. She made little impression on family and friends until she dropped out of college in Oxford and married a young Congress Party worker, Feroze Gandhi. (Feroze was no relation to the Mahatma, but a member of the tiny Parsi minority.) The marriage soon foundered, however, over the conflicting demands of father and husband, or as Indira saw it, her duty to the nation over her loyalty to her marriage. Feroze, a fiercely independent Congress

MP and anticorruption crusader, felt politically and personally stifled, turned to drink and infidelity, and died young in 1960.

When Nehru's successor, Lal Bahadur Shastri, died at the age of sixty-two of a sudden heart attack after peace talks with Pakistan in Tashkent in 1966, the Congress Party stalwarts known as the "Syndicate" picked her as someone who enjoyed national recognition but could be counted upon to take instructions from the party. They mistakenly saw her, in the words of opposition Socialist leader Ram Manohar Lohia, as a *gungi gudiya,* or "dumb doll." Initially, Indira, inarticulate and tentative, overreliant on advisers of dubious competence, stumbled badly in office. The party paid the price in the elections of 1967, losing seats around the country, and seeing motley opposition governments come to power in several states.

At the brink of the abyss, Indira fought back. Sidelining the Syndicate, finding allies among Socialists and ex-Communists, she engineered a split in Congress in 1969 on "ideological" grounds. Having established a populist image and expelled the old bosses, she led her wing of Congress to a resounding victory in 1971, campaigning on the slogan *"Garibi Hatao"* (Remove Poverty). This was swiftly followed by the decisive defeat of Pakistan in the war that created Bangladesh later that year. Her popularity soared; she had reinvented her party, upstaged the older generation of political leaders, and won a decisive war against the country that had, in 1947, vivisected the motherland. India's leading modern painter, the Muslim M. F. Husain, depicted her as a Hindu mother goddess. The imagery was appropriate: indeed, at her peak, Indira Gandhi was both worshiped and maternalized.

But what did she stand for? As Nehru's daughter and political heir, Indira Gandhi had imbibed his vision, but it was distorted by her own proclivities. She took great pride in the fact that she was born in November 1917, at the time of the Russian Revolution. From her father and his friends she had learned to be skeptical of Western claims to stand for freedom and democracy when India's historical experience of colonial oppression and exploitation appeared to bear out the opposite. These convictions fitted in with her domestic left-wing political strategy, her need for Soviet support on the subcontinent against a U.S.-backed Pakistan-China axis, and her dark suspicion, born more out of personal insecurity than of any hard evidence, that the CIA was out to destabilize her government as it had done Allende's.

Nonetheless, Indira Gandhi once memorably confessed, "I don't really have a political philosophy. I can't say I believe in any ism. I wouldn't say I'm interested in socialism as socialism. To me it's just a tool." But tools are used for well-defined purposes, and it was never clear that Indira Gandhi had any, beyond the politically expedient (one observer sardonically said her politics were "somewhere to the left of self-interest"). The 1971 electoral and military triumphs — the first over a sclerotic and discredited political establishment at home, the second over a sclerotic and discredited martial law establishment next door — saw Indira at her pinnacle. But it was not to last. Mrs. Gandhi was skilled at the acquisition and maintenance of power, inept at wielding it for larger purposes. She had no real vision or program beyond campaign slogans; "remove poverty" was a mantra without a method. Her only ideology seemed to be opportunism, garbed in socialist rhetoric.

As mounting protests in 1975 threatened to bring her down, a High Court judge convicted the prime minister on a technicality of electoral malpractice in her crushing 1971 victory. Mrs. Gandhi, it seemed, would have to resign in disgrace. Instead, she struck back. Declaring a state of emergency, Indira Gandhi arrested opponents, censored the press, and postponed elections. As a stacked and compliant Supreme Court overturned her conviction, she proclaimed a "20-point program" for the uplift of the common man. Its provisions — which ranged from rural improvement schemes and the abolition of bonded labor to mass education and urban renewal — remained largely unimplemented. Meanwhile, her thuggish younger son, Sanjay, ordered brutally insensitive campaigns of slum demolitions and forced sterilizations. The Nehruvian compact with the people was ruptured, even as a meretricious slogan spouted by a pliant Congress Party president proclaimed, "Indira is India and India is Indira."

Nehru's daughter had betrayed her father's democratic legacy. But — blinded by the mirrors of her sycophants, deafened by the silence of the intimidated press — Mrs. Gandhi called an election in March 1977, expecting vindication in electoral victory. Instead, she was routed, losing her own seat and the reins of office to an opposition coalition, the Janata (People's) Front. She quietly surrendered the reins; she had flirted with autocracy for twenty-two months, yet she was ultimately the daughter of the man who had done more than most to entrench democracy in India.

But the fractious Janata government could not hold together. By their mistakes, ineptitude, and greed (cynically, if artfully, exploited by Mrs. Gandhi and Sanjay) they opened the way for her improbable comeback. In January 1980, Mrs. Gandhi, having split the Congress once more and unembarrassedly renamed her faction after herself (as Congress-Indira, or "Congress-I") was prime minister of India again.

The rest of the story is more familiar, and all tragic. The reckless Sanjay died in the crash of his stunt plane (one editor, Arun Shourie, wrote that "if he had lived he would have done to the country what he did to the plane"). Mrs. Gandhi, having systematically alienated, excluded, or expelled any leader of standing in her own party who might have been a viable deputy (and thus a potential rival) to her, drafted the only person she could entirely trust — her self-effacing, nonpolitical, and deeply reluctant elder son Rajiv — to fill the breach. (Indira Gandhi's deep mistrust of everyone but her own sons, her blindness to their limitations, and her intolerance of dissent remain profound and inescapable flaws.)

Rajiv had barely begun to grow into the role when Mrs. Gandhi was assassinated by the forces of Sikh extremism, forces she herself had primed, along with Sanjay, for narrow partisan purposes. There is no excusing the cynicism with which she encouraged (and initially financed) the fanaticism of a Sikh fundamentalist preacher, Jarnail

Singh Bhindranwale, in order to undercut her political rivals, the moderate Sikh Akali Dal. As the murders ordered by Bhindranwale mounted, Mrs. Gandhi had little choice but to destroy the monster she had spawned, at a terrible price for Indian democracy and ultimately for the prime minister herself. Mrs. Gandhi had created the problem in the first place and let it mount to the point where the destructive force of "Operation Bluestar" seemed the only solution. Her earlier failure to nip the problem decisively in the bud demonstrated once again the Indira Gandhi paradox: so skilled at acquiring power, so tentative in wielding it. Her murder by her own Sikh security guards came at the end of an inglorious second term of office, at a time when the prospects of reelection had looked remote.

Indira Gandhi's was an extraordinary life, but one which raises too many unanswerable questions. Why did a woman brought up in privilege feel so insecure? Why did her fifteen years in office (with the exception of her annus mirabilis, 1971) have so little to show for them? How did she, with her crushing parliamentary majorities, miss so many opportunities to resolve some of India's most persistent problems? How could she encourage so much sycophancy and corruption, trusting, by her own admission, "men who may not be very bright but on whom I can rely"? What led a secular rationalist — a woman who was so agnostic that she took her oath of office as prime minister without the customary reference to God — to become religious and superstitious in her last years?

Some admirers take Indira Gandhi at her word, seeing a defender of the poor and the wretched where others saw only a political opportunist. Whatever she accomplished for the poor — and the evidence suggests her major "socialist" acts, like bank nationalization, did not do much to benefit them — the balance sheet tilts sadly against her. It is difficult to justify Mrs. Gandhi's deinstitutionalization of Indian democracy, or to explain the grim legacy of failure and paranoia she left the nation. The prime minister's emasculation of party, Parliament, and civil service, and the destructiveness of her actions in Punjab, Kashmir, Andhra Pradesh, and even Sri Lanka in the months leading up to her assassination, were undeniably self-destroying. When she returned to office in 1980 and was asked how it felt to be India's leader again, she snapped at her questioner, "I have always been India's leader."

To many at the time, it seemed that way, and yet, in the almost unrecognizable politics and society of today's India, another epitaph seems more likely to endure. Asked a few months later "what one thing" she wanted to be remembered for, Indira Gandhi bitterly replied, "I do not want to be remembered for anything." Since the party she enfeebled heads a coalition government pursuing policies diametrically opposed to hers, and since India's fractious federalism throws up multiparty coalitions as far removed as imaginable from the centralized "priministerialism" of Indira Gandhi, it seems she may get her wish after all.

31

The Spy Who Came In Through the Heat

I RECENTLY HAD THE GREAT PRIVILEGE OF BEING THE FIRST outsider, unconnected to the security community, to deliver a lecture within the premises of RAW, our country's external intelligence agency. The occasion was the first R. N. Kao Memorial Lecture, on the fifth anniversary of the death of the legendary Rameshwar Nath Kao.

I had never met the man in whose honor I spoke. But his story is a compelling one — from joining the police as a twenty-two-year-old in 1940, moving to the Intelligence Bureau in 1947, winning numerous honors and medals, and serving in 1963 as the first director of the Aviation Research Center, India's first technological intelligence agency. In 1968 Kao took charge as the first head of a new external intelligence agency with the innocuous name of the Research and Analysis Wing. (I am told that many of the agency's professionals prefer to speak of it as "R & AW," whereas like others infected by the media, I like the sound of RAW.)

Kao and RAW proved themselves in the lead-up to and the conduct of the 1971 war with Pakistan; his bureaucratic reward came with elevation to the level of secretary to the government in

1973. After his formal retirement at age fifty-eight, Kao continued to advise the government at the highest levels, providing invaluable advice on various issues relating to the country's national security. Between 1981 and 1984 he served as Security Adviser to the cabinet, in effect as the first National Security Adviser. His role in setting up the Policy and Research Staff as an in-house think tank became the forerunner to today's national Security Council Secretariat. He was a pioneer in intelligence coordination, that bugbear of so many national security systems. The personal links Kao maintained with foreign intelligence chiefs served the country well in many ways that most of us will never learn about. (Kao even set up the intelligence service of Ghana.) And he had a sense of humor — when critics in the bureaucracy described RAW agents as "Kao-boys," he promptly commissioned a fiberglass sculpture of a cowboy and installed it in the foyer of the RAW building.

Kao's own interest in sculpting was, appropriately enough, in iron, and he was known for his fine collection of Gandhara paintings. As a writer, my one regret is that he never wrote his memoirs, despite earning his master's in English literature at Allahabad University. Rather like the reclusive novelist Thomas Pynchon, the legend goes — I heard it from one of his juniors — that R. N. Kao has been photographed in public only twice. There might be an element of exaggeration there, but there is no doubt that his death in January 2002 robbed the country of one whose contribution to building the nation — a safe and secure India — is immeasurable and yet will never be widely known. It is as a consequence of his tireless efforts that the foundations of modern intelligence in India were laid and an edifice constructed that protects the nation to this day. Kao made an enduring impact on the training and professional development of an entire generation of intelligence professionals.

Some of the secrecy that is part of Kao's legacy is natural and understandable. Some of it may merit greater debate. As the Research and Analysis Wing of the Cabinet Secretariat, RAW is not a separate department of government and is therefore not answerable to Parliament. The funds allotted to it are not audited in the usual way, again for understandable reasons, but equally any form of public judgment or performance audit it faces is almost always political rather than professional, with the agency regularly being blamed and traduced in the media without any objective means of defending itself. I suspect that many of the professionals in RAW would benefit from the agency being made accountable in the legal sense, so that they can do their assigned work as a legitimate government body and receive appropriate recognition and criticism for their performance.

I am sure there are many who would disagree with this, and who would celebrate that RAW is relatively little known to the informed international public. Nonetheless, RAW's exact locus within the Indian strategic establishment has remained a puzzle even to many well-informed observers. Our diplomats are not always noted for valuing intelligence inputs in foreign policymaking; our internal intelligence institutions, including the police and the army, do not want RAW's expertise in counterterrorism to amount to meddling in issues of internal security. Indeed, RAW's contribution to Indian foreign policy and national political objectives has never been properly documented: even the study commissioned by R. N. Kao of RAW's work on the 1971 war has never seen the light of day. In any country, an external intelligence organization should always serve as an effective, even if necessarily hidden, arm of foreign policy. But part of that effectiveness comes from a knowledgeable sense of the organization's performance. I think it is a great pity if it is true that, as I am told, secrecy has gone to the point where many who serve in RAW do not have a sense of their own history.

Today, informed knowledge about external threats to the nation, the fight against terrorism, a country's strategic outreach, its geopolitically derived sense of its national interest, and the way in which it articulates and projects its presence on the international stage are all intertwined, and are inseparable from its internal dynamics. There can no longer be a watertight division between intelligence and policymaking, external intelligence and internal reality, foreign policy and domestic society. Indeed, even the image of our intelligence apparatus contributes to the way India is perceived abroad. This is why I welcomed the invitation to speak at RAW. I hope that, in the years to come, its doors will open even wider. R. N. Kao would, I suspect, have grudgingly approved.

32

The Genius Lost to Infinity

THE NEWS THAT THE BRITISH ACTOR-DIRECTOR STEPHEN FRY and our own Dev Benegal will co-write and direct a new film about the tragic mathematical genius Srinivasa Ramanujan is both welcome and worrying. Welcome, because Ramanujan's story deserves to be told for a mass audience; worrying, because the obstacles in the realization of such a project are so great that one fears the tragedy of the genius's life and death might be compounded by the further disappointment of never seeing the movie made.

And what a story it is! In January 1913, a clerk in the Accounts Department of the Port Trust Office at Madras, with no university education, sent the Cambridge mathematician G. H. Hardy nine pages of closely written mathematical formulae, in a rounded schoolboy script. The letter offered startling conclusions on such arcana as divergent series and the negative values of gamma function — and refuted one of Hardy's own papers. At first Hardy thought the author might be a crank; but after studying the theorems he realized that they "could only be written down by a mathematician of the highest class. . . . They must be true because, if they were not true, no one would have the imagination to invent them."

The letter offered only a foretaste of the prodigious calculations to come. For Ramanujan, born so poor he could not afford paper to record his formulae (he wrote many of his calculations in chalk on a slate and erased them with his elbow; sometimes he would write in red ink on paper already written upon) was now summoned to Cambridge, where he embarked on a brilliant career that brought him the world's greatest mathematical honors — and led to his death at the age of thirty-two. When Ramanujan died, at the height of his powers, he left a final notebook full of formulae — 650 theorems devised as his body was being inexorably consumed by tuberculosis. It was a tragedy, his doctor later wrote, "too deep for tears."

A film of this tragedy must vividly portray Ramanujan's humble birth (and a childhood marked by questions like "How far is it between clouds?"), his strong-willed mother, his schoolboy brilliance (a headmaster declared that he "deserved higher than the maximum possible marks"), his Hindu religious convictions ("an equation," Ramanujan once said, "has no meaning unless it expresses a thought of God"). And it must not gloss over the years of neglect and penury until his persistence found him patrons for a shoestring stipend, a clerical job — and the letter to Cambridge that transformed his life.

It is appropriate that the film should be an Indo-British collaboration. The partnership between Ramanujan, a short, dark Tamil with a pockmarked face and glowing eyes, and Hardy, a Fellow of Trinity College, cricket player, and perfectionist who prided himself on the "uselessness" of his purist mathematics, was as unlikely as it was productive. Papers flowed from them amid the ravages of World War I; Hardy polished the rougher edges of his partner's genius and ensured its public acceptance. Ramanujan came up with a succession of astonishing insights that others have proven since. Eminent scholars have devoted decades to the study of Ramanujan's notebooks, and the task is still unfinished. Ramanujan's work retains a compelling relevance; his theorems have found applications in a variety of fields, from computer science to cryptology, particle physics to plastics, statistical mechanics to space travel. President Abdul Kalam has even presented the filmmakers with a paper he has written on Ramanujan's theories on secure communications.

I hope the filmmakers will include among their scenes my

favorite stories of Ramanujan's genius. Attending his first Cambridge lecture and asked by a professor whether he wanted to add anything, Ramanujan went to the blackboard and wrote results the professor had not yet proved — and which he could not have known before. In one episode, Hardy visited his ailing protégé in a nursing home and commented that the license number of the cab he had come in, 1729, was "rather a dull number." Ramanujan reacted instantly: "No, Hardy. It is a very interesting number. It is the smallest number expressible as the sum of two cubes in two different ways."

Ramanujan was convinced, from reading the lines on his palm, that he would die before he was thirty-five. Auto-suggestion in such a religious man could well have had a powerful effect; Ramanujan always saw mathematics as a divine gift, bestowed upon him by his family deity, the goddess Namagiri, in his dreams. Loneliness, neglect, and poor eating habits in an unfamiliar climate also took their toll. Tuberculosis was a common affliction among Indian students in England, and Ramanujan, obsessed by his work, unable to find vegetarian food in an England of wartime shortages, simply wasted away. The enormity of this preventable loss is unbearably moving.

Ramanujan had, in Hardy's words, "a profound and invincible originality," but he was still heir to an ancient Indian mathematical tradition that has given the world its misnamed "Arabic" numerals, that invented the zero in the second century B.C., and that flowered in the theorems of Aryabhatta in the fifth century A.D., Brahmagupta in the seventh, and Bhaskara in the twelfth. Yet he would never have approached the eminence he did were it not for his discovery by (or perhaps one should say of) Hardy. Poverty and colonialism can well be blamed, but today's India must do better at identifying and nurturing new Ramanujans.

It took an Englishman, J. B. S. Haldane, to observe: "If Ramanujan's work had been recognized in India as early as it was in England, he might never have emigrated" — and might have lived to achieve even more. It is a shame that the handful of Indian-born Nobel Prize–winning scientists all triumphed abroad rather than in the land of their birth. Perhaps the film will help change that.

33

The Other Saint Teresa

S HE DIED SEVENTY YEARS BEFORE MOTHER TERESA, in the unremarkable Kerala village of Puthenchira, far from the flashbulbs
of a celebrity-seeking press. Another Servant of God, another
woman who found her calling in ministering to the sick and dying,
another unforgettable heroine to the forgotten. But there was no
state funeral for her, no Nobel Peace Prize, not even a profile in the
big-city papers. Mother Mariam Thresia Chiramel Mankidiyan died,
aged fifty, of a banal wound that would not heal because of her untreated diabetes.

Seventy-four years later, she was beatified in St. Peter's Square
by Pope John Paul II, the penultimate step toward sainthood. I sat
shivering under a gray Roman sky in the Vatican, among tens of
thousands thronging the square for the outdoor ceremony. The atmosphere was a cross between a baptism and an Oscar Awards pre-
sentation. Five venerable servants of the Church were to be
beatified, and as their names were called out raucous cheers rose
from their supporters in the crowd, many of whom were draped in
scarves bearing the colors of their would-be saint. There was a particularly noisy Latin American contingent, and a surprisingly vol-
uble Swedish group bearing the blue and yellow of their national flag
(fortified rather unfairly, I thought, by a large number of Indian nuns

wearing Swedish colors). When Mariam Thresia's name was announced, a ragged little round of applause emerged from the handful of *desis* sporting the orange-and-yellow scarves of her "party." Then the pope shuffled in, and the pomp and magnificence of the Vatican took over, as the organ music swelled and sonorous Latin chants melded with the raised voices of the congregation singing the praises of their Lord. And then the curtains parted to unveil five immense tapestries hanging from the Vatican balconies, the last of a stern Mariam Thresia in her nun's robes, clutching a crucifix and regarding the worshipers with an ascetic eye.

How did this woman transcend the obscurity of her geography and genealogy to receive beatification at the hands of the pope in the Jubilee Year 2000, only the fourth Indian ever to have been beatified? The story of Mariam Thresia is a remarkable one. Born in 1876 into a family in straitened circumstances — the result of a grandfather having had to sell off all his property to get seven daughters married — Mariam Thresia was one of three daughters. Her father and a brother reacted to adversity by turning to drink; Mariam Thresia turned instead to faith. Moved at an early age by intense visions of the Virgin Mary, she took to prayer and night vigils, scourging herself in penitence, donning a barbed wire belt to mortify her own flesh, forsaking meat and "mixing bitter stuff in my curry" (as she later confessed in a brief spiritual autobiography). She took to standing in a crucified position, and blood appeared spontaneously on her hands and feet — the stigmata of Christian lore. Like Saint Teresa of Avila centuries earlier, she suffered seizures during which she levitated: neighbors would come to her family home on Fridays to see her suspended high against the wall in a crucified pose. The Catholic Church was initially suspicious; the local bishop wondered if she was a "plaything of the devil," and in her late twenties she was repeatedly exorcized to rid her of demons. But nothing shook her faith, and soon enough her exorcist, the parish priest of Puthenchira, became her spiritual mentor and ally. Before she turned forty she was allowed to found her own order — the Congregation of the Holy

Family — with three companions. By the time she died in 1926 the three had grown to fifty-five; today there are 1,584 sisters in the order, serving not only in Kerala but in north India, Germany, Italy, and Ghana.

Mariam Thresia was driven not only by her intense visions of the other world but by an equally strong sense of responsibility for the present one. She made it a point to seek out the sick, the deformed, the dying, and tend to them. She bravely nursed victims of smallpox and leprosy at a time when they were shunned even by their own families, caring for people whose illnesses were hideously disfiguring and dangerously contagious. In a caste-ridden society she insisted on going to the homes of the lowest of the low, the poorest of the poor, and sharing her food with them. When these outcasts died, she buried them and took charge of the care of their orphaned children. Her devotion to good works won her a devoted following: it was said she emanated an aura of light and a sweet odor, and that her touch could heal. But she could not heal herself of a wound caused by a falling object. She died just as her tireless work was achieving visible results in the growth of her congregation.

The path to sainthood in the Catholic Church has to be paved with miracles, and many have been attributed to Mariam Thresia. One in particular was thoroughly investigated by the Church and resulted in her beatification. Mathew Pallissery, born with two clubfeet into a family too poor to afford surgery, crawled and hobbled on the sides of his deformed feet till his teens, when his family embarked on forty-one days of prayer and fasting dedicated to Mariam Thresia. On the thirty-third day, he dreamt that Mariam Thresia came to him and rubbed his right foot. He woke and found it had straightened — he could walk on it. A year later, the family prayed and fasted again; this time, on the thirty-ninth day, it was his mother who dreamt of Mariam Thresia, and when she went to her sleeping son she found his left foot had straightened, too. There are "before and after" photographs, x-rays, and the expertise of orthopedic specialists to confirm that the cure could not be explained medically and was, in fact, more complete than surgery could have achieved. Today Mathew is forty-four, employed, married, and the father of two. He was in Rome to witness firsthand the beatification of Mariam Thresia.

Sainthood requires a second miracle, and though Mariam Thresia's followers have produced another case — also of a clubfoot cured through similar prayer — the Church rules are inflexible: only miracles occurring after beatification can lead to sainthood. So Mariam Thresia fans will have to wait for fresh miracles. But her chances of becoming the first Indian Catholic saint — ahead of her better-known near-namesake from Calcutta — appear bright. After all, she did more than help the dying to die with dignity, as the illustrious Nobel Prize–winning nun did.

K. P. Fabian, India's kind and wise ambassador in Rome, and a practicing Catholic himself, wryly remarked to me that Kerala has had Christianity for two thousand years but has only begun producing saints in the last hundred. Clearly, the Church has only recently started to recognize the faith of its darker-hued adherents as equivalent to that of the white originators of their religion. Faith can produce miracles; Hinduism and Islam are replete with similar stories of the lame being able to walk, the blind enabled to see. It is belief that matters, not the particulars of that belief. But the beatification of Mariam Thresia (and of a Colombian alongside her) is an acknowledgment that the future of the Church lies in Asia, Latin America, and Africa, where it finds fertile ground in the intense devotion of ordinary people.

It is this that provides a different context to the unseemly "conversion controversy" of last year. To hear Malayalam recited in St. Peter's alongside half a dozen European languages is, in its own way, satisfying. I am not a Christian, but I rejoice in the magic an Indian woman has brought to Christianity. Perhaps one day it will not just be an Indian saint the world honors in Vatican Square, but an Indian pope. Only the most narrow-minded of our homegrown fanatics would fail to take pride in that.

34

A Polymath's Politics

WHEN PROFESSOR AMARTYA SEN RECEIVED THE NOBEL PRIZE in Economics in 1998, most Indians could barely contain their pride and satisfaction at the honor he had so deservingly earned, and at the near-universal approbation with which his selection was received around the world. By honoring him, most Indians felt, the Nobel Committee reached out to recognize "one of us" — a man steeped in the Indian culture and tradition into which he was born, a citizen of the world who has never relinquished his Indian passport, a Harvard and Cambridge eminence who has always maintained an abiding interest in the nature and future of India.

But Amartya Sen is not just one of us — his contribution to humanity is too great to confine him to that description.

I am not, I am happy to say, an economist. I have tended to keep a safe distance from that dismal science, whose practitioners were once described as people who "knew the price of everything but the value of nothing." Economists as a group were widely seen as people obsessed with arcane theories and endless disputations; George Bernard Shaw once wrote, "If all the economists in the world were laid end to end, they would never reach a conclusion."

The famous disconnection of most economists from everyday realities has even spawned a series of jokes. My favorite one is about the group of five men — a carpenter, a tailor, a sailor, a priest, and an economist — marooned on a desert island, who are trying to figure out a way to escape. "I could chop down the tree there," says the carpenter, "and make a raft." The tailor says he can stitch a few sheets into a mast; the sailor says he can navigate by the stars; the priest says he will pray for favorable winds. All they need now is to chop down the tree. "That's easy," says the economist. "Assume an ax."

Amartya Sen is of this tribe and yet has risen above it. His credentials as a theoretician are impeccable; from his now classic *Collective Choice and Social Welfare* to his extensive work on economic inequality and development, Sen has firmly established himself at the pinnacle of the academic mainstream of his discipline. (So much so that his theoretical work formed the basis for one of the few negative articles on his Nobel, a pernickety piece by Gene Epstein in the New York investment weekly *Barron's* which faulted Sen's "fetish for math-as-method.") Yet, despite being an economist, Sen does reach conclusions — powerful and compelling ones, which have not merely enhanced his scholarly standing but have had direct relevance for public policy in the real world.

Most notably, his work on famine has brought insight and wisdom to the world's understanding of this recurrent tragedy. Sen never forgot his own shattering experience as a nine-year-old during the Great Bengal Famine of 1943, when three million died while precious food either rotted in hoarders' warehouses or was diverted to the British war effort. "I would remember the harrowing scenes vividly," he later recalled, "when more than three decades later I tried to do an economic analysis of the causal antecedents and processes of famines." Sen's work, informed by compassion as well as solid quantitative research, has established the now widely accepted doctrine that famines are nearly always avoidable; that they result not from lack of food but lack of access to food; that distribution is therefore the key; and that democracy is the one system of government that enables food to be distributed widely and fairly. No democracy with a free press, Sen pointed out, has suffered a famine, whereas tyrannies and colonial regimes have.

All this is admirable, but it does a disservice to Sen to honor him merely as an economist. "I believe that economic analysis has something to contribute to substantive ethics in the world in which we live," he modestly suggests. And he has demonstrated the truth of this assertion not merely by the strongly ethical content of his own economic analysis, but by going beyond it into fields that have nothing to do with economics as such. Amartya Sen's writings and lectures on Tagore and Ray, on Indian secularism, on human rights and "Asian values," have all testified to the breadth of vision and the depth of humanity of this remarkable polymath.

One Indian, the old joke goes, is a monologue; two Indians is a debate; three Indians, two political parties. That Indians are argumentative seems beyond dispute. But it takes an economist of the Nobel laureate Amartya Sen's standing to convert that proposition into a magisterial book — The Argumentative Indian — that attests to the depth and eclecticism of his intellectual range.

Amartya Sen is now clearly one of the foremost public intellectuals of our time. "I've always liked arguing with people," he tells me from his home in Cambridge, Massachusetts, in between trips to New York and Florence in his dizzyingly peripatetic (and just as dizzyingly prolific) life. Appropriately enough, he was born (in 1933) on a university campus, that of Vishwa-Bharati, founded by the great Nobel laureate in literature, Rabindranath Tagore, in the West Bengal village of Santiniketan. It was Tagore who prophetically chose the name Amartya ("immortal") for the only other Bengali who has so far emulated his Nobel Prize. Sen won it in economics, though, as his work demonstrates, he could just as convincingly be described as a sociologist, a historian, a Sanskritist, a political analyst, or a moral philosopher.

"I wanted to be a physicist," Sen says, "but my political interests led me to economics." Two things moved him the most as a child: the Great Bengal Famine of 1943, which killed thousands while plentiful harvests ripened in the fields, and the religious violence that preceded the Partition of India in 1947. The teenage Amartya saw a bleeding Muslim laborer, Kader Mia, stumble into his Hindu family's home after being knifed in a communal riot; the man had only ventured into the "wrong" neighborhood because he needed work to feed his family. Kader Mia was rushed to hospital by Amartya's father, but died. Economics, politics, and morality intersected in those episodes, indelibly marking Amartya Sen's growing mind.

Initially, like virtually every Calcutta collegian, Sen's politics were leftist, but leavened by an abiding faith in freedom and an early interest in philosophy. His pioneering work as a "technical economist" in welfare economics and social choice theory (how the wishes of a society can be aggregated from the diverse views of its members) was cited by the Nobel Committee. But he has become better known to a wider audience for his work on famines (in particular the proposition that there has never been a famine in a functioning democracy) and on "development as freedom," which argues compellingly that it is more important to be free than to be rich, and that different kinds of freedom — political, economic, and social — enrich and reinforce each other.

His fame is growing. "I opened the *New York Times* last Sunday," Sen recounts, "and found a full-page ad featuring Laura Bush and Hillary Clinton, with a headline quoting me! It was on the importance of women's education. When I first started working on gender issues in development, it was treated as an eccentricity." Sen's concern for the impoverished, undernourished, and marginalized, especially women, comes through strongly in his essays. His Nobel Prize money has largely gone to two trusts he founded, in India and Bangladesh, focusing particularly on education and health care for the poor. The Nobel citation also lauded his restoration of "an ethical dimension to the discussion of vital economic problems." Though he says he is not interested in the philosophy of economics, a profound moral sense is never absent from his prose.

The Argumentative Indian is not, however, about economics, except tangentially (there's one essay about class in India). It is instead a powerfully constructed case for India's political and cultural heterogeneity, and of the "reach of reason" in India's intellectual traditions. "It's something which has been in my mind for a while," Sen says. He is particularly critical of the Western overemphasis on India's religiosity at the expense of any recognition of the country's equally impressive rationalist, scientific, mathematical, and secular heritage. The son of a professor of soil chemistry, he vividly recalls going to the lab with his father, "testing hypotheses, seeing whether experiments worked out or not." That "scientific spirit of inquiry," he says, has its roots in ancient India. He likes to cite 3,500-year-old verses from the Vedas that speculate skeptically about creation, and details India's contributions to the world of science, rationality, and plural discourse, fields treated by Orientalists as "Western spheres of success."

But debunking Western orientalists who have seen India as an exotic land of delirious worshipers is not Sen's only concern. His targets are homegrown as well. "My view of India is of a very broad civilization, which I've seen being miniaturized by sectarians," he says, alluding to the Hindutva (Hinduness) movement, which has sought to promote a narrowly Hindu identity for India. Sen's book attacks such a "narrow and bellicose" interpretation, while reaffirming his own "capacious idea of India" as an authentically plural and tolerant civilization with a long tradition of intellectual heterodoxy.

Indeed, Hinduism is the only major religion with an explicit tradition of agnosticism within it. Equally important is the tradition of secular tolerance practiced by such rulers as the Buddhist emperor Ashoka and the Muslim emperor Akbar 1,800 years apart. Sen points out that Ashoka's edicts promoted the human rights of all in the third century before Christ, a time when Aristotle's writings on freedom explicitly excluded women and slaves, an exception the Indian monarch did not make. At the time of the Inquisition, when the Catholics of Europe were persecuting Jews and heretics, the Mughal emperor Akbar was proclaiming in Delhi that "no man should be interfered with on account of religion, and anyone is to be allowed to go over to a religion that pleases him." Unlike in the West, Indian secularism has tended not to be about the separation of church from state, but rather about tolerance of a multitude of religions, none of which is favored by the state. To Sen, "The Hindutva movement has entered into a confrontation with the idea of India itself."

Sen has argued that "the need for an intellectual challenge to the sectarians is also important politically." That sense of passionate engagement with India informs much of his writing. On Indian democracy, he is both reasoned and critical. While hailing India's success in preventing the famines that occurred with depressing regularity under British colonial rule, he stresses that this does not mean the problem of chronic and endemic hunger ("a much more complex task") has been solved.

Back at Harvard after serving six years as the first non-English Master of Trinity College, Cambridge, Sen — film and theater buff, cricket fan, and voracious reader — embodies the yearning for eclectic learning. "Teaching is very important for me," Sen says (his official Nobel biography lists, with pride, the accomplishments of many of his students over the years). As a young man he translated a number of George Bernard Shaw's plays into Bengali, but mislaid the manuscripts; perhaps they will turn up, he imagines, in his recently deceased mother's trunkfuls of papers. His most recent book, *Identity and Violence: The Illusion of Destiny*, rests on the seemingly simple proposition that ascribing "singular identities" to people (for example, calling someone a "Muslim" while overlooking other aspects of his individual makeup) leads to the "miniaturization of human beings" and the "belittling of human identity." Sen argues passionately against reducing individuals to a "choiceless singularity" (few people, after all, have a choice about the religion they are born into) when all of us have so much more complexity to our identities. As he rather wittily explains: "The same person can be, without any contradiction, an American citizen, of Caribbean origin, with African ancestry, a Christian, a liberal, a woman, a vegetarian, a long-distance runner, a historian, a schoolteacher, a novelist, a feminist, a heterosexual, a believer in gay and lesbian rights, a theater lover, an environmental activist, a tennis fan, a jazz musician, and someone who is deeply committed to the view that there are intelligent beings in outer space with whom it is extremely urgent to talk (preferably in English)."

Sen's book is concerned not only with the multiplicity of our identities, but also with the way the illusion of a solitary identity, increasingly defined in terms only of religion, has been used to cultivate violence in the world, not least by Islamic terrorists. He inveighs strongly against the Huntingtonian thesis of a "clash of civilizations," pointing out that the argument for the primacy of an individual's religious identity, to the exclusion of other affiliations and associations, ignores the demands of other (explicitly nonreligious) commitments. The separation of Bangladesh from Pakistan, after all, occurred despite their common religious identity, because an ethnic and cultural identity (Bengali) came to mean more than the purely religious label (Muslim). But there is a bigger issue at stake here than intellectual argument. Sen's rejection of Huntington's categorization of humanity in terms of artificially (and religiously) segmented "civilizations" is based on his fear of the political consequences of such an analysis. He sees an implicit alliance between Western parochialism and Islamic extremism in ignoring, or at least undervaluing, the broader history of secular tolerance in Islamic civilization. Too many Westerners, he says, fall into the trap of seeing science and "a sense of individualism and a tradition of individual rights and liberties" as quintessentially and uniquely Western. Instead, Sen argues, they should be celebrating the fact that ideas on mathematics, science, literature, architecture, or tolerance have repeatedly crossed the boundaries of distinct "civilizations."

Western understanding of Arab history ignores Arabic math and science, including algorithmic reasoning, derived from the name of the ninth-century Arab mathematician Al-Khwarizmi (from whose book *Al-Jabr wa al-Muqabalah* the term *algebra* is derived). "If the political leadership of the Arab Muslim world has been shifting toward a greater hold of narrow Islamism, in place of the more old-fashioned pride in the broad achievements of Arab countries," Sen recently argued in an online exchange with the American scholar Robert Kagan, "parochialism in the West has been a substantial contributor to the process."

Similarly, "The Western world has no proprietary right over democratic ideas," he writes in his book. "While modern institutional forms of democracy are relatively new everywhere, the history of democracy in the form of public participation and reasoning is spread across the world." Though Sen writes knowingly of the long traditions of tolerance in Islam, from Saladin to Akbar, he does try to come to grips with the obvious counterargument: the violence of Islamist terror. He argues first that Muslims who pursue peaceful and constructive lives vastly outnumber the rest, and second, that to interpret such violence (which is deliberately cultivated by the terrorists as a political tool) as evidence of an inescapable clash of civilizations would be like claiming from the evidence of twentieth-century history that Germans are doomed to be Nazis. Religion, he avers, is not destiny, and Huntington's civilizational "partitioning" fails to capture the complexity of the world and indeed of each civilization.

I agree with all this — and yet when Amartya Sen asks whether a "religion-centered analysis of the people of the world is a helpful way of understanding humanity," it is fair to say that ignoring religion as a factor in identity is not wise either, especially when so many — from the jihadists of West Asia to the Hindutva chauvinists of Gujarat — continue to harp on it as the basis for their appeal to people's sense of community. We need to understand why so many today, in privileging one among the many identities they could lay claim to, have fallen back on religion. Why are so many political grievances, real or imagined, articulated in religious terms? The answer surely lies in the primordial nature of religious identity. When other avenues of identity mobilization are either restricted (in autocratic states) or difficult (in societies where political patterns are entrenched and admit few interlopers), ordinary people tend to fall back on the one identity that seems basic to them. Secular intellectuals like Amartya Sen may give equal weight to the tag of being a cricket fan or an Oxbridge don to being born in a Hindu family. But we are a minority in today's world, and there remains a great danger to our value system from the larger numbers of passionate sectarians who will never read his humane and enlightened arguments.

Yet a conversation with Amartya Sen underscores the extent to which his Indianness and his cosmopolitanism coexist. He traces his convictions to sources as far-flung as Condorcet and Chakravarti, enjoys a variety of cuisines, and says he cannot think of any one place as home. "I feel very at home in Santiniketan, in Cambridge, Massachusetts, in Cambridge, England, in Italy. If I were told I had to choose one of them and live there only, that I would regard as a very serious loss." Yet he would never contemplate giving up his Indian passport, because it is what entitles him to express political opinions about his own country. He has "never been out of India for more than six months at a stretch" and manages a visit there several times a year. "In our heterogeneity and in our openness lies our pride, not our disgrace," Sen writes. "Satyajit Ray taught us this, and that lesson is profoundly important for India. And for Asia, and for the world."

Amartya Sen has spoken out with courage and conviction about the issues that matter in our country and the world — and he has done so with grace, style, and sharp intelligence. This is what non-economists like myself would have honored him for, whether or not his principal vocation had attracted the attention of the Nobel Committee.

When Amartya Sen was to receive what is officially known as the Bank of Sweden Prize in Economic Sciences in Memory of Alfred Nobel, with a check of $960,000, I wrote in a national newspaper that there should also be a simpler, unbankable prize in the name of the country he has remained so passionately committed to. He has honored our land with his intellect and his heart; he is truly a "jewel of India." Should the country not recognize this, I asked, with the Bharat Ratna? I cannot presume to trace cause and effect, but within three weeks of the appearance of my column, the an-nouncement came from New Delhi that Sen would be so honored. Of course, such decisions take longer to gestate, and columnists should not give themselves airs. But just suppose — perhaps some-body high up in the government of India actually reads the newspa-pers . . . ?

35

Art from the Heart

I T IS NOT ALWAYS THAT I FIND MYSELF TRULY REGRETTING an event I have had to miss because of pressing official commitments elsewhere, but recently my "regrets" at turning down an invitation were not just genuine, they were heartfelt. The event in question was the inauguration of an exhibition in the Peabody Museum in the small Massachusetts town of Salem — an exhibition of M. F. Husain's *Mahabharata* paintings. The irony of this celebration in America, at a time when Husain has been hounded from his own country by the threats of Hindutva chauvinists, did not escape me. So I was all the more sorry to miss this opportunity to pay him tribute, and show him solidarity.

The only time I properly met the incomparable Husain (discounting, that is, the occasional fleeting handshakes in crowded gatherings) was in New York in 1993, over dinner at the home of the Indian then ambassador, Hamid Ansari. Sitting before the book-laden coffee table in the ambassador's Park Avenue living room, I recounted to the master the famous story of what the immortal Pablo Picasso used to say to aspiring artists of the avant-garde. Disregarding their slapdash cubes and squiggles, Picasso would demand: "Draw me a horse." Get the basics right, in other words, before you break free of them. Husain loved the story; he promptly opened the book in front of him, a volume of his own work from Ambassador Ansari's collection, and proceeded to sketch, with astonishing fluidity, a posse of horses on the frontispiece. I have never forgotten the moment: watching the artist's long brown fingers glide over the page, the horses' heads rearing, their manes flying, hooves and tails in the air as Husain left, in a few bold strokes, the indelible imprint of his genius.

So to collaborate on a book with Husain, as I have once done, was an extraordinary privilege. And to do so on the subject of my home state, Kerala, on which Husain has just completed a series of astonishing paintings, made it a special pleasure as well. For horses, in our volume, read elephants. They are everywhere in Husain's extraordinary evocation of Kerala: crashing through the dense foliage, embracing supple maidens with their trunks, and, in miniature, held aloft by triumphant womanhood. The elephants cavort by the waterside, drink, play, gambol, lurk. They are the animal form of the grandeur and gaiety of "God's Own Country." Elephants are indispensable to every Kerala celebration, from weddings to religious festivals; there is nothing in the world like the Thrissur Pooram, when hundreds emerge, bedecked with ornaments and flowers, to receive the homage of the Malayali people. Elephants infuse the Kerala consciousness; they feature in the state's literature, dance, music, films, and art. It is said that the true Keralite can tell one elephant apart from another just by looking at it. In their myriad shapes, sizes, and colors, Husain's elephants embody the magic of Kerala: the extraordinary natural beauty of the state, its lagoons, its forests, its beaches, and above all the startling, many-hued green of the countryside, with its emerald paddy fields and banana groves, and coconut and areca trees swaying in the gentle breeze that whispers its secrets across the land. And in their strength the elephants capture, too, the resilience of Kerala, its defiance of the Indian stereotype, its resolute determination to progress, and above all, its empowerment of women.

What can one say about this remarkable work and its remarkable subject, in this curious collaboration between a great artist who has signed his name in Malayalam, a language he cannot speak, and a writer who traces his roots to Kerala, a homeland he has only visited on his holidays? The *Marunaadan Malayali* — the expatriate Keralite — is so widespread and so common a phenomenon that the phrase has entered the Malayalam language. And here I am, one of the tribe, inspired by the paintings of a man who is the most "inside" of outsiders, seeking to capture in far too many words the insights into Kerala that he has illuminated with the dazzling fluency of his brush.

To get back to the opening I missed in Salem (though I later did go to see it): that M. F. Husain, as a preeminent modern Indian artist, and one of the country's best-known Muslims, should have derived inspiration from an ancient Hindu epic is not in itself surprising. Husain has always felt free to find his images and symbols in the cultural heterogeneity of his native land, and the Mahabharata, unlike its sacred twin, the Ramayana, is essentially a secular epic. It also occupies a unique place in the Indian national consciousness, one that lends itself remarkably well to artistic reinvention. The epic allowed Husain to take characters and images that are laden with epic resonance, and to alter and shape them to paint a contemporary canvas.

As a novelist who did something similar in my own *The Great Indian Novel*, I would argue that the Mahabharata is an ideal vehicle for a creative artist's efforts to affirm and enhance an Indian cultural identity, not as a closed or self-limiting construct, but as a reflection of the pluralism, diversity, and openness of India's kaleidoscopic culture. The first of Husain's paintings in this series was created in 1971, a time of great turbulence in India, with the looming crisis over refugees from Bangladesh that would lead, by year's end, to war with Pakistan. What Husain did in 1971 (and again in later paintings) was to recall, through images starkly familiar to Mahabharata-conscious Indians, the kinds of stories Indian society tells about itself. There are images of battle and conflict, neighing horses and howling elephants caught up in the confusion of Kurukshetra, bloodshed and terror in every brushstroke; but there is also the timeless image of Ganapathi the scribe, merging in Husain's imagination with the sage Ved Vyasa, the epic's author, setting down the transcendent wisdom of the epic that would speak across the ages to the Indians of Husain's time.

In much of Husain's work, Hindu myths and epic narratives both contribute to and reflect the national consciousness that his own creativity has done so much to influence. In reiterating the epic, the artist and his audience both reaffirm the shaping of their own cultural identity. This is an important statement for Husain to make as a Muslim and an Indian: he is staking his claim to a heritage that some chauvinist Hindus have sought to deny to those not of their own persuasion. In recent years these zealots have sought to challenge Husain's right to use Hindu imagery, attacking exhibitions in which he has depicted nude goddesses, denouncing him for sacrilege in his borrowings from the epics. The vast majority of India's art lovers and intellectuals have rallied to his defense — and with the Mahabharata they have rightly asserted that Husain has no case to answer. For, there is nothing restrictive or self-limiting about the Indian identity the Mahabharata asserts: it is large, eclectic, and flexible, containing multitudes.

This is why I have been particularly happy to add my name to the petition circulated by many of our country's leading artists and writers, asking the president to confer upon Husain the highest award of the land, the Bharat Ratna. A number of creative artists have already been so honored: Satyajit Ray, M. S. Subbulakshmi, Ravi Shankar, Bismillah Khan, Lata Mangeshkar. Husain unarguably belongs in this illustrious company. The petition argues that Husain's "life and work are beginning to serve as an allegory for the changing modalities of the secular in modern India — and the challenges that the narrative of the nation holds for many of us. This is the opportune and crucial time to honor him for his dedication and courage to the cultural renaissance of his beloved country."

Looking at the Mahabharata-inspired work in this exhibition, it seems to me that Husain is simultaneously honoring and appropriating the epic. If there is a message to the work that features in this exhibition, it would be that of the continued relevance of the stories, issues, and images he has derived from the Mahabharata. That, in turn, is a twofold message: first, of the need to reexamine the received wisdom of the epic in today's India, to question the certitudes, to acknowledge the weight of the past and face its place in the present; and second, to do so through a reassertion of the epic's dharma, defined not as religion but as the whole complex of values and standards — some derived from myth and tradition, some derived from our history — by which India and Indians must live. In offering his vision of the Mahabharata to India and the world, Husain has paid a fundamental tribute to his own civilization, one which he has, through his reinvention of the past and his reimagining of the present, immeasurably enriched. He deserves the Bharat Ratna.

36

Carrying His Bat

THE BABY LYING IN THE CRIB assigned to Sunil Manohar Gavaskar gurgled happily in his sleep, but Narayan Masurekar was suspicious. The previous day, July 10, 1949, he had visited his newborn nephew and noticed a minor blemish — a small hole near the top of the infant's left earlobe. Now, on the next day, a male baby was sleeping in the crib, but something seemed different about him. All babies look like a cross between Winston Churchill and ET, but Masurekar decided to look more closely. His verdict was stunning. "This," he proclaimed, "is not my nephew."

A frantic search followed. Every male baby in the hospital was examined by desperate seekers for the telltale hole. Finally, the missing infant was found, sleeping beatifically by a fisherwoman. The babies were swapped, and history was made. The child who, had the mistake not been detected, might have revolutionized Indian fishing, grew up to haul in a different kind of catch (108 of them in Tests). For he developed his talents in a cricket-loving middle-class Bombay family instead of a seafarer's shack far from the *maidans*. Were it not for Narayan Masurekar's eagle eyes, somebody else, and not Sunil Gavaskar, would now be known as India's greatest batsman of all time.

Of the many legacies in which the British Raj took pride in leaving to India — railways, universities, the English language, the "steel frame" of the administrative system — the one that has most captured the Indian imagination has been the game of cricket. And on any list of the cricketers who have left their stamp on the national psyche, one name is bound to figure at the top: Sunil Gavaskar.

His plethora of records tells one part of the tale. Statistics can be mind-numbing, but one can no more measure the achievements of Gavaskar without figures than one can describe Mount Everest without them. For those who are interested, a devotee has created a Web site (The Gavaskar File) which comprises no fewer than twenty-one tightly packed pages of statistics, figures, and records held by Sunny Gavaskar.

But though statistics, like book jackets, reveal a great deal, they can only hint at the most interesting parts — those parts that live in the imagination long after precise figures and dates have faded from memory.

How can one explain to today's cricket-crazy generation — weaned on India's winning the World Cup in 1983, used to one-day successes and mammoth private sponsorships, habituated by glowing references to Indian players as being among the world's best batsmen, feeling entitled to expect at least a chance of victory every time India takes the field — what Sunil Gavaskar meant to India when he arrived on the Test scene?

Of course, we had talented cricketers, but their weaknesses were legend. Our batsmen were notoriously suspect against pace even on our benign Indian wickets, and when the selectors met to pick the squad to tour the Caribbean in 1970–71, no Indian opening batsman had scored a hundred in India's preceding nineteen Test matches. So the selectors, preferring ability to experience, picked four opening batsmen for the tour: Ashok Mankad, who did not open for Bombay till that season; Syed Abid Ali, who had not opened for Hyderabad at all but had done so for India; K. Jayantilal, who had had one good season for South Zone; and a twenty-one-year-old Bombay prodigy with four Ranji matches behind him, Sunil Gavaskar.

Gavaskar was not a complete unknown to cricket fans. He had made mountains of runs as a schoolboy, including against the touring London Schoolboys team, and stories abounded about his excellence. As a boy playing street cricket in the Bombay suburb of Chikalwadi, his prodigious talent resulted in a special handicap being devised for him: whereas others defended the usual three stumps chalked on the garage door, Gavaskar would be given out if the ball hit the door at all. He was soon starring for Bombay University (a team stronger, in those days, than most Indian first-class sides). In the 1967–68 season he made his debut for Bombay in the Irani Trophy, aged eighteen, in what was virtually a trial match for the Test tour of Australia and New Zealand to follow. I watched that game at the Brabourne Stadium: two attractive opening batsmen, K. R. Rajagopal and P. K. Belliappa, who had been considered near-certainties for the tour, failed to gain selection after being tormented by the pace and swing of Bombay's Ramakant Desai and Umesh Kulkarni. Instead, Desai and Kulkarni got picked instead, even though they had not been in the list of thirty "probables" announced earlier. The match ended the national hopes of Rajagopal and Belliappa, but in all the drama everyone overlooked the failure of the rookie Gavaskar, who made just five and zero and was promptly dropped by Bombay for the next season.

Recalled nearly two years later for the last two Ranji matches of the 1969–70 season, Gavaskar began with a duck and ended with a century. Two centuries followed in three innings in the 1970–71 season, but surprisingly Gavaskar was not picked for West Zone in the Duleep Trophy. Instead, he captained Bombay University in the interuniversity tournament and made successive scores of 226, 99, 327 (a university record), and 124. That was enough for the new Indian captain, Ajit Wadekar, whose own record Gavaskar had broken in the course of his 327, and for the chairman of selectors, Vijay Merchant. Sunil Gavaskar, who had played just five matches for Bombay and had never even represented West Zone, was picked for the West Indies. Merchant publicly praised Gavaskar for never being content with just a hundred; his seniors, the chairman added, could learn from that.

If Gavaskar felt any pressure as a result of Merchant's comments, it did not reveal itself. Instead of a swollen head, though, the young batsman developed an acutely swollen middle finger on his left hand. A New York specialist, consulted en route to Jamaica, decided to operate immediately; one day's delay, he said, and gangrene would have set in, obliging him to amputate the finger. So Gavaskar, his hand swathed in bandages, missed the first Test. But in those more leisurely days there were other first-class matches to play oneself into form, and he proceeded to score 71, 82, 32 not out, 125, and 63 in his first five innings on the tour. Selection for the second Test at Port-of-Spain was assured.

I remember, as a fourteen-year-old schoolboy, praying that Gavaskar would score a hundred, and then retracting my prayer because none of the seven Indians who had so far scored a Test century on debut had ever scored another one. (Viswanath, Azharuddin, Sourav Ganguly, and Virender Sehwag would later become exceptions to this jinx, to which Surinder Amarnath and Praveen Amre also succumbed.) As it happened, the young batsman batted with remarkable maturity and composure in his first Test, but did not get to a century. His 65 and 67 not out were, however, stamped with class, and helped steer India to an astonishing victory.

From then on it was magical. A century (116) and 64 not out duly followed in the third Test. In the first innings of the fourth, Gavaskar fell, in atrocious light, for one, and Indians wondered if the fairy tale was over. There was no need to worry: in the second innings he scored 117 not out. National jubilation at the unearthing of this gigantic talent knew few bounds. Exhilaration was everywhere; cricket was page-one news across India. Gavaskar went into the fifth Test with 430 runs to his name at an average of 143.33. No one would have believed that the best was yet to come.

Certainly not Gavaskar himself, since he developed a painful abscess in a tooth on the eve of the Test. Denied painkillers because they might have made him drowsy, unable to eat properly or enjoy a cold drink, sleep deprived from tossing and turning in his pain, Gavaskar batted in excruciating agony throughout the six-day match. Despite each run jarring the infected tooth, he scored 124 out of an Indian total of 360 in the first innings. It was not enough; the West Indians, aided by some dubious umpiring, piled on the runs. Opening the second with India 166 runs behind and after twelve hours fielding in the hot sun, Gavaskar became the first Indian since Hazare in 1948 to complete a century in both innings of a Test, and the first Indian ever to score four centuries in a series. The tooth still ached, but he kept going: India was barely 30 ahead when he crossed that landmark. Sobers, the great West Indies captain, tried seven bowlers, but no one could get a ball past Gavaskar. A Trinidadian calypso was composed on the spot by "Lord Relator": "It was Gavaskar/ The real master/Just like a wall/We couldn't out Gavaskar at all/Not at all." He finished with 220 in eight hours and twenty-nine minutes. He hadn't given a chance. Most important, he had saved a Test India had looked likely to lose, and helped clinch a series win against the mightiest Test team in the world.

If Gavaskar had done nothing else in his life, that extraordinary series alone would have written his name in the hearts of his compatriots forever. It is impossible to describe the pride he instilled in our hearts. We had got used to losing, to accepting a sort of perpetual second-class status. We were accustomed to rejoicing in great moments rather than great matches. We were reconciled to batsmen producing flashes of brilliance and fading away. We had even learned to celebrate stirring feats of heroic defiance in a losing cause, like Pataudi's 148 at Headingley in 1967 or Jaisimha's 101 in Brisbane in 1967–68, both magnificent efforts ending in the inevitable defeat. But heroic defiance, brilliance, consistency, *and* victory all together had never been an Indian combination. Gavaskar showed us for the first time that it could be, and so transformed the nation's sporting psyche. By his heroism, he expanded the realm of the possible in Indian cricket. He undid the shackles that had kept us chained to mediocrity; he freed a spirit that soared in countless imaginations across the land.

So Gavaskar did not need to do anything else to leave his stamp on independent India. But he did. After a brief hiccup in his next few Tests — as if to confirm that he was, after all, mortal — the centuries flowed again; the records tumbled; greatness became a quality we learned to take for granted. There were the extraordinary thirteen centuries against the West Indies' feared pace batteries. There was the dazzling 102 in Trinidad in 1975–76 to steer India to an astonishing victory with the then highest-winning target ever successfully chased in a Test. There was the 221 he made against England at the Oval in 1979 when India nearly pulled it off again, chasing an even higher total. There was the 340 he made in 1981–82 in one remorseless inning in the Ranji Trophy. And then, in 1987, after one of the best innings ever seen on an Indian cricket ground — a sublime 96 against Pakistan on a vicious turner at Bangalore — Sunil Gavaskar retired, at the peak of his powers. He wanted to leave when the world was asking "why?" rather than "when?"

I remember Gavaskar in his pomp at the crease, all five foot six inches of him rapt in concentration; the white shirt immaculate, its top two buttons undone, a glint of gold around his neck; the dark eyes steady in their gaze under a wide-brimmed floppy sun hat; the boyish charm supplanted by a wary stillness, ears cocked, knees and back bent, every sinew tensed but ready. And then the calm deliberateness of the stroke, the eyes never leaving the ball: the solidity of the defense, the precision of the offdrive, the liberating punch through midwicket, the sudden unleashing of the cut. He could do it all, and he knew what not to do: it was once said of him, on a spiteful pitch, that his best stroke was one he did not play, at a rearing delivery that a lesser batsman would have edged. When Sunil Gavaskar stood at the crease, it was as if a wall had been constructed across the wicket, and captains and bowlers knew they would have to work very hard for their reward. In 198 Test innings, Gavaskar was bowled just thirty-three times, and on fewer than half those occasions did he miss the ball altogether. In other words, in a career in which he faced some thirty thousand deliveries, he was beaten and bowled by perhaps twenty of them. That is a measure of his skill, of his concentration, and of the impregnability he brought to the top of a fragile Indian batting order. As Sir Gary Sobers reminded the world, his achievement is all the more striking in that he could not make any easy runs off the amiable Indian bowling attack.

Of course, not everything in Gavaskar's career was perfection. Having nearly broken his mother's nose with a hard-hit shot in a game of corridor cricket at home in his boyhood, Gavaskar developed a wary cautiousness that Freud could have explained better than Cardus. It too often translated itself into excessive defensiveness, so that, for all his high scores, Gavaskar never threatened to tear apart an attack. Rather, he frustrated bowlers into submission by wearing them down. His one-day record is, by his standards, modest: an average of 35.13 in 108 matches, with only one century, a tale forever blighted by that bizarre inning in the 1975 World Cup at Lord's when he made 36 not out in sixty overs. (Gavaskar himself gave four reasons for his appalling performance, each of which is worse than the previous one: "1. I didn't play sixty overs myself. 2. I couldn't force the pace and couldn't get out even when I tried to. 3. As soon as the ball was delivered, my feet would move to a position for a defensive shot. 4. The awful noise made by the crowd didn't help my thinking.")

For a man whose temperament at the crease was so calm and measured, Gavaskar also lost his cool surprisingly often in print and on the field. His highly readable but tactless book *Sunny Days* was marred by intemperate references to West Indian crowds (as "savages" who should "go back to the jungles" whence they came) and English umpires ("David Constant was constant — in his support of England"), which caused great offense in those countries. (The resulting hostility to him in the Caribbean led to his pulling out of the 1979–80 tour of the West Indies, which was then canceled.) Worse still was his attempt in Melbourne on the 1980–81 tour of Australia to walk out and concede the match when he was given, as he thought, unjustly out. His action in calling his opening partner, Chetan Chauhan, off the field with him was not only thoughtless, it disrupted Chauhan's concentration, costing him his wicket shortly

THE elephant, THE tiger, AND THE cell phone

thereafter, and it looked even more foolish when India won the Test that Gavaskar had had to be prevented from throwing away.

This episode aside, Gavaskar was also a disappointing captain, leading the side without imagination or vision, showing very little feel for the pace or direction of a game, and proving himself on more than one occasion a particularly poor judge of a declaration. His role in the dropping of Kapil Dev for the Calcutta Test against England in 1984–85 (for "disciplinary" reasons) and his tactics in grinding that match down to one of the most meaningless draws in Test history, led me to attack his captaincy in a cover story for *The Illustrated Weekly of India* that winter. The *Weekly* unfortunately emblazoned their cover with the dramatic query "Is Sunil Gavaskar one of the worst captains India has ever had?" which was a bit over the top. My main point was that as a captain obsessed with drawing matches, and as one who rewarded restraint but punished adventurousness, Gavaskar had shown a profound contempt for the paying public for whom, after all, the game was being played. I added, somewhat unnecessarily, "In the words of a perceptive English critic, Gavaskar has done more than any other person to kill [Test] cricket as a spectator sport in India." With hindsight, the criticism — however perceptive the now-forgotten English critic might have been — seems absurdly overstated, though it is no accident that Gavaskar holds the world record for draws, too (no captain has drawn as many Tests [thirty] as he has)! Within a month of my article, Gavaskar led India to victory in the World Championship of Cricket in Australia — and resigned the captaincy.

One journalist told me that my *Weekly* piece had been a major factor in Gavaskar's desire to quit. I did not believe it, because it was typical of Gavaskar to leave on a high note, with the "World Championship" a symbolic raised finger to his critics. Years later I met Gavaskar socially and was horrified to discover that not only had he read the piece, it still rankled with him. So if that article did hurt the Little Master, this essay is a humble attempt to make amends.

For all his flaws put together do not stack up very high against the immensity of Sunil Gavaskar's contributions to Indian cricket — and more, to India itself. He gave us a self-belief that had been lacking before. He brought in a conscientious professionalism, including on issues of fair monetary reward, that transformed the nature of the sport in India. He gave millions of fans a reason to hope that, with Gavaskar at the helm, nothing was impossible. And if there had been moments of pettiness in his captaincy, the greatness of the man was nowhere made more apparent than off the cricket field, after his retirement — above all in the courage with which he intervened personally during the tragic Bombay riots of 1993 to save a Muslim driver from sectarian assault in his neighborhood.

Gavaskar has always had time for the basic verities. His close and mutually admiring relationship with his contemporary and brother-in-law Gundappa Viswanath is rare at the highest levels of any sport. The touching sincerity of his decision to name his son Rohan Jaivishwa after the three batsmen he most admired (Kanhai, Jaisimha, and Viswanath) is another measure of the simplicity of the man. Nor does Gavaskar consider himself above the concerns of ordinary people. One journalist quoted a letter sent to Gavaskar in 1986 by the father of a paraplegic son: "My son is your great fan, but of late he is not taking his medicines at all. He is getting hysterical and uncontrollable. I request you to kindly send him a letter of encouragement." Gavaskar did.

Imran Khan listed Gavaskar highest among the three batsmen he hated bowling to (ahead of Boycott and Greenidge): "His perfect technique makes him the most difficult batsman alive to dismiss." But technique was not all. Gavaskar's boyhood idol, M. L. Jaisimha, wrote that the qualities Gavaskar brought to his cricket were those that would have made him successful in any walk of life — "concentration, dedication, single-mindedness of purpose and willingness to learn." In this Gavaskar was a true professional in a country where sport had for too long been the domain of the gifted amateur.

When he was a boy, Gavaskar used to visit his uncle Madhav Mantri, and run his fingers lovingly through the former Test player's

India pullovers. But when he asked for one for himself, Mantri was strict: "The Indian colors," he said firmly, "have to be earned." No one has earned them more deservingly than Sunil Manohar Gavaskar. He will always be, in his own way, an embodiment of our coming of age as an independent nation.

37

The Dear Departed

I cannot omit, from a section on the people who made up my sense of "my" India, Indians who are far from famous, but who profoundly touched my life and mind, none more so than my own father.

MY FATHER'S HEART

IT WAS IN 1993, WHEN I WAS THIRTY-SEVEN YEARS OLD and a father myself, that the telephone call I had been dreading for twenty-five years — ever since my father, then thirty-eight, had his first massive coronary — finally came. On October 23, 1993, Chandran Tharoor's heart had finally given in.

For a quarter of a century I had feared this moment. I had grown up thinking that every unexpected call at an unusual hour, every unannounced visitor, was to convey the news that my father had suddenly been taken away. Three times in the previous ten years, I had called home — three of my hundreds of regular, routine, anxious calls home — to discover he was in the hospital. Each time he had pulled through. Once, a decade ago, I had brought him to the United States for open-heart surgery and had experienced the very different anxiety of the hospital waiting room, the awful moment when the doctor emerges and you scan his face for the slightest sign of bad news before he speaks. At that time, too, the outcome had been positive. But the time had come when surgery could afford no new solutions. We hoped that my father's zest for life would itself open up the flow to and from his heart. Certainly, there was nothing in that booming voice, that irrepressible spirit, that boundless type-A do-it-all enthusiasm, to suggest that life was ebbing away, that each day his heart was failing, coming closer to admitting a defeat that my father's own manner had never acknowledged.

I was barely twelve when my father first fought for his life in hospital, while I battled fear and bewilderment and prayed for him to recover. He was the only security my mother and little sisters and I had in the world. His work, his income, his drive, kept us in style, fed and clothed us well, sent us to the best schools in Bombay. I loved him: the word games we played together, the cricket matches he took me to, the magic of his irresistible smile as his warm brown eyes lit up at me, even the daily (and all too uncritical) encouragement he provided my writing. But I also understood that my father's survival was intimately bound up with my own, that his dreams for me could founder on his own mortality.

With each passing year, of course, this became less true. As I finished my studies at breakneck speed (always fearing my luck — his health — would run out before I could attain my goals) and embarked on a career, I shed my material vulnerabilities. But the fear of his loss had become so deeply entrenched that it continued to dominate me, my own heart shuddering whenever the faint hollow whine on the telephone suggested an unexpected international call.

Now it had come, and when at last I put the phone down and stood up shivering, the words that came were, "Forgive me, my father. Forgive me." For I felt that, in recent months, I had not tried hard enough to keep him alive. Into my mind I had admitted the possibility that he would go; and perhaps, in doing so, I had removed the last barrier of desperate need that prevented him from going. For my need of him, my need for his approval, his support, his help, had been diluted over time, while his need of my need had never changed.

He had spent his life always being there for me, pushing me to new heights, nurturing great ambitions. He had had such great satisfaction in introducing himself at publishing parties as "the author's author." And he *was* my author: the flesh-and-blood source of my skills, of the spark in my eyes that I knew mirrored his own, of the impulse to attain what his ambition had instilled in me, and of the haste to achieve what his frailty had intensified. But over the years, I had ceased to need him as much as before. I had allowed the urgency of our bonds to slacken, and now they had snapped for all time.

If my father had lived, I told myself, I would have demanded nothing of him, just the joy of seeing him mellow into rest. But because I had nothing to ask him for, I left him with nothing to give. And it was to give, to go on giving, that he had fought with such determination against successive assaults on his heart. My father stopped being able to live when he stopped being asked to give.

So I believed. Until I learned there was more to his giving than I, self-centered in mourning, had allowed myself to remember.

My parents' apartment was overflowing with family and friends when I arrived. For days the phone never stopped ringing; the postmen staggered in with bundles of letters and telegrams; people made inconvenient journeys to Coimbatore to pay him tribute. Former subordinates called from distant cities to weep their regret on the phone; they had never, they said, worked for a better boss. (And indeed, I found among his papers copies of notes he had sent his own superiors, crediting his staff for his achievements.) Throughout my childhood I had been obliged to make room for a succession of young men my father supported while he helped them learn a trade and find a job. Letters poured in from them, and from others my father had helped. Their grief was palpable, for his great-heartedness had touched them financially, morally, and emotionally. But strangers wrote, too, on the letterheads of professional and cultural associations he had given his energies to, to say how much they had been diminished by his death.

"He was all heart," many of them wrote without conscious irony. With these mourners, the principal reaction was one of disbelief. My father, a physically small man, had for all of them been larger than life; always there when he was needed, always accessible, always willing to try to help, always game for a drink, a party, a session of cards, a new venture, always full of an infectious energy and optimism, a sense of the infinite possibilities of life that he communicated to others. His heart was far larger than that of sturdier men. "I cannot bring myself to mourn for such a man," wrote a much older friend. "I mourn instead for us, that we have lost him."

As his son, I had framed his life within my own needs and fears, but its canvas had proved much broader than I had realized. I could now see that I had lived too long with the possibility of my father's death, while countless others had seen only the possibilities of his life. That, in the end, allows me a kind of celebration.

STANDING TALL

My sisters and I knew him as Valiachan, which in Malayalam is literally "Big Father," for he was our father's elder brother, indeed the eldest. "Big" might have seemed the wrong adjective to apply to him, for Valiachan was a big man in everything but the physical sense: five foot two inches in his socks, with a prematurely bald head and thick-rimmed glasses, he spoke in a soft but rasping voice with a hint of eosinophilia in his pauses. But Valiachan commanded respect, even awe, in all who met him. Height was no handicap for Napoleon, nor was it for Tharoor Parameshwar. For he was one of those people who was not merely a self-made man, but one who had made others; rarer still, he had built institutions that would survive him. In 2004, at the age of eighty-six, Valiachan passed away in Bangalore, and for those who had been touched by his extraordinary life, it was as if an age had passed with him.

Valiachan was born, in February 1918, into a good family that had fallen upon hard times. Historians tell us that at the time of Vasco da Gama, the entire area around Palghat was known as Tharoor Swarupam, but the Tharoors had, over the centuries, been reduced to farming at levels little above subsistence. The usual Kerala solution had to be found to the problem: emigration. So young Param, a brilliant student, dropped out of school after tenth grade, learned typing, and moved to Bombay, aged eighteen, to look for a job. His father had been ailing for years and soon passed away, leaving the financial responsibility for his mother, four brothers, and three sisters upon the teenager. Valiachan found a place in the Ramakrishna Mission at the Bombay suburb of Khar where, in return for cleaning the premises, he was allowed to sleep on the floor and given one free meal a day. Each day he walked twenty kilometers to work in the Fort area and back, because he could not afford the bus fare. But he sent money home. Before he became an adult, Valiachan had become the savior of his family.

At the Mission he studied the sacred Sanskrit texts, memorizing *slokas* that he could recite well into his eighties. But he combined his spiritual inclinations with an utterly realistic sense of his material needs and obligations. After a few temporary jobs he was hired by the largest advertising agency in British India, J. Walter Thompson, as a stenographer. His intelligence, integrity, and drive soon shone through: within a couple of years he was the media manager.

After spending most of the war years in Simla as deputy head of the government of India's propaganda department — poverty had made Valiachan apolitical — he decided to set up shop on his own in London. Advertising was a profession Valiachan instinctively understood, and he knew the Indian media better than anyone. In those days most major Indian businesses were headquartered in London and the consumers were in India, so for five years he ran a successful operation from Fleet Street selling space in Indian newspapers and magazines to British advertisers. While doing this he not only supported his family in Kerala but brought his three youngest brothers to London to study and start their working lives. It was no accident that two of them followed Valiachan into advertising: one was my own father, Chandran Tharoor.

London lost its attractions after independence, so three years in Calcutta followed as advertising manager for the *Amrita Bazar*

Patrika — the old war propagandist, in a nice twist of irony, having been hired by the Indian nationalist paper in London. In 1955 Valiachan returned to Bombay in triumph, as the founder publisher of the Indian edition of the *Reader's Digest*. It was a far cry from sweeping floors at the Ramakrishna Mission, but success had to be earned: he began with an office at home, his secretary operating out of the living room. But Valiachan's tireless energy, his matchless ability to persuade advertisers that space in his pages was worth buying, transformed the *Digest*'s fortunes in India. From representing a nominally "Indian" edition printed in the United Kingdom, he built a national brand that soon had its own Indian editors (starting with the gifted Rahul Singh) and local content.

Param was the *Digest*, and the *Digest*, in India, was Param. But when the Foreign Exchange Regulation Act of 1976 required the *Digest* to dilute its foreign shareholding to 40 percent, the parent company decided to sell out completely. Valiachan found buyers he hoped would uphold the values of the organization he had nurtured for a quarter of a century, but once he retired in 1981, the management of the *Digest* passed into unworthy hands.

Fortunately, the *Digest* was not Valiachan's only institutional legacy. He resurrected the Advertising Club of Bombay, presided over it for many years, and published its newsletter, *Solus* (to which my father contributed a pseudonymous column). Ironically, the club celebrated its fiftieth anniversary the very week Valiachan died, and the city's admen were reminded of how much he had done to recast their profession. He also took a keen interest in education, serving for many years on the Board of Governors of the Lawrence School, Lovedale, where he educated his three sons but — equally important — drafted a constitution, established retirement benefits for the staff, and reformed the school's management. He was an early and active member of the Lion's Club, both locally (he was the president of the Chembur club) and internationally. And after his formal retirement he brought his energies, in an honorary capacity, to professionalize the running of the Bharatiya Vidya Bhavan for many years.

All these institutions were transformed by his involvement, but he never took credit for his role. Quiet but authoritative, it was enough for him to leave his stamp on something whose possibilities he was usually the first to spot. The advertising guru Gerson da Cunha has written of Valiachan's knack for "perceiving competence and talent usually before anybody else did, then giving that person the opportunity and encouragement to occupy the full space of his or her potential." Secure in his own self-esteem and iron self-discipline, he was happy to encourage others, serving as example and inspiration to hundreds. Valiachan was once asked for the secret of good public relations. He replied immediately, "Make friends before you need them."

That he did, around the country. The boy who could not afford to complete his schooling, who walked twenty kilometers to work each day, ended a long and distinguished life as the patriarch of a highly successful and prosperous family, and the revered patron of an entire profession. He was indeed, in the profoundest sense of the word, a big man.

FRIENDS WHO LEFT A VOID

An authentic Indian hero died recently at the tragically young age of fifty-nine. His passing did not merit two lines in our country's papers, because it happened far away, in Pretoria, South Africa. And yet the death of Shunmugan Nganasamantham Chetty — known universally as "Shun," though no one ever shunned him — ended a life of which every Indian should be proud.

Shun Chetty was a courageous lawyer in apartheid-blighted South Africa who fought bravely for the rights of the victims of tyranny until he was obliged to flee for his life in 1979. He had been the solicitor for Steve Biko's widow in a remarkable case charging the white government with responsibility for the Black Consciousness leader's death in prison. (Biko, in one of the most notorious episodes in apartheid's history of repression, had been shackled naked in solitary confinement and beaten to death, but the government had arranged for a white doctor to certify that the thirty-six-year-old anti-apartheid crusader had died of "natural causes.") Chetty's courage was also foolhardy: he had been brave enough to take on cases others shied away from, defending the heroes of the African National Congress whose convictions were a foregone conclusion; he had been humane enough to visit them in prison to look into their conditions of detention; but now he had gone too far in trying to make the government accountable for murder. One did not buck the system beyond a point, and the apartheid regime put the word out: Chetty's number was up.

But Shun was not about to go quietly into the dark labyrinth of the apartheid regime's prison systems. Just after dusk one evening his wife, Fazila, a doctor, headed for the Botswanan border in her car, with an unusual cargo in her trunk. It was Shun, with only a blanket to cover him — yet more than Biko had been given on his last ride in a police van. Near the Botswanan border, Shun got out and Fazila, the daughter of a prominent Indian businessman, drove through the checkpoint while he swam across a river. She picked him up on the other side, and Shun Chetty soon arrived, still dripping, at the home of the British High Commissioner in Gaborone, where he claimed asylum. Though a dinner party was going on, he was expected, and welcomed with relief. South Africa's most celebrated solicitor was now a refugee.

I met him soon after that, when he decided to put his legal skills to good use helping other refugees and joined the organization for which I was then working, the United Nations High Commissioner for Refugees (UNHCR). Shun and Fazila were a warm and popular couple, gregarious and generous to a fault. Their marriage had crossed several of the fault lines in South Africa's notoriously stratified society: he was a Hindu and she was Muslim; he was an anti-government lawyer and she came from a family that had prospered under white rule (her father, Rashid Varachia, was the country's principal distributor of Coca-Cola, and a prominent cricket administrator). But they were united by something else South Africa had evoked in them, in reaction to the system in which they had been born and raised — their shared sense of a common humanity. It was this that endeared them to a wide circle of friends and sustained Shun in his passionate devotion to justice.

Though he worked for refugees in places as far afield as Sudan, Thailand, and Australia, it is in South Africa that his abiding legacy lies. Fazila sent me a sheaf of obituaries by black South Africans, and they brought tears to my eyes. One wrote of Shun's gentle demeanor, which "hid beneath it the steely resolve of a man determined not to bow to abuse." The defense minister, M. Lekota, recalled how Shun had managed to get him married in prison and served as best man. The chairman of the Human Rights Commission, Barney Pityana, another former political prisoner, recalled Shun as "a counselor, a lawyer and caregiver all wrapped in one. . . . We trusted him without any reserve." One columnist began his tribute with the words: "There were lawyers, and then there was Shun Chetty." A letter writer to a Pretoria daily perhaps put it best: "Shun Chetty articulated an ethical doctrine that social justice and racial equality were achievable in our society through successful appeal to the conscience of the individual."

That, of course, is a principle that holds true for all countries, especially ours.

There is so much I have not mentioned about Shun the man, from his passion about nature and wildlife to his obsession with cricket (which we indulged in every one of our international phone calls). But it would take more than a single column to introduce Shun Chetty to Indian readers, and this elegy will have to do.

It is true, of course, that Shun Chetty wasn't Indian; he never carried an Indian passport, though during his years of statelessness under apartheid he explored the possibility of acquiring one. (You need at least one grandparent born in India as defined in the Government of India Act, 1935, to qualify, and Shun's forebears had been South African for too long. But Shun did make one fruitless attempt to find the village in Tamil Nadu from which his ancestors had left a century or more ago.) Born a South African, he died an Australian in his beloved homeland. But a look in the mirror told him what, at heart, he really was: one of us. India had lost a distinguished son, and I have lost a friend.

*

While Shun Chetty was struggling for his life in a Pretoria hospital, I was unaware that another good friend, just fifty-one years old, also lay dying. Nina Sibal, diplomat and novelist, was a friend whose writing I had praised in print, suggesting her memoirs would be worth looking forward to. Those will never be written: breast cancer carried her away in her prime. It was less than a year since I wrote her a recommendation for a fellowship that would have allowed her to take time off from her job to work on a new novel. Now she had run out of time too soon.

Nina Sibal was an extraordinary woman: she had studied literature and law, taught at college, published two well-received novels (*Yatra* and *The Dogs of Justice*) and enjoyed a series of challenging diplomatic assignments, including as India's ambassador to UNESCO in Paris. She was a striking presence at the United Nations in New York, where she served as UNESCO's representative, an elegant sari-clad figure with a shock of black hair falling across her face, energetically pursuing such issues as the promotion of an international "culture of peace." Nina was married to the Indian Supreme Court advocate and Congress Party parliamentarian Kapil Sibal, with whom she maintained a transcontinental relationship in which both spouses were able to pursue exacting careers.

As a writer, Nina Sibal told me, "I'm concerned with the terrors of attachment and how it destroys not only the person herself but everyone around her." The novel she was intending to write would, she said, "probably involve a greater inwardness."

A greater inwardness — no male writer would have said that. Nina Sibal's were books that only a woman could have written. An unusual and remarkable woman, she was a warm and generous — as well as gifted — human being.

Her death came at the end of a grisly six months in which I lost no fewer than seven friends and found myself becoming somewhat morbidly obsessed by the capricious cruelty of death. Nina battled cancer with courage and optimism, as well as remarkable dignity, but she knew the end was coming. In Shun's case there was no reason to anticipate the worst: after mild chest pains, he had gone to the hospital for a routine angiogram. The test revealed there was nothing wrong with him — no blocked arteries — but when the doctors removed their probe, they ruptured his heart. A freak accident, perhaps, but this was in the best hospital in Pretoria, capital of the country that gave us the world's first heart transplant. Massive internal bleeding followed, Shun lapsed into a coma and died without recovering consciousness.

Two of the other deaths I mourned the same year were equally unexpected and inexplicable. I had long known Ansar Husain Khan, author of the polemical *The Rediscovery of India*, which received excellent reviews when Orient Longman published it in 1988. Ansar-bhai's was an exceptional story. One of the first Pakistani officials of the United Nations, he fought for years to obtain an Indian passport because of his rejection of the two-nation theory. When he finally obtained his Indian citizenship, it was at a high price in human terms; he was ostracized by his former compatriots, who refused him a visa even to visit his parents' graves. A man of wide reading and great erudition, this secular Muslim offered me one of the best definitions I know of the Hindu concept of dharma: "That by which we should live." He was living in retirement in Geneva, Switzerland, with his gentle Swiss wife, Anita — whom I often thought of as a better Indian wife than many of the Indian wives I knew — when he pulled out a gun one morning and shot her dead. He called the police, turned himself in, and succumbed to a heart attack in the police station — on, I am told, the very same day.

There are some stories you strain hard to believe, let alone comprehend. I did not even know Ansarbhai owned a gun, let alone that he was capable of using it. And against such a target — the kind, patient, and loving mother of his two teenage sons! What makes people snap, what drives them to acts of such horror that their own hearts cannot abide what they have done? I keep turning over the accounts I have heard of the incident and can find no answers in its terrible finality. For years we had been discussing a summer visit by the Khan family to New York, where I lived; I kept expecting to hear his cheerful voice on the phone, asking me to inquire about apartments available on short-term lease. Life itself, I realize, is something we each have only on a short-term lease. A moment of anger, of madness in a marriage, of carelessness in a hospital, of a rogue gene running amok in your cells, and your lease is up.

Three other dear friends left the world more peacefully in this period, at the culmination of lives full of accomplishment. One did not, strictly speaking, have an Indian connection, other than a great partiality to Indian food: he was a frequent habitué of *desi* restaurants in New York, ever ready to try a new one. Joseph Heller, the author of *Catch-22,* was a delightful companion (especially at the dining table, where he loved my former wife's Indian cooking), a witty and kindhearted man whose literary eminence never impeded his interest in younger writers, to whom he was unfailingly generous. One of my proudest possessions is a photo his wife, Valerie, sent me of Joe stretched out on his sofa reading my novel *Show Business.* A healthy and vigorous seventy-six, he died suddenly one night of a massive heart attack, depriving the world of a brilliantly original satiric voice.

And finally, two remarkable women whom I had known since my childhood passed away after long and debilitating illnesses. Sakuntala Jagannathan, the dynamic head of Maharashtra Tourism in the 1960s and a wise and accessible author (her book on Hinduism is a model of its kind), had written to chide me for giving, in an earlier column, all the credit for Kerala's literacy to its Communist rulers. She felt rightly that I should not have overlooked the earlier contribution of her grandfather, the formidable Dewan of

Travancore, Sir C. P. Ramaswami Aiyar. I promised to make this point when I next returned to the subject; sadly, I never expected it to be in an elegy for her. Pearl Padamsee, my mentor in theater and a close friend and counselor for many years, was someone whose bouncy vivacity I had written about. The last time I saw her, illness had reduced her to a wisp, but her strength of personality shone through. I can imagine her in heaven, organizing a cast of angels to mount a celestial production of *Godspell*.

If there is any consolation at all in the voyage of these seven friends to that undiscovered country from which no traveler returns, it can only lie in their own release from the burdens of this world. No one is truly happy, Euripides wrote two millennia ago, until he is dead. I hope these friends are happy wherever they are; it is us they have left behind who are filled with questions, longings, and regrets.

4

Experiences of India

38

Jewish Portraits, Indian Frames

I T HAS ALWAYS BEEN A MATTER OF PRIDE for me that one of the very few countries in which the Jewish people never suffered any persecution is India. The first Jews came to what is today Kerala following the capture of Jerusalem and the destruction of their first Temple there by the Babylonians under Nebuchadnezzar in 597 B.C. A second wave followed a few centuries later, after the Romans destroyed the second Temple. This migration was not all that surprising; trade routes between the Roman world and the southwestern coast of India were well established, so the refugees were not sailing on uncharted waters. (The Romans even established a port in Kerala, Muziris, one of the great port cities of the ancient world.)

The Jews of Kerala settled down largely around Cranganore and practiced their faith and their customs unhindered. It was only a millennium and a half later that they suffered for being Jews — when the Portuguese, fresh from the Catholic Inquisition, arrived on India's western shores and started persecuting the Jews they found. The Jews then fled Cranganore and established themselves in Kochi, where they built an exquisite synagogue that still stands, though attrition and migration (to Australia, I am told, rather than Israel) has taken its toll, and the community living in the indelicately named "Jewtown" of Kochi has now dwindled to forty-two.

The story of the Kerala Jews came back to me when I read Jael Silliman's fascinating book *Jewish Portraits, Indian Frames.* Not that they are even mentioned in the book, for there are two other distinct Jewish communities in India — the Bene Israel of Maharashtra (the largest numerically, who lived undisturbed for centuries till a wandering rabbi recognized them for what they were) and the "Baghdadi Jews" who migrated from various parts of the Arab world to urban centers in India during the British Raj. It is with the latter that Dr. Silliman is concerned. Jael, whom I knew as a teenager in Calcutta and will therefore call by her first name, is the fourth generation in her family to have lived in the Baghdadi Jewish community of Calcutta, and her story traces the lives of the preceding three — her great-grandmother Farha, her grandmother Miriam, and her mother, Flower. The book is subtitled *Women's Narratives from a Diaspora of Hope.* It tells an eye-opening story.

The four women's lives trace, in intimate fashion, the transformation of the community over a little over a century. Farha, who arrived in Calcutta around 1890, "dwelled almost exclusively in the Baghdadi Jewish community no matter whether she was in Calcutta, Rangoon, or Singapore," Jael writes. Miriam, living in British colonial Calcutta, was more Anglicized, called herself Mary, but still saw herself as part of a close-knit community of Calcutta Jews. Flower came of age with the Indian nationalist movement, lived in an independent India with an eclectic circle of Calcuttan friends, and taught in a Roman Catholic convent. Jael saw herself as Indian first and foremost, went to study in the United States like so many of her contemporaries, married a Bengali Hindu physicist there and is again part of a diaspora — but this time of the Indian disapora rather than the Jewish one.

Their stories are told with an effective blend of historical research and personal anecdote, much of it in the form of family reminiscence by Flower, who lives with Jael and her family today in Iowa City. Though there is enough social and cultural detail to have given Jael material for a novel, she approaches her subject as a scholar, and her analysis is informed by a serious academic's understanding of both colonialism and feminism. But the scholarship, though backed by an impressive collection of endnotes (which the general reader may cheerfully skip), never undermines the readability of her narrative, which unfolds in clear, precise, and sometimes sparkling prose. The text is also brightened by a striking collection of black-and-white photographs, ranging from colonial Calcutta to a Jewish bar mitzvah gathering to Jael's daughters Shikha and Maya in *Bharatanatyam* costume, perfectly tracing the history of these four generations.

The story of Jael and her "foremothers" is an Indian story, because the stories of India cannot be narrowed to the Sanskritic specifications of the Hindutva bigots. The Calcutta Jews, alas, left only a few traces of their presence for a century and a half in that metropolis — three impressive large synagogues, two small prayer halls, two schools, and a cemetery. Two sizable buildings, Ezra Mansions and the Ezra Hospital, still bear the name of the Jewish merchant who built them. Ezra Street and Synagogue Street have been renamed. "Very soon," Jael Silliman observes, "matzohs will no longer be made in Calcutta. The Jewish community will exist only as a memory. . . . The Jewish Girls' School, once the center of community life, has no Jewish girls attending it. It has been increasingly difficult for the synagogues to attain a minyan — the ten men required to conduct a service. The imposing edifices and physical spaces that denote a Jewish presence are hollow, for they are bereft of the people and social relations that gave them their purpose and meaning."

That is a sad ending to a happy story. As the Jewish community of Calcutta dies out, a part of India's history dies with it. It was a remarkable son of this community, Major General J. F. R. Jacob, who helicoptered to Dhaka to negotiate the surrender terms of the Pakistani forces there in December 1971. Indian Jews have left their mark on our national evolution. And yet, as Jael Silliman writes, "The Jewish presence has been written over by contemporary India and is only visible to those in search of it." I am glad, for all our sakes, that she conducted this search.

39

Southern Comfort

WHEN A. P. J. ABDUL KALAM OF TAMIL NADU WAS ELECTED president of India in 2002, I had just finished a visit to his home state's capital, Madras, a city I still cannot bring myself to call Chennai (any more than I would refer to Deutschland when speaking in English of Germany). I grew up between the ages of three and nineteen in three cities — Bombay, Calcutta, and Delhi — where being from the South meant you were generically classified as Madrasi, even if, like myself, you were from another state altogether. In vain did I protest that my parents were from Kerala and we had not spent five minutes in Madras: to most of our neighbors, Madrasis is what we were.

I doubt very much whether, three decades later, "Chennaiyyas" has acquired the same resonance in the suburbs of Matunga or Jodhpur Park. By reducing the term Madras to the petty specificity of "Chennai," the city has lost its claim to stand for an entire peninsula. But this essay is not a lament for the lost redolence of Madras, whose renaming, along with Bombay's, I objected to in print at the time as emblematic of much that was wrong with modern Indian chauvinism (those who cannot create, I suggested somewhat nastily, can only rename). That battle is over, and the votaries of tradition and historical accuracy, not to mention linguistic common sense, have lost it. *The Hindu's* masthead now proclaims that it is published in Chennai. But I took some perverse pleasure in the knowledge that one of my engagements in the city was an evening with the members of a group that still defiantly calls itself the Madras Book Club.

What did it mean to be a Madrasi? To those who used the term, we were a tribe of articulate, bustling people with polysyllabic names, who spoke with astonishing rapidity in a number of incomprehensible languages and were clever enough to have risen high and wide both in government jobs and in private sector corporations. The untiring stenographer, the gnomic bureaucrat, the brilliant professor of mathematics, the formidable nuclear scientist — these were the Madrasis the Delhiite came across in the course of a typical day, and they shaped the stereotype. The average Madrasi was also seen as smaller, darker, and more agile than his northern brethren, who made fun of his accent while secretly admiring him for his competence and dedication. It was always the Madrasi who was scurrying briskly to fulfill every responsibility, who came up with new ideas and was all too willing to put in overtime to implement them, who was the one person to be trusted with the cashbox when the manager was away. Ability, commitment, energy, initiative, integrity — these were the qualities the North saw in Madrasis, and many of us came to believe the stereotype enough to live up to it ourselves.

I spent most of my childhood in the North, visiting the ancestral homes of my parents only on the annual holidays they took to Kerala. When I began working abroad, returning to India meant going to Bombay, Calcutta, and Delhi, where I found family and friends and the familiar associations of my own upbringing. But over the years I began to spend more of my limited vacation time in the South. My mother now lives in Coimbatore, and that is a powerful motivation. But getting to know South India better is only partly an effort to rediscover my roots; it is also an effort to stay connected with the future. For the future of India lies in the South.

No, that is not mere regional chauvinism. Nor am I just referring to Bangalore's "Silicon Plateau" and Mr. Chandrababu Naidu's "Cyberabad," though these are powerful symbols of an India that is wired to the twenty-first century. I am thinking also of the South as the part of our country that is getting the basics right — where literacy rates and educational levels are higher than in the North, where women are respected and empowered, where infrastructure is built and maintained, and where the disadvantage of being born in the wrong caste is less of an obstacle to advancement than elsewhere in the country. Above all, the South is a place of time-honored coexistence among religious communities, where the evil bigotries that have been allowed to flourish in northern India simply have no place. We may have had the odd episode of communal violence — sadly, no place on the subcontinent is immune to rioting — but it is inconceivable that the murderous rampages of Gujarat could ever have occurred anywhere in the five southern states.

For all his delightful idiosyncrasies, A. P. J. Abdul Kalam is still a product of the southern India I cherish — a man who rose from humble beginnings to acquire a decent education and build a brilliant governmental career, a Muslim whose mentor was a Hindu priest, a rocket scientist who writes like an *advaita* philosopher, a college professor whose inspirational vision for India's future is a staple of NRI exchanges on the Internet, a polymath who plays the *veena* and quotes with equal felicity from the Koran and the Bhagavad Gita. The Dravidian cast of his features and complexion, and the Tamil inflections of his English, complete the picture.

The Delhi wallahs who elected him knew what to expect from President Abdul Kalam. He is, you see, a Madrasi — the very best of the breed.

40

God's Own Country

THOUGH I AM A MALAYALI AND A WRITER, I have no claims to be considered a Malayali writer: indeed, despite setting some of my fictional sequences in Kerala and scattering several Menons through my stories, I could not have written my books in Malayalam because I cannot write my own mother tongue. And yet I am not inclined to be defensive about my Kerala heritage, despite the obvious incongruities of an expatriate praising Kerala from abroad and lauding the Malayali heritage in the English language.

As a child of the city, growing up in Bombay, Calcutta, and Delhi, my only experience of village Kerala had been as an initially reluctant vacationer during my parents' annual trips home. For many non-Keralite Malayali children traveling like this, there was often little joy in the compulsory rediscovery of their roots, and many saw it more as an obligation than a pleasure. For city dwellers, rural Kerala (and Kerala is essentially rural, since the countryside envelops the towns in a seamless web) was a world of rustic simplicities and private inconveniences. When I was ten I told my father that this annual migration south was strictly for the birds. But as I grew older, I came to appreciate the magic of Kerala — its beauty, which is apparent to the most casual tourist, and also its ethos, which takes greater engagement to uncover.

We Marunaadan Malayalis are, for the most part, conscious — some would say inordinately proud — of our Malayali cultural heritage. But as we are cut off from its primary source, the source of daily cultural self-regeneration — Kerala itself — we have to evolve our own identities by preserving what we can of our heritage and merging it with those of the others around us. As we grow up outside Kerala, we know that we are not the Malayalis we might have been if our parents had never left Kerala. In due course Onam becomes only as much a part of our culture as any other holiday, and we are as likely to give a younger relative a Christmas present as a *vishukkaineettam* (Kerala New Year gift). We, Malayalis without our *Mathrubhumi* or *Manorama* newspapers, who do not understand the *Ottamthullal* folk dance and have never heard of the great poets Vallathol or Kumaran Asan — are, when we come to visit Kerala, strangers in our own land.

I am such a Malayali — and in towns and cities around India and across the world, thousands more are growing up like us. Our very names are often absurdities in Kerala terms. In my case, my father's *veetu-peru* (house name; the family name handed down from his mother and her female forebears in the Nair matrilineal tradition) has been transmuted into a surname. We speak a pidgin Malayalam at home, stripped of all but the essential household vocabulary, and cannot read or write the language intelligibly. I tried to teach myself the script as a teenager on holidays in Kerala, gave up on the *koottaksharams* (joined letters) and as a result can recognize only 80 percent of the letters and considerably fewer of the words. (When an Indian ambassador in Singapore wanted discreetly to inform me of his imminent replacement by a Kerala politician, he passed me a clipping from a Malayalam newspaper and was startled at my embarrassed incomprehension of the news.) Malayalam books and magazines may be found at home, but they are seen by us as forlorn relics of an insufficiently advanced past and are ignored by the younger generation, whose eager eyes are on the paperbacks, comics, and textbooks of the impatient and Westernized future.

What does it mean, then, for Keralites like me, now living outside Kerala, to lay claim now to our Malayali heritage? What is it of Kerala that we learn to cherish, and of which we remain proud, wherever we are? In many ways my sense of being Malayali is tied up with my sense of being Indian. I grew up in an India where my sense of nationhood lay in a simple insight: the singular thing about India was that you could only speak of it in the plural. The same is true of Kerala. Everything exists in countless variants. There is no uniform standard, no fixed stereotype, no "one way" of doing things. This pluralism emerges from the very nature of the place; for both Kerala and India as a whole, it is made inevitable by geography and reaffirmed by history.

I came to my own Indianness through my Kerala roots. My parents were both born in Kerala of Malayali parents, speakers of Malayalam — the only language in the world with a palindromic name in English — the language of this remarkable sliver of a state in southwest India. Non-Malayalis who know of Kerala associate it with its fabled coast, gilded by immaculate beaches and leafy lagoons (both speckled nowadays with the more discerning among India's deplorably few foreign tourists). But my parents were from the interior of the state, the rice-bowl district of Palghat, nestled in the last major gap near the end of the mountain chain known as the Western Ghats, which runs down the western side of the peninsula like a subsidiary spine. Palghat — or Palakkad, as it is now spelled, to conform to the Malayalam pronunciation — unlike most of the rest of Kerala (which was ruled by maharajahs of an unusually enlightened variety), had been colonized by the British, so that my father discovered his nationalism at a place called Victoria College. The town of Palghat itself is unremarkable, even unattractive; its setting, though, is lushly beautiful, and my parents both belonged to villages an hour away from the district capital, and to families whose principal source of income was agriculture. Their roots lay deep in the Kerala soil, from which has emerged the values that I cherish in the Indian soul.

As Malayalis, the beauty of Kerala is bred into our souls; it animates our very being. Hailing from a land of forty-four rivers and innumerable lakes, with 1,500 kilometers of "backwaters," the Keralite bathes twice a day and dresses immaculately in white or cream. But she also lives in a world of color: from the gold border on her off-white *mundu* and the red of her bodice to the burnished sheen of the brass lamp in her hand whose flame glints against the shine of her jewelry, the golden *kodakaddakan* glittering at her ear. Kerala's women are usually simple and unadorned. But they float on a riot of color: the voluptuous green of the lush Kerala foliage, the rich red of the fecund earth, the brilliant blue of the life-giving waters, the shimmering gold of the beaches and riverbanks.

Yet there is much more to the Kerala experience than its natural beauty. Since my first sojourn as a child in my ancestral village, I have seen remarkable transformations in Kerala society, with land reform, free and universal education, and dramatic changes in caste relations.

It is not often that an American reference seems even mildly appropriate to an Indian case, but a recent study established some astonishing parallels between the United States and the state of Kerala. The life expectancy of a male American is seventy-two, that of a male Keralite seventy. The literacy rate in the United States is 95 percent; in Kerala it is 99 percent. The birthrate in the United States is sixteen per thousand; in Kerala it is eighteen per thousand, but it is falling faster. The gender ratio in the United States is 1,050 females to 1,000 males; in Kerala it is 1,040 to 1,000, and that in a country where neglect of female children has dropped the Indian national ratio to 930 women to 1,000 men. Death rates are also comparable, as are the number of hospital beds per 100,000 population. The major difference is that the annual per capita income in Kerala is around $300 to $350, whereas in the United States it is $22,500, about seventy times as much.

Kerala has, in short, all the demographic indicators commonly associated with "developed" countries, at a small fraction of the cost. Its success is a reflection of what, in my book *India: From Midnight to the Millennium and Beyond*, I have called the "Malayali miracle": a state that has practiced openness and tolerance from time immemorial; which has made religious and ethnic diversity a part of its daily life rather than a source of division; which has overcome caste discrimination and class oppression through education, land reforms, and political democracy; which has honored its women and enabled them to lead productive, fulfilling, and empowered lives.

But that is not all. Kerala's working men and women enjoy greater rights and a higher minimum wage than anywhere else in India. Kerala was the first place on earth to democratically elect a Communist government, remove it from office, reelect it, vote the Communists out, and bring them back again. When the Italian political system saw the emergence of a Communist Party willing to play by the rules of liberal democracy, the world spoke of Euro-Communism, but Kerala had already achieved Indo-Communism much earlier, subordinating the party of proletarian revolution to the ethos of political pluralism. Malayalis are highly politically aware: when other Indian states were electing film stars to Parliament or as chief ministers, a film star tried his political luck in Kerala and lost his security deposit. (Ironically, the first Indian film star to become the chief minister of a state was a Malayali, Marudur Gopalannair Ramachandran — known to all as MGR — but he was elected in the neighboring state of Tamil Nadu, where he had made a career as a Tamilian film hero.) Malayalis rank high in every field of Indian endeavor, from the top national civil servants to the most innovative writers and filmmakers.

More important, Kerala is a microcosm of every religion known to the country; its population is divided into almost equal fourths of Christians, Muslims, caste Hindus, and Scheduled Castes (the former untouchables, now called Dalits), each of whom is economically and politically powerful. Kerala's outcastes — one group of whom, the Pariahs, gave the English language a term for their collective condition — suffered discrimination every bit as vicious and iniquitous as in the rest of India, but overcame their plight far more successfully than their countrymen elsewhere. A combination of enlightened rule by far-thinking maharajahs, progressive reform movements within the Hindu tradition (especially that of the re-markable Ezhava sage Sree Narayana Guru), and changes wrought by a series of left-dominated legislatures since independence have given Kerala's Scheduled Castes a place in society that other Dalits across India are still denied. It is no accident that the first Dalit to become president of India was Kerala's K. R. Narayanan — who was born in a thatched hut with no running water, who as a young man suffered the indignities and oppression that were the lot of his people, but who seized on the opportunities that Kerala provided him to rise above them and ascend, through a brilliant diplomatic and governmental career, to the highest office in the land.

When the artist M. F. Husain painted a series of paintings on Kerala for our joint book, *God's Own Country,* I was struck by what, in his striking style, he chose to depict: the violence and the idealism of the leftist movement, the calm spread of literacy, the turbulence of the quest for rights of the downtrodden, the vivid masks of the Kathakali dancers, the palpable air of tranquil fraternity in village Kerala. And everywhere there are the women: striding confidently through the green, holding aloft their elephants, steering their little boats through a storm, holding their own at the marketplace, and simply — how simply! — reading. The mere fact that every Kerala girl or woman above the age of six can read and write is little short of a miracle, in a country where more women are illiterate than not, and where a state like Bihar enters the twenty-first century with only 27 percent of its women able to decipher an alphabet. A girl born in Kerala can expect to live twenty years longer than one born in Uttar Pradesh, and she can expect to make the important decisions in her life, to attend college, choose a profession, do what others might consider "men's work," and inherit property (something which, be-fore the law was changed in 1956, Indian women could not expect to do, unless they were Malayalis following the *marumakkathayam* matrilineal system). Kerala's women have become doctors and pi-lots, supreme court justices, ambassadors of India; they have shone in sport, politics, and the armed forces. "If Kashmir is all about men and mountains, " Husain once said, "Kerala is all about women and nature." His work in this series has been dubbed *Kalyanikuttyude Keralam* — Kalyanikutty's Kerala, with Kalyanikutty the emblematic Kerala woman, an enlightened modern figure steeped in her traditional culture, rising from it to conquer new worlds while remaining comfortable in her own.

As a child, I grew up listening to my paternal grandmother read aloud from her venerable editions of the Ramayana and the Mahabharata. And I saw, too, my maternal grandmother running a big house and administering the affairs of a large brood of children and grandchildren with firmness and courage. In both cases, they had been widowed relatively young, but in neither case was their gender a disqualification in their assumption of authority. Keralites are used to seeing women ruling the roost. My own mother, now closer to seventy than she would like to admit, still drives her own car to our ancestral home in a Palakkad village, scorning male help. She likes to be in charge.

Fittingly, it was a woman ruler, Rani Gouri Parvati-bai, then queen of Travancore, who decreed in 1817: "The state should defray the entire cost of the education of its people in order that there might be no backwardness in the spread of enlightenment among them, that by diffusion of education they might become better subjects and public servants." Her royal successors followed the policy, and after independence, elected Communist governments in the state and enshrined free, compulsory, and universal education as a basic right. Today, Kerala outspends every Indian state in its tax outlays on education, and Keralites support over fifty newspapers. No village is complete without a "reading room" that serves as a community library, and the sight of villagers reading their newspapers in public is a ubiquitous one, particularly in the *chayakadas* (tea shops) where animated arguments around the day's news over steaming sweet cups of tea are a regular feature of daily life.

It is not accidental that one of Husain's paintings depicts young and old sharing a home life; family bonds are strong in Kerala, though nuclear families are on the increase there as everywhere, and the older generation has an honored place in the lives of the young, who accept the responsibility to care for them. Another reveals an outdoor market, a street scene in which the people are surrounded by bananas, coconuts, fish, and tapioca, the great staples of Kerala cuisine. Men and women are equally present in the painting; indeed, the women seem to be in the position of economic power. It is striking that in the one picture in which Husain depicts the thundering force of the monsoon (which hits Kerala first before it takes on the rest of India, and with such force that it is often described as an invasion of gray elephants, a metaphor the artist underscores), he shows a woman rowing a boat, standing up to the forces of nature. My paternal grandmother would read the Ramayana from start to finish during the rains, and my maternal grandmother would dispense her herbal potions and pills, averring that they would be most effective if taken at this time of year. The monsoon buffets the people but replenishes the land; it affirms life and hope even as it sweeps away the frail and the weak before it. In its awesome impact it offers a clue to the resilience of Kerala's culture.

Not everyone is equally admiring of the "Kerala model"; economists point out it places rather too much emphasis on workers' rights and income distribution, and rather too little on production, productivity, and output. But its results in terms of social development are truly remarkable; and as a Keralite and an Indian, I look forward to the day when Kerala will no longer be the exception in tales of Indian development, but merely the trailblazer.

Part of the secret of Kerala is its openness to the external influences — Arab, Roman, Chinese, British; Islamist, Christian, Marxist — that have gone into the making of the Malayali people. More than two millennia ago Keralites had trade relations not just with other parts of India but with the Arab world, with the Phoenicians, and with the Roman Empire. From those days on, Malayalis have had an open and welcoming attitude to the rest of humanity.

The Christians of Kerala belong to the oldest Christian community in the world outside Palestine, converted by Jesus' disciple Saint Thomas (the "Doubting Thomas" of biblical legend), one of the twelve apostles, who came to the state in 52 a.d. and, so legend has it, was welcomed on land by a flute-playing Jewish girl. So Kerala's Christian traditions are much older than those of Europe — and when Saint Thomas brought Christianity to Kerala, he made converts among the high-born elite, the Namboodiri Brahmins. Islam came to Kerala not by the sword, as it was to do elsewhere in India, but through traders, travelers, and missionaries, who brought its message of equality and brotherhood to the coastal people. Not only was the new faith peacefully embraced, but it found encouragement in attitudes and episodes without parallel elsewhere in the non-Islamic world; in one example, the all-powerful Zamorin of Calicut asked each fisherman's family in his domain to bring up one son as a Muslim for service in his Muslim-run navy, commanded by sailors of Arab descent, the Kunjali Maraicars.

It was probably a Malayali seaman, one of many who routinely plied the Arabian Sea between Kerala and East Africa, who piloted Vasco da Gama, the Portuguese explorer and trader, to Calicut in 1496. (Da Gama, typically, was welcomed by the Zamorin, but when he tried to pass trinkets off as valuables, he was thrown in prison for a while. Malayalis are open and hospitable to a fault, but they are not easily fooled.)

In turn, Malayalis brought their questing spirit to the world. The great Advaita philosopher Shankaracharya was a Malayali who traveled throughout the length and breadth of India on foot in the eighth century A.D., laying the foundations for a reformed and revived Hinduism. To this day, there is a temple in the Himalayas whose priests are Namboodiris from Kerala.

Keralites never suffered from inhibitions about travel: an old joke suggests that so many Keralite typists flocked to stenographic work in Mumbai, Kolkata, and Delhi that "Remington" became the name of a new Malayali subcaste. In the nation's capital, the wags said that you couldn't throw a stone in the Central Secretariat with-out injuring a Keralite bureaucrat. Nor was there, in the Kerala tra-dition, any prohibition on venturing abroad, none of the ritual defilement associated in parts of north India with "crossing the black water." It was no accident that Keralites were the first to take advan-tage of the post oil-shock employment boom in the Arab Gulf coun-tries; at one point in the 1980s, the largest single ethnic group in the Gulf sheikhdom of Bahrain was reported to be not Bahrainis but Keralites. The willingness of Keralites to go anywhere to do anything remains legendary. When Neil Armstrong landed on the moon in 1969, my father's friends joked, he discovered a Malayali already there, offering him tea.

But Keralites are not merely intrepid travelers. They also have behind them a great legacy of achievement. In the fifth century A.D. the Kerala-born astronomer Aryabhatta deduced, one thousand years before his European successors, that the earth is round and that it rotates on its own axis; it was also he who calculated the value of π (3.1416) for the first time. In a totally different discipline from another era, the first great modern Indian painter, the prince Raja Ravi Varma (1848–1906), was a Keralite. (Ravi Varma revolution-ized Indian art by introducing the medium of oil on canvas and in-corporating into his style a distinctively Victorian European realism.) But a recitation of names — for one could invoke great artists, musicians, and poets, enlightened kings, and learned sages through-out history — would only belabor the point. Kerala took from oth-ers, everything from Roman ports to Chinese fishing nets, and gave to the rest of India everything from martial arts (some of which ap-pear to have inspired the better-known disciplines of the Far East) to its systems of classical dance-theater (notably Kathakali, to which I will return, Mohiniattam, and the less well known Koodiyattom, re-cently hailed by UNESCO as a "masterpiece of the oral and intangible heritage of humanity"). And I have not even mentioned Keralite cuisine and traditional medicine, in particular the attractions of Ayurveda, the great health system of ancient India, with its herbs, oils, massages, and other therapies, now revived and attractively presented at dozens of locations around the state.

All this speaks of a rare and precious heritage that is the patrimony of all Malayalis — a heritage of openness and diversity, of pluralism and tolerance, of high aspirations and varied but considerable accomplishment. To be a Malayali is also to lay claim to a rich tradition of literature, dance, and music, of religious diversity, of political courage and intellectual enlightenment — and of energetic entertainment. A visitor must look at Kerala life beyond the sandy beaches. One should not miss the *vallomkali,* or backwater boat races (which during the harvest festival of Onam are among the biggest mass sporting events in the world). One should also go backstage at a Kathakali performance, revealing the *thiranottam* (the prelude to a performance in which the dancer emerges from behind a handheld curtain) and reminding us of the stark morality of color in Kathakali, where characters clad in green, nature's hue, embody goodness and dharma, and those in black represent the darkness of evil. One should also enter the state's myriad places of worship — Orthodox Christian cathedrals, the oldest Muslim mosque in India, and the exquisite synagogue in Kochi's "Jewtown," as well as the famous Hindu temple at Guruvayoor and a smaller village shrine. One could also visit students learning the ancient martial art of *kalaripayattu,* or depict the holistic Ayurvedic treatments offered at the Kottakkal Arya Vaidya Sala, or take in the wildlife sanctuary at Thekkady.

There is an old verse of the poet Vallathol that my late father loved to recite: "*Bharatam ennu ketal, abhimaana-pooritham aavanum, andarangam; Keralam ennu ketalo, thillakkanam chaora namukke njerumbugalil*" (When we hear the name of India, we must swell with pride; When we hear the name of Kerala, the blood must throb in our veins). It is, in some ways, an odd sentiment for a Malayalali poet, for Keralites are not a chauvinistic people: the Keralite liberality and adaptiveness, such great assets in facilitating Malayali emigration and good citizenship anywhere, can serve to slacken, if not cut, the cords that bind expatriate Keralites to their cultural assumptions. And yet

Vallathol was not off the mark, for Keralites tend to take pride in their collective identity as Malayalis; our religion, our caste, our region come later, if at all. There is no paradox in asserting that these are qualities that help make Malayalis good Indians in a plural society. You cannot put better ingredients into the melting pot.

Keralites see the best guarantee of their own security and prosperity in the survival and success of a pluralist India. The Malayali ethos is the same as the best of the Indian ethos — inclusionist, flexible, eclectic, absorptive. The central challenge of India as we enter the twenty-first century is the challenge of accommodating the aspirations of different groups in the national dream. The ethos that I have called both Keralite and Indian is indispensable in helping the nation meet this challenge.

*

"In the exceptional nature of Kerala's social achievements," Amartya Sen has written, "the greater voice of women seems to have been an important factor." The literacy of Kerala women has produced a lower birthrate than China's, without the coercion China needed. But there is a cloud to every silver lining, and as an expatriate male Keralite, I discovered soon enough that not everything about the lives of Kerala's women is ideal.

I have received several striking letters from disillusioned Malayalis attacking their own state's prevailing culture in relation to women. Two of these stand out. The poet Thachom Poyil Rajeevan put it bluntly:

> It's true that Kerala women can read and write (and) are doing better than Bihari women or the women in the neighboring states in the professional and social spheres. There may be pilots, doctors, ambassadors, and Supreme Court judges among them. But they cannot come out of their houses after six in the evening. If anyone dares to do so, she is not safe outside in the

dark. Any man she comes upon on the way is a potential intruder into her modesty. I don't know whether women in Bihar face a similar threat in public places. But I have seen girls in Madurai Kamaraj University in Tamil Nadu walk fearlessly and safely to hostels late at night after completing their work in libraries and laboratories. Yet I cannot expect [to see] a girl after six or seven on the campus of the university where I work. I have seen many Malayali women walk with confidence in Bangalore, Mumbai, and New Delhi. But when they come to Calicut or Trichur, they become timid. Kalyanikuttys, despite all their claims to literacy and empowerment, are not safe in their home state.

That is a sad enough indictment coming from a man, but even more searing are the words of a Malayali woman reader, Prema Nair. "Oh dear, oh dear!!" she begins. "Are you one of those who have seen everything through the tinted lens of the acclaimed 'Kerala model'? Nobody is disputing the favorable development and lifestyle indicators this state has, but please do not confuse well-being with an empowered and independent sense of being. Do we not often also confuse literacy with education?"

Fair point, Ms. Nair. She goes on to assail what she ironically calls the "other glories" of Kerala — a state where women become regular victims of dowry harassment ("Unlike in the north of India, this is prolonged mental harassment leading to suicides") and of domestic violence (she cites scholarly studies from INCLEN and Sakhi confirming the "increasing and alarming rise of domestic violence" in Kerala). "Yes," Prema Nair goes on, "animated arguments are a regular feature of daily life in Kerala. But what happens after? Political parties and politicians play their games; women suffer. The elected women representatives are expected to toe the party line; women's concerns are always given a back seat, except when it can be a means of increasing votes. Women's groups and the autonomous women's network have to consistently intervene (with) regular gender-sensitizing and training programs (in order to) support women and equip them to withstand this masculinization of public spaces."

I am already feeling the telltale symptoms of male inadequacy, but Ms. Nair goes on: "Isn't this the very state that produced the infamous sex rackets, or should we look the other way? Isn't this God's own country and the devil's own people who waltz their way into organized sex-racket gangs (a special feature of Kerala, by the way) victimizing teenage girls, luring them into jobs, and then sexually exploiting them? This is done by the VIPs . . . politicians, civil service officials, businessmen, film stars. Along with the distinction of having women 'doctors, pilots, supreme court justices, ambassadors of India,' we also have the women of Suryanelly, the Ice Cream Parlor sex racket in Kozhikode, the Vithura sex racket in Kiliroor; the list is endless."

And Prema Nair drives the point home: "Isn't this the state where rape happens to a six-month-old baby girl as well as to an eighty-year-old female corpse? Isn't this the state where the latest sex-racket victim breathed her last in a private nursing home, under very suspicious circumstances? Isn't this the state where one of the latest sex-racket victim's brothers killed her, and gave the reason as 'honor killing' (that is another first for Kerala, or maybe not)? Or maybe we should just look the other way; away from the muddy fields to the beautiful backwaters. After all isn't that what we see when we just pass by?"

Citing my reference to the longer life spans of girls born in Kerala, Prema Nair argues that fewer girls are being born now, since studies have shown a declining female birthrate. My other points also get short shift: "Oh, she 'makes the decisions,' yet she cannot choose her own contraceptive. And when she works ('men's work' maybe) she gets paid less than men do. What about the high rate of dowry here, in all communities — one of the highest in the country? 'Enlightened modern figure' who stoops to be trampled? Have we missed something here . . . ?"

I clearly have. "Dear Mr. Shashi Tharoor," Prema Nair concludes, "We are proud of you. But please do get your facts and fiction right, sir — or Kalyanikutty would get angry, for she does know how to read."

She does indeed. I am suitably chastened. But at least I was right about one thing. You can always trust a Kerala woman to put you in your place for praising the lot of Kerala women!

41

Oh, Calcutta!

FOR YEARS IT WAS FASHIONABLE to see Calcutta as the epitome of all the ills of our urban culture. Poverty, pollution, pestilence — you name it, Calcutta had it. (Forgive my alliteration: you could stick to that one letter of the alphabet and still find no difficulty cataloguing Calcutta's woes: power cuts, poverty, potholes, pavement-dwellers, political violence, paralyzed industry.) As business capital and professional talent fled the city from the late 1960s onward, the former First City of the British Empire spiraled into increasing irrelevance. "Calcutta," I found myself writing in my book *India: From Midnight to the Millennium and Beyond,* "has become a backwater."

It wasn't always that way. When, as a twelve-year-old in late 1968, I first learned of my father's transfer from Bombay to Calcutta, I embraced the news with great excitement. Calcutta still had the lingering aura of its old grandeur. It was the bustling commercial metropolis of the jute, tea, coal, and iron and steel industries. More important, it was the city of the greatest cricket stadium in India, Eden Gardens, the pavement bookstalls and animated coffeehouses of College Street, the elegant cakes of Firpo's Restaurant, and — recalling the whispers of wicked uncles — the cabarets of the Golden Slipper, the acme of all Indian nightclubs. It was the city of the visionary

Rabindranath Tagore and the brilliant Satyajit Ray; for juveniles of less exalted cultural inclinations, it had India's first disco (the Park Hotel's suggestively named In and Out) and, in JS, India's only "with it" youth magazine. Former Calcuttans still spoke of the brilliance of the Bengali stage, the erudition of the waiters at the Coffee House, the magic of Park Street at Christmas.

By the mid-1980s, most of that list had disappeared. What remained, instead, was the dirt and the degradation, the despair and the disrepair, that made Calcutta the poster child for the Third World city. The global image of what had once been a great metropolis remained a cross between the "Black Hole" of historical legend and the tragic *City of Joy* of modern cinema. The best you could hope for was salvation in the slums.

Well, I am glad to report that Calcutta has turned the corner. On repeated visits to the city I had felt that nothing had changed, that the only alternative to decline was stagnation. As the twenty-first century gets under way, I have discovered this is no longer true. Two things have happened: the problems are abating, and creativity has returned.

I am not suggesting that Calcutta has suddenly become a paragon of civic virtue. But the streets are cleaner, the garbage is being picked up, hawker encroachments cleared, and power cuts are largely a thing of the past. There are still people sleeping on the pavement, but very much fewer than ever before: reforms in the Bengal countryside mean that destitute villagers no longer flock to Calcutta for survival, and nearly three decades of Left Front rule have given the city a measure of political stability unimaginable even a quarter of a century ago. It may be true that one of the reasons that "load-shedding" does not regularly plunge the city into darkness is that nothing succeeds like failure: the exodus of major industry in the last thirty years has reduced demand for power consumption. But there is also something positive in the air.

The signs of progress are everywhere: in the new roads and housing developments that are expanding the metropolis; in the stylish new buildings that have come up where collapsing colonial structures used to stand; in the new high-tech Science City, which both amuses and educates the young; in the gleaming Vidyasagar Setu, which bids fair to rival the great Howrah Bridge as both artery and symbol; in the dazzling prosperity of Salt Lake City, which used to be a mangrove swamp on the way to the airport; in the air-conditioned supermarkets and restaurants that are attracting a new breed of affluent customers. Calcutta feels like a real city once more.

But most important, Calcuttans are innovating again. One businessman I met — Harsh Neotia, a large and gentle forty-something — epitomizes the revived spirit of the city. His three current projects encapsulated for me the reasons to hope again about Calcutta. First, he has taken over the decaying eighteenth-century Town Hall and given it a multicrore-rupee facelift as a renewed symbol of Calcuttan splendor. Second, he has given middle-class Calcuttans a weekend escape from the city by constructing a residential resort at a bend in the Hooghly at Raichak an hour and a half from the city, a place where city dwellers can swim, boat, play tennis, watch a cultural performance, or simply enjoy the sunset from the balcony of their well-appointed room. Third and most important, he has worked with the state government to create India's first joint-sector public housing project, a twenty-five-acre development called Udayan, a beautifully landscaped complex designed by Balkrishna Doshi in which half the flats are reserved for the city's lower- and middle-income groups. The below-cost sale of these small but practical flats is subsidized by the popularity of the more expensive luxury apartments in the same development. HUDCO's dynamic former national chief, V. Suresh, has called the concept a "revolution" in the country's housing sector. It is not the kind of revolution Calcutta had become famous for.

These are just three projects pursued by one man; there are undoubtedly other Harsh Neotias in the city. It used to be said that when Calcutta catches a cold, the rest of India sneezes. The Neotia virus is the kind one hopes is infectious.

42

Urbs Maxima in Indis

To some of us, the story of Bombay is a story of decline. I lived in Bombay from 1959 to 1969, the formative years of my childhood, and in those days everything exciting and vital in India appeared to be happening there. As late as 1979, the only Indian selection in Time-Life Books' Great Cities of the World series was, inevitably, Bombay (elegantly evoked by Dom Moraes and a clutch of brilliant photographers). A plaque outside the Gateway of India reminds us that it is known as *"Urbs Prima in Indis."* But Bombay has been increasingly overtaken by Delhi. In the last two decades, Delhi has grown, sucking up the nation's resources and talents like a sponge — money, art, theater, publishing. Delhi is now the capital of virtually all the things that Bombayites used to pride themselves on. Gaining fast, especially on the livability index, is Bangalore, flourishing on our own Silicon Plateau.

What makes Bombay Bombay is not just that it is India's commercial capital, the home of its stock exchange, a city that generates nearly 40 percent (38 percent at last count) of the country's taxes; nor that it manufactures the grandiose dreams of Bollywood (making five times as many films annually as the United States); nor that it houses the country's most opulent hotels and boasts of commercial

293

rents higher than Manhattan or Tokyo (in a city where half the population is homeless); nor even that Bombay supports India's most innovative theaters and art galleries and 150 diet clinics while millions
of its residents eke out a bare subsistence in the world's largest slums.
No, what makes Bombay Bombay is that it is a microcosm of the best
and worst of India. Its 17.5 million inhabitants — more than the entire populations of Norway, Denmark, and Finland put together —
hail from every part of the subcontinent. On Bombay's bustling
streets you can hear every one of India's twenty-three major languages, see all of its styles of dress, taste all of the astonishing variety
of its cuisines, buy and sell any of its products, pray to any of its gods.
Bombay is India writ small — a marvel of cosmopolitanism, of the
country's pluralism and collective energy. It is living, thriving evidence that India's diversity, when channeled productively, is its richest asset.

The expatriate writer Suketu Mehta portrayed Bombay as still
the biggest, richest, most murderous city in India, in his stunning
debut, *Maximum City.* Bombay, Mehta points out, is a city of appalling contrasts — a bottle of Champagne at the Oberoi Hotel sells
for one and a half times the national average annual income when
40 percent of the city has no safe drinking water; the world's largest
film industry thrives in a city where plumbing, telephones, and
law and order break down regularly; millions starve in filthy slums
while the city supports several hundred slimming clinics. Such contrasts can be found elsewhere, but is there any other place on earth
to which immigrants continue to flock while the trains in the city
alone kill four thousand people a year? Where a thug buys chickens
in the morning from Muslims he will butcher in the afternoon?
("Bombayites understand that business comes first," Mehta quotes
him as saying.) Where a ragpicker can be hired to kill a man for a
sum of money that would not buy a cup of coffee at a good hotel in
the city?

And yet to say this is to overlook Bombay's eclectic architecture, its fine museums and art galleries, its commercial life; to forget

about a boat trip in the choppy seas to Bombay's premier attraction, the Elephanta Caves, with their remarkable ancient Hindu carvings; a visit to the cooperative Aarey milk colony; paying homage at Mani Bhavan, the house where Mahatma Gandhi lived and where many of his possessions can still be seen, as well as an intriguing series of dioramas on his life. To focus only on the crime and the corruption is to neglect the remarkable buildings and beautiful views (especially from the Hanging Gardens on Malabar Hill). And if either the heat or the rains drives one indoors, one must seek shelter at the Prince of Wales Museum, which houses one of the finest collections of Indian miniature paintings in the country. Most date from the sixteenth, seventeenth, and eighteenth centuries and are from the Deccani, Mughal, and Pahari schools. There is a particularly interesting series of paintings portraying the moods of the classical ragas, and some exquisite, but poorly labeled, temple statuary.

In other words, Bombay must not be reduced to its seamy underside. How can a visitor ignore, for instance, its fabled Taj Mahal Hotel, built in 1903 and still perhaps India's finest hotel, a grand crenellated edifice facing the sea near the historic arch of the Gateway of India? Legend has it that the hotel was born when Sir Jamsetji Tata, India's leading industrialist in the 1890s, was refused entry, together with a group of Indian friends, to the British-owned Pyrke's Apollo Hotel. Tata, a visionary steel magnate, vowed to build a hotel that would exceed the Apollo in quality but admit patrons of all races. He succeeded spectacularly, so that the Taj has now sprouted a modern twenty-two-story annex and is the flagship of a chain that has acquired the Pierre in New York and the Ritz-Carlton in Boston while Pyrke's is buried in the mists of colonial memory.

Legend also has it that the Taj's architect, William Chambers, visited the hotel only when its construction was complete and, discovering to his horror that the plans had been misread and the building built back to front, killed himself. Romantics should best not explore the veracity of this tale too closely, since it is almost certainly apocryphal, though the hotel staff is careful neither to confirm nor deny it.

Which is altogether the right approach to take to the great stories of a great city.

43

Of Cows Sacred and Profane

THE OTHER DAY I RECEIVED BY E-MAIL one of those Internet jokes that constantly do the rounds, particularly among expatriate Indians, whose appetite for *desi* humor, usually self-deprecating, knows no bounds. It purported to be an essay written by a Bihari candidate at the Union Public Service Commission (UPSC) examinations for the Indian Administrative Service (IAS). The sender quoted what was allegedly the candidate's essay on the subject of "The Indian Cow," which, for the benefit of those fortunate enough not to be assailed daily by the Internet, I reproduce below almost in full:

He is the cow. The cow is a successful animal. Also he is four-footed. And because he is female, he give milks, but will do so when he is got child. He is same like-God, sacred to Hindus and useful to man. But he has got four legs together. Two are forward and two are afterwards. His whole body can be utilized for use. More so the milk. Milk comes from 4 taps attached to his basement. Horses do not have any such attachment. What can it do? Various ghee, butter, cream, curd, why and the condensed milk and so forth. Also he is useful to cobbler, watermans and mankind generally.

His motion is slow only because he is of lazy species. Also his other motion (gobar) is much useful to trees, plants as well as for making flat cakes like

Pizza, in hand, and drying in the sun. Cow is the only animal that extri-
cates his feeding after eating. . . . His only attacking and defending organ
is the horns, specially so when he is got child. This is done by knowing his
head whereby he causes the weapons to be paralleled to the ground of the
earth and instantly proceed with great velocity forwards.

He has got tails also, situated in the backyard, but not like similar animals.
It has hairs on the other end of the other side. This is done to frighten away
the flies which alight on his body whereupon he gives hit with it.

It goes on for a few sentences more in similar vein, and then the
e-mailer added the following footnote: "We are reliably informed
that the candidate passed the exam and is now an IAS officer somewhere in Bihar."

Now let's put aside the obvious implausibilities of this story —
the unlikelihood of an IAS exam paper being posted on the Web, the
even greater unlikelihood that the IAS would ask its examinees to
write an essay on the cow — and consider the sneering that lies behind it. The anonymous candidate is, of course, supposed to be from
Bihar, which over the last couple of decades has become a sort of national symbol for corruption, venality, and incompetence in Indian
governance, at least among the urban Anglophone classes. (This
phenomenon has, of course, accelerated since the ascent of unprincipled rusticity to high office in that state, as embodied in the person
of Shri and Smt Laloo Prasad Yadav.) Worse still, the e-mail claims
the howler-laden essay actually got its author into the IAS. This is
startling, because it suggests that the stock of that institution, once
considered the home of the best and the brightest in our society, has
fallen lower than any of us could have imagined, at least in the eyes
of our nouveaux riches computer-owning yuppies and their NRI
friends. In the old days, the IAS officer was the paragon of authority
and power, the prospective bridegroom who commanded the highest
price on the marriage market. Today, as multinationals and dot-coms
(and better still, multinational dot-coms) reward their executives
with riches and perks that a mere *sarkari babu* can only dream of, the

once-august IAS man can even be portrayed as a semi-illiterate *de-hati* who can't write a sensible English paragraph but still gets sent off to rule over the masses, at least in Bihar.

I may be making far too much of a silly Internet joke, but I wonder what its wide circulation (I have received it from at least three different people) reveals about the way Indian society is changing. I once wrote about the insidious divisions being promoted between "India" and "Bharat" — between a slice of our country that is seen as cosmopolitan, liberal, Anglophone, technologically savvy, and secular, and the undifferentiated rest that is thought of as traditional, casteist, superstition-ridden, backward, and vernacular. It worries me that, in this era of greater communication, complete interdependence, and the leveling influence of mass television, the gulf of empathy between the "Indians" and the Bharatvasis seems to be widening rather than shrinking. There is probably room here for more serious sociological enquiry than I am capable of. I hope it is undertaken by someone in Bihar.

But I don't want to leave the subject of classroom howlers before making the defensively feeble observation that Biharis, or for that matter Indians, are not their only perpetrators. Anders Henriksson, an American professor of history (at the not particularly well known Shepherd College in West Virginia) has compiled a volume he has titled *Non Campus Mentis*, a collection of egregious errors taken word for word from term papers and exams conducted at American and Canadian colleges. His chronicle runs from such prehistorical periods as "the Stoned Age" to the more contemporary dramas of "the Berlin Mall." In his account, Julius Caesar is assassinated on "the Yikes of March" and bursts out while dying, "Me too, Brutus!"

In the student essays the good professor has trawled, there are knowing references to "Judyism" as a "monolithic" religion (whose adherents, in a contemporary computer-age error, worship the god "Yahoo"). Columbus's benefactors, Ferdinand and Isabella, conquer not Grenada but "Granola." Martin Luther King Jr. (the student even left out the surname "King," confusing the black American

Nobel winner with the fifteenth-century German Protestant re-
former) makes a historic "If I Had a Hammer" speech (the title of a
pop song — King had, in reality, famously declared, "I have a
dream"). Hitler is depicted as terrorizing his enemies with his feared
"Gespacho," a conflation of the Spanish soup, or gazpacho, with the
dreaded Gestapo. Kennedy resolves the "Canadian Missile Crisis,"
not the Cuban. And so on.

Ignorance, in other words, knows no boundaries. Not even national ones. I don't know how much they might know about the cow,
but I have no doubt that none of the American students in Professor
Hendriksson's book would have gotten into the IAS.

44

Of Vows and Vowels

THE NEWS THAT THE ERSTWHILE (or should one say "once and future"?) chief minister of Tamil Nadu, Jayalalitha, has decided to add an extra "a" to the end of her name because a numerologically minded astrologer told her it would be more propitious is the kind of Indian story foreigners find almost impossible to believe. There is no other society on earth in which a leading public figure would change the spelling of her name in such a manner, and for a reason that most non-Indians would find frivolous. And yet we take it so cheerfully in stride in our country because we manage to live in that rare combination of modernity and superstition that defines us as a breed apart from the other peoples of the world.

Where else, after all, is so much made of an individual's astrological chart, that mysterious database which determines his opportunities in life, his marital prospects, his willingness to undertake certain risks? I once wrote that an Indian without a horoscope is like an American without a credit card, and the truth of that observation shows no signs of fading away in the twenty-first century. It seems particularly entrenched in our political world. As one who is what we like to call a "God-fearing" Hindu, I make no claims to be a pure rationalist myself, but I am still bemused to read of the swearing-in of a minister delayed because a politician's astrologer told him the time was not auspicious to take the oath, or of a candidate's nomination papers being filed at the last possible minute to avoid the malign influences of raahu-kaalam. My favorite story is of the chief minister who refused to move into his official residence because a pundit claimed it was not built according to the principles of vastu (the Indian forerunner of feng shui) and he would not fare well in it. The bungalow was accordingly redone, at great public expense, with new doorways made and windows realigned to satisfy the pundit. At last the chief minister moved in — only to lose his job and his new home the next day, the vagaries of politics having outstripped the benefits of vastu.

Why on earth do otherwise intelligent, educated people put themselves in thrall to such superstition? I am all in favor of the innate human desire to propitiate the heavens, and I am even prepared to entertain the notion that the cosmos might be sending us signals in every planetary realignment, but what makes us so credulous as to believe that our godmen understand the code? I suppose it is entirely possible that Ms. Jayalalithaa will attain political successes that a mere Ms. Jayalalitha might not have, but on what possible basis can it be argued that the addition of a superfluous vowel made all the difference? I remember when I was about to publish *The Great Indian Novel* and a friend's guru advised me solemnly that all that was lacking was an extra vowel in the title. Put in another *a,* he advised, and success was certain; otherwise the book's prospects could not be guaranteed. I could scarcely believe he was suggesting that a retelling of the Mahabharata would work better as *The Great Indiana Novel,* or that a 432-page tome could get away with calling itself *The Great Indian Novella.* So I ignored the advice, and I am glad to say the novel is currently in its eighteenth printing while the godman himself, having been arrested a couple of years later under Section 420 of the Indian Penal Code, is now spending his eighteenth year in prison.

I must confess, however, that there has been a spelling change in the bosom of my own family. My son Ishaan was named Ishan on his birth certificate, but growing up in America he soon tired of people pronouncing his name as if it rhymed with "I can," and around age seven he did a Jayalalithaa and baptized himself Ishaan — a spelling less liable, he felt, to mispronunciation. (His twin is named Kanishk, without the conventional final vowel, which puts us doubly out of sorts, since to the purist Ishaan has one *a* too many and Kanishk one *a* too few.)

I was quite willing to accept this precocious act of individual affirmation by my little son, but had he based his preference on the suggestion of a trusted astrologer, I would have resisted it stoutly. I do not believe God dispenses his favors according to the number of vowels in his creatures' names.

Bollywood, of course, disagrees with me; our cinematic history is full of the titles of movies being chosen, amended, or misspelled on astrological or numerological grounds. (Think of that absurd second *u* in *Ek Duuje Ke Liye* or the bizarre extra *e* in *Kabhi Khushi Kabhie Ghum*.) Actors, too, have had their names tampered with for luck: I recall the actor Rakesh Roshan, after a couple of undeserved flops, trying his hand at being Raakesh Roshan for a film or two before giving up and finding success behind the camera rather than in front of it. And wasn't Raaj Kumar a plain "Rajkumar" once upon a time?

Not that other fields are immune from the contagion. As a longtime cricket fan, few things drove me as much up the wall about the exhilarating and exasperating Krishnamachari Srikkanth as that irritating second *k* in his surname. Was it idiosyncrasy, illiteracy, or numerology? After all, no Indian language renders this Sanskritic name with a double *k* sound.

But in all fairness, I have to admit that the rendering of Indian names into English follows few consistent principles to begin with. Why do many Maharashtrian names end in *e* (as in Borde or Godse) when they could as easily be spelt with an *ay* (as in Mhambray or Thipsay)? Even more confusingly, why do the Sinhalese use the same *e* ending (as in Ranasinghe) to convey not the *ay* sound but the "uh," the half vowel that comes at the end of many Sanskritic names? Yet that only reaffirms my point: spellings vary for assorted reasons, so do people's fates, but a correlation would be impossible to find.

Do Naidus, Nayudus, and Naidoos enjoy different kinds of divine benediction? And what about those Bengalis who spell their common name Mukherjee, Mukherji, Mukherjea, Mookerjee, and even Mukherjei, because the Brits couldn't wrap their tongues around Mukhopadhyaya?

Spelling cannot disguise, let alone alter, the essential nature of the thing itself — the person, the name, the title, the book, the film so labeled. As Gertrude Stein so memorably put it, a rose is a rose is a rose, whatever else you choose to call it, and Shakespeare beat her to it by famously asking whether a rose by any other name wouldn't smell as sweet. (If it were spelled "roase," though, it might not look as attractive.) Bollywood might hope that a different spelling on the marquee would alter an actress's fortunes, but would it matter whether a woman was Priti, Preeti, Preety, or even Preity as long as she was pretty?

Of course not. But nonetheless, we are all wedded to our own spellings — to the ways in which we are used to seeing our own names written down. I can only hope that some Indians will stop writing to me as Sasi Tarur.

45

Indian Realities,
Virtual and Spiritual

O
N A RECENT HOLIDAY IN BANGALORE, I made two trips out of the city that captured, within a span of forty-eight hours, a simple truth about the Indian reality.

Late one night I set out on a four-hour drive with my mother to the town of Puttaparthi in the southern Indian state of Andhra Pradesh. We arrived after 2 A.M. in a remarkably well-lit and orderly town. Buildings gleamed white against the streetlights; the sidewalks, patrolled by volunteers even at that hour, seemed freshly scrubbed. Puttaparthi, once a humble Andhra village like so many others, had become a boomtown as the birthplace and headquarters of the spiritual leader Sathya Sai Baba.

My mother had been a devotee for eighteen years, attending prayer meetings of Sai Baba followers around the world and singing devotional *bhajans*. I was a skeptic myself, but joined her among the early-morning gathering of thousands, all waiting patiently for a glimpse of the great man. Sai Baba emerged in his long ochre robe and made a stately progress through the throng. He paused here and there to accept a petition from a believer, or to materialize *vibhuti* (sacred ash) from his palm into the cupped hands of a worshiper. We were privileged to be invited through an ornate door into a small room for a private audience. There we were joined by two other groups that had been similarly favored: an Indian family of three and half a dozen Iranian pilgrims, wearing green scarves that proclaimed their Islamic faith. They looked up at him with folded hands, their adoration glistening in their eyes.

"Would you like something from me?" Sai Baba asked me.

"Peace of mind for my mother," I replied.

"Yes, yes," he said somewhat impatiently, "but would you like a gift from me?"

"Whatever you give me is for my mother," I replied. He waved his hand in the air and opened his palm. In it nestled a gold ring with nine embedded stones, a *navratan*. He slipped it on my finger, remarking, "See how well it fits. Even a goldsmith would have needed to measure your finger." He shook some *vibhuti* into my mother's grateful hands before taking the Indian family into an inner chamber for what devotees called an "interview."

While they were gone, my mother expressed disappointment about the meager quantity of the ash she had received. But soon it was our turn for a private interview, and no sooner were we alone with Baba than he materialized a little silver urn for her, overflowing with *vibhuti*. "It was as if he had heard what I wanted," my mother breathed.

The encounter was indeed astonishing at several levels. In our private talk, Sai Baba uttered insights about my family and myself that he could not possibly have known. He has a habit, disconcerting at first, of turning his palm quizzically outward and staring off into the distance, as if silently interrogating an unseen, all-knowing source. Sometimes he scribbles in the air with a finger as if dashing off a note to a celestial messenger. And then he says things which are sometimes banal, sometimes profound, and sometimes both (if only because so much of what he says has become worn out by repetition and frequent quotation, including in signs on the streets outside). His manifesting gifts from thin air is startling; he "transformed" a metal ring worn by one of the Iranians to a gold one, then returned his original to him as well.

But a skilled magician can do that, and it would be wrong to see Sai Baba as a conjurer. He has channeled the hopes and energies of his followers into constructive directions, both spiritual and philanthropic.

Everything at his complex is staffed by volunteers who rotate through Puttaparthi at well-organized two-week intervals; while we were there, the volunteers were all from Madhya Pradesh, and it was to be Orissa's turn next. Many left distinguished positions behind to serve. ("I once asked a man washing a window where he was from," mused a visitor, "and he said he was the Chief Justice of Sikkim.") The free hospital in Puttaparthi, which I visited, is one of the best in India; many reputed doctors volunteer their services to him. Sai Baba has built schools and colleges, and is currently undertaking a project to bring irrigation to a number of parched southern districts.

The next day I drove from Bangalore in a different direction, to the campus of Infosys, India's leading computer technology firm. It, too, wore the clean and scrubbed look I had seen at Puttaparthi. But there were no temples here, no pavilions thronged with devotees. Instead, escorted by the company's affable CEO, Nandan Nilekani, I saw the world's leading software museum, a state-of-the-art teleconference center, classrooms with sophisticated video equipment, and a work environment that could not be bettered in any developed country. Infosys is a world leader in information technology services, providing consulting, systems integration, and applications development services to some of the biggest firms in the world. Infosys's then thirteen thousand staff (known in the company's argot as "Infoscions") worked in over thirty offices around the world. In Bangalore they sit amid lush landscaped greenery dotted with pools, recharge themselves at an ultramodern gym ("the best in Asia," Nandan said lightly), display their creativity at a company art gallery, and enjoy a choice of nine food courts for their lunchtime snacks. I marveled at the sophistication and affluence visible in every square inch of the campus. "We wanted to prove," Nandan explained, "that this could be done in India."

Sai Baba and Infosys are both faces of twenty-first-century India. One produces rings out of the ether and urges people to be better human beings; the other deals in a different form of virtual reality and helps human beings to better themselves. One runs free hospitals and schools; the other seeks to bring the benefits of technology to a country still mired in millennial poverty. In the 1950s, Prime Minister Jawaharlal Nehru declared dams and factories to be "the new temples of modern India." What he failed to recognize was that the old temples continued to maintain their hold on the Indian imagination. The software programs of the new information technology companies dotting Bangalore's "Silicon Plateau" may be the new mantras of India, but they supplement, rather than supplant, the old mantras. Programming and prayers are both part of the contemporary Indian reality.

Sai Baba and Infosys are emblematic of an India that somehow manages to live in several centuries at once. On our way out of Puttaparthi, my mother and I had a brief word with a devotee who was lining up to buy a packet of *vibhuti* to take home with him. "What do you do?" I asked.

"I am," he replied proudly, a cell phone glinting in his shirt pocket, "a project manager at Infosys."

46

The Prehistory of Indian Science

WHILE WORKING ON A SHORT BIOGRAPHY of Jawaharlal Nehru (*Nehru: The Invention of India*), I became conscious of the extent to which we have taken for granted one vital legacy of his: the creation of an infrastructure for excellence in science and technology, which has become a source of great self-confidence and competitive advantage for the country today. Nehru was always fascinated by science and scientists. He made it a point to attend the annual Indian Science Congress every year, and he gave free rein (and taxpayers' money) to scientists in whom he had confidence to build high-quality institutions. Men like Homi Bhabha and Vikram Sarabhai constructed the platform for Indian accomplishments in the fields of atomic energy and space research; they and their successors have given the country a scientific establishment without peer in the developing world.

Nehru's establishment of the Indian Institutes of Technology (and the spur they provided to other lesser institutions) has produced many of the finest minds in America's Silicon Valley. Today, an IIT degree is held in the same reverence in the United States as one from MIT or Caltech, and India's extraordinary leadership in the software industry is the indirect result of Jawaharlal Nehru's faith in scientific education. Nehru left India with the world's second-largest pool of trained scientists and engineers integrated into the global intellectual system, to a degree without parallel outside the developed West.

And yet the roots of Indian science and technology go far deeper than Nehru. I was reminded of this yet again by a remarkable book, *Lost Discoveries,* by the American writer Dick Teresi. Teresi's book studies the ancient non-Western foundations of modern science, and though he ranges from the Babylonians and Mayans to Egyptians and other Africans, it is his references to India that caught my eye. And how astonishing those are! The Rig Veda asserted that gravitation held the universe together twenty-four centuries before the apple fell on Newton's head. The Vedic civilization — broadly, that of Aryan India from 1500 B.C. to 500 A.D. — subscribed to the idea of a spherical earth at a time when everyone else, even the Greeks, assumed the earth was flat. By the fifth century A.D. Indians had calculated that the age of the earth was 4.3 billion years; as late as the nineteenth century, English scientists believed the earth was 100 million years old, and it was only in the late twentieth century that Western scientists estimated the earth to be about 4.6 billion years old.

If I were to pick one field to focus on, it would be that of mathematics. India invented modern numerals (known to the world as "Arabic" numerals because the West got them from the Arabs, who learned them from us!). It was an Indian who first conceived of the zero, *shunya;* the concept of nothingness, *shunyata,* integral to Hindu and Buddhist thinking, simply did not exist in the West. ("In the history of culture," wrote Tobias Dantzig in 1930, "the invention of zero will always stand out as one of the greatest single achievements of the human race.") The concept of infinite sets of rational numbers was understood by Jain thinkers in the sixth century B.C. Our forefathers can take credit for geometry, trigonometry, and calculus; the "Bakhshali manuscript," seventy leaves of bark dating back to the early centuries of the Christian era, reveals fractions, simultaneous equations, quadratic equations, geometric progressions, and even calculations of profit and loss, with interest.

Indian mathematicians invented negative numbers: the British mathematician Lancelot Hogben, grudgingly acknowledging this, suggested ungraciously that "perhaps because the Hindus were in debt more often than not, it occurred to them that it would also be useful to have a number which represents the amount of money one owes." (That theory would no doubt also explain why Indians were the first to understand how to add, multiply, and subtract from zero — because zero was all, in Western eyes, we ever had.)

The Sulba Sutras, composed between 800 and 500 B.C., demonstrate that India had Pythagoras's theorem before the great Greek was born, and a way of getting the square root of two correct to five decimal places. (Vedic Indians solved square roots in order to build sacrificial altars of the proper size.) The Kerala mathematician Nilakantha wrote sophisticated explanations of the irrationality of pi before the West had heard of the concept. The Vedanga Jyotisha, an astrological treatise written around 500 B.C., declares: "Like the crest of a peacock, like the gem on the head of a snake, so is mathematics at the head of all knowledge." (Our mathematicians were poets, too!) But one could go back even earlier, to the Harappan civilization, for evidence of a highly sophisticated system of weights and measures in use around 3000 B.C.

Archaeologists also found a "ruler" made with lines drawn precisely 6.7 millimeters apart with an astonishing level of accuracy. The "Indus inch" was a measure in consistent use throughout the area. The Harappans also invented kiln-fired bricks, less permeable to rain and floodwater than the mud bricks used by other civilizations of the time. The bricks contained no straw or other binding material and so turned out to be usable five thousand years later when a British contractor dug them up to construct a railway line between Multan and Lahore. And though they were made in fifteen different sizes, the Harappan bricks were amazingly consistent: their length, width, and thickness were invariably in the ratio of 4:2:1.

"Indian mathematical innovations," writes Teresi, "had a profound effect on neighboring cultures." The greatest impact was on Islamic culture, which borrowed heavily from Indian numerals, trigonometry, and analemma. Indian numbers probably arrived in the Arab world in 773 A.D. with the diplomatic mission sent by the Hindu ruler of Sind to the court of the Caliph al-Mansur. This gave rise to the famous arithmetical text of al-Khwarizmi, written around 820 A.D., which contains a detailed exposition of Indian mathematics, in particular the usefulness of the zero. With Islamic civilization's rise and spread, knowledge of Indian mathematics reached as far afield as Central Asia, North Africa, and Spain. "In serving as a conduit for incoming ideas and a catalyst for influencing others," Teresi adds, "India played a pivotal role."

For a nation still obsessed by astrology, it is ironic that Indians established the field of planetary astronomy, identifying the relative distance of the known planets from the sun, and figured out that the moon is nearer to the earth than the sun. A hymn of the Rig Veda extols *"nakshatra-vidya"*; the Vedas' awareness of the importance of the sun and the stars is manifest in several places. The Siddhantas are among the world's earliest texts on astronomy and mathematics; the Surya Siddhanta, written about 400 A.D., includes a method for finding the times of planetary ascensions and eclipses. The notion of gravitation, or *gurutvakarshan,* is found in these early texts. "Two hundred years before Pythagoras," writes Teresi, "philosophers in northern India had understood that gravitation held the solar system together, and that therefore the sun, the most massive object, had to be at its center."

The Kerala-born genius Aryabhata was the first human being to explain, in 499 A.D., that the daily rotation of the earth on its axis is what accounted for the daily rising and setting of the sun. (His ideas were so far in advance of his time that many later editors of his awe-inspiring *Aryabhattiya* altered the text to save his reputation from what they thought were serious errors.) Aryabhata conceived of the elliptical orbits of the planets a thousand years before Kepler, in the West, came to the same conclusion (having assumed, like all Europeans, that planetary orbits were circular rather than elliptical). Aryabhata even estimated the value of the year at 365 days, six hours, twelve minutes, and thirty seconds; in this he was only a few minutes off (the correct figure is just under 365 days and six hours). The translation of the *Aryabhattiya* into Latin in the thirteenth century taught Europeans a great deal; it also revealed to them that an Indian had known things that Europe would only learn of a millennium later.

If Aryabhata was a giant of world science, his successors as the great Indian astronomers, Varamahira and Brahmagupta, have left behind vitally important texts that space does not allow me to summarize here. The mathematical excellence of Indian science sparkles through their work; Indian astronomers advanced their field by calculations rather than deductions from nature. Teresi says that "Indian astronomy, perhaps more than any other, has served as the crossroads and catalyst between the past and the future of the science." Inevitably, Indian cosmology was also in advance of the rest of the world. Teresi's book has a fascinating section relating Hindu creation myths to modern cosmology; he discusses the notion of great intermeshing cycles of creation and destruction and draws stimulating parallels with the big bang theory that currently commands the field.

The ancient Indians were no slouches in chemistry, which emerges in several verses of the Atharva Veda, composed around 1000 B.C. Two thousand years later, Indian practical chemistry was still more advanced than Europe's. The historian Will Durant wrote that the Vedic Indians were "ahead of Europe in industrial chemistry; they were masters of calcination, distillation, sublimation, steaming, fixation, the production of light without heat, the mixing of anesthetic and soporific powders, and the preparation of metallic salts, compounds, and alloys." An Indian researcher, Udayana, studied gases by filling bladders and balloons with smoke, air, and assorted gases. The ancient Jain thinkers predicted the notion of opposite electrical charges and advanced a notion of the "spin" of particles, which would not be discovered by the West till the twentieth century.

So what about physics? Indian metaphysicists came upon the idea of atoms centuries before the Greek Democritus, known in the West as the father of particle physics. In 600 B.C. Kanada established a theory of atoms in his Vaisesika Sutra; the Jains went further in later years, expounding a concept of elementary particles. Indians also came closer to quantum physics and other current theories than anyone else in the ancient world.

The Upanishadic concepts of *svabhava* — the inherent nature of material objects — and *yadrchha* (the randomness of causality) are startlingly modern. The Upanishads developed the first classifications of matter, evolving into an awareness of the five elements and later of the five senses. When the Samkhya philosophers explained, in the sixth century B.C., that "the material universe emanates out of *prakriti,* the rootless root of the universe," they anticipated Aristotle. And when Indian philosophers spoke of *maya,* or that which gives illusory weight to the universe, they did so in terms that evoke the twentieth-century idea of the Higgs field, the all-pervasive invisible field so beloved of particle physicists, which gives substance to illusion.

Which brings us back to technology. Did India have any technology of its own before the IITs? The answer is an emphatic yes. I have already mentioned the extraordinary achievements of the Harappan civilization, which included terra-cotta ceramics fired at high temperatures, a sophisticated system of weights and measures, and sanitary engineering skills in advance of the West of the nineteenth century. Our skill at digging up, cutting, and polishing diamonds goes back millennia. In the sixth century A.D. India made the highest-quality sword steel in the world. Iron suspension bridges came from Kashmir; printing and papermaking were known in India before anywhere in the West; Europeans sought Indian shipbuilding expertise; our textiles were rated the best in the world till well into the colonial era. But we were never very good with machinery; we made our greatest products with skilled labor. That was, in the end, how the British defeated us.

47

The Anatomy of Civil Conflict

ESPITE HAVING EARNED A PH.D. IN INTERNATIONAL POLITICS twenty-nine years ago, I have always squirmed a little at the expression "political science." For all its fountains of theory and the associated outpourings of academic jargon, I always suspected that political studies were not and could not be a science because the best political analyses, in my view, were those that drew from the art of understanding human behavior. A journalist's eye, even a novelist's heart, I felt, were preferable in this field to a scientist's microscope and petri dish.

An Indian scholar has proved me wrong. Ashutosh Varshney, a forty-five-year-old scholar from Allahabad, currently associate professor of political science at the University of Michigan — by way of Massachusetts Institute of Technology, Harvard, and Notre Dame — has published a book, *Ethnic Conflict and Civil Life: Hindus and Muslims in India,* that has been ten years in the making and seems likely to prove seminal in its impact on the field. And it is indeed a work of science, based on comprehensive and wide-ranging field research, overflowing with charts and graphs and tables, testing a hypothesis assuredly as any lab scientist in a white coat, and coming up with answers (and further questions) that should offer further possibilities to a whole generation of political scientists to follow.

The thesis is deceptively simple: the greater the patterns of intercommunal civic engagement in a city, the lower the likelihood of violent conflict and communal riots. To prove this, Varshney examines three pairs of Indian cities: Aligarh and Calicut (Kozhikode); Hyderabad and Lucknow; Ahmedabad and Surat. In each pair, the demographics of the two cities are similar, with broadly comparable percentages of Muslims, but one of the pair is riot prone and the other is not.

Varshney asks, why not? What is there about Calicut that makes it a less likely site of Hindu-Muslim violence than Aligarh? He delves into history, studies the social and cultural factors, analyzes the politics of each place — but concludes that the real difference is that in Calicut but not in Aligarh, Hindus and Muslims engage with one another in strong associational forms of civic life, from political parties and nonreligious movements for social justice or land reform to trade unions and business groups. In Calicut, caste is a more important divider than religion, whereas in Aligarh much of Muslim civic life takes place within the Muslim community. Varshney extends the analysis, with obvious variations for local color, to the other pairs of cities, and arrives at the same conclusion.

Varshney's central insight is invaluable, and its buttressing with an impressive array of facts and figures from over seven years of research means that it is solidly grounded. Varshney has no illusions about how riots are instigated and manipulated: whatever the proximate trigger for violence, there is always a politician with an ax to grind, pulling the strings, inflaming passions, exploiting the victims for purely political ends. But his point remains that the chances for success of such politicians (he calls the breed "riot-entrepreneurs") would be remarkably lower if there is vigorous and communally integrated civic life, not just through everyday casual contact but through formal associations that consolidate the mutual engagement of the two communities. The Hindus of Varanasi would not attack the Muslim artisans who make the masks and effigies for the annual Ram Lila, even if an irresponsible and bigoted politician egged them on to do so.

Since the tragic events in Gujarat shook my faith in this economically highly developed state, Varshney's chapters on Ahmedabad and Surat are particularly fascinating. Varshney describes two cities, which were largely peaceful communally but succumbed later. Since 1969, Ahmedabad has been one of the most riot-prone cities in the nation, and Surat's shantytowns suffered terribly after 1992. He asks why the civic structures of peace broke down in these cities. His answer is troubling. From the 1920s onward, Gandhian nationalism created a strong level of civic associational activity across communal lines, with the cadre-based Congress Party creating labor unions and mass-rooted social organizations that welded the society together before Partition. Gujarat's business associations were also intercommunal.

But the weakening of the Congress Party as a civic institution following its rise to power, the enfeeblement of the trade unions, and the emergence of new, less communally integrated organizations made the descent to violence in recent years possible. If Varshney is right, the increasing polarization we are seeing in the aftermath of the Gujarat horrors will make matters worse, not better, since the prospects for an integrated civic life in many parts of the state have worsened after the riots.

It has to be asked — and Varshney raises the question toward the end of his fine book — whether his findings could be relevant to the rest of the world. He seems to think so, though he acknowledges that much more research will have to be done. Having dealt with the former Yugoslavia myself, I think his thesis would falter there, because this was a thoroughly integrated society where 22 percent of the population either lived in mixed marriages or was the product of them. Yet people turned against each other in the most brutal way, with neighbors killing and raping neighbors — the very people with whom they went to school or belonged to the same chess club (or the same branch of the local Communist Party).

This might be the exception that proves Varshney's rule; perhaps one day a scholar will apply the same level of scientific rigor to research civic life in the former Yugoslavia as Varshney has in India.

317

The results would be worth waiting for. Ashutosh Varshney has written a rich, complex book, meticulously researched, exhaustively analytical, and carefully argued. It is a fine work of scholarship that has broken new ground in the field of political science. But its greatest value lies not in academics but with those who must make public policy — the politicians and policemen in whose hands lies the safety of Indian citizens the next time a riot is instigated.

The promotion of Hindu-Muslim civic engagement, Varshney has demonstrated, is now an urgent priority for India's leaders if we are to prevent the spiraling descent into communal violence whose worst manifestations were seen in Gujarat.

48

Stephanians in the House

THE STARTLING NEWS THAT NO FEWER THAN TWELVE of my fellow Stephanians — alumni of that bastion of elite liberal education, Delhi's St. Stephen's College — currently hold seats in Parliament, and that eight of them were actually elected to the Lok Sabha, has provoked in me a mild state of astonishment.

The roster of Stephanians in the Lower House is impressive enough: Mani Shankar Aiyer, Kapil Sibal, Lakshman Singh, Sachin Pilot, Manvendra Shaha, Dushyant Singh, Sandeep Dikshit, and Rahul Gandhi. Add to these Natwar Singh, Ashwani Kumar, Arun Shourie, and Chandan Mitra in the Rajya Sabha, and one's surprise is complete. In my time Stephanians were expected to go into the IAS and IFS, not to enter politics. And they conquered *babu*dom in large numbers every year, rising to the highest ranks of the civil service but believing profoundly that politics was not for them.

I have never forgotten the college's annual "Games Dinner" of 1974–75, which I, never proficient at games of any sort, was invited to attend as the elected president of the College Students' Union. Our guest speaker that night was a distinguished Stephanian of royal descent, an Additional Secretary to the government of India and a civil servant known to be well connected to the ruling family. He surveyed us, seventeen- to twenty-two-year-olds with bright eyes

319

and scrubbed faces, and chose to express a candor none of us was accustomed to from Indian officialdom. "I look at you all," he said bluntly, "the best and the brightest of our fair land, smart, honest, and able, and my heart sinks. Because I know that most of you will do what I did and take the civil service examinations, little realizing that if you succeed, your fate will be to take orders from the dregs of our society — the politicians." He could see the shock on the faces of his audience as he went on: "Don't make the mistake I did. Do something else with your lives."

I have never forgotten the speech, thinking about which kept me awake most of that night — and helped change my own career plans. If someone as successful and important in the bureaucracy as he could feel this way, I wondered, what satisfaction could ordinary people without his rank or connections derive from government service?

Nor have I forgotten the speaker, whom I have had the privilege of meeting many times since. He was Kanwar Natwar Singh, star of the IFS, who went on to put his money where his mouth was: he resigned from the government before he could attain the foreign secretaryship that most of his peers considered inevitable, and entered politics instead. This gave him a stint as minister of state for external affairs, where he could give orders to the foreign secretary of the day; and for two years he was India's foreign minister.

This transformation from diplomacy to politics — from pinstripes to *khadi* — was extremely unusual even when Mani Shankar Aiyar followed in Natwar Singh's footsteps. But it became possible because of the unexpected ascent of Rajiv Gandhi to the prime ministry in 1984, which brought to power the kind of Indian almost completely unrepresented in Indian politics. The Stephanian kind.

How can one describe them? There are many of us, but, among India's multitudes, we are few. We have grown up in the cities of India, secure in a national rather than local identity, which we express in English better than in any Indian language. We rejoice in the complexity and diversity of our India, of which we feel a conscious part; we have friends of every caste and religious community, and we marry across such sectarian lines. We see the poverty, suffering, and conflict in which a majority of our fellow citizens are mired, and we clamor for new solutions to these old problems, solutions we believe can come from the skills and efficiency of the modern world. We are secular, not in the sense that we are irreligious or unaware of the forces of religion, but that we believe religion should not determine public policy or individual opportunity.

And, in Indian politics, we used to be pretty much irrelevant.

Usually, we don't get a look in. We don't enter the fray because we can't win. We tell ourselves ruefully that we are able, but not electable. We don't have the votes: there are too few of us, and we don't speak the idiom of the masses. Instead we have learned to talk about political issues without the expectation that we would be able to do anything about them.

Rajiv Gandhi epitomized the breed, dismissed by so many as the *baba-log* (pampered children). When he came to office he was unlike any Indian political figure I had ever met. He had nothing in common with the professional politicians we had taught ourselves to despise, sanctimonious windbags clad hypocritically in homespun who spouted socialist rhetoric while amassing private wealth through the manipulation of political favors. And at a time when casteists and religious fanatics were attempting to redefine India and Indianness on their own terms, I was proud to have an Indian leader who belonged to no single region, caste, or community, but to the all-embracing India I called my own. By simply being Rajiv Gandhi, he represented a choice it was vital for India to have.

It didn't last. He failed at his first attempt in office, and I was not alone in regretting that he did not more effectively act upon the convictions of his upbringing. At the second attempt, a suicide bomber deprived India of that choice. With Rajiv Gandhi's passing, there was no longer any Indian political leader of whom it could be said that his appeal was truly national, and in the spectrum of alternatives available to Indians, that loss was disenfranchisement indeed.

All that is now changing. Twelve Stephanians in Parliament, with more (the likes of Salman Khurshid, Montek Singh Ahluwalia, and Sheila Dikshit) behind the throne! And, to paraphrase Macaulay, others in politics who may not have earned the Stephanian label but are "Stephanian in tastes, in opinions, in morals, and in intellect" (like ministers P. Chidambaram, Praful Patel, and Jairam Ramesh and parliamentarians like Milind Deora). The political landscape may not have been irretrievably transformed, but we at last have a breed of politicians who have a chance to prove they can do better than "the dregs of society."

Of course, as that very phrase suggests, there is a danger here, too. The very name St. Stephen's conjures up in the minds of some critics three overlapping concepts, none of which is meant to be flattering: elitism, Anglophilia, and deracination.

Whether it is a good thing that so many Stephanians are in Parliament, there is certainly a spirit that can be called Stephanian: I spent three years (1972–75) living and celebrating it. Stephania was both an ethos and a condition to which we aspired. Elitism was part of it, but by no means the whole. In any case, the college's elitism was still elitism in an Indian context, albeit one shaped, like so many Indian institutions, by a colonial legacy. There is no denying that the aim of the Cambridge Brotherhood in founding St. Stephen's in 1881 was to produce more obedient subjects to serve Her Britannic Majesty; their idea of constructive missionary activity was to bring the intellectual and social atmosphere of Camside to the dry dust plains of Delhi. Improbably enough, they succeeded, and the resultant hybrid outlasted the Raj. St. Stephen's in the early 1970s was an institution whose students sustained a Shakespeare Society and a Criterion Club, staged avant-garde plays and wrote execrable poetry, ran India's only faculty-sanctioned practical joke competition (in memory of P. G. Wodehouse's irrepressible Lord Ickenham), invented the "Winter Festival" of collegiate cultural competition, which was imitated at universities across the country, invariably reached the annual intercollegiate cricket final (and turned up in large numbers to cheer the Stephanian cricketers on to their accustomed victory), maintained a careful distinction between the Junior Common Room and the Senior Combination Room, and allowed the world's only non-Cantabrigian "gyps" to serve their meals and make their beds. And if the punts never came to the Jamuna, the puns flowed on the pages of *Kooler Talk* and the cyclostyled *Spice* (whose typing mistakes, under the impish editorship of Ramu Damodaran, were deliberate, and deliberately hilarious). And Stephanians wryly acknowledged the charge of disconnection from the masses by organizing union debates on such subjects as "In the opinion of this House, the opinion of this House does not matter."

This was the St. Stephen's I knew, and none of us who lived and breathed the Stephanian air saw any alien affectation in it. For one thing, St. Stephen's also embraced the Hindi movies at Kamla Nagar, the trips to Sukhiya's *dhaba* and the chowchow at TibMon (as the Tibetan Monastery was called); the nocturnal Informal Discussion Group saw articulate discussion of political issues, and the Social Service League actually went out and performed social service; and even for the "pseuds," the height of career aspiration was the IAS, not some foreign multinational. The Stephanian could hardly be deracinated and still manage to bloom. It was against Indian targets that the Stephanian set his goals, and by Indian assumptions that he sought to attain them. (Feminists, please do not object to my pronouns: I only knew St. Stephen's before its coedification.)

At the same time St. Stephen's was, astonishingly for a college in Delhi, insulated to a remarkable extent from the prejudices of middle-class Indian life. It mattered little where you were from, which Indian language you spoke at home, what religious faith you espoused. When I joined college in 1972 from Calcutta, the son of a Keralite newspaper executive, I did not have to worry about fitting in: we were all minorities at St. Stephen's and all part of one eclectic polychrome culture. Five of the preceding ten Student Union presidents had been non-Delhiite non-Hindus (four Muslims and a Christian), and they had all been fairly elected against candidates from the "majority" community.

But at St. Stephen's, religion and region were not the distinctions that mattered: what counted was whether you were "in residence" or a "dayski" (day scholar), a "science type" or a "ShakSoc type," a sportsman or a univ topper (or best of all, both). Caste and creed were no bar, but these other categories determined your share of the Stephanian experience.

This blurring of conventional distinctions was a crucial element of Stephania. "Sparing" (or hanging about) with the more congenial of your comrades in residence — though it could leave you with a near-fatal faith in coffee, conversation, and crosswords as ends in themselves — was manifestly more important than attending classes. (And in any case, you learned as much from approachable faculty members like David Baker and Mohammed Amin outside the classroom as inside it.) Being ragged outside the back gate of Miranda House, having a late coffee in your block tutor's room, hearing outrageous (and largely apocryphal) tales about recent Stephanians who were no longer around to contradict them, seeing your name punned with in *Kooler Talk,* all were integral parts of the Stephanian culture, and of the ways in which this culture was transmitted to each successive batch of Stephanians.

Three years is, of course, a small — and decreasing — proportion of my life, and of course I was at St. Stephen's at an age when any experience would have had a lasting effect. But in celebrating Stephania I think of its atmosphere and history, its student body and teaching staff, its sense of itself and how that sense was communicated to each individual character in the Stephanian story. Too many Indian colleges are places for lectures, rote learning, memorizing, regurgitation; St. Stephen's encouraged random reading, individual note-taking, personal tutorials, extracurricular development. Elsewhere you learned to answer the questions, at college to question the answers. Some of us went further, and questioned the questions.

Politics has never been a noble profession, but in every democracy it is a necessary one. The quality of our politicians inevitably affects the quality of our democracy. Perhaps it is time for more Stephanians to set aside their preparations for the IAS exams and seek to serve their country in elective office instead.

49

Ayurveda Takes Off

"AYURVEDA GOES GLOBAL," BLAZED THE HEADLINE in a leading Indian weekly. The cover story waxed eloquent about the West's discovery of this five-thousand-year-old Indian discipline, dropping the names of celebrities who have turned to our traditional remedies to cure their postmodern ailments — Naomi Campbell, Demi Moore, Cherie Blair, and the ubiquitous Madonna were prominently mentioned. "Ayurveda continues to grow rapidly as one of the most important systems of mind-body medicine, natural healing, and traditional medicine," the article quoted a Dr. David Frawley as saying, "as the need for natural therapies, disease prevention, and a more spiritual approach to life becomes ever more important in this ecological age." That sounds like an appropriately New Age sentiment, but tellingly, the article calculates the success of this otherworldly science in material terms: ayurveda, it seems, accounts for $60 billion of a $120 billion "global herbal market."

And therein, if I may coin a phrase, lies the rub. There is no argument about the increasing popularity of ayurveda: clinics professing to offer ayurvedic treatments are sprouting like herbs in places as far afield as London and the Italian Dolomites, and "ayurvedic tourism" is already a significant money earner for our national exchequer.

Kerala has long attracted tourists to its abundant natural beauty, but these days even a glimpse of paradise is not enough to lure jaded international tourists. So Kerala has turned to the past to improve its present. It has resurrected the ancient life-science of ayurveda, which uses herbs and oils concocted millennia ago to promote health and longevity. The state is now dotted with about as many ayurvedic clinics as mango trees. No Kerala hotel worth its name fails to offer, at a minimum, an ayurvedic massage, with more esoteric treatments — a half-hour drip of oils onto your forehead, medicated oil infusions into your nostrils — available at most places. Even several five-star hotels, which not so long ago would have looked down at anything so *desi,* have cashed in on the rage.

But what exactly is it that they are selling? Tourist brochures show a winsome blonde in a bikini being massaged by a lady in a traditional red-bordered white Kerala sari, with jasmine in her hair and a brass lamp at her side. This is effectively packaged exotica: not ayurveda as a remedy for disease, but rather as an upmarket beauty treatment — a relaxation cure for the jaded. A five-thousand-year-old science has become the diversion of choice of the era of the fifteen-second sound bite. "Pamper yourself with the wisdom of the ancients," the slogan might as well say.

"This is not ayurveda," says Dr. Ramkumar of the venerable Arya Vaidya Pharmacy in Coimbatore, which offers the more traditional treatments. "This is a travesty of ayurveda. People are taking what is meant to be a total system of medicine and reducing it to a few superficial treatments. Ayurveda is meant to diagnose and treat the entire person, not one part of his or her body. And the principle behind our treatments is vital. Our massages, for example, are not intended for transient pleasure. In fact, massage is the wrong word for them — they are really oil applications. A doctor determines what are the right oils you need, and they are then applied systematically over a period of time. The benefit of the treatment comes from the oil, not from the rubbing. But instead it is the massage that is being promoted rather than the medicinal purpose of the oil."

True enough. Professional *ayurveds* are also critical of the way in which the cosmetics industry has latched on to ayurveda. The hottest range of beauty products in North America these days — soaps and moisturizers, anti-wrinkle creams and conditioning shampoos — claims to be based on ayurveda. But it calls itself "Aveda," a more digestible brand name, in order to appeal to a mainstream clientele. "Aveda," snorts one *ayurved* dismissively, "that means against the Veda!"

Purists sneer at what they consider the rampant commercialization of a hallowed practice. "Ayurveda is a holistic science," one expert explained to me. "The oils, the herbs, the foods are all part of the treatment. It's not something you can dispense with a pill or an oil rub in an air-conditioned spa."

The Arya Vaidya Pharmacy is doing tremendous work to popularize "real" ayurveda across the country — both former prime minister Vajpayee and former president Narayanan were beneficiaries of their treatments — but it is more of a challenge to get the word out around the world. Most countries — not just in the West — do not recognize ayurveda as a system of medicine, which makes it impossible to export medicines and oils except as "herbal dietary supplements." Ayurvedic practitioners are also not recognized as doctors (though many of them have graduated from a rigorous four-year course taught by the Central College of Ayurveda in India), and as such would not be licensed to treat illnesses. This leaves them little choice but to offer the cosmetic treatments, especially massages, which have less exacting licensing requirements. An ancient science has been reduced to a modern fad.

"You wouldn't go for a bypass and ask the doctor to short-circuit some of the procedures," says Dr. Ramkumar. "Why should you ask an ayurved to do so?"

The answer is that no one has a bypass for pleasure, but some ayurvedic treatments are indeed pleasurable, whether or not they serve a larger medical purpose. One August day, I drove up to the Tamil Nadu hill resort of Kotagiri to spend a blissful twenty-four hours at the Arya Vaidya Pharmacy's Ayurprastha retreat, the former palace of the Travancore Maharajah. I walked in the bracing mountain air, ate organic vegetarian Kerala meals, and treated myself to two ayurvedic massages by an expert therapist. I knew perfectly well that twenty-four hours was not going to redress anything fundamentally wrong with my constitution, but twenty-four hours was all I had, and even if the effects could not possibly be lasting, I felt reinvigorated for the next few days. Is that such a bad thing for India to offer the rushed visitor?

Our ancient traditions evolved in ancient times; if we can adapt them to the present and in the process bring a few of those sixty billion dollars into our country, what's the harm in doing so? We're never going to become a major tourist destination because of our beaches or our shopping malls; no one is going to come to us for our spectacular historic sites because they are so badly maintained and so poorly supported by our infrastructure. The one commodity we have in abundance that the world wants is our ancient wisdom — the spiritual teachings of our sages, including the practice of ayurveda. The purists like Dr. Ramkumar are right that what is being promoted is really "Ayurveda Lite," but let us not allow the best to become the enemy of the good.

No one wants the basic principles of ayurveda to be compromised. But perhaps by popularizing ayurveda in this way we will generate the resources the *ayurveds* need to do their serious work better.

*

"The palace?" the excitement in my mother's voice was palpable. "We're going to stay at the palace?"

"I suppose so," I replied. In booking my annual holiday in India, I opted this year for a change from the usual round of visits to friends and relatives. My mother, my sons, and I would instead play tourist in our native Kerala — and check in to the tony resorts that have recently sprung up around the state. How, I wondered, had the backwater I knew as a kid become a tourist destination?

Each winter, my sisters and I round up our British- and American-reared children and head for Kerala, rather self-consciously "renewing our roots" and instilling in the new generation our same sense of obligation.

But this time, as we visited our crumbling two-hundred-year-old ancestral home in a seemingly timeless village, it was Kerala that had changed. Savvy tourism promoters have lately come to appreciate the region's exceptional beauty. And because Kerala is also the spiritual center of the ancient life-science of ayurveda, with its aromatic oil massages and yoga, New Age travelers have come flocking.

I worked out our itinerary: five top-class resorts in fifteen days — a trip "home" doubling as a real vacation, with us trying out ayurvedic treatments at half a dozen different resorts, many run by the ecologically savvy CGH Earth Group, which offers its guests tours of the compost-processing biogas plants at its hotels.

Some resorts definitely traded authenticity for a more cosmopolitan allure: you could sip a Singapore sling poolside before going in for a massage, blissfully unaware that alcohol is prohibited in ayurveda.

But the majority have clung to ayurveda's origins as Kerala's indigenous medical system, insisting on an on-site interview with a registered ayurvedic practitioner before arranging the appropriate treatments. And only one, the newly restored Kalari Kovilakom in Kollengode, went the whole way, offering its guests all ayurveda, all the time.

My mother couldn't believe it when I e-mailed her. "The palace!"

"What's the big deal?" I asked. "Tourists in Rajasthan have been staying in converted palaces for decades. It's the one thing palaces are good for in our democratic age — serving as hotels."

"You don't understand," Mother replied, "this is the Kovilakom in Kollengode."

Then I caught on. Kollengode, a tiny town miles from anyplace, was where she was born. "When I was a little girl, I used to walk along the outer walls of the palace every day on my way to school," she said. "It looked so immense, so forbidding. It was unimaginable that I could even step into it, let alone stay there. The biggest thrill of my life was when your father and I were invited to tea by the rajah nearly fifty years ago. But even then we sat on an open porch. Visitors were not allowed inside. And now we're going to stay there?"

"Four nights," I said. "The authentic ayurvedic spa experience."

As lunch arrived I looked covetously at the steaming dishes placed before my sons. "I'd like some of what they're having," I said.

The waiter grinned a bit sheepishly. "Sorry, sir," he said, "the doctor has prescribed a different lunch for you."

"You mean my lunch requires a prescription?" I exclaimed. The waiter nodded, unabashed. Welcome, his smile seemed to say, to the serious world of ayurvedic tourism.

No sooner had I checked in than I was interviewed by the resident doctor, Dr. Sreelatha. Her searching questions about my medical history sought to establish which of the three basic ayurvedic "humors" my body ran to — *vaata* (air), *pitta* (bile), or *kapha* (phlegm). Then she determined the types of treatment I'd undergo and the precise combination of oils that would be mixed for my massages. Dr. Sreelatha prescribed the last thing I'd drink at night and the hot water, lemon, and honey with which I'd be roused at 6 A.M. And, as I found out at my first lunch, she decided what I was allowed to eat.

"Ayurveda is not like Western medicine, which treats an individual symptom," she explained. "Your entire lifestyle has to be treated."

And so it was. I sat with my sons on yoga mats with coconut trees swaying in the gentle breeze around us as an Australian swami in saffron robes took us through our exercises. Mother woke up in a royal bedroom and had her breakfast on the very porch she'd visited when young. And just down the road, our ancestral village slumbered on, as farmers with yoked bullocks plowed the fields as their forebears had done for centuries.

I smiled at my mother when she returned from an hour-long ayurvedic massage meant to ease her arthritis. "Welcome home," I said.

Under the good doctor's care, and with wholesome organic vegetarian fare, I began to glow — and even to lose weight. But we were on holiday, and five days after checking in, it was time for me to move on to the beach.

Dr. Sreelatha wouldn't accept my thanks. "You should have stayed at least a month," she said disapprovingly. "Five days of ayurveda isn't enough."

"I'll be back," I promised.

That, of course, is the point of ayurvedic tourism. Don't just get people to come in and breeze out: get them to stay, and to return. In Dr. Sreelatha's words, treat their lifestyle. Even if it means denying them what they want for lunch.

50

In Defense of Delhi

OST OF US INDIANS ARE, I SUPPOSE, ambivalent about our capital city. Its broad avenues, late-colonial architecture, and a general air of well-ordered self-importance goes well with popular notions of what the nation's premier city and seat of government should be like. When Lutyens's aging imperial model was given a multicrore-rupee facelift before the 1982 Asian Games, the new highways, overpasses, and tourist hotels made our rajdhani presentable as well as patrician. New Delhi, its inhabitants tended to assure impressed visitors, wasn't like the rest of India. And they meant it as a compliment.

But, at the same time, another stereotype also existed. The chattering classes lament that Delhi typifies an India that has lost its soul, that it's the epitome of a new concrete culture of "black money," five-star hotels, and shopping malls divorced from tradition, the arts, or the refinements of the higher life. All that was worth cherishing in old Delhi, they moan, has now given way to the overpass and the fast-food counter, both occupied by hustling Punjabis who feel no real sense of belonging to the city and don't even know the history behind the addresses on their visiting cards.

But so what if New Delhi is, as the intelligentsia claim, a parvenu city? It was re-created by those who had lost everything in the partition of the subcontinent — men and women of the Punjab, Sikhs, and Hindus uprooted from the land that had been the home of their ancestors for countless generations, rejects of history who had to carve out their own futures. They worked and struggled and sweated to make it. They were unencumbered by the baggage of the past, for the past had betrayed them. They succeeded; and as a result of their efforts, they created the first truly postcolonial Indian city.

So families that had trudged across the frontier as refugees to-day drive shining Suzukis across superhighways; people whose parents had lost their houses now sip imported wine in fancy restaurants. But instead of applauding them, educated Indians from Kolkata or Chennai tend to curl their refined lips in scorn. The crass materialism of the archetypal Delhiite is sniffed at, his lack of culture ridiculed, his ignorance of history deplored. Literate North India, for its part, laments the transformation of a Delhi that was once a by-word for elegant poetry, Mughal manners, and courtly civilization.

Old Delhi may indeed have had its attractions, but it was also a moribund place steeped in decay and disease, ossified in communal and caste divisions, exploitative, and unjust. Today's New Delhi — not the musty bureaucratic edifices of government, but the throbbing, thriving agglomeration of factories and TV studios, industrial fairgrounds and software consultancies, nightclubs and restaurants — is a city that reflects the vigor and vitality of those who have made it. It is far and away India's richest city; it provides and reflects a stimulus, unfamiliar to the Indian intelligentsia, of enterprise and risk taking; its people are open and outward-looking. They may have forgotten their history but they remember their politics. They may not know why but they know how.

New Delhi has enshrined performance and effectiveness as more important measures of human worth than family name or pedigree. If, in the process, it has also placed a premium on vulgar ostentation rather than discreet opulence, so be it. The new rich could not have run the old clubs, so they built the new hotels and restaurants. The "five-star culture," for all its vulgarity, is more authentically Indian than the club culture it has supplanted, a musty relic of proto-colonial dress codes and insipid English menus.

It is true that New Delhi lacks a coherent cultural focus. Its physical sprawl, its disaggregated "colonies," ensures that the capital is really twenty townships in search of a city. But as the ambitious new Metro railway proves, it is not a city indifferent to the basic needs of its citizens. Nor is it lacking in creative endeavor. Today, fueled by the money and the people that have poured into the city, there are more plays, exhibitions, and concerts on any single day in New Delhi than anywhere else in India.

New Delhi is also, uniquely, a cosmopolitan society in the international sense. We have always been an overly self-obsessed people; our decades of protectionist policies also drastically reduced, in most other Indian cities, the frequency of routine contact and interchange between Indians and foreigners. Thanks to the diplomats and journalists based there, New Delhi is the one place where Indians of every class benefit from relating to, and seeing themselves in the eyes of, the outside world. (Bangalore is getting there, too, but not on the same scale.)

In its urban openness and economic energy, Delhi reminds me of the bustling coastal ports of a bygone era. With the advent of jet travel and the World Wide Web, you don't need port cities as your principal contacts with the outside world: the "coast" can move inland. New Delhi is India's contemporary equivalent — bustling, heterodox, anti-ritual, prosperous. For all its inadequacies, it is a symbol of a country on the move, the urban flagship of a better tomorrow. It has led India into the twenty-first century, even at the price of forgetting all that happened in the other twenty.

51

NRIs — The "Now Required Indians"

INDIA HAS AN OFFICIAL ACRONYM for its expatriates — NRIs, for "Non-Resident Indians." In my book *India: From Midnight to the Millennium and Beyond,* I jokingly suggested that the real debate was whether NRI stood for "Not Really Indian" or "Never Relinquished India." The nearly twenty-five million people of Indian descent who live abroad fall, of course, into both categories. And in recent years, as the government has set about cultivating them through generous new policies, the establishment of a ministry for overseas Indian affairs and annual Pravsai Bharatiya Divas (Overseas Indians' Day) events in India, it's clear one can apply a third variant to the acronym: "Now Required Indians."

The 1,600 to 2,000 delegates who have flocked annually to India from over sixty different countries for the Pravasi Bharatiya Divas celebrations were firmly in the "Never Relinquished India" camp. They were in India to affirm their claim to it.

I attended one of the Pravasi Bharatiya weekends — the third one, in 2005, which fell on the ninetieth anniversary of the return to India of the most famous NRI of them all, Mahatma Gandhi, who alighted from his South African ship at Bombay's Apollo Bunder port on January 9, 1915. The nativism that has seen Bombay being renamed Mumbai has not diluted the city's dynamic cosmopolitanism.

It still remains the gateway to India, a thriving, bustling, industrious, polyglot beehive of trade and exchange. If Mumbai seems sometimes to be choking on its own traffic, the city's aspirations, both literally and metaphorically, seem limitless. It was the right place to bring the world's largest gathering of NRIs together.

And they came in larger numbers than ever, their enthusiasm undampened by the grim news of the tsunami disaster just two weeks earlier. The vice presidents of Suriname and Mauritius, the former prime ministers of Fiji and Trinidad and Tobago, Malaysian politicians and Gulf-based entrepreneurs, tycoons from Hong Kong and titans from the United States, all united by the simple fact of shared heritage — the undeniable reality that even exiles cannot escape when they look in the mirror. They were united, too, in the words of the typically thoughtful and inspiring inaugural address by Prime Minister Manmohan Singh, by an "idea of Indianness." It is an idea that enshrines the diversity and pluralism both of our country and of its diaspora. In a land and a city that is home to Indians of every conceivable caste and creed, the Pravasi Bharatiya Divas celebrations afforded to Indians — including former Indians — of every conceivable caste and creed the welcome assurance that they were indeed at home.

In his speech, the prime minister traced what he characterized as four waves of Indian emigration: the first, in precolonial times, featured Indians leaving our shores as travelers, teachers, and traders; the second involved the enforced migration of Indian labor as indentured servants of the British Empire; the third, the tragic displacement of millions by the horrors of Partition; and the fourth, the contemporary phenomenon of skilled Indians seeking opportunity and challenge in our globalized world.

I would probably divide the fourth wave further into two distinct categories: one of highly educated Indians, often staying on after studies abroad in places like the United States, and the other of more modestly qualified but even harder-working migrants, from taxi drivers to shop assistants, who for the most part see their migration as temporary and who remit a larger proportion of their funds home to India than their higher-earning counterparts. But in today's world both sets of "fourth wave" migrants remain closely connected to the *matrbhumi* (motherland): ease of communications and travel makes it possible for expatriates to be engaged with the country they left behind in a way that was simply not available to the plantation worker in Mauritius or Guyana a century ago. To tap in to this sense of allegiance and loyalty through an organized public gathering was an inspired idea of the previous government, one that the present government has built upon through its creation of a "one-stop shop" in the form of a dedicated ministry.

So I was mildly surprised by the cynicism of the many *desi* journalists who thrust microphones into my face during the weekend and asked me if it wasn't all a waste of time. "What does a conference like this actually achieve?" they wanted to know. "How is it useful?" This was a remarkably utilitarian approach to the occasion, and I suppose I could have responded by pointing to the many parallel seminars being run by state governments to attract NRI investment, or the session on disaster-management that had been added in the wake of the tsunami.

Many shared the negativism of the journalists. "These NRIs have left the motherland and gone off to make their fortunes elsewhere," wrote A. Mukesh. "They have abandoned India. India does not owe them anything. Indeed, it is they who owe the country that has educated them and given them the opportunity to better their lives abroad." To Mukesh, "The money spent on celebrating the Pravasi Bharatiya Divas would be better spent reconstructing the fishing villages of Tamil Nadu."

Now, with the greatest of respect to Mukesh, I would like to take issue with him (and others who have, in whole or part, echoed his arguments) on several points. First, I was not suggesting that India "owed" its NRIs anything, other than an occasion to affirm their Indianness. Second, while it is a fact that many, perhaps most, of the recent wave of Indian emigrants have benefited from a subsidized education in India before going off to make their living elsewhere, that is not true of many of the *pravasis* in attendance, who are descended from earlier waves of (often forced) emigration to the far-flung outposts of the British Raj a century or more ago, and who return unburdened by any reason for guilt. Third, the reconstruction of fishing villages is, if I may be pardoned the metaphor, a red herring. The choice is a false one: the NRIs are as committed as any resident Indian to tsunami relief and have raised a great deal of money for the purpose. The expenditure on the Pravasi Bharatiya Divas is not diverted from more worthwhile national causes but is, rather, raised specifically for this purpose from sponsors, notably the Federation of Indian Chambers of Commerce and Industry (FICCI), which bears the organizational burden entirely.

But I preferred to make a larger point: sometimes the real value of a conference lies in the conferring. Perhaps it is time we realized that instead of counting how many new millions were raised for tourism in Rajasthan or pledged for reconstruction in Port Blair, we should appreciate how much it means to allow NRIs from sixty-one different lands the chance to share their experiences, celebrate their commonalities, offer their ideas, and swap business cards. Because when India allows its *pravasis* to feel at home, it is India itself that is strengthened.

After all, one can ask the core question: Why do NRIs matter to India?

The answer is simple: as a source of pride, as a source of support, and as a source of investments. It is entirely natural for Indians to take pride in the successes of their erstwhile compatriots abroad. I once remarked rather cruelly to an interviewer that the only country where Indians as a whole did not succeed was India. That is fortunately no longer the case, as signs of Indians' growing prosperity are increasingly evident everywhere one travels in India, but Indians abroad have certainly given us all a great deal to be proud of. One recent statistic from the United States shows that the Indian-American family's median income is nearly $71,000 a year, the same as Japanese-Americans, but nearly $20,000 higher than the figure for all American families. That kind of success is not merely at the elite end of the scale: in England today, Indian curry houses employ more people than the iron and steel, coal, and shipbuilding industries combined. (Many are the ways, indeed, in which the Empire can strike back.)

So we can be proud of the impact Indians have made on foreign societies. But pride is not merely an intangible asset. Living in the United States, I have been struck by the extent to which the success of our NRIs has transformed the public perception of India here. A generation ago, in 1975, when I first traveled to the United States as a graduate student, India was widely seen as a land of snake charmers and begging bowls — poverty marginally leavened by exotica. Today, if there is a stereotypical view of India, it is that of a country of fast-talking high achievers who are wizards at math and are capable of doing most Americans' jobs better, faster, and more cheaply in Bangalore. Today IIT is a brand name as respected in certain American circles as MIT or Caltech. If Indians are treated with more respect as a result, so is India, as the land that produces them. Let us not underestimate the importance of such global respect in our globalizing world.

The presence of successful and influential NRIs in so many countries also becomes a source of direct support for India, as they influence not just popular attitudes, but governmental policies, to the benefit of the mother country. And I haven't even mentioned NRI investments in India — from the remittances of working-class Indians in West Asia that have transformed the Kerala countryside to the millions poured into cutting-edge high-tech businesses in Bangalore or Gurgaon by investors from Silicon Valley. But we shouldn't get carried away — overseas Indians still invest a lower proportion of their resources in India than overseas Chinese do in China. Encouraging them to do more — and giving them reasons to do more — is certainly a worthwhile task for the newly established ministry for overseas Indian affairs in New Delhi.

Which is why I was concerned to hear rumors that the government was contemplating reducing the frequency of the hitherto annual Pravasi Bharatiya gatherings to one every other year. I was quite sure that the minister and his mandarins had not road-tested the

341

idea with a cross section of the attendees. My own conversations, across the board, left me in no doubt that this would be a mistake, since the occasion has clearly acquired a momentum that it would be a shame to disrupt. When a locomotive has been gathering steam, why apply the brakes?

Perhaps the fear is that, with dual citizenship granted, there is not enough new for the government to offer the *pravasis* each time. But that is, in my view, beside the point. The interactions are worthwhile as ends in themselves. No doubt this will mean putting up with new demands from NRIs — voting rights, for instance (India, shamefully, is one of the few democracies that denies the vote to its own expatriate citizens). But so what? A government that seeks the allegiance, support, and money of its diaspora should also be willing to be accountable to it. Hosting a forum once a year where the *pravasis* can make their views known seems to me a very small price to pay indeed.

The dialogue between India and its diaspora has only just begun. Let us not interrupt it.

*

"Oh, you'll feel right at home," a friend from Delhi said when she learned I was traveling to the Gulf for the first time. "The place is crawling with Indians. And most of them aren't just Indians, they're Keralites like you."

This didn't entirely surprise me. My home state of Kerala, with its long sliver of coastline, had long been known for its intrepid travelers. Keralites had plied the waters of the Arabian Sea for millennia, taking cloth and spices to the Arab world, and returning with dates — and gold. Keralites sailed to the Gulf as if it were an outpost of their own land. They brought back wealth and ideas. Islam came to Kerala on the lips of traders and travelers, not by the sword. A society evolved in Kerala of Hindus, Muslims, Christians, and Jews living amicably side by side, open to the influences of the rest of the world. The Chinese came, and either acquired or left behind their fabled fishing-nets. Keralite sailors went to China, and returned with the favorite cooking pot of the Kerala housewife, a wok known in Malayalam as a *cheen-chetti* — literally, a "Chinese pot." Xenophobia is as unknown to the Keralite as snow is to a Bedouin.

As a result, Keralites are all too willing to travel to make their fortunes. And harsh economic reality makes travel necessary. Kerala is an overcrowded place with little industry, so many Keralites have no choice but to seek employment elsewhere. Under the British, the route to advancement for hardworking Kerala men was to learn to type in English and take up clerical work in cities across the subcontinent.

So it was entirely in keeping with the Kerala spirit that, when oil-fueled prosperity caused a boom in the Gulf countries in the 1970s, the people of my home state leapt at the opportunities that arose. There was far more work available than locals to do it, and so Keralites flocked to the Gulf in droves. They took every job, from salesclerks in shops to schoolteachers and yes, stenographers. Perhaps a million Keralites have worked in the Gulf at one time or another; it is estimated that they account for a quarter of all the expatriate workers who have lent their sweat to the Gulf sheikhdoms. At one point in the late 1970s, it was reliably reported that the most populous ethnic group in the Gulf state of Bahrain was not Bahrainis but Keralites.

A generation later, this is no longer true. Economies were not the only things that boomed in the Gulf; demography did, too, and many of the Gulf states doubled and even trebled their populations, leaving fewer openings for foreigners to fill. War and terrorism have not diminished the attractiveness of Gulf salaries, but the first Gulf war witnessed the expulsions of Keralite labor from Kuwait and some of its neighbors, and, though many returned, the numbers just aren't the same. No longer does every other Kerala family boast of at least one member who is remitting part of a Gulf salary home every month. The Malabar Coast is dotted with incongruously fancy abodes rising among thatched-roof dwellings, built on the proceeds of employment in the "Gelf" (as Keralites pronounce it). But today there are fewer garish new mansions being built in Kerala's villages. So I wasn't as sanguine as my Delhiite friend. "I'll believe it," I replied, "when I see it."

Indeed, when I landed in Doha, the capital of the Emirate of Qatar, to be greeted by a young Arab in flowing robes and then driven to my hotel by a chauffeur who spoke only Arabic, I made a mental note to tell my friend how out of date her information was. And there seemed to be more Romanians than Indians on the staff of my five-star hotel. But then, for my first dinner in the country, my host invited me to a fancy restaurant on the water's edge, and I realized I should have stowed my skepticism. The maître d' who greeted us bore a common Muslim name — but he had only to utter a few words to give his identity away. The accent was unmistakable: he was a Keralite. It was the same story with the waiter who took our order and the busboy who cleared the dishes. "Where are you from?" I asked each of them in Malayalam as soon as I heard their accent, each time earning an enthusiastic response and terrific service.

The next day, I visited the offices of Qatar's leading English-language newspaper, the *Gulf Times*. I was formally received by the editor in chief, a distinguished Arab gentleman in robes whose modest conversational English suggested he served as the paper's presiding deity rather than as the wielder of the blue pencil. That role clearly belonged to his vice editor, an experienced Englishman from Liverpool, who duly suggested that I might wish to pay a visit to the newsroom. I gladly shook hands with each of the journalists on duty. And then it struck me: every single one of them, without exception, was from my home state.

"Is there anyone here who isn't from Kerala?" I rather crassly asked the news editor, K. T. Chacko, who was taking me around.

"Oh, there's Ramesh Mathew," came the reply. "He's from Bombay." A sheepish look came over the news editor's face. "But his parents were from Kerala."

Clearly my Delhi friend was absolutely right. Even Doubting Thomas would have felt right at home.

*

"Here," said Mr. Shankardass, leading me to his garden, "we live in heaven."

I looked around the lush African foliage, multicolored flowers ablaze amid the verdant Nairobi green. "It certainly looks like paradise," I replied.

"I don't mean the garden," my eighty-six-year-old host replied. "I mean Kenya." Mr. Shankardass's garden was a metaphor: a fertile place in magnificent bloom, it stood for the life that Indians were able to lead in this corner of East Africa.

Mr. Shankardass and his wife were both born in Kenya, when it was a British colony. They had grown up amid anticolonial ferment, in which most Asians — descended mainly from nineteenth-century migrants and indentured workers from the Indian subcontinent — made common cause with their African fellow subjects. But when independence came, some Africans looked on the Asians as interlopers, foreigners depriving the locals of jobs and economic opportunity. In next-door Uganda in 1972, the dictator Idi Amin gave his entire Asian population seventy-two hours to leave the country for good. The mass expulsion of Ugandan Asians, mainly people who had never known any other home, sent tremors through the Asian community in Kenya and Tanzania as well. But their fears proved unfounded. Asians stayed on in Kenya as honored and respected citizens, building flourishing businesses and excelling in the professions. Mr. Shankardass's garden was emblematic of that.

But I couldn't help wondering, as I devoured a delicious Punjabi lunch on his porch with three generations of his Kenya-born family, whether the garden was an oasis as well, isolating the Asians from the Africans among whom they prospered. Indians abroad are often an insular people, focusing on their own community, customs, and (as I could savor it) cuisine. Did Mr. Shankardass's heaven have room for African angels, too?

It didn't take me long to find out I needn't have worried. Later that day I attended a party in my honor thrown by another Kenyan

Asian, the media entrepreneur Sudhir Vidyarthi, to whom I had been introduced by my good friend and former UN colleague Salim Lone, a Kashmiri Kenyan. Vidyarthi's father had run an anti-British newspaper, the *Colonial Times,* in which the legendary Jomo Kenyatta had first published his nationalist screeds. The elder Vidyarthi had gone to jail for his pains, and his son had continued in the family tradition as a courageous antiestablishment publisher.

Sudhir Vidyarthi's garden, with its outdoor deck and outsized bar, was even grander and more impressive than Mr. Shankardass's, but as fifty guests milled about on the patio, what struck me most was their ethnic mix. An Indian DJ bantered with the African CEO of a rival radio station; a Ugandan Asian journalist questioned the newly appointed government spokesman; a senior government official, a striking woman with a vivid tribal scar down her cheek, held forth to an older lady in a graceful sari. Asians and Africans melded seamlessly into one. "We're all Kenyans here," my host said simply.

A group of Kenyan South Asians was publishing a magazine called Awaaz, subtitled The Authoritative Journal of Kenyan South Asian History. I was given a copy of the latest issue. On the cover was a photo of the recently deceased Pranlal Sheth, a hero of Kenyan independence who was then deported from his country by the Kenyatta government and died in exile in England. If that seemed discouraging, the same issue carried a review of a new play by a Kenyan-Indian playwright Kuldip Sondhi, dealing with shop demolitions in Mombasa. And a portfolio of photographs by the legendary Mohammed Amin, who first broke the news of the Ethiopian famine with his searing pictures, lost a leg in the Somali civil war but went on immortalizing East Africa through his lens till he was killed in a plane crash in 1996.

There was much talk at the party about a new exhibition that had just been mounted by the National Museum of Kenya. It was called "The Asian African Heritage: Identity and History"; through photographs, documents, and artifacts, the exhibition depicted two centuries of Asian assimilation in Kenya. Indian labor had built forts

346

in Kenya as early as the sixteenth century; Indian masons and carpenters had practiced their craft in even larger numbers from 1820; and over 31,000 contract laborers from Punjab and Gujarat had built the famous Mombasa railroad, 2,500 of them perishing in the process. The city of Nairobi (like forty-three other railway towns along the line) was erected by Indian hands.

"This is our home," said Pheroze Nowrojee, who had written the text of the exhibition. "Our social identity rests on our bicontinental tradition. We are both Asian and African. We are Asian African."

Sudhir Vidyarthi soon emerged, proudly holding a little black toddler in his arms. "Meet my new daughter," he beamed. "She's been with us since she was four months old; the official adoption comes through next week." His excitement was as palpable as his affection for the girl, who nibbled at Indian hors d'oeuvres from his palm. "Give Daddy a kiss," he told her in Swahili, and the tiny tot, bits of samosa and kebab still on her lips, duly obliged.

I looked at them — Asian father, African daughter, sharing Indian food and chatting in an East African tongue — and I raised a silent toast to their Kenyan garden. I only wished I knew the Swahili word for heaven.

*

As an Indian who, without actually emigrating, has found himself working abroad all his adult life, I have always had some sympathy for my fellow NRIs. The argument that Indians who work abroad are doing a disservice to their country seems to me misplaced, especially in recent years as Indians abroad gave back to their homeland so much more than they could ever have contributed while staying there. The old fears of a "brain drain" seemed to me to have been supplanted by hopes of a "brain gain," as desi software designers and high-tech gurus from Silicon Valley have opened thriving firms in India, employing their countrymen and women, increasing the country's export revenues and pumping up the national GDP. Indians going abroad after their studies have done a great deal to benefit the Indians who stayed at home.

But one category of Indian professional who emigrates still troubles me. I know it's unfair, but though I am unfazed by the expatriation of our engineers and economists, our scientists and scholars, it still bothers me when I see an Indian doctor settle abroad.

Don't get me wrong. Some of my best friends in the United States are Indian doctors, and I feel no personal desire to uproot them from their lives here and send them back. But whereas our country is so abundantly supplied with talent that few of us living abroad can truly claim that our absence from our native shores makes any negative difference to India, doctors strike me as a different case, mainly for two reasons: they possess knowledge and training that is still in short supply in our country, and the government of India, through its generous subsidies for higher education, has spent a large sum of money helping them to acquire the skills they are taking abroad.

The problem came back to me when I read that Indian doctors in the United States are discovering a new means of staying on legally in America. They are serving the poor.

Under U.S. immigration rules, a foreign doctor — even if he completes his medical schooling in the United States, or does an internship or residency at an American hospital — is obliged to return to his homeland for a period of at least two years before he can seek employment in the United States. There is, however, an exception built into the law. The U.S. government has designated 2,100 areas, mostly impoverished districts at the nadir of the economic recession, as "medically underserved." If a foreign doctor agrees to work in one of these areas, the standard requirement of two years outside the States before working here is lifted. The much sought-after green card, entitling the doctor to permanent residence in the United States, is just a few prescriptions away.

As a result, the brain drain of doctors from developing countries continues while ensuring Americans get medical care even in areas where American doctors wouldn't want to work. There are some 600,000 licensed medical practitioners in the United States, of whom about 120,000 are foreigners. The largest single group of foreign doctors is, of course, from India — no fewer than 25,000. The irony of Indian doctors, who have no lack of poor patients needing their medical skills in their own country, coming to help the American underclass, is considerable.

Few American doctors want to build a practice or make a home in some of the places where Indians are prepared to serve. I remember one *New York Times* piece years ago about one such "medically underserved" area, the town of Welch, West Virginia. The journalist described Welch, a remote outpost in the Appalachian Mountains, as "an economic sinkhole whose coal-mining jobs have been vanishing." Towns like Welch, populated largely by the very poor and the often sick, have little appeal for American doctors, whose principal objective is to earn back the quarter of a million dollars they have spent on their medical education. Even graduates of West Virginian medical schools refuse to work at the local hospital. So Welch has made use of its federal designation to import its doctors. Fifteen of the nineteen doctors in the town hospital were from abroad, including India.

As with lesser professions, from janitors to cab drivers, immigrants are always willing to do the jobs the locals consider beneath them. The easier route to a green card may not, however, be the only incentive for the foreign doctors. The *New York Times* wrote that many found greater professional opportunity in these blighted rural communities, less professional discrimination — and greater material comforts. Typical earnings, the newspaper reported, ranged from $80,000 to $200,000 a year. Only in America can you make that much by serving the poor.

No wonder Indian doctors prefer to work in Welch than in Warangal or Wardha. But must the Indian taxpayer subsidize them for seven years to do so? As is usually the case, the responses from

Indian readers who considered this question can broadly be divided into two categories: agreement (sometimes enthusiastic) and disagreement (often vehement). But many in both categories of respondents are willing to see some merit in the opposite point of view.

Dr. N. R. Ramesh Masthi, who teaches in a medical college in India and has served as a doctor in several remote rural areas, "fully agrees" with me, saying that in his experience, "nearly forty to fifty percent of the students migrate from every medical college each year." He notes that "ninety to ninety-five percent of the students who join medical college are from urban areas, mostly capital cities, and [are] just not interested in working even thirty kilometers from an urban area." Barely 2 percent of the students admitted are from rural or government schools. Dr. Masthi says with feeling: "If we cannot retain our doctors, the whole notion of merit in education has no value for people like me who are paying a very high tax to subsidize their education in the hope that they will give back something to the community which sponsored them." He would rather have an average student joining a medical college and staying on to serve India than a bright student who goes abroad "because ultimately in medicine it is experience and commitment which makes a doctor good."

Dr. Vishwa P. Rath from Canada says that medical education is no longer as attractive as it used to be to the younger generation. "The youngsters feel medical studies are time-consuming, less paid, makes one look thirty years older than one's age, and [offers] limited scope." A computer science or technical degree, Dr. Rath says, provides a far better lifestyle. The solution is to offer Indian doctors better financial incentives and more attractive working conditions: "If a patient dies, a doctor should not be beaten in the corridor!" The good Dr. Rath adds, "Even if twenty percent of [doctors] emigrate, we still have eighty percent to serve our nation. Personally, I belong to a family of doctors serving in the Indian Air Force, Indian Navy, and other government assignments. Therefore subsidy is essential because for a family like mine this generous help has contributed seven doctors to our nation."

An NRI blogger named "Seeji" (Dr. C. G. Prasanna) lists the

"minimal number of postgraduate seats not catering to the thousands of [medical] graduates, illogical reservation system, a very low pay package compared to other professions" among the reasons doctors emigrate. Seeji asks: "How justified is it to blame doctors alone when even IITians and IIM guys have studied with the same taxpayers' money?" But he proposes the passage of a law that would bind graduates to work in India for a specified number of years. "That should be applied to doctors as well as engineers," he suggests. A regular reader, Anju Chandel, agrees that "the Indian government should first ensure a basic level of comfort, safety, and salary for young doctors and then enforce mandatory service in medically underserved areas for a stipulated time."

The issue of subsidies for medical education elicits the most informed and contentious debate. Blogger T. A. Abinandan in Bangalore points out that subsidies apply to "everyone — nonmedicos or medicos, irrespective of whether they work in India or elsewhere." Noting that tuition fees are a pittance, he states that "such low fees do not allow our colleges and universities to upgrade their infrastructure and hire high-quality faculty. On the other hand, making every college student pay — up front — the true cost of higher education may render it inaccessible to the deserving among the poor."

Mr. Abinadan suggests an "Australian model," under which every college student (whether in public or private colleges) benefits from a loan from the government that he repays by paying taxes at a higher tax rate. "This additional tax kicks in only when the income exceeds a certain minimum, thereby protecting those individuals who fall on hard times." The great flaw in this model, however, is that it does nothing to address the problem of doctors emigrating. If repayment is solely through the tax system, how will the government recoup its investment from doctors who, having emigrated, no longer pay Indian taxes?

Dr. J. Mariano Anto Bruno Mascarenhas of Tuticorin sent me a lengthy philippic explaining that the subsidy argument is a myth. Medical colleges have some twenty departments, of which most also treat patients; only three (anatomy, physiology, and pharmacology) are exclusively for students. So "98 percent of the subsidy is for health and less than 1.5 percent is for education. . . . The truth is that even if a medical college does not admit MBBS students, it will still have 98 percent of its expenses for treating patients." Dr. Mascarenhas considers the main reason for emigration to be the poor remuneration for doctors. "Please understand one simple fact," he declares. "No one will want to work in another country for money alone if he can earn enough in India."

That may well explain why we can only expect the tribe of NRIs to grow and prosper.

52

Ajanta and Ellora in the Monsoon

I T IS TO AN ELUSIVE LION that we owe our rediscovery of the magnificent cave temples of Ajanta. A party of British officers, out hunting in 1819, pursued their quarry into a gorge in the thickly wooded Sahyadri Hills of west-central India. The animal retreated into the dense jungle, but the dazzling sun revealed, through the seemingly impenetrable foliage, the outlines of a horseshoe-shaped cave. The British officers followed, crossing a river to investigate — and soon forgot all about their hunting.

For they had stumbled upon a site lost for centuries — a series of thirty caves cut into the hill by Buddhist monks between 200 B.C. and 650 A.D., to serve as residences, temples, and schools. Each is adorned with statuary chiseled into the rock face by the monks, and in many cases by remarkable paintings, telling stories both religious and secular. "They took our breath away," one of the officers reported, and they have continued to do so for generations of visitors since.

History does not record what happened to the lion, but the leader of the hunting party etched his name into the wall across a priceless painting: "John Smith, 20 April 1819." (Fitting, perhaps, that so extravagant a treasure should have been found by one with so prosaic a name, and so barbarous an attitude.) The Ajanta cave-temples joined those at Ellora, forty miles away as the crow flies (and which had not been reclaimed by the jungle), as extraordinary monuments to human artistic accomplishment. Ellora has few surviving paintings, but its carvings, which represent three different faiths (Buddhism, Hinduism, and Jainism) and were created between 350 and 700 A.D., offer even finer examples of the skill, virtuosity, and determination of ancient India's artists and sculptors.

"Ajanta and Ellora, in the monsoon?" asked my then wife, Minu, when I suggested we visit the caves in the summer of 1998, when our twin sons, Ishaan and Kanishk, then fourteen, would be enjoying their school break. We were planning to go to India anyway, but Minu's idea of a monsoon holiday was to put her feet up at her parents' home in Calcutta and consume vast quantities of mangoes, the season's great fruit. "We'll get soaked. And the flights will be delayed by the weather."

That seemed to make sense, until I ran into a bibulous Indian guest at a diplomatic party in New York.

"Have you heard they're going to close the caves to visitors?" he asked. "Too many visitors. All that hot breath and tramping feet, causing damage to the paintings and sculptures. So they'll be closing them all to the general public."

"When?" I asked, horrified.

"Next year, I believe."

That did it. Monsoon or no monsoon, we were going to catch a glimpse of Ajanta and Ellora before the curtains came down on either place.

After recovering from our transcontinental jetlag with two days in Bombay, we flew 375 kilometers inland to the city of Aurangabad, northeast of Bombay, for our excursions to Ajanta and Ellora. Aurangabad, a manufacturing town of some 1.1 million people, has the nearest airport to the caves, as well as several fine hotels. We had a bit of a drama coming in: Kanishk, whose hospitability to visiting bugs is a source of family legend, threw up copiously and looked decidedly queasy. Our first hour after landing in Aurangabad was therefore spent driving in the gloom to every building that looked like a hospital. Aurangabad, a prosperous and spread-out town, green and dusty in equal measure, had several of these. After knocking fruitlessly at the doors of a couple of maternity clinics with a retching boy in tow, which rather confused the doctors in the labor wards, we took Kanishk to our hotel, the spanking new Taj Residency, whose in-house doctor promptly prescribed something that cured him in twenty-four hours.

As a concession to Kanishk's state, we reversed the traditional order of doing things and decided to go to Ellora first. (A leisurely start even allowed me to use the hotel's gym, which made a change from my usual form of exercise — jumping to conclusions.) The Residency equipped our rented car with packed lunches, chilled drinks, and even umbrellas to ward off the depredations of the monsoon, of which, to Minu's relief, we saw little evidence.

Our twenty-something tourist guide, Srikant Jadhav, had been in the business only four years, but he made up for inexperience with a fund of historical knowledge and a small stock of witticisms he tested on the boys ("Why is the number six afraid of seven? Because seven ate nine.") It also helped that he was slim enough to squeeze into the front seat of our air-conditioned Ambassador car with the driver, Mohammed Nissar, and me (which, given Kanishk's condition, was probably the safest place to be in the vehicle.)

Ellora is less than an hour's drive from Aurangabad, across lush farming country, on a good road. Even if Ishaan and Kanishk hadn't announced, at age seven, their desire to lead the Mongol hordes or, failing that, to become military historians, we would have made one stop on the way. This was at the Daulatabad Fort, a soaring citadel on a conical hill that commands the land approaches from both north and east. This thirteenth-century edifice was widely reputed to be invincible, so intricate was its pyramidal construction atop the hill. The rock-hewn fort had several layers of walls, iron gates with elephant-deterring spikes, a forty-foot-deep moat, and a narrow, twisting subterranean passage that could be blocked by the intense heat generated by a large brazier at one end. It is a bit of a hike to the top, and Minu soon gave up the climb, preferring to sit under a mango tree with a lazily solicitous Ishaan, while Kanishk, miraculously revived by the sight of cannon, trudged up with me.

The fort is well worth the effort. A medieval sultan of Delhi, Muhammad bin Tughlaq, was so impressed by its impregnability that he moved his capital to Daulatabad. (The experiment failed, however; Tughlaq and his displaced citizens marched back to Delhi, and he has gone down in history as the "mad monarch.") Among the fort's incongruities is an ancient Hindu temple, its roof supported by a hundred and fifty pillars, that today houses a modern idol — a kitsch figure of "Mother India," draped in a gaudy sari, her eight arms brandishing an assortment of implements, including a sword, a sharp-pointed trishul (the Hindu trident), and a somewhat startled-looking snake. No one seems to know who invented this deity, except that the statue is clearly of fairly recent provenance, a post-independence version of the powerful mother goddess (worshiped variously as Durga, Kali, and Shakti, but not, other than here, as "Bharat Mata," Mother India).

Before leaving the fort's attractive setting, Ishaan pulled out our camera, and Minu and I looked expectantly at each other to produce a new roll of film. We had left seven at the hotel, but our condition immediately attracted a swarm of boys clutching Kodak packages. "A hundred and fifty rupees," one said, offering a 35mm ISO 200 film with twenty-four exposures. Since the rupee's post-nuclear depreciation in 1998 (at that point it had fallen to forty to the dollar) meant that this was less than four dollars, we gladly bought two. Five minutes later another youth came by to sell us two more rolls at a hundred and twenty. Scarcely able to believe our good fortune, we bought them as well. We were almost back in our car when a sad-eyed teenager begged us to take at least one roll for a hundred; he was the only peddler who hadn't made us a sale. By this time Minu was convinced the film canisters would all turn out to be empty. They weren't, and the film was fine; what we found out later was that Kodak manufactures the film in India, where each roll normally retails for eighty to ninety rupees in photo stores.

On our way to Ellora, we also took in two contrasting graves. The first was that of the Emperor Aurangzeb, the last of the Great Mughals, after whom Aurangabad is named — a simple and austere slab of marble paid for by the sale of prayer caps the devout monarch had stitched himself. (He had forbidden any other expenditure on a tomb.) The second grave, the Bibi-ka-Maqbara, was that of his wife, Rabia Durani, a grand imitation Taj Mahal startlingly reminiscent of the original, but without the Taj's perfect proportions and majesty. In other circumstances it might have been an attractive resting place, but Minu didn't think so. "Wonder what it's like for her," she said sympathetically, "to know she's buried in a travesty and her mother-in-law's tomb is where the real action is?"

Ellora itself was exquisite. In a little over four hours, we took in all thirty-four caves, sequentially admiring the work of artists of different faiths. This meant starting with the Buddhist (constructed 550–750 A.D.), then working our way through the Hindu caves (600–875 A.D.) to the Jain ones (800–1000 A.D.). The tour was not arduous, not even with Kanishk still a bit wobbly at the knees. The monsoon finally sprinkled us, but briefly and rather halfheartedly, as if it didn't really want to get in the way of our view. We took in the rolling hills, rock-laden and stately, all around; the golden *gulmohur* blossoms, flaming insolent and tender in every garden; and then, in the afternoon sun, the caves themselves, opening into the earth like a secret prayer.

The caves are numbered, logically enough, for visitors' convenience. We walked through them in order, marveling at the paucity of people. The previous year we had taken the boys to Italy, where they had gotten accustomed to the throngs at every site; here, being able to enjoy the splendors without crowds, to sense the space available, made each cave, each carving, more approachable, our discovery of it more intimate. Remarkably, every pillar, alcove, and niche is carved from solid rock. We admired the contrast between Cave 5, in the Mahayana style (the more ostentatious "Great Vehicle" tradition of Buddhism), whose treasures include a magnificent "praying Buddha," and the plain and austere lines of Caves 1 and 7, in the Hinayana

(Little Vehicle) tradition, of which Aurangzeb might have approved (if only his Islamic fundamentalist bigotry had made it possible for him to approve of any other faith).

We could see why Cave 6 might have been "afraid of 7." It seemed the work, perhaps, of lay sculptors rather than monks, because it overflows with lush carvings: dancing dwarves play musical instruments; busty goddesses disport themselves, every detail of their clothing, ornaments, and headdresses rendered with minute precision; on one wall, a student toils at a desk, oblivious to temptation. Cave 10 is spectacular: with its vaulted arches and intricate interior carvings; it reminded the boys of a Roman basilica, except that it had been hewn entirely out of a rocky hillside, and there are no gelati on sale outside.

"You mean they didn't actually carry a single stone into the cave?" Ishaan asked incredulously. They didn't. Though the temples are referred to as caves, they are the work of men, hammering and chiseling diligently away for centuries, creating principally two kinds of structures — monasteries, or *viharas,* and halls of worship, or *chaityas.* Their method required great technical expertise, aesthetic dexterity, and infinite patience. The monks seem to have marked an outline on the surface of the hill and dug downward, cutting away the rock to create the entrances, columns, and chambers. Imagine the drama of it, turning mountain faces into works of art, sanctuaries, temples; year after year, working only with natural light, the metronomic poetry of hammer and chisel against rock. It is possible to imagine one set of sculptors working dexterously on the ceilings while muscular excavators hacked away beneath them to reach the floor. The artists and painters must have followed, though age, moisture, and vandalism have left little trace of their work in Ellora.

One remarkable feat of skillful labor is Cave 12, a three-storied edifice carved in the seventh century to serve as a hostel for the monks. Each "room" cut into the rock has a carved stone bed for the monk to sleep on, complete with stone pillow, and a niche cut into the wall for his lamp. To complete the dormitory effect, there is a room for an attendant on each floor. "Look," said our guide, Srikant, pointing to a rectangular depression in the stone, "they even had a notice board." Ishaan and Kanishk, overwhelmed by the sense that they were in a two-thousand-year-old boarding school, refused to climb to the headmaster's floor. Minu and I followed our guide to the top level, where a row of seven meditating Buddhas sits alongside another row of seven who have already attained enlightenment, as attested to by the stone umbrellas over their beatific heads. Here, too, are faded remnants of paintings on the ceiling, a faint hint of what is to come in Ajanta.

The Hindu Cave 16 goes one better: it is the largest monolithic carving in the world, a gigantic temple called Kailash, after the god Shiva's mountain abode, which took eight hundred workmen a century and a half to complete and is twice the size of the Parthenon. The sculptors' vision was that of a flying chariot, and the cave is carved like one. It is embellished with vivid statuary depicting various Hindu legends, a particularly astonishing piece being that of the goddess Durga slaying the demon Mahishasura amid a stone flurry of flailing arms and weapons. This was the sort of authenticity missing in the ersatz idol at Daulatabad.

"Hey, Dad," said Kanishk irreverently, "the Great Indian Novel." He had just finished reading my book of that name, a reinvention of the ancient Mahabharata epic as a twentieth-century political satire, and was pointing to a series of friezes bringing episodes of the epic to life on the temple's plinth. Then the rain came again, and we sheltered under one of Kailash's many ribbed cupolas, marveling at the sheer scale of the architectural achievement. In a curiously modern touch, the sculptors have carved a statue outside of their principal donor, King Krishna Raya II of the Rashtrakuta dynasty, his palm open in generous giving. Other contemporary resonances echoed in statues of Shiva playing a game of dice with his consort Parvati, and one of their wedding, with Parvati as a nervous bride, her head bent in modesty, shyly placing one foot against the other as she receives her husband.

We ate our picnic lunch at a spot where Cave 29 overlooks a waterfall. There was something incongruous about biting into

sandwiches a few feet away from pillars that had been carved labori-
ously a thousand years before sandwiches were invented by an impatient earl. We sat on an ancient ledge and looked out to where the
water cascaded sudden and silvery from the hillside like a gasp. When
the food was finished and we tried to venture farther into the cave,
we found it had been cut so deeply into the hill that no sunlight ever
reached its deepest interior. The back of the cave smelled strongly of
the droppings of bats, who whirled furiously past us in the dark.

We ended our tour of Ellora at the massive double-storied Jain
Indrasabha, Cave 32, a relatively late construction (eleventh century) notable for more than one statue of Siddhayika, a female attendant of the founder of the Jain faith, Mahavira. An exquisitely carved
lotus on the ceiling caught our eye. And then I couldn't resist telling
Minu we could have done without the film at Daulatabad after all.
For there, in stone, was a *yakshi* (a demoness) sitting on a lion under
a mango tree, for all the world like the pair Kanishk and I had left behind on our trudge up to the top of the fort. It was a striking piece of
work, for the ripe beauty of the doe-eyed woman seemed at odds
with the legendary asceticism of the Jain faith. But the caves were
carved in lushly prosperous times, and asceticism always thrives better in penury.

Ellora and the medieval distractions on our way prepared us
well for the wonder that is Ajanta. We woke a little earlier on the
second day, since the sixty-five-mile journey from Aurangabad takes
almost two hours by road, and we had a flight to catch back to Bombay at the end of the day. The long trip provided my sons the opportunity to ask why questions: Why were the caves created here,
Ishaan asked, and Why, Kanishk added, in this form? Part of the answer lay in political stability: the area was ruled by two enlightened
dynasties, the Satavahanas and the Vakatakas, during the first eight
hundred years of the Christian era, a period of great prosperity and
growth during which art and culture flourished under royal patronage. The second reason is more functional: the basalt rock of the
Deccan plateau proved ideal for the sculptors, solid but easy to hew,

which is why there are other examples of rock-cut caves scattered throughout the area, including in Aurangabad itself.

Ajanta looks more like an organized tourist destination. As soon as we parked, we were inundated with hawkers offering tchotchkes with the most tenuous connection to the caves we had come to see. Young boys thrust mineralized chunks of rock into our hands as free gifts to entice us into their shops. We fled, but were drawn up short at a paved ascent that curved upward from the parking lot to the caves. A wiry porter emerged to carry our possessions for us — eighty rupees (two dollars) for the entire duration of our visit. I accepted with alacrity, since the Taj Residency appeared to have given us an even more generous supply of bottled drinks than on the previous day. Two more individuals appeared, looking as if a couple of the larger sculptures had come to life. They were palanquin bearers, enterprising young men ready to carry the less energetic visitor up to the caves in a stuffed chair mounted on two long poles. Minu looked wistfully at the palanquin, but the shocked disapproval of our sons sent her off, abashed. ("They need the work," she muttered as she reluctantly turned away. "It's their livelihood.") But the ascent was less arduous than at Daulatabad Fort, and the palanquins were not missed.

There weren't enough foreigners around to remind us that we were tourists, but the pressure of tourism is felt more keenly at Ajanta than at Ellora: the four main caves admit only forty visitors at a time, for a maximum of fifteen minutes. It was just as well that we were there in the relatively unpopular monsoon, for we found an intimidating queue only at one cave, to which we were able to return later. For years, attendants used to stand outside the caves with large mirrors to reflect the sunlight onto the art within, but today Ajanta employs a "lighting attendant" in selected caves, whose job it is to shine a large electric lamp upon certain paintings pointed out by your guide.

Ajanta, which was created in the second century B.C., had disappeared from popular consciousness around the eighth century A.D., when Buddhism faded away in India, largely absorbed by a reformed and resurgent Hinduism. Eleven hundred years of neglect have preserved it well, particularly its paintings, though we wondered about the long-term effects of the helpful ministrations of the lighting attendant. We were grateful that he existed, though, because there would have been no other way to have captured, from three angles, the extraordinarily enigmatic expression of the Padmapani Bodhisattava in Cave 1, an amazing work that invites comparisons to Da Vinci's *Gioconda.* The young male figure, his elongated eyes both brooding and reverential, a lotus in his hand, his expression soulful in the fullest sense of that overused word, seems both of this world and beyond it. The cave carvings and paintings are positioned so as to catch natural light at certain moments of the day, and if one had all day one could have waited to see how different rays of sunlight might have illuminated different aspects of the face and figure portrayed in this magnificent painting. But even five minutes under electric light told us we were in the presence of a work of genius.

Buddhist monks lived and learned in the womb-shaped caves, which served as their monasteries and seats of learning. The paintings of tales from the Buddhist Jatakas and the nondevotional images of princesses and nymphs suggest the caves were also intended to attract lay visitors. Our guide had an attentive eye for signs of modern life in ancient art, pointing out figures carrying such items of daily use as Coke-shaped bottles, glass tumblers, and playing cards. ("Ancient India had Coke," he smiled proudly.) With the football World Cup going on, he showed Ishaan and Kanishk a figure in a blue striped garment that might have been a soccer jersey. But when he suggested that a hanger-on in one Buddhist painting was actually wearing blue jeans, I called a halt to his appropriations of the past. The truth was remarkable enough: many of the paintings testified to an amazing degree of international contact and trade. The ceiling in Cave 2 is covered with portraits of visiting princes, including a Persian monarch and his consort; Hellenic influences are reflected in bacchanalian figures wearing stockings and hats; all this two thousand years before "international relations" became a subject of study rather than what you acquired if you married abroad.

The desire to astonish sometimes takes tourists too far. In Cave 6, our guide asked an attendant to thump a series of pillars with the heel of his palm to produce musical sounds; amusing, but it seems highly unlikely that the monks ever used the rock pillars for an orchestra. No, it's the paintings that made Ajanta special for us. The art of Ajanta has a standing comparable in the history of Asian art to the place that the frescoes of Siena and Florence enjoy in the development of European art. The Ajanta painters used a tempera technique, applying their colors onto a thin layer of dry plaster rather than directly on the walls themselves. The plaster was composed of organic material, including vegetable fibers and rice husks, mixed with fine sand. The paints themselves, in vivid chromatic colors, were derived from locally available minerals, though the blue is believed to have come from lapis lazuli imported from Central Asia. Legend has it that several attempts to reconstitute the paints after chemical analysis failed — the ancients knew a thing or two that the moderns cannot replicate.

Apart from the Padmapani figure in Cave 1, I was most struck by a painting in Cave 16. It portrays the emotional scene of the conversion of Prince Nanda by the Buddha, as his princess swoons, realizing she is to lose her husband to the world-renouncing faith of his preceptor. The narrative painting, depicting the mournful messenger bearing the news, an attendant bringing the prince's rejected crown, and melancholy ladies-in-waiting consoling the grieving princess, is an extraordinary evocation of the price of faith, rendered with exquisite sensitivity. In a different mood is a flying *apsara* (celestial nymph) in Cave 17, a figure of joy and glitter, her necklace studded with diamonds and sapphires that glint fifteen centuries after she was painted, her ribbons trailing gaily as she swings forward.

In Cave 17, devoted largely to the good deeds of the brave and devout Prince Simhala — beginning with the shipwreck of his expedition to Sri Lanka and ending with his coronation there — the artists have entered into prodigious evocations of detail, including a particularly grisly image of a wounded soldier with his large intestine spilling out of his slashed midriff. Even Ishaan and Kanishk seemed momentarily to have mislaid their war lust at the sight. They moved silently along to another painting on an adjoining wall, a moving depiction of the legend of a captured elephant being returned to its blind parents.

This is art revealing a high level of technical skill, with a subtle use of shading and highlighting to achieve a three-dimensional effect. Often, the eyes of the painted subject seem to follow the viewer. There are curiosities: the women in the pictures are all dark, the men all fair, and it is not clear whether this was an artistic convention or the reflection of some ancient colonizing sensibility. With their varied themes, their sophisticated execution, and their vivid depictions of human and animal forms, the paintings of Ajanta made a tremendous impact across Asia, becoming a model for artists throughout the Buddhist world. But it isn't just their age or beauty that imprints the Ajanta paintings on our consciousness; it's their vitality, the energy and social acuity of their creators. Today their art is an invaluable record of the past, but in its time it had immediate validity as a depiction of what mattered in the world and of the images that drew the community together. To think of this stunning work being created, day after day in those precious moments of sunlight, backbreaking work with anonymity its only reward, is to sense the devotion of these artists to a higher calling than art itself.

We returned to Aurangabad after five hours, including a quick lunch, consuming the Taj's packed offerings in a gazebo a hundred steps below the cave level. Our patient porter had sensibly waited downstairs, rather than dog our footsteps as we climbed, and he laid claim to the gazebo before anyone else had the same idea. Oddly enough, there is no concession stand, let alone a restaurant, in the complex. Though there is no shortage of peddlers offering everything from postcards to samples of local rock, you have to bring your own food.

D. M. Yadav, the knowledgeable senior tourism official in Aurangabad, tried to talk us into extending our stay by another two days. He urged us not to leave Aurangabad without making two more excursions: to Paithan, two hours away, the old capital of the Satavahanas and seat of a legendary weaving tradition, famed throughout the ancient world, which still produces wondrous saris and other fine cloth; and to Lonar, a four-hour drive, the site where a meteorite struck the earth some fifty thousand years ago, leaving a crater with a radius of five kilometers. We had commitments in Bombay that obliged us to make our plane, though Minu pointedly observed that she had no Paithani sari in her collection. "And we have no fragments of meteorite, either, Ma," Ishaan retorted.

Before boarding the aircraft, I did ask Yadav about the threatened closure of the caves to tourists. He seemed puzzled. "Why would we do that?" he asked. "People have been coming daily to Ellora for two thousand years, to Ajanta for somewhat less. Why stop them now?"

"Never believe all that you hear at diplomatic parties," the twins chimed in. But I was grateful for the misinformation, which had sent us scurrying here in the monsoon. We had seen the caves, encountered no crowds, and stuck to our schedule. What's more, not a single flight was canceled because of the weather. And we didn't even really get wet.

5

The Transformation of India

53

The Davos Economy

THE ANNUAL GATHERING OF THE GREAT and the good at the
World Economic Forum in Davos, Switzerland, has become a
pilgrimage site for the twenty-first-century Indian. I was not
able to attend in 2007, but saw a list of the Indian delegates who did.
They're a "Who's Who" of the country's business and industry, with
an impressive sprinkling of top politicians and bureaucrats alongside.
Among the sixty-seven names on the list were enough movers and
shakers to cause a small earthquake, and the number of zeroes in
their collective net worth would probably fill the rest of this chapter.
But impressive though that is, it's not the whole story of the Indian
numbers at the World Economic Forum. I asked a prominent NRI
businessman I know why he didn't go this year. "Oh, I did," he said.
"But since I'm based in London, I'm not included in the Indian list."

The Indian presence in Davos is emblematic of a larger transformation in India, and in the way India is perceived internationally.
It reflects the discovery of India by the world's financial markets.
When I first went to Davos in the early 1990s Indians were present,
of course, but they bore the faint whiff of the exotic minority, notice-
able but hardly worth noticing. The annual Indian reception thrown
by the Confederation of Indian Industry in those days was a semi-
forlorn affair, overpopulated by official *desis* in bulging *bandhgalas*

wolfing down samosas and scotch. Today it's the hottest ticket in the town of the Magic Mountain; the lines of well-heeled international businessmen queuing up to shake the hand of Finance Minister Chidambaram are reminiscent of those involving ticket-holders to the World Cup final. Indians are sought after because India, indubitably, matters to the world.

And why shouldn't it? India's gross domestic product is rising by 7.5 percent a year, which means that India is annually becoming richer by $200 billion, an increase in one year that exceeds the total GDP of Portugal or Norway. The level of investment in 2006–7 crossed 40 percent of GDP; just five years ago, it stood at 25 percent. If McKinsey is to be believed, some nine million jobs may be moved to India from the developed West in the next eight years. India's foreign reserves have exceeded $140 billion, enough to cover fifteen months' worth of imports; fifteen years ago, the country had to mortgage its gold in London because the foreign exchange coffers were dry. The speed of India's growth is so remarkable that the IMF this year even warned of the risks of the economy "overheating." In *Forbes* magazine's published list of the world's billionaires, twenty-seven of the world's richest people are Indians, and even more surprising, only four of them live abroad: Indian wealth is staying in India, and it's growing.

Of course, a rather large portion of the world's poorest people live in India, too. Our country's poor live below a poverty line that seems to be drawn just this side of the funeral pyre. And yet, for all the tragic news of farmers committing suicide and the undeniably sad sight of human beings reduced to begging on our city sidewalks, there have been positive developments as well. In 1991, 36 percent of India's population (in those days, 846 million people), lived on less than one dollar a day, the World Bank's classic measure of absolute poverty. That added up to nearly 305 million people, giving India the dubious distinction of being home to the largest collection of poor people in the world. In 2001, our population had grown to 1.02 billion people, but after a decade of economic reforms, however fitful, the percentage of those living on less than a dollar a day had fallen to 26 percent, or some 267 million people. In other words, even though India had added 156 million more people to its population in the decade between those two censuses, the number of poor Indians had actually fallen by 37 million. The liberalized and liberated Indian economy had, in effect, lifted 94 million people out of absolute poverty in ten years — a feat on a scale that no country on earth, other than China, had ever accomplished. Today, five years later, estimates of people below the poverty level stand at 22 percent. Economic growth is steadily chipping away at poverty, and it is doing so far faster than in the first four decades of independence, when statist economic policies ruled the commanding heights in Delhi.

None of this is grounds for complacency. We still have a long way to go; 22 percent is still 250 million people living in conditions that are a blot on our individual and collective consciences. The necessary steps must be taken to ensure that every Indian is given the means to live a decent life, to feed his or her family, and to acquire the education that will enable him or her to fulfill their creative potential. As an Indian, I'm chuffed at India's prominence at Davos, but to me that's not the most important measure of the country's international standing. I'm much more proud that India has shown a willingness to use its newfound prosperity to benefit others: it's an article of pride, for instance, that the government has written off the debt owed to it for years by African countries. Let us celebrate, too, that India was quick to respond to the devastation that followed the tsunami and helped lead international relief efforts in Sri Lanka, even though Indian victims needed attention. India must show the world that it can go to Davos and stay true to its soul as well.

54

The Myth of the Indian Middle Class

WHENEVER I HEAR FOREIGNERS TALKING ABOUT the Indian "middle class," I wonder what they mean. Much of the clamor about economic reforms has focused on this group, which may be sociological but is not entirely logical. The conventional wisdom is that this middle class is some 300 million strong — larger than the entire domestic market of the United states, say the marketing gurus — and, together with a very rich upper class, has both the purchasing power and the inclinations of the American middle class.

Today's economic mythology sees this new Indian middle class as ripe for international consumer goods. Our television channels and glossy magazines overflow with ads for foreign brand-name products, from Daewoo Cielo cars to Ray-Ban sunglasses. This is why Kellogg's rushed in with their corn flakes; Nike got our then cricket captain, Mohammed Azharuddin, to endorse their sports shoes (sparking off an unintended controversy since his name is also that of the Prophet and could not adorn an item so lowly as footwear); Mercedes-Benzes began rolling off the automotive production lines; and Johnny Walker Black Label scotch has become an Indian brand, not just one purveyed by smugglers. It was once said that more bottles of Johnny Walker Black Label were sold in India than were distilled in Scotland: now the joke may literally come true.

But all these manufacturers, I hear, have been dismayed by the weak response of the market, for the Indian middle class is not quite what it's cracked up to be. A survey conducted between 1986 and 1994 by the National Council of Applied Economic Research (NCAER) in New Delhi had already found that India's consumers could be divided into five classes, not three: the very rich, of six million people (or one million households), the "consuming class" of some 150 million (half the conventional estimate), the "climbers" (a lower middle class of 275 million), the "aspirants" (another 275 million who in America or Europe would be classified as "poor"), and finally the destitute (210 million). The numbers have gone up by another 100 million or so in the decade since the survey was conducted, but the relative balance among these five classes, despite some progress in all of them, is unlikely to have changed dramatically.

Thomas Friedman's enthusiasm for a newly "flattened" world risks adding to the myth of the Indian middle class. The first misconception is the nature of the state itself, whose withering away Friedman posits with an almost Marxian glee. Yet the state is still indispensable to most people. It provides, or should provide, physical security, law and order, economic infrastructure, and basic services. For most people in the world, however, and certainly in many parts of India, the problem is that their state is not strong enough to deliver on those vital requirements. One can rejoice at the rising living standards of Indians working at call centers, tracing lost luggage, and reading CAT scans for Americans, but what is the condition of the country they return to? Friedman waxes lyrical about the Infosys campus outside Bangalore, an oasis I too have visited, which would not be out of place in the West, but the managers of Infosys have to organize their own electricity, their own "mass" transportation, their own health club, and so on, because these facilities are absent, unreliable, or dilapidated in the city itself.

The worst news for foreign consumer goods marketers is that it is only among the one million households of the very rich that there exists a sustainable interest in the products of Kellogg, Nike, Mercedes-Benz, or Johnny Walker. Of course, the others buy goods — but these are more basic, and cheaper, than multinational corporations produce. If you're selling tea or cooking oil, you have a vast Indian market, spanning all five classes; leather sandals and ready-made shirts reach half the population; rubber thongs and plastic buckets delve even deeper; but sports shoes that cost a chauffeur's monthly take-home pay? Forget all but the smallest group at the top.

Not that Indians aren't spending more and acquiring more: since the 1980s, there has been a veritable boom of buying. On my visits to rural southern India — Tamil Nadu and Kerala — I am increasingly struck by how many village houses are of pukka construction rather than mud or thatch, and even more by how many have some sort of vehicle parked outside — in most cases a bicycle, but there were also scooters, other two-wheelers, and in some cases cars. An astonishing number of roofs sprout television antennae, and a few houses even sport a satellite dish. This empirical, if unscientific, evidence is confirmed by the NCAER study: TV ownership is rising, and all but the most destitute own wristwatches, bicycles, and portable radios. Smaller but still significant numbers buy electric irons and kitchen equipment. But this is a far cry from preferring Macallan to Kingfisher, let alone buying a Mercedes-Benz.

Cumulatively, the NCAER survey concluded, India has a "consuming population" of 168 million to 504 million people. But what they consume, and how much they can afford to pay for it, is another matter altogether. One thing that is noticeably changing is our national indifference to global brand names, which is the legacy both of four thousand years of traditional civilization and nearly five decades of self-reliant protectionism. But change is still slow in global terms; and in any case, the items most Indians buy, from household detergents to hair oil, and from cigarettes to snack food, are those where Indian brands have an advantage in both familiarity and price.

All of which suggests that, though we do have a middle-class, in many respects it consumes fewer goods than the working class in the West. The economic transformation of India since liberalization is real, but it will be a while before the average middle-class Indian tosses her Lakmé aside for a Lancome, or trades in her handmade *salwar kameez* for a Ralph Lauren pantsuit. After all, why shouldn't globalization speak with an Indian accent?

55

Connecting to the Future

O NE OF MY FAVORITE PHOTOGRAPHS ABOUT INDIA was from
the last Kumbh *mela*, the great religious festival that takes
place four times every twelve years and is thronged by
millions of Indian pilgrims. It showed a *sadhu* right out of central
casting — naked body, long matted hair and beard, ash-smeared
forehead and all — chatting away on a mobile phone. The contrast
says so much about the land of paradoxes that is today's India — a
country that, as I wrote many years ago, manages to live in several
centuries at the same time.

There are other photographs I have seen over the years that illustrate the same phenomenon — laborers carrying TV sets on their
heads, a bullock-cart transporting rocket parts, a motorcar overtaking an elephant, and so on. But there's something particularly
special about the *sadhu* and his cell phone. Because it is in communications that the transformation of India in recent years has been
most dramatic. In recent months, for the first time, seven million
Indians subscribed to new mobile phones. That's a world record. In
September 2006, India overtook China for the first time in the number of new telephone subscribers per month. We're still way behind
China in the total number of cell phone users (just over 140 million

against their 450 million), but each month the gap is narrowing. By 2010, the Indian government tells us, there will be 500 million Indian telephone users. China will probably still be ahead, but on a per capita basis there will be little to choose between the two.

Now, to anyone who grew up in pre-liberalization India, that's astonishing. Bureaucratic statism committed a long list of sins against the Indian people, but communications was high up on the list; the woeful state of India's telephones right up to the 1990s, with only eight million connections and a further twenty million on waiting lists, would have been a joke if it wasn't also a tragedy — and a man made one at that. India had possibly the worst telephone penetration rates in the world. The government's indifferent attitude to the need to improve India's communications infrastructure was epitomized by Prime Minister Indira Gandhi's communications minister, C. M. Stephen, who declared in Parliament, in response to questions decrying the rampant telephone breakdowns in the country, that telephones were a luxury, not a right, and that any Indian who was not satisfied with his telephone service could return his phone — since there was an eight-year waiting list of people seeking this supposedly inadequate product.

Mr. Stephen's statement captured perfectly everything that was wrong about the government's attitude. It was ignorant (he clearly had no idea of the colossal socioeconomic losses caused by poor communications), wrongheaded (he saw a practical problem only as an opportunity to score a political point), unconstructive (responding to complaints by seeking a solution apparently did not occur to him), self-righteous (the socialist cant about telephones being a luxury, not a right), complacent (taking pride in a waiting list that should have been a source of shame, since its existence pointed to the poor performance of his own ministry in putting up telephone lines and manufacturing equipment), unresponsive (feeling no obligation to provide a service in return for the patience, and the fees, of the country's telephone subscribers), and insulting (asking long-suffering telephone subscribers to return their instruments instead of doing anything about their complaints). It was altogether typical of

378

an approach to governance in the economic arena that assumed the government knew what was good for the country, felt no obligation to prove it by actual performance, and didn't, in any case, care what anyone else thought.

So the cell phone revolution in India is exciting not only as a sign of India's economic transformation into a twenty-first-century success story, but as a symptom of something far more important, a change in the attitude of our ruling classes. The government is marginal to this success story, since we don't need it to lay telephone lines across the country anymore, and the private sector telecom companies develop their own connectivity. Perhaps the key contribution of the government has lain in getting out of the way — in cutting license fees and streamlining tariffs, easing the overly complex regulations and restrictions that discouraged investors from coming into the Indian market, and allowing foreign firms to own up to 74 percent of their Indian subsidiary companies. The Telecom Regulatory Authority of India (TRAI) has also been a model of its kind, a regulatory agency that saw its role as facilitating the growth of the business it was regulating, rather than stifling it with rules and restrictions.

All this is to the good. But I am not merely celebrating a triumph for the capitalists of India. What is truly wonderful about the "mobile miracle" (and I'm not embarrassed to call it that) is that it has accomplished something socialist policies talked about but did little to achieve — it has empowered the less fortunate. The beneficiaries of the new mobile telephones are not just the affluent, but people who in the old days would not even have dreamt of joining those twenty-year-long waiting lists.

It's a source of constant delight to me to find cell phones in the hands of the unlikeliest of my fellow citizens: taxi drivers, *paanwallahs*, farmers, fisher folk. As long as our tax policies keep telecommunications costs low and it's cheap for people to call on their cell phones, the greatest growth in the use of mobile phones will be in this sector. Communications, in the new India, is the great leveler. Pity Mr. Stephen is no longer around to see how wrong he was.

56

The Strange Rise of Planet India

O NE NEW INDICATION OF THE MOUNTING INTERNATIONAL interest in India can be found in foreign bookstores, where books about our country are proliferating like bougainvillea. Edward Luce's excellent *In Spite of the Gods* (a superb portrait of contemporary India, marred only by its awful title) attracted a great deal of well-deserved attention in 2006 and 2007. Hot on its heels comes Mira Kamdar's *Planet India*, whose subtitle runs, *How the Fastest-Growing Democracy Is Transforming America and the World.*

"India," Winston Churchill once barked, "is merely a geographical expression. It is no more a single country than the Equator." Churchill was rarely right about India, but it is true that no other country in the world embraces the extraordinary mixture of ethnic groups, the profusion of mutually incomprehensible languages, the varieties of topography and climate, the diversity of religions and cultural practices, and the range of levels of economic development that India does. Any truism about India can be immediately contradicted by another truism about India. I once jokingly observed that "anything you can say about India, the opposite is also true."

And yet India is more than the sum of its contradictions. How does one come to grips with a land of such bewildering contrasts?

The world's largest democracy that is also the home of the ageless caste system; a land steeped in superstition and spirituality that is a world leader in information technology; the nation of Mahatma Gandhi, the apostle of nonviolence, that is convulsed by periodic bloodletting — the paradoxes abound. The country's national motto, emblazoned on its governmental crest, is "Satyameva Jayaté" — Truth Alone Triumphs. The question remains, however: Whose truth?

Edward Luce, a British journalist who headed the *Financial Times* bureau in Delhi at the cusp of the new century, ventures an answer in his insightful and engaging book. In the sharp-witted prose of a keenly observant journalist, Luce brings India to life with insight and irreverence ("If Gandhi had not been cremated, he would be turning in his grave"). His writing is richly evocative of place and mood, and sparkles with the kind of telling detail that illuminates an anecdote and lifts it above mere reportage. Almost the only thing not worth admiring in this book is its title, which suggests a nation struggling against the heavens, a thesis that has nothing to do with Luce's sophisticated and sympathetic narrative.

Advised early on that in India it is not enough to meet the "right people," Luce travels through the country meeting the "wrong people" as well. He explores economic development from the ground up while never losing sight of the big picture (a "booming service economy in a sea of indifferent farmland"), punctures the myths surrounding India's IT explosion (which he correctly argues will not solve India's fundamental employment problems), and depicts the continuing allure of the secure and corruption-laden "government job." Few foreigners have written with as much understanding of the skills and limitations of India's senior government bureaucrats, of their idealism and inefficiency, of the vested interests impeding growth and progress, as well as the extraordinary triumphs of India despite these obstacles.

On my annual visits home, I discover that India is anything but the unchanging land of cliché. There is an extraordinary degree of change and ferment. Dramatic transformations are taking place that amount to little short of a revolution — in politics, economics, society, and culture. In politics, single-party governance has given way to an era of multiparty coalitions. In economics, India has leapt from protectionism to liberalization, even if it is with the hesitancy of governments looking over their electoral shoulders. In caste and social relations, India has witnessed convulsive changes. And yet all this, which would have rent a lesser country asunder, has been managed through an accommodative and pluralist democracy. Luce tells this story remarkably well.

There is a gently sympathetic portrait of Sonia Gandhi, the Italian-born leader of the ruling Congress Party, for whom "the political is very personal." Luce, who is married to an Indian, clearly admires much of India's culture: "If world trade were to be conducted purely in cultural products," he writes, "then India would have a thumping annual surplus." He answers the famous question of why Indian Muslims don't join al-Qaeda: "the political system under which they live" guarantees them "freedom of speech, expression, worship, and movement." But Luce is a far from uncritical admirer. He is unsparing on the corruption that infests Indian politics and society, on the ersatz Westernization that has seen sonograms used to facilitate female feticide, on the "unimpressive politicians" who run India's "impressive democracy."

No one speaks seriously anymore of the dangers of disintegration that, for years, India was said to be facing. Luce demonstrates credibly that, for all its flaws, India's democratic experiment has worked. Though there have been caste conflicts, linguistic clashes, interreligious riots, and threats to the nation from separatist groups, political democracy has helped to defuse each of these. The explosive potential of caste division has also been channeled through the ballot box. Most strikingly, the power of electoral numbers has given high office to the lowest of India's low. Who could have imagined, for three thousand years, that an "untouchable" woman would rule as chief minister of India's most populous state? Yet that has happened three times, most recently in mid-2007.

In 2004, in an event unprecedented in human history, a nation of a billion people, after the planet's largest exercise in free elections, saw a Roman Catholic political leader (Sonia Gandhi) make way for a Sikh (Manmohan Singh) to be sworn in as prime minister by a Muslim (President Abdul Kalam) — in a country 81 percent Hindu. Luce is right to list the many problems the country faces, the poor quality of much of its political leadership, the rampant corruption, the criminalization of politics. But I'd like to have read a little more about the strengths of India's vibrant civil society: Nongovernmental organizations actively defend human rights, promoting environmentalism, fighting injustice. The press is free, lively, irreverent, disdainful of sacred cows. India is the only country in the English-speaking world where the print media is expanding rather than contracting, and the country supports the world's largest number of all-news TV channels. Luce disappointingly tells us nothing of this.

But these are minor cavils. Luce clearly loves the country he writes about — an essential attribute for a book like this — but he is tough-minded, and his judgment is invariably sound. Luce quotes a colleague as telling him, "In India, things are never as good or as bad as they seem." If you want to understand how that might be, read his wonderful book.

*

As her subtitle suggests, and despite her Indian name, Mira Kamdar, whose mother was Danish, is an American writing for American readers. But her book is all the more interesting to Indians for that, because it helps answer an intriguing question: What does a sensitive, engaged American writer ("I wrote this book because I believe that India matters as never before to the future of a world in crisis") feel her compatriots need to know about India? *Planet India* is a thoroughly researched depiction, warts and all, of today's India. Kamdar has visited the country frequently since her childhood and sprinkles her narrative with personal anecdotes and references to her father's family there, but she has also put in a great deal of research, and her book bristles with statistics. She traveled extensively through the country in the course of a year, conducted wide-ranging interviews and conversations with an astonishing array of Indians, and has taken pains to cover all the key topics that a comprehensive examination of the country demands. It's all here — the IT boom, the television explosion, nuclear weapons, biotech research — and no booster of "India Shining" can have reason to complain: Kamdar even quotes a young NRI filmmaker in New York, Smriti Mundhra, saying, "Who needs the American audience? There are only three hundred million people here." (What's the Hindi equivalent of chutzpah?)

But to Kamdar's credit, she doesn't stop with the good news. *Planet India* is also unsparing in its portrayal of rural poverty, fetid slums, throat-searing pollution, inadequate health care, crippling water shortages, cities choking on themselves. And as a writer of Gujarati descent, her own despair about the pogrom overseen by Narendra Modi and the Gujarat police in 2002 is painfully evident. Not everything is rosy on Planet India, and Kamdar is realistic about the desperation of many people's lives and the scale of the challenge facing India's rulers and policymakers. She could have said more about corruption (which Luce tackled more fully) and about the sterling work of social activists combating communalism, like Harsh Mander, Teesta Setalvad, or Shabnam Hashmi.

Planet India is a worthy addition to the burgeoning shelf of serious books about twenty-first-century India. Despite seeing all the tragedies and limitations, Kamdar comes down firmly on the side of the optimists about India. "One day soon," she writes, "when a critical mass of the talent, the money, and the market is in Asia, a tipping point will be reached, and India will move from joining the game, or even winning the game, to inventing new rules for new games."

It's a striking thought. And the last word should probably belong to an Indian, the man behind the success of Ambootia Tea, Sanjay Bhansal, who lends Kamdar a laptop so that she can take notes more efficiently during their interview. After describing his work and his plans, Bhansal remarks pithily, "So this is what is happening in India. My father could not have dreamt of what I am planning to do." In that simple statement lies a world of hope for our country and our people.

57

Calls from the Center

I T HAS BECOME FASHIONABLE OF LATE, among our bien-pensant classes, to sneer at the success of India's business process outsourcing industry — the call centers and the like that have become the visible face of globalization in our formerly protectionist land. Some seven hundred thousand Indians work in the BPO business, which contributes an estimated $17 billion to the burgeoning Indian economy. The call center has become the symbol of India's newly globalized workforce: while traditional India sleeps, a dynamic young cohort of highly skilled, articulate professionals works through the night, functioning on U.S. time under made-up American aliases, pretending familiarity with a culture and climate they've never actually experienced, earning salaries that were undreamt of by their elders (but a fraction of what an American would make), and enjoying a lifestyle that's a cocktail of premature affluence and Westernization transplanted to an Indian setting.

It's been a major breakthrough for India and Indians, one that Anglophone countries in Africa, like Ghana and Kenya, are striving to emulate. But many in India see the call centers as soul-destroying sweatshops soaking up the talents and energies of young Indians who could and should be doing better for themselves and their country.

Chetan Bhagat's best seller, *One Night @ the Call Center,* for instance, inveighs against young Indians wasting their time catering to
the unreasonable and petty demands of American customers —
customers so stupid, in Bhagat's telling, that an instructor teaches
call center trainees the formula 10 = 35: "Remember, a thirty-five-
year-old American's brain and IQ is the same as a ten-year-old
Indian's." As one of Bhagat's protagonists puts it in the novel's cli-
mactic scene: "An entire generation up all night, providing crutches
for the white morons to run their lives . . . while bad bosses and stupid Americans suck the lifeblood out of our country's most productive generation." One elitist friend of mine put it even more pithily:
"All we're doing is providing coolie labor — carrying the excess baggage of globalization that's too clunky for the West to bother to lift."

It's a harsh judgment, one that's genuinely unfair to the talent,
dedication, and creativity of the young people who make the call
centers work. But it's also out of date. If what India is doing is providing coolie labor, then today the coolies are scheduling the trains.

The evidence is striking. The business processes that are being
outsourced are no longer just the airline reservations or customer
billing or even minor technical troubleshooting that earlier made up
the bulk of the call centers' work. Today Indians are reading MRIs
for American hospitals, running consulting services for global U.S.
firms, handling actuarial work for British insurance companies, ana-
lyzing U.S. and European company stocks for Western institutional
investors, and writing software that will prevent Boeing and Airbus
planes from colliding in midair. Hardly menial tasks.

And there's more. When the U.S. pharmaceutical company Eli
Lilly discovered a molecule recently that it needed to shepherd
through extensive clinical research and human trials before it could
be placed on the market, it gave the task to an Indian firm, Nicholas
Piramal. Anand Giridharadas, who reported this in the *New York
Times,* added that Infosys is designing part of the wing of the Airbus
A380, Tata Consultancy Services is building the software for the
cockpits, and a third Indian firm is designing the plane's doors. This
is not just back-office work; it's the sort of fundamental responsibil-

ity that Western firms traditionally carried out in their national HQs, on the assumption that that was the only way they could guarantee quality. Today, they see India as a country that can provide the same quality — and a lot more cheaply.

The employment figures of multinational corporations in India tell their own story. By December 2007, Accenture should have more employees in India than in the United States, its headquarters. In the last fifteen years, IBM has increased its Indian workforce by 52,000 while reducing its American employees by 31,000. When Citigroup recently announced major job cuts in the States, its 22,000 Indian staff were unaffected, and if anything are likely to increase. The proportion of these companies' workforces in India as a percentage of their global labor pool is going up steadily. As technology advances, there's almost no limit to the kind of work that can be outsourced, and India is in the prime position to pick up the offerings. Today, as long as you have the fiber-optic cables and the bandwidth to communicate with the other side of the globe, geography is merely a circumstance, not a determining factor.

This is a welcome development, but we shouldn't be content with it. The next stage must be for Indians to develop such services for our own market. Doing outsourced work for the United States and Europe is all very well, but there's a lot more we could be doing for India and Indians, too. The skills we are able to market for foreign employers can also be turned toward improving the prospects of our fellow citizens — finding solutions for the problems of Indians and not just Americans or Brits. Perhaps the next level of outsourcing will come when smart scientists in Bangalore farm out processes to young engineers in Dharwar to cater to the needs of consumers in Hubli.

58

Looking to the Future with Brand IIT

EW SUBJECTS WARRANT AS OPTIMISTIC A LOOK TO THE FUTURE as Indian science and technology. Living as I am these days in the United States, I have had the particular pleasure of seeing some of the prospects firsthand, having been asked to address a global gathering of IIT alumni in Mumbai just before Christmas 2006.

Demographic projections suggest that the next U.S. census will find more Indian Americans than American Indians. When I was admitted to an American graduate school in 1975, not too many history majors were making the journey to America. Already, though, our counterparts at India's elite technological universities and engineering colleges — especially those from the Indian Institutes of Technology or IITs — had begun to snap up the fellowships that American munificence provided. They went on to form the creative backbone of the global information revolution with their quick minds and developed crucial innovations that changed the way Americans live.

IITians dominate what Americans call the "honor roll." Arun Netravali, former president of Bell Laboratories, received the Presidential Medal of Technology for pioneering the technology that enabled high-definition television, HDTV, and Internet streaming videos. Raj and Neera Singh, an entrepreneurial couple, pioneered the use of cell phone and pager technology in forty countries. Mohamed Zaidi, as president of Alcoa in Germany, pioneered the first aluminum-based automobiles for various models of Audi, Mercedes, Jaguar, Volvo, and Porsche. Dr. Mani Bhaumik invented the cold laser technique, which is used for laser eye-surgery machines and has benefited over fifteen million patients worldwide. Padma Warrior as CTO of Motorola is creating more affordable mobile phones for the Indian rural markets. (These stars and many more — 101 global IITians in all — are featured in a book by IIT alumnus Ranjan Pant, published in 2007.)

The success of these IITians and several thousand more transformed the image of their homeland and its people. To the American mind, the stereotypical Indian is no longer a snake charmer but a software guru. Today an Indian student with decent grades has a better than ever chance of admission to an American university of his or her choice, with a substantial scholarship. This blossoming of the Indian diaspora has happened because of seeds sown decades ago by the founders of great institutions like the IITs.

When I wrote my short biography of Jawaharlal Nehru (*Nehru: The Invention of India*), I became conscious of the extent to which we have taken for granted one vital legacy of his: the creation of an infrastructure for excellence in science and technology, which has become a source of great self-confidence and competitive advantage for India today.

Men like Homi Bhabha and Vikram Sarabhai constructed the platform for Indian accomplishments in the fields of atomic energy and space research. They and their successors have given India a scientific establishment without peer in the developing world.

Nehru's establishment of the IITs (and the spur they provided to other institutions like Birla Institutes of Technology and Indian Institutes of Management) have produced many of the finest minds in America's Silicon Valley and Fortune 500 corporations. Today, an IIT degree is held in the same reverence in the United States as one from MIT or Caltech. The next step is for IITians in India and

IITians abroad to strengthen their bonds and combine their intellectual talents, resources, and skills to help each other expand into one another's markets.

One can imagine IIT alumni abroad enhancing opportunities for their businesses by partnering with Indian companies led by IITians, and vice versa. Such "IIT alumni to IIT alumni trade" could apply to many industries and even to higher education, where IIT alumni professors from Indian institutions and those attending from abroad can plan to exchange students and faculty and collaborate across borders on research.

India's extraordinary emergence in new industries — software, information technology, and business process outsourcing — is the indirect result of Jawaharlal Nehru's faith in scientific education. Nehru left India with the world's second-largest pool of trained scientists and engineers, integrated into the global intellectual system, to a degree without parallel outside the developed West.

His legacy is not one we can afford to be complacent about. After all, the roots of Indian science and technology go far deeper than Nehru. The Rig Veda asserted that gravitation held the universe together twenty-four centuries before the apple fell on Newton's head. The Vedic civilization subscribed to the idea of a spherical earth at a time when everyone else, even the Greeks, assumed the earth was flat.

And yet we lost the global lead in science and technology for over a millennium. It is time to resolve that we will never allow ourselves to slip behind again. That will require resources — serious money for research, world-class lab facilities. But above all, it will require one commodity India is not short of — brains (and the determination to use them).

"Brand IIT" has shown the way. We must start to scale this up to the point where one day "Brand India" becomes synonymous not with cheap products or services but with the highest standards of scientific and technological excellence.

59

India and Soft Power

"POWER," WROTE HARVARD'S JOSEPH NYE, "is the ability to alter the behavior of others to get what you want, and there are three ways to do that: coercion (sticks), payments (carrots), and attraction (soft power). If you are able to attract others, you can economize on the sticks and carrots."

It is increasingly axiomatic today that the old calculations of "hard power" are no longer sufficient to guide a country's conduct in world affairs. Informed knowledge about external threats to the nation, the fight against terrorism, a country's strategic outreach, its geopolitically derived sense of its national interest, and the way in which it articulates and projects its presence on the international stage, are all intertwined, and are also conjoined with its internal dynamics. There can no longer be a foolproof separation of information management from policymaking, of external intelligence and internal reality, of foreign policy and domestic culture. A country's role on the world stage is seen more and more as a reflection of its society.

At the same time, states operate in an era of competition with others, seeking to promote their security by leveraging their assets. And this is where "soft power" comes in. "The soft power of a country," Nye explained, "rests primarily on three resources: its culture (in places where it is attractive to others), its political values (when it lives up to them at home and abroad), and its foreign policies (when they are seen as legitimate and having moral authority)."

*

As an Indian, I am a little concerned about those who speak of our country as a future "world leader" or even as "the next superpower." Many Indian thinkers and writers I respect have spoken of India's geostrategic advantages, its economic dynamism, political stability, proven military capabilities, its nuclear, space, and missile programs, the entrepreneurial energy of our people, and the country's growing pool of young and skilled manpower as assuring India "great power" status as a "world leader" in the new century.

The notion of "world leadership" is a curiously archaic one; the very phrase is redolent of Kipling ballads and James Bondian adventures. What makes a country a world leader? Is it population, in which case India is on course to top the charts, overtaking China as the world's most populous country by 2050? Is it military strength (India's is already the world's fourth-largest army) or nuclear capacity (India's status having been made clear, if not formally recognized, in 1998)? Is it economic development? There, India has made extraordinary strides in recent years; it is already the world's fifth-largest economy in PPP (purchasing-power parity) terms and continues to climb, though too many of its people still live in destitution, amid despair and disrepair. Or could it be a combination of all these, allied to something altogether more difficult to define — the power of example?

In answering this question, India must determine where its strengths lie as it seeks to make the twenty-first century its own. Much of the conventional analyses of India's stature in the world relies on the all-too-familiar indices of GDP, impressive economic growth rates (7 percent a year over the last five years, and talk of even 10 percent in the next five), and our undoubted military power.

But if there is one attribute of independent India to which increasing attention is now being paid around the globe, it is the quality that we would do well to cherish and develop in today's world: our soft power.

The notion of "soft power" is relatively new in international discourse. The term was coined by Nye to describe the extraordinary strengths of the United States that went well beyond American military dominance. Traditionally, Nye explains, power in world politics was seen in terms of military power: the side with the larger army was likely to win. But even in the past, this wasn't enough; after all, the United States lost the Vietnam War, and the Soviet Union was defeated in Afghanistan. Enter soft power.

For Nye, the United States is the archetypal exponent of soft power. The United States is the home of Boeing and Intel, GM and the iPod, Microsoft and MTV, Hollywood and Disneyland, McDonald's and Starbucks — in short, home of most of the major products that dominate daily life around our globe. The attractiveness of these assets, and of the American lifestyle of which they are emblematic, is that they permit the United States to maximize what Nye called its soft power — the ability to attract and persuade others to adopt the U.S. agenda, rather than relying purely on the dissuasive or coercive hard power of military force. Its subtly deployed soft power is therefore as important to the United States as — perhaps more so — than its well-established hard power.

In his book *The Paradox of American Power* Nye took the analysis of soft power beyond the United States; other nations, too, he suggested, could acquire it. In today's information era, he wrote, three types of countries are likely to gain soft power and so succeed: "those whose dominant cultures and ideals are closer to prevailing global norms (which now emphasize liberalism, pluralism, autonomy); those with the most access to multiple channels of communication and thus more influence over how issues are framed; and those whose credibility is enhanced by their domestic and international performance."

At first glance this seems to be a prescription for reaffirming to-day's reality of U.S. dominance, since it is clear that no country scores more highly on all three categories than the United States. But Nye himself admits this is not so: soft power has been pursued with success by other countries over the years. When France lost the war of 1870 to Prussia, one of its most important steps to rebuild the nation's shattered morale and enhance its prestige was to create the Alliance Française to promote French language and literature throughout the world. French culture has remained a major selling point for French diplomacy ever since. The U.K. has the British Council, the Swiss have Pro Helvetia, and Germany, Spain, Italy, and Portugal have, respectively, institutes named for Goethe, Cervantes, Dante Alighieri, and Camoës. Today, China has started establishing "Confucius institutes" to promote Chinese culture internationally. But soft power does not rely merely on governmental action: Hollywood and MTV have done more to promote the idea of America as a desirable and admirable society than the Voice of America or the Fulbright scholarships. "Soft power," Nye says, "is created partly by governments and partly in spite of them."

What does this mean for India? It means giving attention, encouragement, and active support to the aspects and products of our society that the world would find attractive — not in order to directly persuade others to support India, but rather to enhance our country's intangible standing in their eyes. Bollywood is already doing this by bringing its brand of glitzy entertainment not just to the Indian diaspora in the U.S. or U.K. but to the screens of Syrians and Senegalese — who may not understand the Hindi dialogue but catch the spirit of the films, and look at India with stars in their eyes as a result. (An Indian diplomat friend in Damascus a few years ago told me that the only publicly displayed portraits that were as big as those of then president Hafez al-Assad were those of Amitabh Bachchan.) Indian art, classical music, and dance have the same effect. So does the work of Indian fashion designers, which not long ago dominated the show windows of New York's chic Lord and Taylor department store. Indian cuisine, spreading around the world, raises our culture higher in people's reckoning; the way to foreigners' hearts is through their palates.

When India's cricket team triumphs or its tennis players claim grand slams; when a bhangra beat is infused into a Western pop record or an Indian choreographer invents a fusion of *kathak* and ballet; when Indian women sweep the Miss World and Miss Universe contests, or when *Monsoon Wedding* wows the critics and *Lagaan* claims an Oscar nomination; when Indian writers win the Booker or Pulitzer Prizes; when each of these things happens, our country's soft power is enhanced. (Ask yourself how many Chinese novelists the typical literate American reader can name. Indeed, how many non-Western countries can claim a presence in the Occidental mind comparable to India's?) And when Americans speak of the IITs with the same reverence they used to accord to MIT or Caltech, and the Indianness of engineers and software developers is taken as synonymous with mathematical and scientific excellence, it is India that gains in respect.

In the information age, Joseph Nye has argued, it is often the side that has the better story that wins. India must remain the "land of the better story." As a society with a free press and a thriving mass media, with a people whose creative energies are daily encouraged to express themselves in a variety of appealing ways, India has an extraordinary ability to tell stories that are more persuasive and attractive than those of its rivals. This is not about propaganda; indeed, it will not work if it is directed from above, least of all by government. But its impact, though intangible, can be huge.

To take one example: Afghanistan is clearly a crucial country for our national security. Our foreign policy mandarins have their work cut out for them there, and I would be surprised if Afghanistan isn't a priority for the Research and Analysis Wing (RAW). But the most interesting asset for India in Afghanistan doesn't come out of one of our famous consulates in the border regions. It comes, instead, from one simple fact: don't try to telephone an Afghan at 8:30 in the evening. That's when the Indian TV soap opera *Saas Bhi Kabhi Bahu Thi*, dubbed into Dari, is telecast on Tolo TV, and no one wishes to miss it. It's the most popular television show in Afghan history, considered directly responsible for a spike in the sale of generator sets and even for absences from religious functions that clash with its broadcast times. *Saas* has so thoroughly captured the public imagination in Afghanistan that, in this deeply conservative Islamic country where family problems are usually hidden behind the veil, it's an Indian TV show that has come to dominate society's discussion of family issues. I have read reports of wedding banquets being interrupted so that the guests could huddle around the television for half an hour, and even of an increase in crime at 8:30 P.M. because watchmen are sneaking a look at the TV rather than minding the store. One Reuters dispatch recounted how robbers in Mazar-i-Sharif stripped a vehicle of its wheels and mirrors recently during the telecast time and wrote on the car, in an allusion to the show's heroine, "Thanks, Tulsi." That's soft power, and India does not have to thank the government or charge the taxpayer for its exercise. Instead, Indians too can simply say, "Thanks, Tulsi."

Of course, official government policy can also play a role. Pavan Varma, the current head of the Indian Council on Cultural Relations (ICCR), has argued that "culturally India is a superpower" and that cultural diplomacy must be pursued for political ends, "keeping in mind our priorities on a global scale." A casual glance at the 2006 calendar shows how India is consciously seeking to leverage its soft power in Europe. India dominated discussions of the "creative imperative" at Davos in January 2006, was "partner country" for the Hanover Trade Fair in May, then "theme country" at the Bonn Biennale, a cultural festival for theater lovers. It starred at the Frankfurt Book Fair in October 2006, where it was the guest and country of honor, before November saw the Festival of India attract throngs in Brussels. The Festival of India was an interesting example of what India is consciously trying to showcase, incorporating as it did a classic exhibition called Tejas (or effulgence) highlighting early images of iconic Indian art from the last 1,500 years, somewhat more recent fare featuring exquisite paintings in the Kangra style, to contemporary photographic expositions on Satyajit Ray, performances by some of India's world-renowned artists in music, dance, and theater, a food festival, a fashion show — and, inevitably, a section on business opportunities in India.

That's all very well, and kudos to the ICCR for organizing it. But I would argue that soft power is not just what we can deliberately and consciously exhibit or put on display; it is rather how others see what we are, whether or not we are trying to show it to the world.

So it is not just material accomplishments that enhances our soft power. Even more important are the values and principles for which India stands. After all, Mahatma Gandhi won us our independence through the use of soft power — because nonviolence and satyagraha were indeed classic uses of soft power before the term was even coined. Pandit Nehru was also a skilled exponent of soft power: he developed a role for India in the world based entirely on its civilizational history and its moral standing, making India the voice of the oppressed and the marginalized against the big power hegemons of the day. This gave the country enormous standing and prestige across the world for some years, and strengthened our own self-respect as we stood, proud and independent, on the world stage. But the great flaw in Nehru's approach was that his soft power was unrelated to any acquisition of hard power; as the humiliation of 1962 demonstrated, soft power has crippling limitations. Instead of Theodore Roosevelt's maxim "Speak softly and carry a big stick," we spoke loudly but had no stick at all. Soft power becomes credible when there is hard power behind it; that is why the United States has been able to make so much of its soft power. Let us be clear: soft power by itself is no guarantee of security.

As Joseph Nye himself has admitted, "Drinking Coke or watching a Bollywood film does not automatically convey power for the U.S. or India. Whether the possession of soft power resources actually produces favorable outcomes depends upon the context." That context is often one of hard geopolitics. Soft power is one arrow in a nation's security quiver. It is not an all-purpose panacea.

So I have little patience for those who would naively suggest that soft power can solve all our security challenges. That is absurd:

a jihadi who enjoys a Bollywood movie will still have no compunction about setting off a bomb in Mumbai, and the United States has already learned that the perpetrators of 9/11 ate their last dinner at a McDonald's. To counter the terrorist threat there is no substitute for hard power. But there can be a complement to it. Where soft power works is in attracting enough goodwill from ordinary people to reduce the sources of support and succor that the terrorists enjoy, and without which they cannot function.

But this means we also need to solve our internal problems. When Joseph Nye wrote of the prospects for India developing its soft power, he observed that our country "still faces challenges of poverty with 260 million people surviving on less than one dollar a day, inequality tied to a caste system, and corruption and inefficiency in the provision of public services." In other words, until we can tackle and eliminate such problems, the negative perceptions they generate will continue to undermine our appeal.

So as we speak of leveraging our soft power, we must also look within. We must ensure that we do enough to keep our people healthy, well fed, and secure not just from jihadi terrorism but from the daily terror of poverty, hunger, and ill health. Progress is being made: we can take satisfaction from India's success in carrying out three kinds of revolutions in feeding our people — the "green revolution" in food grains, the "white revolution" in milk production, and, at least to some degree, a "blue revolution" in the development of our fisheries. But the benefits of these revolutions have not yet reached the third of our population still living below the poverty line. We must ensure they do, or our soft power will ring hollow, at home and abroad.

At the same time, if we want to be a source of attraction to others, it is not enough to attend to these basic needs. We must preserve the precious pluralism that is such a civilizational asset in our globalizing world. Our democracy, our thriving free media, our contentious NGOs, our energetic human rights groups, and the repeated spectacle of our remarkable general elections, have all made of India a rare example of the successful management of diversity in the developing world. But every time there is a Babri Masjid or a pogrom like the savagery in Gujarat in 2002, India suffers a huge setback to our soft power. Those who condoned the killings in Gujarat have done more damage to India's national security than they can even begin to realize. India must reclaim its true heritage in the eyes of the world.

India's civilizational ethos has been an immeasurable asset for our country. Let us not allow the specter of religious intolerance and political opportunism to undermine the soft power that is India's greatest asset in the world of the twenty-first century. Maintain that, and true world leadership in promoting global security — the kind that has to do with principles, values, and standards — will follow.

60

The Thrilling Face of a Bold New India

W E ALL KNOW INDIA HAS CHANGED DRAMATICALLY in recent years: the country I left when I first went abroad as a
student in 1975 would be barely recognizable to the
young Indians of today.

To those who remember the old India, there's visible evidence
of change all around, from the variety of makes of car on the roads
to the number of channels on my mother's television set, not to
mention the malls now sprouting like mushrooms in chic suburbs
that used to be dusty and forlorn mofussils.

But what about the invisible evidence of change? How does
one capture the transformation of attitude that's as essential a part
of what India has become?

Sometimes a simple event encapsulates something far larger
than itself. Journalists are overly fond of "defining moments," I know.
And one should always be wary of making too much of anything that
transpires on that theater of the evanescent, the sports field.

But my epiphany about the new India came in December 2006,
in just such a setting, during the telecast of the first cricket Test
against South Africa at the Wanderers' ground in Johannesburg.

India's new bowling hero, Shantakumaran "Gopu" Sreesanth,
was batting, facing the charged-up South African speedster André

Nel. "As soon as I walked in to bat, Nel said, 'I can smell blood, I can smell blood,'" Sreesanth later revealed. His first ball beat the Indian tail ender all ends-up.

Nel then marched up to the young Indian, taunting him that he didn't have the heart to stand up to the big man's pace bowling. "You don't have the fire, man. You should have a big heart to play me," Nel reportedly said, thumping his own chest in full view of the TV cameras. "You are like a bunny to me." He then declared that he would "get" Sreesanth with his next delivery. Nel ostentatiously changed the field for the next ball, moving the short-leg fieldsman to deep square-leg and informing wicket-keeper Mark Boucher, in Sreesanth's hearing, that he would be bowling a bouncer.

The young Indian was not fooled. "I am a fast bowler," Sreesanth said later, "and I was sure that he would bowl a length ball." Sure enough, Nel charged in, believing the batsman was expecting a short-pitched delivery, and bowled a fast, full-length ball on the middle stump.

Sreesanth, having guessed correctly, stepped back and with an almighty swing hit the ball back over the fast bowler's head into the stands for six. What followed is now one of television's most memorable moments.

No one who saw it can forget Sreesanth running down the pitch in triumph, twirling his bat like a bandleader's baton, then breaking into a dance that combined both relief and exhilaration: the relief of the plucky kid on the beach who has kicked sand back into the bully's face and the exhilaration of one who knows that, after essaying so foolhardy a deed, he had gotten away with it.

Nel was left not merely speechless but defanged; the sheepish expression on his face was worth almost as much as the priceless, laugh-out-loud joy of Sreesanth's impromptu breakdance.

Everything about the episode emblazoned a story of transformational change. In the old India, a tail ender, confronted with a fast bowler's aggression, would have been cowed. He would have either backed away from the imminent threat of decapitation or (at best) put his head down and attempted to block the next ball.

He would have been grateful to have survived at all; there would have been no doubt that the foreign paceman would have maintained his psychological ascendancy. It would certainly never have occurred to the Indian to think like a fast bowler, and it would have been beyond imagining that he would decide to meet fire with fire.

Sreesanth's extraordinary hit over Nel's head for six encapsulated for me all that is different about the new India: courage, assertiveness, a refusal to be intimidated, a willingness to take risks, and ultimately the confidence to stand up to the best that the outside world can fling at us.

This goes well beyond the cricket field. Sreesanth's India is the land that throws out the intruders of Kargil, that (in the shape of L. N. Mittal's takeover of Arcedor) acquires Europe's largest steel conglomerate in the face of taunts of "monkey money," that exports more films abroad than it imports, that challenges the traditional assumption of superiority by others, that wins Booker Prizes and Miss Universe contests.

It doesn't matter, then, that India lost the next Test, in Durban. It doesn't even matter that the entire series "went south" in Cape Town. Because this is not about cricket anymore. It's about a state of mind — a state of mind that will also change the Indian state.

What Sreesanth demonstrated was an attitude that has transformed the younger generation into a breed apart from its parents. It is the attitude of an India that can hold its nerve and flex its sinews, an India whose self-confidence is rooted in the sober certitude of self-knowledge ("*I am a fast bowler,*" said Sreesanth), an India that says to the future, "Come on; I am not afraid of you."

Let us cheer on the prospects of this India, an India whose reach and imagination can soar like a six into the skies above.

61

The Branding of India

THERE'S A NEW BUZZWORD THESE DAYS about our country: "Brand India." It's an idea, says the subtitle of a forthcoming book by London-based Niclas Ljungberg, whose time has come.

But what is that idea? What, for that matter, is Brand India? A brand, the marketing gurus tell us, is a symbol embodying all the key information about a product or a service: it could be a name, a slogan, a logo, a graphic design. When the brand is mentioned, it carries with it a whole series of associations in the public mind, as well as expectations of how it will perform. The brand can be built up by skillful advertising, so that certain phrases or moods pop up the moment one thinks of the brand; but ultimately the only real guarantee of the brand's continued worth is the actual performance of the product or service it stands for. If the brand delivers what it promises — if it proves to be a reliable indicator of what the consumer can expect, time after time — then it becomes a great asset in itself. Properly managed, the brand can increase the perceived value of a product or service in the eyes of the consumer. Badly managed, a tarnished brand can undermine the product itself.

So can India be a brand? A country isn't a soft drink or a cigarette, but its very name can conjure certain associations in the minds of others. This is why our first prime minister, Jawaharlal Nehru, insisted on retaining the name "India" for the newly independent country, in the face of resistance from nativists who wanted it renamed "Bharat." "India" had a number of associations in the eyes of the world: it was a fabled and exotic land, much sought after by travelers and traders for centuries, the "jewel in the crown" of Her Britannic Majesty Victoria, whose proudest title was that of "Empress of India." Nehru wanted people to understand that the India he was leading was heir to that precious heritage. He wanted, in other words, to hold on to the brand, though it was not a term he was likely to have employed.

For a while, it worked. India retained its exoticism, its bejeweled maharajahs and caparisoned elephants against a backdrop of the fabled Taj Mahal while simultaneously striding the world stage as a moral force for peace and justice in the vein of Mahatma Gandhi. But it couldn't last. As poverty and famine stalked the land, and the exotic images became replaced in the global media with pictures of suffering and despair, the brand became soiled. It stood, in many people's eyes, for a mendicant with a begging bowl, a hungry and skeletal child by his side. It was no longer a brand that could attract the world.

Today, the brand is changing again. As India transforms itself economically from a lumbering elephant to a bounding tiger, it needs a fresh brand image to keep up with the times. The government even set up, with the collaboration of the business association the Confederation of Indian Industry (CII), an India Brand Equity Foundation. They were tasked with coming up with a slogan that encapsulated the new brand in time for the 2006 World Economic Forum session in Davos, where India was the guest of honor. They did. "India: Fastest-Growing Free Market Democracy" was emblazoned all over the Swiss resort. Brand India was born.

But though it's a great slogan, is it enough? Coca-Cola, for years, offered the "pause that refreshes": it told you all you needed to know about the product. Does "fastest-growing free market democracy" do the same? India's rapid economic growth is worth drawing attention to, as is the fact that it's a free market (we want foreigners to invest, after all) and a democracy (that's what distinguishes us from that other place over there, which for years has grown faster than us). But isn't there more to us as a country than that?

In fairness to the smart people who coined the phrase, the more attributes you try to get in, the clunkier the phrase and the less memorable it becomes. It's easier for smaller countries that aim for one-issue branding. The Bahamas came up with the great message "It's better in the Bahamas." Puerto Rico sold itself as a "tropical paradise," and there's "surprisingly Singapore." But what do we want the world to think of when they hear the name "India"? Clearly we'd prefer "fastest-growing free market democracy" to replace the old images of poverty and despair. But surely there are other elements we want to build into the brand: the exquisite natural beauty of much of our country, encapsulated in the "Incredible India!" advertising campaign conducted by the Tourism Department; the glitz and glamour of Bollywood and Indian fashion and jewelry designs; the unparalleled diversity of our plural society, with people of every conceivable religious, linguistic, and ethnic extraction living side by side in harmony; and the richness of our cultural heritage, to name just four obvious examples. Yet it would be impossible to fit all that into a poster, a banner, or even a TV commercial. (And we'd still have left out a host of essentials, from ayurveda to IT.)

So the challenge of building Brand India continues. But one essential fact remains: what really matters is not the image but the reality. If we can make India a healthy and prosperous place for all Indians, the brand will be burnished all by itself. Then, and only then, we might even return to "India Shining."

62

India, Jones, and the Template of Dhoom

O NE OF THE MORE STRIKING INDICATIONS of the way in which perceptions of India have changed around the world lies in your answer to a simple question: Could Steven Spielberg make a film like *Indiana Jones and the Temple of Doom* today? It's been just over two decades since that blockbuster swept the world's movie screens, taking boy-wonder Spielberg (who'd already gone from the dental — *Jaws* — to the transcendental — *Close Encounters of the Third Kind*) into the cinematic stratosphere. Despite lame dialogue, contrived plotlines, and a visual gloominess that makes you wonder why anyone sat through the thing at all, the real problem with the second film in the Indiana Jones trilogy was undoubtedly its grotesque depiction of India.

The heart of Spielberg's story lay (along with the hearts of assorted human unfortunates) in the eponymous Temple of Doom beneath a palace somewhere in northern India, near the Himalayan border with China. Indiana Jones accompanied by a blond moll and a Chinese sidekick (actually played by a Vietnamese, but the filmmakers probably figured that all Asians look alike) enter an Indian temple in quest of a translucent *Sivalingam* that belongs to an impoverished village. The intrepid trio proceeds to annihilate a bloodthirsty cult of Kali worshipers there and liberate a swarm of children the villains have enslaved. At the end they return the kids and the stone to the village, now prosperous and green again. Virtue has triumphed over evil.

Sounds pretty good, I suppose. The critics thought so (the film scores an astonishing 93 percent favorable rating on the Web site rottentomatoes.com) and so did the fans, who flocked to cinemas from Sacramento to Sydney. Stepping goggle-eyed off Spielberg's celluloid roller coaster, hundreds of millions of people, mostly young and impressionable — people who almost certainly had never set foot on the subcontinent, met an Indian family, or read an exposition of Hinduism — acquired an abiding image of India. It was of a country where kings and courtiers feasted on stewed snakes and monkey brains, where Kali worshipers plucked out the hearts of their victims and embroiled them in flaming pits, and where evil, poverty, and destitution reigned until the Great White Hero could intervene to restore justice and prosperity.

Never mind that anyone with some education and a little common sense should have been able to see how absurd these propositions were — the filmmakers correctly assumed they wouldn't. Given both the relative youth of the audience and the colossal global ignorance about India in those days, the Indiana Jones view of India was swallowed without challenge by cinegoers around the world. (Many NRIs recounted tales of foreigners canceling prior commitments to dinner for fear of being served stewed snakes and monkey brains by their Indian hosts!) Of course, Steven Spielberg and his accomplices weren't involved in any sinister conspiracy to denigrate India; what was at work was not bias but indifference, even sloppiness. Spielberg may well have learned of the exotic culinary practices of some Chinese in Hong Kong, found them sufficiently revolting to be filmed, and put them quite literally into the mouths of Indians. Who knows the difference, he may well have thought, and who cares?

It was in the same vein, then, as his supposedly "Himalayan" village populated not by stocky, high-cheekboned Gurkhas or Garhwalis, but by dark-skinned, long-limbed Sinhalese speakers:

those were the extras he found on location in Sri Lanka, and all foreign languages sound alike anyway, don't they? So too the scenes in the temple — he knew what kind of horror would make his shrieking patrons choke on their popcorn, he knew just how his phantasmagorical Temple of Doom should be depicted, and if neither bore any relation to any kind of Indian reality, who would give a damn? After all, an Indian actor was prepared to drag one of his goddesses into the gore and to mouth lines about his religion's desire to stop the spread of Christianity by any means. Why blame Spielberg, if Amrish Puri could sell his self-respect for several fistfuls of dollars?

I can imagine Spielberg's fans rising to his defense with the argument that the film wasn't meant to be taken seriously. But entertainment is a highly effective method of instruction, and the fantasy in *Indiana Jones* is always anchored in reality: thus, there is a real city (Shanghai), a real country (China), and a real mountain range (the Himalayas), which no one suggests are figments of Spielberg's fancy. But he does not invest any of them with nonexistent sins. India, Indians, and Hinduism, however, do not escape so lightly. The filmmakers are cavalier in their disregard. If they had to show Indians, a notoriously vegetarian people, eating yuckily, why with the worst excesses of Chinese carnivorism? If they had to libel a cult, why not invent one, rather than abuse a goddess revered by millions? (The film is set in the 1930s, when Kali worship did not include human sacrifice — a century after the elimination of the Thugs, who by comparison with Spielberg's Amrish Puri, seem positively humanitarian.) Where in a Hindu temple would one worship grotesque skulls and skeletons, and find slogans on Kali scrawled on the walls like so much political graffiti? The reason all these feature in this appalling film is, quite simply, that the filmmakers knew they would get away with it. No one would care — except Indians, and we didn't matter.

Well, now we do. What has changed in the years since *Indiana Jones and the Temple of Doom* is that India has ceased being a land that could be relegated to the margins, a place of exotic inconveniences, full of snake charmers impaled on beds of nails. It's now a country that counts, populated by software geeks who might be making your airline reservations and reading your MRIs, a land that foreigners can no longer afford to be ignorant about. Even Hollywood moguls. If Jones ever got out of Indiana, what he'd find in our country today isn't a temple of doom, but something quite different. Call it a template of *dhoom* — the Hindi word for having a blast.

63

Heroines of Rural Development

URING A RECENT VISIT TO KERALA I addressed what was among the most remarkable audiences I have ever seen: some seven thousand rural women, gathered under a tent in the courtyard of a school in the small dusty town of Kollengode. Many of them had traveled great distances to attend an event celebrating the Society for Rural Improvement, a microcredit venture run by an ex-NRI returned from America, Dr. "Ron" Prabhakar, which had touched their lives directly in ways that decades of official development projects had not.

We all know that poverty persists in our country, and we have to stop regarding it as a sad but inescapable aspect of the human condition. We know from example after example around the world that, over a very short time, poverty and maternal and infant mortality can be dramatically reduced, while education and gender equality can be dramatically advanced. Rural microcredit projects like SRI (as Dr. Prabhakar's society dubs itself) are showing the way.

The poor rural women I addressed have exploded the myth that they are not credit-worthy. They have proven that, if given the opportunity, they know how to wisely invest their money for economically viable and environmentally sustainable income generating activities, repay their loans with almost a 100 percent repayment rate, and become the masters of their own destiny without the interference of their men. This idea was first tested, and proven, in Bangladesh by the Grameen Bank of Dr. Muhammad Yunus, who was awarded last year's Nobel Peace Prize for his achievements. Dr. Prabhakar has taken the same idea and successfully replicated the Grameen Banking System of Bangladesh in Kerala's Palakkad District.

It is no accident that microcredit is provided only to women. The fact is that in most of the world, poverty has a female face. Women experience poverty more than men. Generally, when money is given to men it seldom trickles down to the family: the toddy shops of Kerala flourish on the self-indulgent spending habits of men. Women take far more seriously the responsibility of bringing up their children, and they bear the brunt of this task. The result is that when a woman is empowered, a family is empowered.

So the women patiently assembled from several villages around Kollengode were the true heroines of development. They had shown yet again that we must not underestimate the entrepreneurial skills of poor rural women merely because they are poor. In turn, SRI accepts that its job is to help the women to help themselves — not to micromanage the efforts of the rural women, but to provide the necessary assistance, guidance, leadership, and capital and let the women themselves get on with their own work to pull themselves out of poverty.

Of course, poverty alleviation is not simply throwing money into the hands of poor women and enforcing repayment. This is done by unscrupulous agents who go from door to door in the villages (opportunistic people who lend money to poor women at exorbitant interest, exploit their vulnerable situation, and addict them to perpetual borrowing). These lending agents in the villages are called "blade companies" because of their cutthroat interest rates.

SRI is different: it seeks to build social assets along with economic assets. Poor work ethics and a distorted notion of the dignity of labor have limited the development of Kerala. The SRI project — whose beneficiaries make and sell reusable, economical, and eco-friendly items using indigenous material like areca nut leaves — is breeding a new-generation workforce, imbued with professionalism and a sense of customer service. Dr. Prabhakar has taught them that there is no greater dignity of labor than doing your work well and with pride.

In addition, SRI is providing free education and computer training to about two hundred poor and needy students. Learning is important, but besides academic subjects, they are taught the basic tenets of discipline, good behavior, and civic duties. If they cannot only overcome poverty but be groomed into responsible, productive, and law-abiding citizens when they grow up, society will be the winner.

Microcredit is not a panacea: it cannot be the perfect solution for all our socioeconomic ills. But it can be a precious tool in the empowerment of poor rural women. Yet not everyone in Kerala has shown the open-mindedness to support such creative and innovative efforts. Dr. Prabhakar tells me that the banking system is still cumbersome, complicating his efforts to deliver the small loans on which his microcredit system depends. Credit delayed can be worse than credit denied, and it is time that our banks and government funding agencies showed flexibility and imagination in supporting microcredit efforts.

SRI has proved that the Grameen Banking System, with suitable modifications, can be successfully replicated worldwide. A Chinese proverb says that those who say something is impossible should not stop those who are actually doing it. Projects like SRI's can show us all that ending poverty is not only *not* impossible — it is happening in the lives of our own people in India, here and now.

64

Kerala: Open for Business

DESPITE ALL THE STRENGTHS OF KERALA — ITS LIBERALITY, its pluralism, its literacy, its empowerment of women, its openness to the world — it's difficult to deny that the state has acquired a less than positive reputation as a place to invest. "Keralites are far too conscious of their rights and not enough of their duties," one expatriate Malayali businessman told me. "It's impossible to get any work done by a Keralite labor force — and then there are those unions!" He sighed. "Every time we persuade an industrialist to invest in Kerala, it ends badly. The late G. D. Birla put a Gwalior Rayons plant in Mavoor — it has long since closed. The Doshis of Mumbai started the Premier Tyre factory in Kalamassery — you know the fate of that plant? The late Raunaq Singh set up the first Apollo Tyres plant in Chalakudi, but all the expansions of Apollo Tyres since then went to other states such as Gujarat, as neither Raunaq or his son Omkar could deal with the politically charged trade unions." He shook his head. "I am a Malayali," he declared, "but I would not advise anyone to invest in Kerala."

It was with his words ringing in my ears that I stepped gingerly into my home state in May 2007. Newly freed from my career as a UN official, I wanted to see what I could do for Kerala's development, in particular by opening the eyes of foreign investors to what the state had to offer. What I saw and heard there convinces me that my friend's pessimism is, at the very least, out of date.

For one thing, the attitude of the workforce is not what it was. It's always been a curious paradox that Keralites put in long hours in places like the Gulf, where they have earned a reputation for being hardworking and utterly reliable, though at home they are seen as indolent and strike-prone. Surely the same people couldn't be so different in two different places? And yet they were — for one simple reason: the politicized environment at home. It's a reputation that has come to haunt Kerala. Several people told me the story of how BMW had been persuaded to install a car-manufacturing plant in the state, thanks to generous concessions by the government. But the very day the BMW executives arrived in Kerala to sign the deal, they were greeted by a bandh (strike): the state had shut down over some marginal political issue, cars were being blocked on the streets, shops were closed by a hartal. It had nothing to do with BMW or with foreign investment, but the executives — or so I was told — beat a hasty retreat. The plant has now been set up in neighboring Tamil Nadu.

Kerala's political and business leaders are aware of this story. But few are aware of the counternarrative. Last year I met Antony Prince, a Malayali long settled in the Bahamas, who is president of a major ship design company there, GTR Campbell (GTRC). GTRC had built many ships around the world, and its contracts had helped revive China's Xingang shipyard. Why not try to do the same in his native land, Prince wondered. Ignoring all the friendly (negative) advice he was given, he decided to get one of his huge "Trader" double-hull bulk carriers built at Kerala's Kochi shipyard. This was a major undertaking: GTRC's Trader-class ships are thirty thousand tons deadweight, have cargo holds of forty thousand cubic meters in capacity, and are meant to sail over a range of 15,500 nautical miles, so the task would have challenged a more experienced shipyard. But as the work unfolded, Prince realized he need not have worried. Not only was there not a single strike or work stoppage, but the shipyard workers took pride in having been given such a major assignment. They finished the job to GTRC's complete satisfaction — ahead of deadline. Five more ships will now be built in Kochi; it's the ship-yard's largest-ever order.

But the potential is even greater. Working with GTRC had transformed Xingang into a world-class shipbuilder; there is no rea-son why the same cannot happen in Kochi. Mr. Prince was enthusi-astic about the prospects. "The officers and workers in the Kochi yard have proved that they can do it, launching the first vessel on schedule, with first-rate quality and meeting international shipbuild-ing standards," he said. "I hope the message will spread."

It should. The interesting point is that shipbuilding is a highly labor-intensive industry; some 30 percent of the input is human la-bor, which is what makes it ideal for a country like India. The work-ers at Kochi shipyard — unionized to a man — demonstrated that labor remains India's greatest asset, even in Kerala. It is not, as skit-tish investors had long feared, a liability.

A visit to Trivandrum's Technopark confirmed my impression that the skeptics are behind the curve. CEO after CEO told me in glowing terms of their satisfaction with the work environment in Kerala, the quality of the local engineering graduates, and the beauty of the lush and tranquil surroundings. Indeed, Kerala's past failures at attracting and retaining heavy industry are now working in the state's favor. One Technopark firm, U.S. Technologies, told me of having bid for a contract with a Houston-based company which had drawn up a short list of Indian service providers and placed the Trivandrum-based company last. The American executives making the final decision flew down to India to inspect the six short-listed Indian firms. After three harrowing days plowing through the traffic congestion and pollution of Bombay, Bangalore, and Delhi, they ar-rived in Trivandrum, checked into the Leela at Kovalam Beach, sipped a drink by the seaside at sunset — and voted unanimously to give the contract to U.S. Technologies. "If we have to visit India from time to time to see how our contract is doing," the chief said, "we'd rather visit Kerala than any other place in India."

As they say in the United States: Sounds like a plan! It is time that Indian investors took notice as well. God's own country no longer deserves the business reputation of being the devil's playground.

65

Shaking Hands

HANDSHAKES ARE NOT OFTEN TERMED "HISTORIC," but the one between Indian Prime Minister Atal Behari Vajpayee and Pakistan's President Pervez Musharraf in Islamabad in 2004 readily earned the adjective. After three years of bristling hostility verging on war, and less than five years after a bloody clash of arms across the snowy wastes that divide them in Kashmir, not to mention the fifty-six years of mutual tension that had marked their relationship, the two countries seemed genuinely on the verge of a real and lasting peace.

In the southern Indian city of Hyderabad, a striking example of the confluence of Islam and Hinduism on the subcontinent, the talk for days after the handshake was of the possibilities it had opened up. One idea that had seized the Hyderabad public's imagination (and many inches in its newspapers) was of the city "twinning" with its namesake, the city of Hyderabad in Pakistan. Till the British partitioned India in 1947, the two had been known as "Hyderabad, Deccan" and "Hyderabad, Sind" to distinguish them from each other in conversation. The drawing of hard lines on a map had made this unnecessary; it was enough to know which side of the border you were on to know which Hyderabad you were referring to. The other was simply out of reach.

The Indian Hyderabad is a good place to look at the subcontinent's past — and its future. Exquisite Muslim architecture abounds, especially palaces and mosques, including the famous Mecca Masjid where the faithful congregate in the thousands every Friday. But at the foot of the city's most famous monument, the four-turreted Charminar, sits a Hindu temple to the goddess Mahalakshmi, the priests chanting their mantras for centuries under the celebrated Muslim minarets. And beyond the old city of Hyderabad gleams the high-tech crucible of "Cyberabad," a pet project of the state's laptop-toting former chief minister, Chandrababu Naidu, where Indian software engineers of all faiths click their country's way into the twenty-first century.

Here the past poses no impediment to the future. But that has not been quite as true for the subcontinent as a whole, which has for more than five decades seemed a prisoner of the past, handcuffed to a pessimist's reading of history.

Muslims and Hindus (as well as followers of many other creeds) have shared the same civilizational space on the subcontinent for over a thousand years. Islam came to India as early as the eighth century A.D., to Sind in the north with the Arab armies of Mohammed bin Qasim, and to Kerala in the south with traders and travelers across the Arabia sea. For the most part the two big faiths coexisted for centuries; though persecution and violence were not unknown, few saw religion as the primary determinant of their loyalties. In the great revolt of 1857 against the British, Hindus and Muslims rose as one against the foreign occupier, rallying under the banner of the last Mughal king. But the Hindu-Muslim unity seen in that revolt led the alarmed British to adopt a policy of "divide and rule," which sowed mutual suspicions and hatreds. The policy found its culmination ninety years later in Partition.

The tragic flash point of Kashmir, which has twice brought the two countries to war and several times to the brink of it, is described by some in Pakistan as the "unfinished business of Partition." When a student at Cambridge, Chaudhury Rehmat Ali invented the name

Pakistan (land of the pure) for the country he hoped would be created for his coreligionists, the *k* in his neologism stood for Kashmir. But Kashmir's Hindu maharajah, facing invaders at his door, acceded to India, and the resultant conflict left both countries with a portion of the state, and a dotted line (the Line of Control) across the map. Pakistan argues that the Muslim-majority state should have always been part of the Muslim country; India points to Kashmir's Muslim majority as proof of the pluralism of its secular democracy.

So for years the talk has been of war, militancy, terrorism, and now the nuclear threat. And yet history entwines the two countries together with bonds of paradox. India derives its name from the river Indus, which flows in Pakistan. The Partition of 1947 created a state for India's Muslims, but there are more Muslims in secular India than in Islamic Pakistan. The two countries share common languages, costumes, customs, and cuisines; when their citizens meet abroad, they slip easily into camaraderie. (Many is the time a Pakistani cabbie in New York has refused to take money from an Indian passenger, saying only, "You are my brother.") Indian films, music, and clothes remain wildly popular across the border, and Pakistani cricketers and musicians are lionized in India. A national of either country visiting the other is soon overwhelmed with the hospitality showered upon him by anyone discovering where he is from.

Strikingly, as part of his peace overture in Islamabad, Prime Minister Vajpayee, once a leading member of a party whose platform called for the undoing of Partition and the re-creation of an "undivided India," suggested that the two countries and their sibling, Bangladesh (once East Pakistan), jointly commemorate the 150th anniversary of the great revolt of 1857. His proposal was received warily; history has so far been a force for division on the subcontinent, not of unity. But Vajpayee had proved he could transcend the past by paying tribute at the Minar-e-Pakistan in Lahore, a shrine to that country's founding. And Musharraf, a trained man of war whose own family left India for Pakistan upon Partition, has shown signs of his determination to reinvent himself as a man of peace.

"History has been made," President Musharraf told a news conference after his meeting with Prime Minister Vajpayee. The challenge for both countries is now to demonstrate that history has also been overcome. Till then, those who contemplate peace also find their hands shaking — with fear of the alternative.

66

Trade for Peace

FOR YEARS, INDIA SEEMED PERVERSELY PROUD of its declining foreign trade. During the first four decades of our independence, our exports of manufactured goods grew at an annual rate of 0.1 percent until 1985; as a result, India's share of world trade fell by four-fifths, or 80 percent, from 1947 to 1987. This was perhaps understandable in the postcolonial context because India's closed and statist economic policies were principally a political and cultural reaction to British imperialism. After all, the East India Company had come to trade and stayed on to rule. So our idea of self-reliance combined a Nehruvian concern for distributive social justice with a profound mistrust of the international economic forces that had enslaved the country for two hundred years. Economic self-reliance was seen as synonymous with independence itself. So who needed trade when we were going to make everything we needed ourselves?

The attitude sank deep roots in the national consciousness. We saw it as recently as the mid-1990s, in the hue and cry that erupted over the "Uruguay round" negotiations of the General Agreement on Tariffs and Trade (GATT), which culminated in the establishment of the World Trade Organization (WTO). Ideologues fearful that free trade would involve surrender to foreign imperialist interests made common cause with protected industries anxious about new patent rules; both were supported by idealists dreading the effects of free trade on the common man (for instance, the end of affordable medication for the Indian poor). Of course, many of the fears were exaggerated, but agitators called for India to pull out of GATT/WTO altogether, even if this would have been calamitous for the country.

How different things have been with India's leading role in the WTO on the current "Doha round" of trade negotiations. The most significant proof of India's maturity as an independent country has been the willingness of our leadership to accept, at long last, that economic interdependence is not incompatible with political independence. Around the world, leaders have realized that the main reason developing countries have not caught up more rapidly with developed ones is that they were closed to the world economy and therefore to the benefits of increased trade and foreign investment. Whereas not very long ago, 90 percent of the developing nations — members of the "Group of 77," which actually comprises over a hundred countries — ran closed economies, today only Myanmar (and that too not entirely) resists the siren call of the global marketplace. In every country, trade barriers are being lowered, imports and exports increased, foreign capital avidly sought, legal systems are being brought into line with the needs of international business, tax and property laws are being reexamined against foreign standards, and restrictive rules and regulations are being scrapped. More and more economies are being "plugged in" to the global system in what is a self-reinforcing process.

What is true at the global level is not, however, what is practiced next door to home. India-Pakistan trade is negligible. The two countries, which shared the same economic and political space before Partition, and which should logically be each other's major trading partner (as Canada is to the United States, or Belgium is to the Netherlands) hardly buy from each other. Only 0.2 percent to 0.4 percent of our exports go to Pakistan, and only 0.2 to 0.6 percent of our imports come from there. (Of course, a great deal of illegal trade is being conducted by smugglers on both sides, but one can scarcely count that.) The general assumption is that the tensions and the history of conflict between the two countries condemns us to a continuation of this pattern; indeed, given that for nine years (1965–74) there was no trade at all between us, the attitude is that the modest level of trade we have is better than nothing.

Indians also point out that much of the reluctance to open up trading relations comes from the Pakistani side, both out of a fear of being swamped by Indian products and from a policy posture that normal economic relations cannot be established until Kashmir is solved to Islamabad's satisfaction. That being the case, the conventional wisdom is that any Indian argument for free trade across the border is essentially self-interested. So I was all the more intrigued to read an essay by Karachi-based social scientist S. Akbar Zaidi in the quarterly *South Asian Journal* arguing that not only do both countries stand to gain from freer trade between them, but that Pakistan stands to gain more.

The case is clear enough. Pakistani consumers are still buying Indian goods — but they are buying at double or triple the price by importing them from countries like the United Arab Emirates, which repackage Indian-made products for profitable resale to Pakistan. Yet, even at times of political tension, India remains the only obvious source of immediate essential food supplies whenever shortages arise in Pakistan. In 1990, Zaidi writes, India "helped Pakistan tide over a potato and onion crisis," and during a sugar shortage in 1997, it imported fifty thousand tons of Indian sugar. Where else could Pakistan have acquired food supplies on an emergency basis but from its biggest neighbor?

Zaidi cites a study from Pakistan's Ministry of Commerce pointing to various practical advantages — lower transportation costs, cultural affinities, similar tastes — which point to complementarities between India and Pakistan as trading partners. The ministry concluded that "the economic benefits of liberalizing trade with India outweigh the costs." Not only would Pakistanis pay lower prices for Indian goods, thereby increasing their purchasing power, but smuggling would decrease, leading to improved revenue for the government of Pakistan from legal trade. The Karachi Chamber of Commerce and Industry has conducted a sector-by-sector survey of the impact of greater trade with India on the Pakistan economy and argued that even the obvious negatives had positive implications. For instance, though cheaper iron and steel from India would impact on those industries in Pakistan, they would also reduce high inventory costs in Pakistan's engineering sector. Cheaper Indian raw materials could revive ailing Pakistani businesses and help generate more employment. And, of course, a vast Indian market would open up for Pakistani manufacturers. No wonder Zaidi concludes that, from a Pakistani point of view, trade with India is "a win-win situation."

And it's not just about the exchange of rupees. As Zaidi points out, "Trade normalization is likely to improve the overall atmosphere in which India and Pakistan address all contentious issues." It is hard to disagree. The old cliché used to be, "If you want peace, prepare for war." In today's world, it is time for a new formula: If you want peace, prepare to trade.

67

The Dangers to India's Future

"You're becoming known as a champion booster of the new India," writes a friend. "But we all know nothing is perfect in our country. What do you see as the vulnerabilities that might throw India off course?"

FAIR QUESTION, BECAUSE OURS IS A COUNTRY where predictions are both ubiquitous and foolhardy, and where the future is never quite what it used to be. So in reply to that question, I ventured a quick "top ten" checklist of the major dangers that could still retard, if not scuttle, our country's confident march into the twenty-first century.

1. The Threat to India's Pluralism

Everyone in India, irrespective of the circumstances of their birth, must feel they have a stake in the country, that they can create a decent life for themselves (and, for that matter, attain the highest office in the land), regardless of which ethnic or religious or linguistic background they hail from. The whole point about being Indian is that you can be many things and one thing: you can be a good Muslim, a good Gujarati, and a good Indian all at once. I've celebrated that a country that is 81 percent Hindu has a Muslim president, a Sikh prime minister, a Catholic leader of the ruling coalition, and now, a Dalit chief justice. But ours is also a country where religious riots have scarred the face of our land, where untouchability still condemns millions to degrading lives, and where the dangers of a triumphant majoritarianism are ever present. The moment we allow the pettiest and most bigoted of our politicians to create an India that reduces some Indians to second-class status is the moment when we fail ourselves and betray our future. An India that is denied to some of us will one day be an India that is denied to all of us.

2. The Danger to India's Democracy

Democracy is indispensable to India's survival as a pluralist state. For all its flaws, the miracle of democracy, with its exchange of demands and promises, hopes and compromises, has enabled India to manage its own diversity and deal with the extraordinary challenges of growth and development. But India's democracy has largely been ill-served by its political leaders; with honorable exceptions, mainly at the very top, an indispensable and impressive system is today overrun by unprincipled and unimpressive operators. Corruption and criminalization have taken their toll on people's faith in our democracy. That 113 of our 543 members of the Lok Sabha, the lower house of the Indian Parliament, should have criminal cases pending against them is an abomination. Despite the encouraging entry of bright, educated young politicians into Parliament in recent years, the continuance in office of venal and violent men could gravely discredit the system by undermining people's faith in their elected representatives.

3. The Persistence of Poverty

Despite all the good economic news I have celebrated in this book, 22 percent of our population — some 250 million people — are still living below the poverty line, in conditions that are a blot on our individual and collective consciences. By poverty I don't simply mean the kind of poverty that economists refer to, measured in the numbers of people living below a dollar a day. Our poor cannot afford to feed themselves, but I am equally concerned about their lack of opportunities in our society, which prevents the complete participation of large masses of Indians in their nation's democracy, and in our country's governance. We must take the necessary steps to ensure that every Indian is given the means to live a decent life, to feed his or her family, and to acquire the education that will enable him or her to fulfill their creative potential. Failure to accomplish this will be a real threat to India's future.

4. The Strains of Overpopulation

Most Indians have tended to take as an article of pride rather than shame that we are a nation of 1.2 billion people who are likely to overtake China in the next three decades to become the world's most populous nation. There is little doubt that the larger our population, the more difficult it will be for our society and economy to sustain it. Indeed, the size of our population both reflects and underscores our poverty. I have often argued, echoing Mahmood Mamdani, that people are not poor because they have too many children, but that they have too many children because they are poor. For the poor, children are an asset (they can be put to work) rather than a liability (they aren't being expensively educated); and in the long term, they are a guarantor of their parents' future, their only social security safety net, since only their own children will provide for them and look after them in their old age. So overpopulation needs to be tackled, but we have to tackle poverty, too. If we *hatao garibi* — "abolish poverty," as the country was promised in 1971 — people who are less insecure about their future will have fewer children.

5. The Risks of Unemployment

A major challenge amid our country's impressive economic

growth is that of employing all those millions of Indians who come of age and seek to enter the workforce each year but remain without jobs. It is not only important that the economy grows at a pace that can absorb all the job seekers; it must also expand in activities that generate jobs, whether in manufacturing or in tourism (our fabled IT firms and BPO centers employ only a million Indians out of a billion). Those frustrated in their attempts to find employment and earn a decent livelihood are often those who turn to violence and terrorism. It is no accident that there are few Maoists in Gurgaon or Gandhinagar.

6. The Politicization of Development

It's unavoidable, in a fiercely contentious democracy like ours, that decisions on economic development are made as the consequence of a political process. But the great successes of our economy in recent years have lain where the government played no role at all (information technology), got out of the way after a bad start (cell phones), or eased stifling restrictions (television). When politicians intrude, development almost invariably suffers, as the half-complete overpasses of Bangalore and the saga of the Tata car factory at Singrur (whose construction has been blocked for months by protesting farmers and their political sponsors) testify. The great challenge for government is to strengthen or renovate our dilapidated infrastructure — rutted roads, choked ports, antediluvian airports, collapsing bridges, corroded pipes. Much of this must be left to the private sector, given the many limitations of our public sector. And this requires accepting that quite often a few may profit but all will benefit. That means politicians will have to resist the chronic temptation to put self-interest before the national interest and let results be delivered regardless of political or financial advantage to themselves. The chances of that happening, it has to be admitted, are slight.

7. The Failure to Curb Corruption

The rampant corruption in public services in India is not just a sorry shame but one of the biggest obstacles to India's entry into the developed world. We have managed to become a society in which politicians and bureaucrats seek to profit from the power to permit and where every officeholder, however insignificant, seeks to leverage his position for private gain. Corruption drains resources from productive investment, distorts the true costs of doing business, undermines efficiency, and rewards influence rather than performance. That we have managed to grow and develop despite the rampant corruption is a small miracle, and proof of our remarkable strength as a society and an economy. But as long as corruption persists, we will find ourselves running the race of globalization with our ankles tied together.

8. The Risks of Demographic Imbalance

When people speak of demographics in India, it is usually to talk about the "youth bulge," a population pattern that ensures India a majority of people in their most productive years whereas the rest of the world is aging. That's all to the good, but there is another phenomenon that has gone largely unremarked — the unbalanced growth of our population, with skyrocketing numbers in the poorer and illiterate parts of the country, mainly in the north, and declining growth in the more educated and developed south. The obvious danger is not just of the poor reproducing their poverty and illiteracy and "dragging the country down"; there is also the political danger that a fair reapportionment of parliamentary constituencies according to population would grant the north many more seats in Parliament, while the south may actually lose a few. This would potentially enable the rough-hewn political hacks of the Cow Belt to override the representatives of the south; alarmists even conjure up fears of a revival of southern separatism in response. I am personally convinced that, after six decades of independence, we are beginning to see ourselves more as Indians than just as north or south Indians; I marvel at how masala dosas, the southern spice crêpes, are just as easy to get in Delhi as chhole bature, the classic northern fried bread and chickpea platter. But we should not be completely insensible to the danger of "two Indias" emerging, in which the north has the numbers, while southern India fuels the economic growth — with all the risks of resentment that could breed.

9. The Limitations of Federalism

I have long been convinced that a country the size of India must be a genuine federation — that not every question asked in Dharwar needs to be answered in Delhi. The increasing power and influence of regional and state parties in an era of coalition governments in Delhi should not, however, give way to complacency. Because it is not enough merely to transfer powers from the center to the states, genuine decentralization must involve empowering the *zilla parishads* and the village *panchayats*, the district and village-level institutions that reflect Indian democracy at the grass roots. The only way that Indians will be able to determine their own destinies is if our political system enables them to be responsible for their own lives. The centralism of the past might have served a purpose in the first decades after 1947 (to consolidate national unity); thereafter it proved a serious handicap to the country's development. Today, it is increasingly clear: that government is best that centralizes least.

10. Neglecting the "Software" of Human Development

We are right to focus on the urgent need to upgrade our national "hardware" — the country's collapsing infrastructure. But we must not neglect the "software" — the human capital without which no country develops. We must do much more to promote education, health care, and an end to caste and gender discrimination. Only then can we produce Indians truly ready to take India to the top in the twenty-first century.

6

An A to Z of Being Indian

68

An A to Z of Being Indian

WHAT DOES IT MEAN TO BE AN INDIAN? Our nation is such a conglomeration of languages, cultures, and ethnicities that it is tempting to dismiss the question as unanswerable. How can one define a country that has two thousand castes and subcastes, 22,000 languages and dialects, and three hundred different ways of cooking the potato? Sixty years after independence, however, it will no longer do to duck the question. For amid our diversities we have all acquired a sense of what we have in common: the assumptions, the habits, and the shared reference points that constitute the cultural and intellectual baggage of every thinking Indian.

India's complexities make the task a little more difficult than that of the British friend who defined Englishness as "cricket, Shakespeare, the BBC." Any Indian equivalent — "cricket, Bollywood, the Mahabharata"? — would be far more contentious. Instead of a phrase, therefore, one would need an entire glossary, an A to Z of Indianness. And since each Indian has his or her own view of India, this glossary must be treated as being as singular and idiosyncratic, as wide-ranging and maddeningly provocative as India itself.

And there is, of course, the great danger of obsolescence. If ever there was a time when India's cultural assumptions might have been timeless and unchanging, it certainly is not now, at the start of the twenty-first-century. Just a couple of decades ago I would have had to begin my glossary with All-India Radio — "Akashvani: The Voice of the Sky," which was also the voice of millions of radio receivers, transistors, and loudspeakers blaring forth from *puja pandals* and tea shops. Its ubiquitousness reflected the indispensability of radio in a country where most people could not read, and where television was largely absent (can anyone still remember those days?). Despite the often heavy hand of government on its programs, the anodyne cadences of its newsreaders and the requests for *filmi-geet* from improbably remote locations, All-India Radio mirrored the triumphs and trivialities that engaged the nation.

But its moderation also meant mediocrity. In the first five decades of our independence, when an Indian wanted real news, he switched on the BBC; for detailed analyses, he turned to the newspapers; for entertainment, he went to the movies. The rest of the time, he listened to Akashvani. Today AIR's monopoly has long since given way to a proliferation of cable television channels and the mushrooming of FM stations.

So no Akashvani, but even now one cannot eliminate our first entry:

AMBASSADOR: The classic symbol of India's post-independence industrial development. Outdated even when new, inefficient and clumsy, wasteful of steel and gas, overpriced and overweight, with a steering mechanism like an oxcart's and a frame like a tank's, Ambassador cars dominated Indian routes for decades, protected and patronized in the name of self-reliance. Foreigners were constantly amazed that this graceless contraption of quite spectacular ugliness enjoyed two-year waiting lists at all the dealers right up to the 1990s. What they didn't realize is that if they had to drive on Indian roads in Indian traffic conditions, they'd have preferred Ambassadors, too.

AMITABH: The star who refuses to fade away, the "Angry Young Man" of yesteryear who epitomized the hopes and dreams of a nation for nearly three decades. Bachchan remains a superstar in an overladen firmament, a cinema hero of unprecedented popularity whose impact on the nation has been out of all proportion to his talent. To appreciate Amitabh Bachchan, you have to confuse action with acting and prefer height to depth, but there's no denying the way in which the now Complacent Middle-Aged Man has hummed and hammed his way into the nation's hearts. When he had a serious ailment, the nation prayed for his recovery; every vendor of garlands and coconuts stood poised for celebration or mourning. When the ruling party wanted to capture a difficult parliamentary seat and dispose of an inconveniently strong opponent, it turned to Amitabh Bachchan. When he realized politics couldn't be enacted like the movies, he quit, went into business, flirted with bankruptcy, and reinvented himself as a TV game-show host, before returning to the big screen with a beard to complement his baritone. Through it all, Amitabh has remained the "Big B," but in a glossary of India, he leads the "A" list.

AMRITSAR: Engraved on every Indian heart, the City of the Pool of Nectar drips blood onto the pages of India's history. The tragedy of the massacre of unarmed protesters by British troops at Jallianwalla Bagh in 1917 gave a focus and a cause to the incipient struggle for nationhood — a nationhood on which the deaths in the Golden Temple in 1984 did more than anything else to cast a shadow.

ASHOKA: The great conqueror-turned-pacifist is the one figure of history who has most inspired independent India's schizoid governmental ethos. For decades, his tolerance and humanitarianism, his devotion to peace and justice, infused our declarations of policy; his military might, his imposition of a Pax Indica on his neighbors, informed our practice. Our national spokesmen inherited his missionary belief that what was good for India was good for the world. And in choosing a national symbol our government preferred his powerful trinity of lions to the spinning wheel advocated by Mahatma Gandhi. Typically, though, the only institution they saw fit to give his name to was a five-star hotel.

ASTROLOGY: Not only has it survived, it has grown in importance, as more and more important decisions are made by those who believe in it. Marriages are not arranged, flights not planned, elections not called until astrological charts are drawn up and consulted. An Indian without a horoscope is like an American without a credit card, and he is subject to many of the same disadvantages in life.

BABRI MASJID: This mosque stood for nearly 470 years in Ayodhya before being demolished by a howling, chanting mob who never understood that you can never revenge yourself upon history, for history is its own revenge. The Babri Masjid became the site where contending versions of history and faith fought over the rubble, where the very character and limitations of the Indian state were put on display for the world. Its destruction typifies a great national failure; the continuing impasse over what to put in its place reveals our talent for temporizing while the fundamental questions raised by the event remain unresolved. What could be better than a restored mosque side by side with a Ram *mandir* (temple)?

BIDIS: Along with *paan,* India's most original and long-lasting vice. There are few more authentically Indian sights than a five-rupee bundle of *bidis* — brown-green leaves rolled around a sprinkling of tobacco and tied together with a string of pink cotton. They also represent one of India's great unfulfilled marketing opportunities. Made of wholly natural ingredients, low tar, and instantly biodegradable, *bidis* should prove eminently exportable to the ecology-conscious international smoking public. If a cigarette had these qualities it would rapidly become the brand leader in its class. And there's no proven link between *bidis* and cancer, mainly because chronic *bidi* smokers usually die of something else first. In other words, for once we have the technology and are ahead of the competition. Is anyone in computer land listening?

BIRLA: A name attached to a number of leading Indian institutions: *mandirs,* planetariums, trusts, schools, clinics, institutes of technology, all of which have been made possible by a number of other leading institutions to which the *Birla* name is not attached, like Century Mills and Ambassador cars. (Also see *Tata*.)

BLACK MONEY: The real currency of traditional Indian business, the fuel of election campaigns, the high octane of film star contracts, the spark of real estate deals. The vast majority who don't have any of it are condemned to irrelevance; the lack of black money is the real explanation for the relative weakness of the salaried middle classes, with their printed pay slips and taxes deducted at source. Undeclared income is so widespread that its existence no longer shocks anyone; for all the years of liberalization, the black economy is probably as large as the white one. If it's any consolation, this also means that all the official figures for India's GNP should be doubled to reflect reality, so the average Indian is only half as poor as he thought he was.

BOLLYWOOD: Indian culture's secret weapon, producing five times as many films as Hollywood — and taking India to the world by bringing its brand of glitzy entertainment not just to the Indian diaspora in the U.S. or U.K. but to the screens of Syrians and Senegalese. Without Bollywood, India would simply not loom as large in the global popular imagination.

BUREAUCRACY: Simultaneously the most crippling of Indian diseases and the highest of Indian art forms. No other country has elevated to such a pinnacle of refinement the quintuplication of procedures and the slow unfolding of delays. It is almost a philosophical statement about Indian society: everything has its place and takes its time, and must go through the ritual process of passing through a number of hands, each of which has an allotted function to perform in the endless chain. Every official act in our country has five more stages to it than anywhere else and takes five times more people to fulfill. (Also see *Unemployment*.)

BUSES: Indians' favorite means of transport, whether rattling along country roads taking villagers to *melas* or screeching through cities overladen with office-goers clinging to the sides, the window bars, and the shirttails of other passengers. India knows a great variety of them, from dilapidated double-deckers to maniacal minibuses, which collectively constitute the cheapest mass public transportation system in the world. Regrettably, the bus drivers' tendency to plow into pedestrians and drive off bridges also makes it among the most dangerous.

CALL CENTERS: The quintessential symbol of India's globalization. While traditional India sleeps, a dynamic young cohort of highly skilled, articulate professionals work through the night, functioning on U.S. time under made-up American aliases, pretending familiarity with a culture and climate they've never actually experienced, earning salaries undreamt of by their elders (but a fraction of what an American would make), and enjoying a lifestyle of premature affluence and Westernization transplanted to an Indian setting. Critics argue that this is "coolie work" (see chapter 59), but it's transforming lives, boosting our economy, and altering our society. When the story of the New India is written, call centers will play a large part in the narrative.

CASTE: Described as the glue that binds Indian society together, but thanks to the Indian Constitution and decades of democracy, its worst features are beginning to come unstuck. Whereas in the villages caste may still dictate where you live, whom you eat with, and whom you marry, it is more difficult in the cities to pick the shoulders you might rub up against on the bus, and this is leading to a major decrease in urban caste-consciousness. On the other hand, the extension of affirmative action quotas to "backward castes" and not just "scheduled castes" (formerly "untouchable"), as recommended by the Mandal Commission, and (more simply) the politics of opportunism, have preserved the institution into the twenty-first-century.

After all, in much of rural India, when you cast your vote, you vote your caste. So the main thing that keeps caste going today is not negative discrimination but positive: the "affirmative action" programs with their quotas and reservations have created a vested interest in social backwardness. Not that the privileges for the scheduled castes and tribes are unjustified: after centuries of oppression, it is the least that can be done for those who have known millennia of suffering. (But today there are many parts of the country where you can't go forward if you're not a Backward.) Caste isn't what it used to be, an ineradicable stigma that could make or break your prospects. Perhaps the most important C-word of all in our glossary should be *Change*.

CELL PHONES: The instrument that has truly networked India. We don't have as many as China, but we're now selling more every month (7 million) than any country on earth. Not only does it cost Indians less to use a cell phone than anyone else on the planet, but the handy little devices have done something that decades of socialism could not — they've empowered the less fortunate. Cell phones are wielded today by people who could not have dreamt of joining the eight-year waiting lists our country used to have for landline connections — drivers, farmers, fisher folk. It is difficult to imagine a greater transformation than one wrought by the communications revolution in India, and the cell phone is its triumphant symbol.

CENSORSHIP: Holds a strange status in India: unacceptable and even unthinkable with respect to the national print media but perfectly applicable to radio, TV, cinema, and (in times of trouble) the provincial press. This is part of the elitism of the guardians of our public morals: those with the education and good taste to read the *Times of India* will not overreact to its contents, but the peasant in the villages must be protected from the pernicious effects of too much freedom. Sentiments we take for granted in the editorial pages of our big-city papers are thus carefully excised from All-India Radio discussions; fashion shows on TV are rigorously screened to weed out nonconformist attire that might shock the sensibilities of the custodians of *bharatiya sanskriti*. Though nudes appear in urban glossy magazines to titillate the bourgeoisie, villagers for whom partially clad women are a daily sight are spared the view of bare Bollywood bosoms by our city-based censors. Violence is illegal but is rife on our screens; love is legal but is reduced to coyness by our censors. It's time our democracy decided we're mature enough to do away with censorship altogether.

CLUBS: Thought likely, by Forster and other critics of colonialism, to be the first British institution to die with imperialism. In India, however, they simply passed into the hands of another elite and have carried on gloriously unchanged, with week-old British papers still available in the members' reading rooms and areas off-limits to women. Clubs are harmless enough as pleasant places to escape from the bustle of the city and to catch a game of tennis or a cucumber sandwich. But when they preserve the worst of the colonial legacy without the slightest imagination or national self-respect, as far too many do, they are worse than absurd. As a child, I was thrown out of the Breach Candy swimming pool in Bombay for being an Indian, a state of existence my innocent American host had not imagined would pose a problem in India; as a teenager I have been upbraided by a committee member for not taking a fork and knife to my naan at dinner; in another club I have had to tuck a kurta into the waistband of my trousers, since a flowing *desi* garment was not considered appropriate attire. The Communist minister who led a party of sweat-strained Santhal tribals into the pool of a whites-only club in Calcutta in 1969 expressed the feelings of millions of his countrymen. What a pity the tribals could not then be elected to the club's committee to put its affairs straight for good.

COMMUNAL VIOLENCE: Tragically, a sad reality and an avoidable stain on the Indian societal map. Every Indian carries with him the shame of the periodic bouts of bloodletting that hit the world's headlines: Hindu-Muslim, Thakur-Harijan, Assamese-Bengali, Sikh-Hindu, Shia-Sunni. One of the costs of being a composite nation proud of its storied "unity in diversity" is that diversity sometimes asserts itself at the expense of unity. When the madness passes, as it always does, what is left amid the wreckage is the belated recognition of intertwined destinies.

CONGRESS: The name of our national movement before it became reduced to that of a political party, and new generations of Indians are continuing to discover how vital its magic is. Shorn of its associations, Congress is even a faintly absurd name, for all it means is "assembly," but it is the association with the freedom struggle that makes "Congress" such a sought-after suffix even for opposition parties (from the Tamil Maanila Congress to the Trinamool Congress). No other political party in the developing world has as old or as seminal a history, as agglomerative a nature, and as many offspring (with Congresses — I, O, R, S, J, and even U at one stage). The Indian National Congress even inspired the African National Congress in South Africa and a host of lesser parties around the globe. That is why, even as it is reduced to heading a minority government, the Congress — as a movement and a model — should remain a source of pride for all Indians, even those who utterly reject its performance after independence.

CORRUPTION: Endemic in our society, even if it is never quite as all-pervasive as we ourselves proclaim it is. Indians are givers and takers of bribes, adulterators of foodstuffs, black marketeers of cinema tickets, resellers of train reservations, payers of capitation fees. Our soil nurtures bootleggers, smugglers, hoarders, and touts of all descriptions. Perhaps this is because there are so many laws and regulations that some will always have to be violated; perhaps it is that in any situation of resource scarcity, temptation will always be reinforced by need; perhaps it is simply that we have so many underpaid officials exercising power out of all proportion to their earnings that some are bound to want to narrow the gap by profiting from the power to permit. Perhaps, as Gibbon remarked about the Roman Empire, corruption is merely "the infallible symptom of constitutional liberty" — how else can politicians afford to run for election, after all? Or perhaps we should stop making excuses and find within ourselves a Hercules to clean out our Augean stables.

COWS: As much a symbol of India as of Switzerland, though ours do not contribute to a flourishing cheese and chocolate industry. But the veneration of the cow and its ubiquitousness have become something of a cliché, masking the often depressing reality of the conditions in which Indian cows live and die.

CRICKET: Not considered our national sport until quite recently (when I was growing up, it was supposed to be hockey), but the crowds at cricket matches and the media coverage of the game confirm the new reality. In how many countries would work crawl practically to a halt during a major match, crowds stay awake till the wee hours of the morning to hear a result from abroad, and pilots interrupt their passengers' reveries to announce the latest score? The range and subtlety of cricket, its infinite variations and complexities, its vulnerability to the caprices of the weather and its inability to guarantee a result make it perfectly suited to the Indian temperament. Now that our players' performances are beginning (World Cup aside) to match the spectators' enthusiasm, now that talent scouts and coaches are moving to the villages, now that the money in the game is attracting players of ability from all walks (and runs!) of life, now that 80 percent of the sport's global revenues come from India, it is time to celebrate the truth in Ashis Nandy's claim that cricket is really an Indian game accidentally discovered by the British.

CROWDS: An inescapable feature of Indian life. If foreigners stepping onto Indian streets for the first time were asked to name what struck them most about India, it would not be the heat, the dust, or the poverty but simply the crowds — the enormous pressure of people on every available space. Pavements and parks, *maidans* and markets, buildings and buses are all full to an extent never seen elsewhere. There is no such thing in India as a deserted street, an empty train, or even a secluded spot. Every act that takes place in public, from a farewell kiss to a film shooting, immediately attracts an audience; every inch of open space has at least two claimants; open air offers no release from claustrophobia. The fact that Indians manage to live, function, and order their creative energies in these circumstances is a remarkable feat of social organization.

DACOITS: An Indian peculiarity — the word doesn't exist anywhere else ("bandits" somehow doesn't convey enough). Though they flourish in varying degrees all over the country, the image conjured up by the word is that of the mustachioed bandits of the Chambal ravines, with their blood feuds, their codes of honor, their glamorous "bandit queens." In their tyranny over innocent villagers, their rapacious plunder (Veerappan despoiled the natural resources of his jungle as ruthlessly as any contractor), and the toll they have taken in human lives, the *dacoits* have exceeded the worst excesses of the Wild West, but it is typically Indian that the main method of bringing them to justice has not been the gunfight at the O.K. Corral but the extraordinary "mass surrenders" masterminded by assorted Gandhians.

DANCE: Curiously schizoid in status in India. The revival of classical dance since independence has helped Indians rediscover a precious heritage of great beauty and skill, and the encouragement of folk dancing has brought respectability and public attention to such expressions of rural exuberance as the bhangra or the *ottamthullal.* But for the mass of the urban public, dance is still something to be viewed on the stage rather than a participatory activity, and social dancing is still widely disapproved of as decadence on legs, confined to discos and nightclubs patronized by a tiny and Westernized elite.

DHABAS: Even if they are called *kadais* in Tamil Nadu and other things elsewhere, these food stalls are so much more than India's version of McDonald's. Few Indians have not bought tea, cigarettes, soft drinks, or even an impromptu meal at a *dhaba*. Roughly constructed of thatch or aluminum sheeting with a rudimentary wooden bench (if anything) to sit on, these sheds invariably offer more pleasure, and better food, than most five-star hotels. Which is why fancy hotels are setting up five-star fare in places they disingenuously call "Dhaba."

DISINVESTMENT: A charming Indian euphemism for getting the government out of businesses it has no business being involved in. (See *Privatization.*)

DOODHWALAS: These milkmen are still features of Indian life, despite the recent mushrooming of "milk booths" on certain city corners and the availability of packaged milk in supermarkets. They testify to the persistence of India's traditional social relations in the face of the encroachments of urbanization; and more prosaically to the lethargy of the Indian consumer, who would rather put up with watered milk delivered to his doorstep than pick up a quality-controlled bottle of it elsewhere.

DOWRY: The classic Indian social evil: the cause of much rural indebtedness, a great deal of human misery, and sometimes the death of an unwanted bride, usually in a "kitchen accident." There are still those who justify dowry as recompense for the parents of the son, and many who, more "progressively," argue that it is really intended for the bridal couple to make their start in life. Whatever the arguments, nothing can justify the misery caused by dowry; yet, despite years of campaigning for its abolition, and four decades during which the giving or receiving of dowry has been formally illegal, the iniquitous practice continues. In our country, social pressures are more powerful than legal or moral ones — even when the pressure is to do the wrong thing.

ELECTIONS: A great Indian *tamasha*, conducted at irregular intervals and various levels amid much fanfare. It takes the felling of a sizable forest to furnish enough paper for 600 million ballots, and every election has at least one story of returning officers battling through snow or jungle to ensure that the democratic wishes of remote constituents are duly recorded. Nor is any election coverage complete without at least one photo of a female voter whose enthusiasm for suffrage is undimmed by the fact that she is old, blind, crippled, toothless, or purdah-clad, or any combination of the above. Ballot boxes are stuffed, booths are "captured," the occasional election worker/candidate/voter is assaulted/kidnapped/shot, but nothing stops the franchise. At every election someone discovers a new chemical that will remove the indelible stain on your fingernail and permit you to vote twice (as if this convenience made any great difference in constituencies the size of ours); at every election some distinguished voter claims his name is missing from the rolls, or that someone has already cast his vote (but usually not both). At every election some ingenious accountant produces a set of figures to show that only a tenth of what was actually spent was spent; somebody makes a speech urging that the legal limit for expenditure be raised, so that less ingenuity might be required to cook the books, and everyone goes home happy. Elections are an enduring spectacle of free India, and give a number of foreign journalists the opportunity to remind us and the world that we are the world's largest democracy. But they are also an astonishing achievement that we take for granted at our peril.

ELECTION SYMBOLS: Lend both color and clarity to our political landscape. The great Indian achievement of reducing the differences among a bewildering array of parties to the graphic simplicity of bicycles and banyan trees has been deservedly imitated elsewhere. (Although there is somewhat less universal appeal for a dhoti-clad farmer and his plow, and the right to be identified by two yoked bullocks might not be so bitterly contested by political parties abroad, the principle remains worthy of emulation.) Symbols can, however, cause their own confusions, as when a number of electors in the early 1980s cast their votes for the wrong Congress Party, thinking that the woman on its symbol was meant to represent Indira Gandhi. In the mid-1990s the Election Commission forbade parties from choosing small animals or birds as symbols — after one candidate chose a parrot and his rival proceeded to wring a real parrot's neck to show what he would do in the contest. An elephant would have been safer!

EMERGENCY: A period almost everyone would rather forget, during which elections were suspended but jail sentences for politicians were not, and censorship suddenly involved more than osculatory activity on celluloid. For many Indians it was a watershed in their political growth, because the assumptions they had always made about the kind of polity in which they lived were so rudely shaken. For others, it was merely a period of fewer strikes and power cuts, when prices were stable, and yes, the trains ran on time. But those were the side effects of a far more fundamental change of system — and you don't need an Emergency to attain those ends. The phase ended happily, with free elections that defenestrated the government, but it demonstrated the fragility of institutions Indians had begun to take for granted and so strengthened the determination of those who wished to protect them. Ironically, the Emergency's most lasting legacy was the impetus it gave the press upon its withdrawal. Courage, innovation, and investigative journalism, all conspicuously lacking in the pre-Emergency press, became hallmarks of the newly freed media. There's nothing like losing your freedom to make you realize how much you can do with it; Indians are among the very few peoples in the world to have been given the opportunity to act on that realization.

EVE-TEASING: A uniquely Indian activity. It is not that Italians and Indonesians don't have the same proclivities, simply that the term itself doesn't exist anywhere else. "Eve-teasing," with its coy suggestion of innocent fun, is another of the numerous euphemisms that conceal the less savory aspects of our national life. Anyone who has seen eve-teasing in operation in Delhi knows that the term masks sordid and often vicious behavior by depraved youths against victims often in no condition to resist. Calling it "assault" or "molestation" would be more honest and might do more to raise public consciousness against it.

FAMILY PLANNING: Despite the many problems encountered in its implementation, family planning has already taken a hold on the popular imagination in a way that few could have predicted at the campaign's inception. The standard portrait of the four-member "happy family" (not so standard because the posters in southern India give the happy father a pencil-line mustache rather than the curler on display north of the Godavari) is now part of our national consciousness, as is the symbol of an inverted red triangle. Our vasectomy camps of the 1970s and 1980s, where thousands of men went for a quick snip and a transistor, are already the stuff of sociological legend, and who could have imagined the brazenness of government-sponsored advertisements for condoms in a country where a public kiss can provoke a riot? The achievements of family planning were done a great disservice by the excess of zeal, which led to forced sterilizations and to villagers living in fear of being dragged off to fulfill arbitrary Emergency quotas. Ironically, when governments changed, one of the first victims was the name itself, which became diluted to the neo-euphemistic "family welfare." The urgency went out of the effort. Today we are on course to top the global population charts, overtaking China as the world's most populous nation by 2034. Family planning cannot afford to be forgotten, though. Euphemisms do not prevent babies.

FASTS: These never worked half as well anywhere else as they have in India. Only Indians could have devised a method of political bargaining based on the threat of harm to yourself rather than to your opponent. As a weapon, fasts are effective only when the target of your action values your life more than his convictions — or at least feels that society as a whole does. So they were ideally suited to a nonviolent, moral national leader like Mahatma Gandhi (despite the resentment of a couple of viceroys, who thought his fasts akin to a child browbeating an adult by threatening to hold his breath until he turned purple). Gandhi's example was effectively emulated by other Gandhians: Potti Sriramulu's fast unto death in 1952 led to the reorganization of states on linguistic lines; Morarji Desai's in 1975 led to elections being called in Gularat. But when used by lesser mortals with considerably less claim to the moral high ground and no great record of devotion to principle, fasts are just another insidious form of blackmail, abused and overused in agitation-ridden India. It might have been worse, though. If more politicians had the courage to fast in the face of what they saw as transcendent wrong, governments might have found it impossible to govern. But too many would-be fasters proclaim their self-denial and then retreat to surreptitious meals behind the curtain, which makes their demands easier to resist since there is no likelihood of their doing any real harm to themselves. Inevitably, fasts have suffered the ultimate Indian fate of being reduced to the symbolic. What could be more absurd than the widely practiced "relay fast," where different people take it in turns to miss their meals in public? Since no one starves long enough to create any problems for himself or others, the entire point of Gandhi's original idea is lost. All we are left with is the drama without the sacrifice — and isn't that a metaphor for Indian politics today?

FASTS, PERSONAL: The individual, rather than political, fast is another Indian institution for which there is no equivalent abroad, except among expatriate Indians. Indians starve on certain days of the week, deny themselves their favorite foods, eliminate essentials for their diets, all to accumulate moral rather than physical credit. Where a Western woman misses a meal in the interest of her figure, her Indian sister dedicates her starvation to a cause, usually a male one (think of *karva chauth,* when women starve for their husbands' well-being). Her husband or son never responds in kind: he manifests his appreciation of her sacrifice by enjoying a larger helping of her cooking.

FILMS: The great Indian national pastime, an institution of such overwhelming importance that this glossary can barely hint at their impact on the national ethos. Films are the dominant and in many cases sole form of mass entertainment available to the vast majority of our people. India produces more films than any other country in the world, and these are seen several times each by people who have fewer alternative forms of distraction. Film stars are better known than most politicians, sportsmen, or writers and are the most potent symbols of the hopes and aspirations of ordinary Indians. There is no limit to their mass appeal: several have been elected to Parliament, three have founded political movements, and two have become chief ministers of their states. (One of them, NTR, still has a temple dedicated to him in Andhra Pradesh; the other, MGR, might easily have, too, but for the inconvenient fact that he was an atheist.) For decades there was virtually no popular music in India but film music, though this is now changing. The most widely read Indian journals in any language are film magazines, and even general interest publications cannot do without a film gossip column.

Films are the nation's most participatory activity: they attract larger audiences and employ more people than any other industry. They are a perennial growth sector in periods of economic stagnation; if so many of their financial transactions were not sub rosa, films might constitute one of the largest single determinants of our GNP. There is hardly any corner of our vast land that has not been touched by that great manifestation of popular art, the film poster. In other countries, films are threatened by television, but in India the most popular television programs are song sequences from films, or movies themselves. Films, also spelled (and pronounced) "fillums," are not to be confused with cinema, which is the exclusive domain of auteurs either Bengali or Benegali whose reputations abroad generally exceed their receipts at home. (See also *Bollywood*).

GANDHI: (1) A legendary, almost mythical figure, shrouded in the mists of history and the masks of textbooks, whose precepts, like God's, are cited more often than obeyed. The father of our nation, with a billion children and no followers. (2) An award-winning Hollywood film starring Candice Bergen, which won more golden statuettes than anything else ever sponsored by the Indian taxpayer. (3) A magic name that guarantees its bearer short odds of being offered the prime ministership (though it gains in luster if the prime ministry is refused).

GANGA: The country's great river, which to some degree is ironic since the names India, Indian, Hindu, and Hindustan all derive from the river Indus, which now flows through Pakistan. It is the Ganga, though, that irrigates northern India's great alluvial plain, waters many of Hinduism's holy places, and washes away the sins of believers. Nehru waxed lyrical about the Ganga in his will; to him it was "the river of India, beloved of her people, round which are intertwined her racial memories, her hopes and fears, her songs of triumph, her victories and her defeats. She has been a symbol of India's age-long culture and civilization, ever-changing, ever-flowing, and yet ever the same Ganga, a memory of the past of India, running into the present, and flowing in to the great ocean of the future." To Nehru, the most sacred river of Hinduism was a force for cultural unity, a torrent that unites history with hope. When his grandson Rajiv Gandhi was elected prime minister he used his first post-election broadcast to announce the setting up of a Central Ganga Authority to cleanse and safeguard this "symbol of India's culture, the source of our legend and poetry, the sustainer of millions" and "to restore its pristine purity" after centuries of neglect and pollution. Two decades later the Ganga is less neglected but more polluted.

GAVASKAR, SUNIL: A cricket player is one of contemporary India's first authentic national heroes — somebody good enough at his chosen vocation to be numbered among the best in the world at it. Who can forget his memorable debut series of 774 runs in four Tests against the West Indies, and what it meant for a generation of Indian cricket fans who were becoming inured to defeat? Since then his innumerable batting records have fallen to others, most memorably the highest number of Test centuries ever scored and the most runs ever made in Test cricket, but they were records he set in a sport where Indians did not use to set records. Even if his captaincy never quite measured up to expectations, Gavaskar's batting, as he stood up to the world's fastest and most fearsome bowling attacks, did as much for national pride as it did for Indian cricket.

GHERAOS: India's contribution to the art of industrial disputes. The notion of getting your own way by blockading your opponent in his office may have little in common with that of the self-sacrificial fast, but as a tactic of coercion it is used at least as often in India. Regrettably, there is no equivalent Indian invention on the conciliation side of the process.

GODMEN: More prosaically, "gurus," India's major export of the second half of the twentieth century, offering manna and mysticism to an assortment of foreign seekers in need of it, though some of the biggest and best of the tribe remain on our shores. Godmen appeal to the deep-seated reverence in Indians (by no means only Hindus) for spiritual wisdom and inner peace, perhaps because the conditions of Indian life make it so difficult for most of us to acquire either. Many also prey on the credulous by seeking to demonstrate their divinity through their mastery of magic, a device used for millennia by those who seek to impress themselves on others. The majority, however, are content to manifest their sanctity by sanctimoniousness, producing long and barely intelligible discourses into which their listeners can read whatever meaning they wish. If religion is the opium of the Indian people, then godmen are God's little *chillums*.

GULF, THE: Not a body of water, but a magic land in faraway

Araby, paved with gold, cheap electronics, and the hopes of Indian immigrants. Someone will no doubt do a study one day on the number of Indians who sold land, jewelry, or the family home to abandon a reasonably viable existence in India for the life of a laborer, clerk, driver, or shop assistant in the Gulf, offering ten times the income, five times the hardship, and half the joy. It has been a long tradition, particularly in Kerala, to seek work in distant places, live frugally, remit the bulk of one's earnings home, and hope to retire on the accumulations of a lifetime of privation, but the Gulf changed the scale of the whole enterprise, dramatically increasing the stakes. The Gulf began to attract highly educated and well-qualified expatriates as well. Though there is growing consciousness of the problems encountered by working-class Indian emigrants in the area and frequent reports of broken promises, dishonest or tyrannical employers, abysmal living conditions, terrible loneliness, and lack of legal rights, there are very few signs as yet that the Gulf dream is fading. That will take something else — a narrowing of the vast gulf of affluence that separates life in the Gulf from the life of lower-middle-class Indians in India.

HARIJANS: "Sons of God," is what Gandhiji called the untouchables in an effort to remove the stigma of that term. Unfortunately, the word has quickly become another typical Indian palliative — a means of concealing a problem by changing its name. No wonder that Harijans themselves prefer "Dalit" — the oppressed. Nothing like calling a spade a bloody shovel when it comes to labeling social injustice.

HINDI: The language of 51 percent of our people, a vernacular two hundred years old with practically no history, little tradition, and minimal literature, which is no doubt why it enjoys the elevated status of our "national" language. Every two-bit northern politician demands that it be the sole official language of India; the loudest clamor usually comes from politicos who are busy educating their own children in the English medium to ensure they have the very opportunities they propose to deny the rest of the populace. One chauvinist central minister addressed a letter in Hindi to West Bengal's then chief minister Jyoti Basu, who duly replied in Bengali; that ended the correspondence. On the other hand, Hindi is the language in which Bollywood's film producers reach their biggest markets, so there must be something to be said for it — as long as you don't say it in Chennai or Kolkata.

HINDUISM: The religion of over 80 percent of Indians. As a way of life it pervades almost all things Indian, bringing to politics, work, and social relations the same flexibility of doctrine, reverence for custom, and absorptive eclecticism that characterize the religion — as well as the same tendency to respect outworn superstition, worship sacred cows, and offer undue deference to gurus. (See also *Congress*.) Hinduism is also the sole major religion that doesn't claim to be the only true religion, and the only religious tradition that allows for such eclecticism of doctrine that there is no such thing as a Hindu heresy. This hasn't prevented self-appointed votaries of the faith from developing their own brand of Hindu fundamentalism, even though Hinduism is uniquely a faith without fundamentals. What they don't seem to realize is that Hinduism is a civilization, not a dogma. It's ironic that those who claim to be its defenders define Hinduism in a way that makes it something it isn't — narrow-minded, exclusive, and intolerant.

HOSPITALITY: The great Indian virtue, practiced indiscriminately and unhesitatingly irrespective of such unworthy considerations as whether one can afford it. Indians throw open their doors to strangers, offering their time, their food, and the use of their homes at the drop of a mat. After dowry, hospitality is probably the greatest single cause of Indian indebtedness. There is one catch, though: we are usually hospitable only to those we consider our social equals or betters. Oddly enough, foreigners inevitably seem to qualify.

IITs: Perhaps Jawaharlal Nehru's most consequential legacy, they epitomize his creation of an infrastructure for excellence in science and technology, which has become a source of great self-confidence and competitive advantage for India today. Nehru's establishment of the Indian Institutes of Technology has led to India's reputation for engineering excellence, and its effects have been felt abroad, since the IITs produced many of the finest minds in America's Silicon Valley and Fortune 500 corporations. Today, an IIT degree is held in the same reverence in the United States as one from MIT or Caltech. There are not too many Indian institutions of which anything comparable can be said.

ILLITERACY: Remains rife, with just under half our population unable to read or write in any of our several dozens of scripts. This may well be, as Indira Gandhi once suggested, because half our population is either too young or too old to read or write, but the real reason is that our society is not so constructed as to make illiteracy the kind of handicap it would be in the developed world. We are a particularly verbal people, reading aloud to each other in village tea shops, communicating fact, rumor, and interpretation without the intermediaries of pen, paper, and ink. But we can no longer afford the attitude that literacy is an extravagance (requiring implements to write with, material to write on, and light to read the results by, none of which is easily available in our rural areas). In today's information age, no country can succeed economically without a population that is wholly literate and that can use every keyboard it can gain access to. Allowing illiteracy to prevail is to handicap our people in a twenty-first-century race they have no choice but to run. It is true that illiteracy is not a sign of lack of intelligence: most Indian illiterates have a native shrewdness and sense of personal conviction that would put a city lawyer to shame. But it does reflect a lack of opportunity that remains a serious blot on our society.

INDIAN ENGLISH: A popular native dialect, spoken with varying accents and intonations across the country. It has not been greatly codified, its practitioners preferring to believe they speak the language of a distant Queen, even if she couldn't tell a dak bungalow from a burning ghat or a zamindar from a boxwallah. The point about this truly national language is that it has its roots in India and incorporates terms not found among the nine hundred "words of Indian origin" listed in the *Oxford English Dictionary*. The *OED*'s Indianisms are pretty tame stuff, like jungle, shampoo, and thug, whereas the true speaker — and reader — of Indian English doesn't blink at a lathi-charge on a sarvodaya leader emerging from a pandal after a bhajan on his way to consume some ghee-fried double-roti at a paan shop near the thana (none of which would make any sense under the, er, Queen's very rules). Indians are at home with Vedic rituals and goondaism, can distinguish between a ryot and a riot, wear banians under their kurtas, and still function in the language of Macaulay and Churchill. Our criminal classes, alone in the Commonwealth, are populated by dacoits, miscreants, and antisocials who are usually absconding; if these 420s are then nabbed by the cops, they become undertrials or detenus. Indian English has its own rules of syntax ("Why you didn't come? It was good, no?"), number ("I give my blessings to the youths of the country"), usage ("I am seeing this comedy drama thrice already"), convention (we eat toasts off quarter-plates instead of pieces of toast off side plates), and logic ("Have some Indian-made foreign liquor"). After our chhota-pegs we sign chit-books; the next day we don our dhotis and Gandhi-topis and do pranam when felicitating the PM at his daily darshan. These are not merely the mantras of babus: each term has a specific meaning within the Indian context that would be impossible (and unnatural) to convey in an "English" translation. Which is why the ultra-chauvinists who upbraid us for speaking a "foreign" language don't have a leg to stand on. As far as I'm concerned, Indian English Zindabad!

INDIRA: In a land of a million Indiras, there was still only one "Indira." Indira Gandhi's domination, not just of India but of India's consciousness of itself and of the perception of India abroad, has finally begun to fade from the public memory, two decades after the tragic circumstances of her departure from the national scene. (Even in death, she was larger than life.) She did much to transform Indian politics and to promote Indian culture and the arts, but she will sadly be remembered for the excesses of the Emergency (q.v.) and for fostering a culture of sycophancy epitomized by D. K. Borooah's fatuous pronouncement, "Indira is India and India is Indira." As the voters responded in 1977: Not.

INFORMATION AGE, THE: The era India entered when a superabundance of fiber-optic cabling and the imminence of the Y2K scare suddenly made the country's hardworking computer geeks indispensable to the rest of the world. Today, India's young software programmers have gone well beyond the menial labor of ensuring that American computers didn't crash at the end of the previous millennium: they write original code and devise creative approaches that make the world's infotech networks buzz. Today an IIT degree adds a gilt edge to any resumé. And the stereotypes are catching up: a friend recounts being accosted at a European airport by a frantic traveler saying, "Hey, you're Indian — I have a problem with my laptop, I'm sure you can help me!" The stereotyped Indian used to be the *sadhu* or the snake charmer, now it's the software guru.

JOKES: A staple of the national conversational diet; it was not so long ago that most Indian magazines ran a pageful of them. Indian jokes are almost always directed at Indians, either archetypally (as in the host of jokes about an American, a Russian, a Chinese, and an Indian, in which the Indian "wins" by being cussed or obtuse or both) or sectionally (Bengali jokes about Oriyas, Nair jokes about Namboodiris, Sikh jokes about Sikhs). Jokes in Indian English are in a class by themselves because they are cheerfully bicultural and often involve elaborate (and untranslatable) Hindi-English puns. The "Ajit" jokes remain the classics of the genre, featuring lines of imaginary film dialogue that the famously *dehati* villain would never have dreamt of uttering ("*Raabert, isko centrifuge mein daal do. Pata chal jayega ki chakkar kya hai*").

JP: The simple name by which one of India's simplest men was known. Jayaprakash Narayan was the Mahatma of 1977, but he was a flawed Mahatma. A man of insight and compassion, humanity and principle, JP stood above his peers, a secular saint whose commitment to truth, honesty, and justice was beyond question. But though his loyalty to the ideals of a democratic and egalitarian India could not be challenged, JP's abhorrence of power made him unfit to wield it. He offered inspiration but not involvement, charisma but not change, hope but no harness. Having abandoned politics when he seemed the heir-apparent to Nehru, he was reluctant to return to it after the fall of Nehru's daughter, and so let the revolution he had wrought fall into the hands of lesser men whose application was unworthy of his appeal. JP died a deeply disappointed man, but his legacy lives on in the subsequent conduct of the Indian people — to whom, in the last analysis, he taught their own strength.

KAMA SUTRA: May well be the only Indian book that has been read by more lascivious foreigners than Indians, unless one counts the works of Sasthi Brata. It is for the most part a treatise on the social etiquette of ancient Indian courtship, and those who think of its author Vatsyayana as some sort of fourth-century Harold Robbins are usually sorely disappointed to go through his careful catalogue of amatory activities, which reads more like a textbook than a thriller. Nonetheless, it never ceases to amaze me that a civilization so capable of sexual candor should be steeped in the ignorance, superstition, and prurience that characterize Indian sexual attitudes today. Perhaps the problem is that the *Kama Sutra*'s refined brand of bedroom chivalry cannot go very far in a country of so many women and so few bedrooms.

KARGIL: The war that wasn't a war. The conflict in 1999 that claimed hundreds of soldiers' lives, fought against an enemy that wouldn't acknowledge it was there and would not even reclaim the corpses of its dead (in order to protect its denials). An unnecessary war that sowed more mistrust in Delhi toward Islamabad than the officially declared wars had ever done, the Kargil conflict nonetheless played a huge part in awakening a sense of patriotism among the Indian people — who had just begun to slip into the cynical self-centeredness of our postmodern age.

KASHMIR: For years the fabled playground of favored tourists, a status it has yet to regain after nearly two decades of violent conflict. But it was always much more than a land of snowcapped mountains, exquisite carpets, and idyllic houseboat holidays. Kashmir has had to bear the burden of being a testament to the Indian secular democratic ideal, an affirmation that religion has nothing to do with nationhood and that Indian pluralism admits of no exceptions. The idea of India can only succeed if it embraces justice in Kashmir. That is what makes Kashmir so important for the future of India.

KHALISTAN: (1) An imaginary homeland for the pure of faith, the land of the Khalsa; (2) also *khali-sthan*, the space between its advocates' ears; (3) in the words of Khushwant Singh, a "duffer state."

KHAN: One of five unrelated cinematic heartthrobs who rule the hearts of Indian filmgoers and the wallets of the industry's bankrollers. Each of them — Shah Rukh, Aamir, Saif Ali, Salman, and Fardeen — has variously been dubbed "King Khan" by unimaginative assistant editors. But they may all have to make way, in critical acclaim, for a namesake who doesn't chase actresses around trees but can really act — the quietly impressive Irrfan.

KOLKATA: More a state of mind than a city, it epitomizes all that is magnificent and all that is squalid about urban India: its people, its theaters, its coffeehouses, and its bookshops set against some of the most depressing slums, the most wretched pavement hovels, the most noxious pollution, the most irreparable decay in the world. It seems a city without hope, a soot-and-concrete wasteland of power cuts, potholes, and poverty, yet it inspires some of the country's greatest creative talent. To the true Kolkatan there is no other city quite like it: if one tires of Kolkata, to paraphrase Samuel Johnson about old London, one tires of life.

LATA: Still doesn't need a surname to be recognized, indeed she doesn't even need a face; her ageless voice alone means magic to millions. The holder of various world records for the number of songs sung and hits achieved, Lata Mangeshkar has no equivalent in any other civilization, a singer at the top of the charts for over five decades. The late Piloo Mody once defined All-India Radio as an institution designed for the promotion of two women: Indira Gandhi and Lata Mangeshkar. He was half wrong. Lata has done far more for All-India Radio than All-India Radio can ever do for her.

LAW: Rivals cricket as the major national sport of the urban elite. Both litigation and cricket are slow, complex, and costly; both involve far more people than need to be active at any given point in the process; both call for skill, strength, and guile in varying combinations at different times; both benefit from more breaks in the action than spectators consider necessary; both occur at the expense of, and often disrupt, more productive economic activity; and both frequently meander to conclusions, punctuated by appeals, that satisfy none of the participants. Yet both are dear to Indian hearts and attract some of the country's finest talent. And in both cases, the case for reform seems more and more irresistible, as results fail to keep up with the nation's legitimate expectations. Unlike cricket, though, the problem with law is one of popular access to it. As an eminent judge once put it, the law courts of India are open to the masses, like the doors of the Taj Mahal Hotel.

LAXMAN, R. K.: You don't need to read the *Times of India* to be a fan of the first Indian Magsaysay Award winner for journalism, who won for his images rather than his words — the spry, smiling cartoonist whose audience exceeds even his newspaper's. Three generations have delighted at his rapier-sharp wit, his telling eye for instantly recognizable human foibles, his brilliance at capturing an insight in an image. And his enduring creation — the frail, perpetually bewildered, balding, check-coated "common man" — remains an abiding symbol of our day.

MAHARAJA: (1) Ancient feudal ruler, extinct as a species since 1947 and as a class since 1969; (2) title of some of India's better hoteliers; (3) symbol of Air India, usually depicted in turban, waxed mustache, and leggings bowing deeply from the waist, an act of which most real maharajas were incapable.

MANGOES: What more can one say about the king of fruits (though it now sells at prices that make it the fruit of kings)? It seems that the immortal Ghalib was frequently ribbed by his friends about his passion for the fruit. One day, they spotted a donkey going up to a mound of mango skins, sniffing it, and turning away. "See," they chortled, *"gadha bhi nahin khata hai"* (even a donkey doesn't eat it). "Yes," Ghalib replied quietly, *"gadha nahin khata hai"* (a *donkey* doesn't eat it). The greatest news story of 2007 in Indo-American relations is undoubtedly not the nuclear deal but the import of Indian mangoes to the United States — bringing hope of civilization to a land that had only tasted the fibrous, insipid, flavor-challenged American versions of the fruit before.

MARUTI: (1) ca. 1500 B.C., the Hindu wind god; (2) ca. 1975–76, a wheeled object in the shape of an inverted bathtub, with scooter tires and a smuggled West German engine, five of which were produced, as a "People's Car," by an unqualified engineer with government funds in a striking example of democratic socialism; (3) ca. 1982–present, a Japanese car, manufactured under an Indian name in keeping with the nation's commitment to indigenization, sold to the masses in ever-larger numbers, with the government's participation in the profits declining in inverse proportion to its sales. (See also *Ambassador.*)

MATRIMONIAL ADS: Seized upon by every hack journalist who wants to ridicule India for fun and profit, but they are no more amusing or pathetic than the lonely hearts announcements that litter the personal columns of the Western press. Indeed, they have an even more valid role to play in Indian society than elsewhere, for they harness modernity to the preservation of a traditional cultural practice, that of the arranged marriage. Matrimonial advertisements have brought together families who might never have heard of each other if they had stuck to the local barber. At the same time, the ads are a microcosm of Indian social preoccupations and prejudices, with their excruciating specificities about caste, age, salaries, and the intactness of hymens. But Indian typesetters always find ways to relieve any tensions with deftly placed printers' devils like the ones that, in one day's issue of a Delhi paper, invited proposals for a "fair-complected young widow, aged 92," declared the liberality of a "U.S.-based unclear scientist" who proclaimed "caste, color, no bras," and touted the attractions of a young divorcee "holding respectable job in pubic relations." I don't know if any of the advertisers achieved the desired results, but they could have made a remarkable ménage à trois.

MINORITIES: What we all are — for no one single Indian group can claim majority status in our country. A Hindi-speaking Hindu male might consider himself a representative of the "majority community," to use the term much abused by the less industrious of our journalists, but a majority of the country does not speak Hindi, and Hinduism is no guarantee of majorityhood since his caste automatically places him in a minority as well. Amid India's variegated communal divisions we are all minorities. Even in the days of "India is Indira and Indira is India," Indira Gandhi herself represented this condition: she was a Kashmiri ruling a majority of non-Kashmiris, a Brahmin among a majority of non-Brahmins, a UP-ite facing a majority of non-UP-ites, and (lest we forget) a woman leading a majority of men. Indian democracy is quintessentially about minority rule.

MONSOON: Not, as a Doon School student once put it, a French gentleman, but the season that sets our climate apart from the rest of the world's. Other lands have cold and fog and snow, and some tropical countries enjoy hot and hotter climates relieved by bursts of wetness, but few know the exhilaration of being lashed by monsoon rains for weeks on end, the frustration of vehicles stalled in the 180th successive year of flooded streets, the camaraderie of wading knee-deep in water with shins bared by the privileged and the proletarian alike, and, let's face it, the relief of avoiding our responsibilities as life spirals helplessly to a halt. In our rural areas the monsoon is life-giving, the harbinger of hope for the next harvest, nourishing the parched earth, flooding the paddy fields and filling the wells that sustain people, animals, and plants. The monsoon is integral to the Indian experience; centuries ago, Kalidasa wrote these immortal lines about the monsoon: "A source of fascination to amorous women, the constant friend to trees, shrubs and creepers, the very life and breath of all living beings, this season of rains." No one who has experienced the monsoon can treat the rains of Western climes as anything but a nuisance; our rains, however, are an event.

MOTHER TERESA: With her compassion, her vigor, and her faith, Mother Teresa brought light into the lives — and the deaths — of many miserable human beings who might never have known what it was to be touched by grace. Yet for all her undoubted greatness, I cannot help squirming at the perversity of those Indians who take pride in her Nobel Prize, who instead of being shamed by the conditions that made the prize possible, organized "committees of felicitation" when Mother Teresa returned to Kolkata with a Norwegian certificate clutched with her Indian passport. We Indians should be striving to create the kind of society that makes a Mother Teresa unnecessary.

MUSIC: Enters every Indian ear; from the classical cadences of the sitar and the sarod to the lyrical lilt of catchy film tunes, music is impossible to escape in India, whether blaring from your neighbor's radio in the morning, broadcast on loudspeakers outside temples and tea stalls all day, or nocturnally available in the all-night concerts of classicians. To the undiscriminating connoisseur there is a vast range to be traversed between Carnatic and Hindustani music, morning ragas and mourning ragas, Ravi Shankar and Lata Mangeshkar. With Muslim ustads playing Hindu devotional ragas and Bollywood playback singers chanting Urdu lyrics, the music of India is the collective anthem of a hybrid civilization. But music represents an even larger metaphor, for it sets the tone for the political life of modern India — in which, rather like traditional Indian music, the broad basic rules are firmly set, but within them one is free to improvise, unshackled by a written score.

NATIONALIZATION: An act of socialist governance that consists of transferring banks, insurance companies, industries, and other functioning institutions from the hands of competent capitalists into those of bumbling bureaucrats. The prevalence of nationalization in the face of widespread evidence of its shortcomings, inefficiencies, and failures testifies to the curious Indian credo that public losses are preferable to private profits. In other countries, this would be known as cutting off your nose to spite your face. (See also *Privatization*.)

NEHRU: As much the father of modern India as Mahatma Gandhi was of Indian independence. Nehru was a moody idealist intellectual who felt an almost mystical empathy with the toiling peasant masses; an aristocrat, accustomed to privilege, who had passionate socialist convictions; an Anglicized product of Harrow and Cambridge, who spent over ten years in British jails; an agnostic radical, who became an unlikely protégé of the saintly Mahatma. Few national political leaders have made as much of an impact on their nation's ethos. It is to Jawaharlal Nehru that we owe the "socialistic pattern of society," the dominance of the public sector over the "commanding heights of the economy," parliamentary democracy, nonalignment, secularism, the electoral system, respect for the judiciary, freedom of the press, the Nehru jacket, the Congress cap, and, at several removes, Rahul Gandhi. (Since I've written an entire book about him, *Nehru: The Invention of India,* I'll leave it there.)

NEPOTISM: Nepotism, or uncles granting jobs and favors to nephews, does not exist in India. None of our prime ministers, for instance, had uncles of any consequence.

NONALIGNMENT: Was (and in theory still is) the basis of India's foreign policy and consists of equidistance from the superpowers, a concept challenged by both geography and reality, not to mention the lack of a second superpower to be equidistant from. Nonetheless, nonalignment is still paid ritual obeisance by Indian diplomacy, which has been defined by a former doyen of the Ministry of External Affairs as being "like the love-making of an elephant: it is conducted at a high level, accompanied by much bellowing, and the results are not known for two years."

OPINIONS: As may be readily apparent from this glossary, opinions flow from Indian tongues like the Ganga through Benares: profuse, stimulating, and muddied with other people's waste matter. From village tea shops to urban coffeehouses, Indians give free rein to their opinions, which often, like those who express them, do not have visible means of support. On most issues, however, these are unrelated to any expectation of action, and the Indian public as a whole largely acquiesces in governmental policies even when they are contrary to its professed beliefs. In India, the expression of public opinions is no proof of the existence of public opinion.

PAAN: A concoction of spices wrapped in betel leaf is India's answer to French wine as the essential adjunct to a good meal. It is a useful if mildly intoxicating aid to digestion and the most national of liquid vices, though each consumer is obliged to generate his own liquid and to dispose of it against the most convenient wall. (This even led one Japanese health expert to declare that acute TB was endemic in India because he had seen so many people spitting blood.) The distinctions between a Calcutta *patta* and a Banarasi *mitha* are at least as significant as those between a Bordeaux and a Burgundy, but *paan* chewing is too down to earth to have evolved the same pretentious vocabulary as its French counterpart. It is time we established our own *paan* columnists to wax lyrical about the "strong body" and "delicate coconut fragrance" of a 2007 Madrasi *beeda*, contrasting it, perhaps, with the "heady bouquet" and "lingering aftertaste" of a silver-wrapped Mumbai concoction.

PARSIS: see *Zoroastrians*. (I had to have something beginning with Z, didn't I?)

PARTITION: The scar inflicted by history upon the nation when Pakistan was carved out of India's stooped shoulders by the departing British. Its human cost in lives, in the tragedies of displacement and flight, in lost faith and comradeship across communal divides, in the surrender by people on both sides of a part of their national heritage, was appalling enough; but it was further augmented by the colossal waste of resources thereafter in mutual defense preparedness and in actual military conflict. Partition betrayed both those Hindus who lived in what became Pakistan and those Muslims who were abandoned in India by the more affluent and vocal of their co-religionists. Above all, it betrayed all those, irrespective of religion, who believed that nationhood transcended creed and credo.

POLITICAL PARTIES: They grow in India like mushrooms, split like amoeba, and are as productive and original as mules. The old saw that two Indians equals an argument and three Indians equals two political parties can almost be taken literally, as every "leader" disgruntled with his lot in one party takes off to found another. (Shri Ajit Singh, if memory serves, has actually "led" eleven parties in the last ten years.) As a result, most of India's so-called national parties, with the sole exception of the BJP, are variants of the Congress (or variants of variants of the Congress), even when they have been founded with explicitly anti-Congress aims. The proliferation of regional parties, often with appeals that do not go beyond a single state, has further complicated this situation and virtually guaranteed coalition governance in perpetuity in Delhi. Although there is something to be said for the view that a multiplicity of parties is inevitable in a pluralist polity like India's, where a number of groups contend to defend their interests, a total fragmentation of political representation can hardly be in the national interest. And it is difficult to be entirely enthusiastic about a system in which a political party, rather than being the vehicle for the expression of a coherent set of ideas and interests, is merely a convenient cloak for the ambitions of an individual leader, to be cast off (or stitched to another's raiment) whenever it suits him.

POLLUTION: Indians have learned to live with pollution, inhaling more particles each day than a chain smoker might in the West, and boiling their water for fear of being laid low by every imaginable liquid-borne pollutant (and many a poison, including arsenic). India's cities are among the world's dirtiest. The air in Kolkata or Delhi is all but unbreathable in winter as car-exhaust fumes, unchecked industrial emissions, and smoke rising from countless charcoal braziers are trapped by descending mist and fog. When the Australian cricket team played in Delhi, its coach complained the smog-laden air gave the home team an unfair advantage — by impairing his players' performance. Factories belch forth noxious black clouds. Effluents pour untreated into rivers. Sewage systems reek and overflow. Governments pass regulations, then ignore them. Meanwhile, more and more cars ply the congested roads, and more small factories open up that do not meet pollution-control standards. Cardiovascular and respiratory illness are rampant, with attendant health costs estimated at 4.5 percent of India's GDP. In other words, more than half of India's annual economic growth is wiped out by pollution, and development is taking place largely at the expense of the environment. But given a choice between living more modestly in a "green society" and becoming more prosperous in the midst of brown, most Indians would be happy to gasp and wheeze all the way to the bank.

POPULATION: India's greatest asset, but some assets are better when they are not growing. We add an Australia every year to our population, which would be fine if we could also add Australia's resources to ours every year. By the year 2034 we will have overtaken China, by the year 2050 every fifth human being on earth will be an Indian. The nation's great challenge will be to ensure that she is a well-fed, healthy, clothed, and educated Indian. (See also *Family Planning.*)

PRIVATIZATION: The "third rail" of Indian politics, which cannot be touched for fear of electrocuting yourself. Privatization is essential in a society where the government finds itself running businesses for which it has neither the aptitude nor the mandate, and where the public sector's rampant inefficiencies both slow down the economy and impede growth, but the politics of the issue oblige even governments in favor of privatization to tread warily — so that even those who do it call it something else (disinvestment). It is an axiom of Indian politics that our political consensus prefers public losses to the prospect of private profits.

PUBLIC SCHOOLS: Like most British legacies, these are not what they seem; they are in fact private schools, set up to make better maharajas, Indian civil servants, tea planters, and boxwallahs out of their dusky charges. The tradition has continued after independence, so that our public school products can generally be found with a glass in one hand, a sporting implement in the other, and a languid lady within reach. Their recent switch of emphasis from garden parties to political ones has sociological implications that are yet to be studied.

QUEUES: Orderly lines of individuals seeking the use of public facilities and services. They were last spotted at a Delhi bus stop in February 1977, and have never been the same since. Indians don't mind their peace in queues.

RAILWAYS: Vital to Indian unity because they guarantee the mobility that makes Indians conscious of India. And they are also the institution that has made the Indian elite look at Laloo Prasad Yadav — the country bumpkin politico who turned around the fortunes of the Railway Ministry — with respect. For all their inadequacies, our trains are still the best value for money in the country, getting you farther for fewer rupees than any other mode of mechanized locomotion available in the world. Much is made of their lack of punctuality, but being a few minutes late should hardly be held against them in a civilization that rarely takes notice of the passage of years. The railways have spawned an entire subculture, from the congested life on station platforms to the comradeship of what used to be called third-class sleepers (since dubbed second-class in another fit of egalitarian euphemism, as if a change of rank might make them more comfortable). The management of millions of train reservations made, entered, and kept up to date by hand is a human miracle that the most sophisticated computers have only just been able to match. The art of railway traveling is also one that has reached great heights in India — literally, if you take a look at the rooftop passengers on many carriages. India offers more kilometers of passenger railways than any other country, more varieties of gauges (broad, narrow, and meter) and more kinds of train (from the palace-on-wheels that tours Rajasthan to the suburban electric trains of Bombay, from the air-conditioned Rajdhani express to the "toy train" that winds its way to Darjeeling). And Indian Railways doesn't just mean trains. Who can forget such marvelous ancillary institutions as the sumptuous SER Hotel in Puri, with its fabled cuisine, and the famous Railways hockey team?

RAY, SATYAJIT: The late Master, under whom Indian cinema came of age. Artist, musician, children's storyteller par excellence, Ray's creative genius would have won him a following even if he had not happened to be one of the world's greatest filmmakers as well. When he made *Pather Panchali* with a 35-mm handheld camera, this Renaissance man placed India on the cinematographic map of the globe and confirmed its place there with a series of celluloid master-pieces that captured the soul of his people. His success, directly or indirectly, inspired others — Sen, Karnad, Sathyu, Gopalakrishnan, Benegal, and many more — to lift Indian cinema out of the morass of commercial formulae and earn it the respect of the world. But above all, he gave the Indian subcontinent a cinematic voice whose equivalent India had found in literature with the works of Ra-bindranath Tagore.

RELIANCE: The company that gave us a founding father who in-spired a Bollywood blockbuster, suitings that not "only Vimal" could wear, one of the world's largest petrochemical plants, a high-tech communications network, a family feud to rival any soap opera, and a cricket World Cup. Now split into two empires, each headed by a billionaire.

RELIGION: Ever-present in Indian life. Whether it is the loud-speaker-aided call of the Lucknow muezzin or the raucous din of the Kolkata *puja-pandal*, the stray half-starved cow meandering through a gully, or the profusion of fruitcake in the stores at Christmas, the presence and influence of religion is everywhere apparent. Hardly a foundation stone is laid, ship launched, or hazardous ascent by car begun without the ritual smashing of a coconut or the offering of a *puja* to propitiate the gods. Fundamentally, Indians are a religious people, even if (as in the case of the enthusiastic young Kolkatans who collect "donations" for the betterment of their local Durga Puja Pandal) they claim to be Communist. Three of the world's major faiths — Hinduism, Buddhism, and Sikhism — originated on Indian soil, as did several of the minor ones (the Jains and the Qadianis, for instance) and most of the others — notably Islam, Christianity,

Judaism, and Zoroastrianism — have found fertile ground here. Unfortunately, in India as elsewhere, religion has also served to justify injustice, to provoke division, and to whip up hatred: the faithful rarely live up to the gentle precepts of their faiths. But India, of all countries, remains the living embodiment of the dictum that there is only one religion, though there are a hundred varieties of it.

RENAMING: A highly developed art for Indian streets and monuments, though nowhere is it more refined than in Kolkata, where a Left Front government managed, during the Vietnam War, to rename the street that housed the U.S. consulate after Ho Chi Minh. (The Americans, however, were cleverer, changing their letterheads to reflect a side gate that opened onto the less disconcerting Little Russell Street, which was not named for Bertrand.) Where this becomes more disconcerting is when whole cities are renamed: in the 1990s Pune, Mumbai, Chennai, and Kolkata entered the consciousness of English speakers. The nativism this bespeaks sits ill with the cosmopolitanism to which India has been laying claim at the beginning of the twenty-first century, but we have to list it among the many contradictions that constitute the Indian paradox. It's a great pity, though, to lose centuries of brand-name building, especially for Bombay and Madras; and to do so out of nothing but a petty chauvinism, a reassertion of pride in the right to label rather than the capacity to build. As I wrote at the time, our civic leaders seemed to be saying, in an admission of their own smallness: if we can't create, we can at least rename.

RICE: The great Indian food, whatever northerners may think about the merits of wheat. There are few more lyrical sights in India than the lush green of the paddy fields, and few happier ones than a Tamil or a Bengali before a plateful of rice. At the basic level rice is a sustainer of millions, the source of more energy for Indians than any other food, the vital staple of our land. At the level of culinary art, rice is the essential ingredient of those triumphs of Indian cuisine, the *idli* and the *dosa*. An India without rice would no longer be India.

SARI: Is to Indian dress what rice is to Indian food, its prose as well as its poetry. No more graceful garment has been invented by man, nor one more truly flattering, for the sari can conceal flaws that other dresses only accentuate and hint at features that other costumes only hide. It has adorned Indian womanhood for at least two thousand years, but it has never gone out of fashion, primarily because it has adapted with the times. Worn straight or pleated between the legs, with *pallavs* flung over the left or the right shoulder, below long-sleeved high-necked blouses or backless *cholis*, saris have retained an appeal that cuts across all distinctions of rank, religion, age, or shape. Tied primly beneath the breastbone or low in "hipster" style, knotted at the waist or pinned to an undergarment, in plain colors or patterned prints, polyester or poplin, heavy silk or sturdy cotton, saris have survived every sartorial change from the burqa to the miniskirt. In Pakistan, the sari has resisted the blandishments of the official *churidar* culture and is triumphantly worn on special occasions; in Bangladesh, the battle did not even need to be fought. In India, alas, its use by the impatient younger generation is fading, and when I once appealed to "save the sari from a sorry fate," I was met with a feminist backlash that left me reeling. So there is something of rueful defiance in this glossary entry: the sari is a triumphant achievement of Indian culture, but only Indian women can save it from being reduced to ritual wear, donned only to temples and weddings.

SECULARISM: An article of faith in the Indian political ethos, but where dictionaries define it in opposition to religion, Indians equate it to toleration of all religions. Either way, secularism presumes that the state shall grant no favor on the basis of religion, even though 81 percent of the population may have one in common. In an intensely religious nation like India, this credo is easier stated than adhered to, but there is widespread recognition among opinion leaders that India can no more abandon secularism than it can democracy. At least at the top, secularism has worked well, with armed services chiefs having represented every major community and Rashtrapati Bhavan having been home to presidents of three leading faiths. The important thing, however, is that for all the attacks upon "pseudo-secularism," the overwhelming majority of Indians remain noncommunal, wedded to the chronic pluralism of our civilization, of which secularism is merely the official reflection.

SINGH, KHUSHWANT: If one were to single out an Indian journalist whose name has evoked instant reactions across the land for the longest time, one would not look beyond Khushwant Singh. No other man could be remembered for two achievements so different as revealing the existence of the female torso to the incredulous readership of the formerly staid *Illustrated Weekly of India* and returning his Padma Shri Award to an equally stunned President Zail Singh. Khushwant Singh is revered by many for making bluntness and candor respectable in a profession that thrived on euphemism and ellipsis, for teaching journalists that it was not incompatible with their trade to get up from their desks, and for showing readers for the first time that writing was meant to be enjoyed as much as admired. He is condemned by an equal number of critics for what they see as his salivating lasciviousness, his tiresomely idiosyncratic obsessions, and his complete lack of either taste or discretion. No English-speaking Indian reader is neutral about Khushwant Singh: the one thing he does not do is leave his readers cold. May he live to be a hundred, and may he continue to amuse, delight, and provoke well past that landmark.

SOCIALISM: The political credo of India's left wing. It was also the credo of India's right wing (remember when the BJP claimed "Gandhian Socialism" as its ruling ideology?), its center, its ruling party, and all its editorialists. You could own land, fancy apartments, and cars and call yourself a socialist; the dominant principle of Indian socialism is "do as I say, not as I do." It is only since 1991 that it has become acceptable in India for some people not to be socialists, but the vast majority still pays lip service to the creed, whether or not they implement its tenets in policy or practice.

TAGORE, RABINDRANATH: The Shakespeare of the country, our greatest litterateur and a genius on the Da Vinci scale, who wrote novels, short stories, plays, poems, and songs, who founded a new discipline of music (Rabindra Sangeet) and a new university of the arts (Santiniketan), and whose work, even in a poor translation, won India's first Nobel Prize in 1913 (and its only one for literature). Tagore towers over India's cultural consciousness. His *Gitanjali* still evokes admiration wherever it is read; his "Kabuliwallah" is among the few short stories most Indians remember; and his famous poem, "Where the mind is without fear and the head is held high," inspires generations of Indian schoolchildren long after the context of its composition has been forgotten. Rabindranath Tagore is also the only human being in the world to have composed the words and music to two separate national anthems, those of India and Bangladesh. Tagore would have won immortality in any of his chosen fields; instead he remains immortal in all.

TAJ MAHAL: The motif for India on countless tourist posters and has probably had more camera shutters clicked at it than any other edifice on the face of this earth. How easily one forgets that this unequaled monument of love is in fact a tomb, the burial place of a woman who suffered thirteen times the pain of childbirth and died in agony at the fourteenth attempt. Perhaps that makes it all the more appropriate as a symbol of India — a land of beauty and grandeur amid suffering and death.

TATA: The dynasty that long represented the acceptable face of Indian capitalism: efficient, progressive, productive, honest, profitable, and socially conscious. For their pains, the Tatas were pilloried as tyrants and exploiters by a variety of leading politicians whose party coffers they proceeded thereafter to fill. (This peculiarly Indian dialectic was a tribute to the patience of capitalists and the elasticity of politicians.) The Tatas gave India its first indigenous steel industry, its first five-star hotel, its first company town (Jamshedpur), its first IT firm, and its first airline. Whether it can notch up any more firsts in the twenty-first century remains to be seen.

TENDULKAR, SACHIN: The sobriquet "The Little Master" was already taken, but Sachin Tendulkar was our sole "Boy Wonder." By the time he was fourteen people were speaking of him as potentially India's greatest batsman ever, and after breaking onto the international cricket scene as a precocious sixteen-year-old, he proceeded to fulfill that potential brilliantly. His records will long remain the stuff of cricketing legend, but what future generations will never know is the extraordinary weight of expectation that Sachin carried on his young shoulders every time he went out to bat, and the palpable sense of deflation that accompanied his every return to the pavilion.

TIGERS: India's most significant, yet most fragile, conservation achievement. In 1900 there were about 35,000 tigers in India; by the time tiger shooting was banned under a 1972 law there were only 1,872 left, a decimation rate of 95 percent in seventy years. Thanks largely to Project Tiger, established in 1973, that figure has slowly climbed up toward three thousand. The problem is that the tiger remains gravely endangered and conservation requires political sacrifices that are not easily made, notably the relocation of villages to create tiger sanctuaries, and the maintenance of adequate prey to sustain tiger populations. Tigers need large areas of land relatively free from incompatible human uses, but how can India reconcile the agreed ecological goal of protecting tigers with the pursuit of equitable socioeconomic development for the people of the affected areas? The prime minister's "Tiger Task Force" came up with ideas that, conservationists agree, have not yet solved the problem. Unless real political will is put behind it, India risks the extinction in the wild of this magnificent specimen of our natural diversity.

TRAFFIC: The bane of all Indian commuters. Chaos and crowds are hardly unknown elsewhere, but our extraordinary variety of means of transportation has long since outstripped the length and breadth of our roads, and the problem gets worse each month. The constituents of Indian traffic make for fairly remarkable conditions. Only in India can one get stuck in a jam at a nonfunctioning traffic light amid six Ambassadors in various states of disrepair, five Korean vehicles of assorted sizes, a Maruti almost crushed underfoot by a Tata Sumo, two minibuses facing each other and both on the wrong side of the road, a tram madly if impotently ringing its bell, three buses heading in different directions with passengers dangling from the tailboards and from each other, six rickshaws, one auto-rickshaw with a broken silencer, a homesick cow, a small flock of goats milling about at the zebra crossing, and some three hundred pedestrians picking their way gingerly through the confusion. Exaggeration? It happened to me on my last visit to Kolkata.

UNDERDEVELOPMENT: Used to be the condition erroneously ascribed to India by economic theoreticians, who looked at some of our labor-intensive agricultural techniques and promptly concluded that we were primitive. In fact, everything in India is overdeveloped, particularly the social structure, the bureaucracy, the political process, the monetary system, the university network, the industrial base, and (as Galbraith tactlessly observed) the women. Given its economic and imperial history in a number of previous Golden Ages under Ashoka, Vikramaditya, and Akbar, India is not underdeveloped at all; it is, as I argued in *The Great Indian Novel*, a highly developed country in an advanced state of decay. Now that we are cleaning up the dilapidation and glitzy malls are sprouting all over what used to be our mofussil areas, and real estate values are going through the roof (usually before the roof is even constructed), India may soon give "overdevelopment" a whole new meaning.

UNEMPLOYMENT: A serious social evil, with the talents and skills of a vast army of ill-educated people being wasted because the economy is unable to absorb them. There are more unemployed engineers in India than there are qualified engineers in the whole of East Africa. Part of the problem is that a number of Indians are being educated out of a job; their learning makes them unsuitable for the work that is available. But there is also an urgent need to create more manufacturing and service industries to absorb and employ people (the entire IT industry only accounts for a million jobs in a country of over a billion people). And remedial training, to make up for the deficiencies of some of our less prominent educational institutions, is also essential: companies would have people they could hire if they were prepared to invest in training them to par. The unemployment statistics would look even worse if they took into account the vast army of those who actually hold jobs but have nothing to do in them, a form of unemployment particularly prevalent in government service and which therefore carries great social prestige.

UP: Or Uttar Pradesh, is a state in north India that accounts for 10 percent of our population, 20 percent of our industry, 40 percent of our pollution, and 60 percent of our prime ministers.

VARANASI: The new(ish) name for Benares. It was also the old name for Benares, which is why it has been revived, but there is an older name still, Kashi, and that's where most southern Indian pilgrims think they're going when they buy a ticket to Varanasi. It is a town that still attracts sadhus, mendicants, and long-haired seekers of truth to its ghats and temples. The Ganga at Varanasi is the best place for Hindus to wash their sins away, and after what the press has revealed about police brutality in the city's jails and thanas, that may be just as well.

VEGETARIANISM: Doesn't have it so good elsewhere. India enjoys a long tradition of respectable vegetarian cuisine, which is more than can be said for almost any other culture on earth (Chinese being the only exception, but then the Chinese dress up their vegetarian fare to look and taste as much like meat as possible, which rather misses the point). Only in India can one attend a dinner in the certainty of not having to starve for one's principles; only in India do restaurants and five-star hotels serve buffets with separate tables marked "veg" and "nonveg"; and only our country's airlines offer you the choice of a vegetarian meal without having to pre-book it. Vegetarianism in India, particularly if it is for religious reasons, can range from a total rejection of animal products to a refusal to contemplate even vegetables that have grown underground, though an increasing number of "vegans" and "eggetarians" simply don't want to bite into anything that, in its natural state, might have bitten them back.

VILLAGES: Where two-thirds of Indians still live. They are, for the most part, neither the dregs of misery they are sometimes portrayed to be (living conditions in our city slums are surely far worse) nor the idealized self-sufficient communities our Gandhians wish they were (there are too many inequalities and vested interests, and too few opportunities, for that). Our villages are just as susceptible to the encroachments of change, to the influence of the nearest movie theater, to the ideas of the loudest politician, as any of our cities. They have simply lasted longer and changed more slowly because neither the attempts nor the resources have been geared for dramatic transformation. But village India is changing — few villages can claim to be identical in every respect to the way they were even a decade ago — and the pace of change can only accelerate. As urbanization proceeds apace within the lifetime of many readers, villages will no longer house a majority of India's population. And then, as the joke goes, if Gandhiji hadn't been cremated he would surely have rolled over in his grave.

WEDDINGS: The classic Indian social event, glittering occasions for conspicuous consumption, outrageous overdressing, and free food. In a culture where marriage is mostly a family arrangement rather than a legal contract, the wedding is the real opportunity to proclaim a new relationship to society, and brings together friends, business contacts, relatives, and spongers in orgiastic celebration of the act of union. Beneath the surface bonhomie and backslapping jollity, however, lurk the real tensions, as the bride's father asks himself, "Are the groom's party really happy with the dowry? Can I trust the chap who's collecting the presents?"

XEROX: A relatively new feature of Indian life. The cost of photocopying, though it has been dropping, is still prohibitive enough to dissuade all but companies, scholars, and the occasional spy from resorting too freely to it. But the existence of so many roadside sheds with Xerox machines in them is, like our STD booths, a contribution of Indian democracy to the popularization of technology.

YES-MEN: Known north of the Vindhyas as *chamchas*, yes-men have existed throughout Indian history and will no doubt continue to do so. Their role is sanctified by the tradition of deference, the power of position, the fact of overpopulation, and the alternative of unemployment. No one with money, power, or position moves alone when he can be accompanied by a host of sycophants ready to echo his every nod. Yes-men are not necessarily at the bottom of the social scale; the role can be played at various levels. Thus a peasant can be a yes-man to a contractor who is a yes-man to a landlord who is a yes-man to a party boss who is a yes-man to a chief minister who is a yes-man to a cabinet member who is a yes-man to the prime minister. At no stage in the process does anyone actually think anything other than, "What does my boss want me to think?" Fortunately for the country, somebody up there values the word no.

ZOROASTRIANISM: See *Parsis*. (This is part of the typical Indian habit of observing the letter of an undertaking, while violating its spirit. It is also known as having the last laugh.)

Index